GENERATION VET

GENERATION VET

*Composition, Student-Veterans, and
the Post-9/11 University*

Edited by
Sue Doe and Lisa Langstraat

UTAH STATE UNIVERSITY PRESS
Logan

CA-P
G284
2014

Published by Utah State University Press
An imprint of University Press of Colorado
5589 Arapahoe Avenue, Suite 206C
Boulder, Colorado 80303

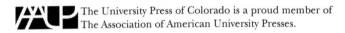 The University Press of Colorado is a proud member of
The Association of American University Presses.

The University Press of Colorado is a cooperative publishing enterprise supported,
in part, by Adams State College, Colorado State University, Fort Lewis College,
Metropolitan State College of Denver, Regis University, University of Colorado,
University of Northern Colorado, Utah State University, and Western State College of
Colorado.

Cover design by Daniel Pratt

ISBN: 978-0-87421-941-8 (paper)
ISBN: 978-0-87421-942-5 (e-book)

Library of Congress Cataloging-in-Publication Data

Generation vet : composition, student-veterans, and the post-9/11
university / edited by Sue Doe and Lisa Langstraat.
     pages cm
  ISBN 978-0-87421-941-8 (pbk.) — ISBN 978-0-87421-942-5 (ebook)
1. Veterans—Education (Higher)—United States. 2. English language—Rhetoric—
Study and teaching (Higher) 3. Academic writing—Study and teaching (Higher)
4. Afghan War, 2001—Veterans—Services for—United States. 5. Iraq War, 2003–2011—
Veterans—Services for—United States. 6. College students—Services for—United
States. I. Doe, Sue, 1957– editor of compilation author. II. Langstraat, Lisa, editor of
compilation.
  UB357.G44 2014
  378.1'9826970973—dc23
                                     2013035014

Cover photograph © Shutterstock/Nattika

CONTENTS

ACKNOWLEDGMENTS

We are grateful to the many student-veterans with whom we've had the pleasure to work, and who have generously agreed to participate in our research. You have entrusted us with your time, your stories, your wisdom, your sense of humor. Thanks for your many "just-to-shoot-the-breeze" visits to our offices. It has been a pleasure and an honor. We learn from you every day. Thank you to our publisher, Utah State Press and the University Press of Colorado, and especially to our editor, Michael Spooner, whose belief in this project helped us to believe in it as well. Thank you to the wonderful contributors to this collection; we thank you for your patience and your willingness to work hard on this challenging project as it evolved. Thanks also to our graduate student research assistants, Sam Iacovetta, Becky McIntyre, Erin Hadlock, and Sondra Harrington; our sponsors, partners, and advocates at Colorado State University, the Department of English, the College of Liberal Arts, and community sponsors of the Faculty Development Fund; The Institute for Teaching and Learning; the Adult Learners and Veterans Services Office (ALVS) including especially our colleague, friend, and ALVS Director, COL (Ret) Jenny Pickett. Finally, thank you to the many members of the CSU community who have participated in our faculty development workshops on teaching and learning with student-veterans.

With love, I thank my husband of over 30 years, Dr. William W. Doe, III, LTC Retired, United States Army, whose own military service and whose invaluable support, research expertise, military knowledge, and dedication to veterans inspire and humble me every day. Thanks as well to my three wonderful children—Adam, Steve, and Maggie—who never shirked the title "Army Brat." Your formative years were deeply affected by our life as a military family, but you always adjusted better than I. To my dad, Ward Winchester Rowe, WWII veteran, who often described his time in the service as the "best time of his life" and the only opportunity he had, as a man of modest means, to see the French Riviera. To my brother, Samuel Rustin Rowe, whose draft number in 1969 was #4, putting him among the first of Vietnam-era vets for whom the rescission of the college deferment program resulted in withdrawal from college and military service that had lifelong effects; Sam, I'm so happy that you were finally able to use your GI Bill benefits this past year to get your commercial driver's license! Thanks as well to my chapter co-author, MAJ Erin Hadlock, whose MA thesis and personal knowledge of military genres contributed importantly to my understanding. Thanks especially to my colleague and co-editor, Lisa Langstraat, whose brainchild this collection is. Lisa, you have not only steered me toward an entirely new research direction at a critical juncture in my career but you have consistently opened doors to professional opportunities I would not otherwise have had the courage to undertake.

Sue Doe, Colorado State University, 2013

My deepest gratitude to my parents, Alice Langstraat and Richard Langstraat, CW4 Retired, United States Army. Because my father made the army his home, his identity, his passion, our whole family served in the military, and I thank my parents for the many opportunities that our army life afforded. My father served for twenty-seven years, completing a tour of duty in Vietnam during the Tet Offensive, and accruing 696 parachute jumps. He was a complex man, a man of honor, who taught me the worth of deep and abiding loyalty, a commitment to service, and the import of always, always speaking truth to power. With remarkable strength, my mother shouldered the challenge of 21 moves in 51 years of marriage and hundreds of TDY's that often left her, a crackerjack nurse with a demanding career, to handle three rather challenging daughters on her own. Like so many military spouses and family members, she found ways to balance the joys and sacrifices of military life and deserves honor and recognition. Thanks to my many friends and colleagues who suffered through my ruminations (okay, concerned diatribes) about opportunities for veterans today. Thanks to my nephews, Daniel and Ryan who never cease to amaze me. Finally, my heartfelt gratitude to Sue Doe, whose integrity, creativity, and friendship are always inspiring. I'm grateful that we share the Army lexicon, and after this project, may you get some R&R before you start kicking ass and taking names.

Lisa Langstraat, Colorado State University, 2013

GENERATION VET

INTRODUCTION

Sue Doe and Lisa Langstraat

The Army wants its trainees to know how to read, how to recite well in class, and how to write simple and correct English without too much flourish or attention to technical details. Let us teachers again bestir ourselves to aid these boys who are fighting many battles of mind and soul.
—H. Adelbert White

Veterans have sacrificed much to attend our institutions of higher education, and our college must assume a responsibility toward each veteran accepted as a student, or there may be dangerous repercussions in the years to come from the cynicism of alumni veterans.
—Edward C. McDonagh

The excerpt from H. Adelbert White's (1944) essay "Clear Thinking for Army Trainees" appeared in *College English* in the same year that the Servicemen's Readjustment Act of 1944, better known as the GI Bill of Rights, was ratified. Only three years later, when McDonagh's (1947) comments appeared in *the Journal of Higher Education*, the United States was at the peak of GI Bill college enrollment with veterans representing nearly 50 percent of all college students. By 1956, when the original GI Bill was terminated, 7.8 million World War II veterans had used GI Bill benefits for college or vocational training programs ("History and Timeline," US Department of Veteran Affairs 2013). This influx of veterans on college campuses dramatically influenced postsecondary instruction, including composition curricula. Now, over sixty years later, the 2009 Post-9/11 GI Bill, one of the most generous social programs in US history, has enabled a new generation of veterans to pursue higher education. The *Chronicle of Higher Education* reports Department of Defense statistics showing that the number of veterans enrolled in colleges and universities increased from just under 35,000 to over half a million between 2009 and 2011 ("Who Benefits from the Post-9/11 GI Bill?" 2012). The Pat Tillman Foundation (2013) reports that over 900,000 veterans had used the new GI Bill benefit by 2012. It seems clear that we are experiencing the largest influx of a unique student group since

DOI: 10.7330/9780874219425.c000

World War II, and it is probable that veterans will substantially transform postsecondary classroom dynamics, relationships across campus and in the community, and our understanding of the kinds of literacies students bring to our courses. Also, at this writing, members of Congress have introduced over a dozen bills, including the Military and Veterans Educational Reform Act, designed to protect student-veterans from the predatory recruitment practices of and insufficient student support services at a number of for-profit colleges and universities (Sander 2012b). Since much of this legislation will affect national policy, not only for student-veterans but for all postsecondary students and institutions, it is safe to say that the post-9/11 GI Bill will shape higher education for decades to come.

A burgeoning body of research in student services addresses postsecondary institutions' efforts to identify and reduce barriers to veterans' educational goals, to assist veterans as they transition from active duty to college life, and to provide timely and accurate information about veterans' benefits and services. Literary studies similarly has a long tradition of scholarly inquiry into war fiction and veterans' memoirs. However, rarely does student-services scholarship address veterans' literacy practices or rhetorical strategies, and rarely do literary studies address student-veterans' presence in our classrooms and the pedagogical approaches that may facilitate their learning. Certainly, with the development of institutes and centers for the study of veterans and their families, such as Purdue University's Military Family Research Institute and Syracuse University's Institute for Veterans and Military Families, we are likely to see vital, longitudinal research emerge in upcoming years. And the CCCC-sponsored research project by Alexis D. Hart and Roger Thompson (2013) has provided new and essential information about veterans' programs across the nation. Their surveys and site visits found that the majority of faculty are not aware of campus services for student-veterans and have not had training regarding teaching and learning with veterans. Most faculty report being aware of greater numbers of student-veterans on campus but also report that their institutions do not provide classes arranged especially for them. Describing such classes as veteran only, veteran focused, and veteran friendly, Hart and Thompson imply that these designations suggest directions for additional research. Despite these important but relatively rare contributions to the literature, including the invaluable *Teaching English in the Two-Year College* (2009) special issue on student-veterans, composition studies has only begun to wrangle with the implications of working with and learning from this new generation of students.

Composition studies can offer great insights into the pedagogical, rhetorical, and programmatic implications of working with student-veteran populations. Just as student-veterans are changed by their college experiences, post-9/11 universities will be changed by student-veterans' presence. Given the numbers of veterans entering writing courses, we face the exciting and challenging prospect of teaching and learning new forms of rhetorical agency that promise to alter our social and political lives. Composition courses, particularly first-year courses, play an integral role in the retention of student-veterans in part because most composition courses are smaller in size than other core, first-year courses, and in part because newly enrolled veterans often take writing courses in their first semesters of college, often as they are "transitioning" from military to civilian life. Similarly, many composition curricula foster or even require personal writing, and student-veterans may find themselves writing about traumatic experiences that may, in turn, pose ethical and pedagogical challenges for writing instructors. At the very least, writing courses are probable sites of significant cultural exchanges—even clashes—as veterans, whether they have been in combat or not, bring to our courses the values, rhetorical traditions, and communication styles they have learned in the military. These perspectives will likely challenge the values and beliefs of not only traditional college students but faculty as well.

Questions of citizenship, subjectivity, disability, activism, community-campus relationships—all come to the fore as we work with veterans in writing-intensive courses and community contexts, and all demand well-researched rhetorical, pedagogical, and programmatic responses. *Generation Vet: Composition, Veterans, and the Post-9/11 University* contributes to the conversation about these issues. Our title is a nod to two competing representations of post-9/11 veterans, representations that this volume complicates and critiques. On the one hand, referencing Tom Brokaw's (1998) book, *The Greatest Generation, Time* magazine featured the cover story "The New Greatest Generation" (Klein 2011). This issue of the magazine garnered significant national attention; its optimistic depiction of wounded warriors clearly resonated with readers searching for confirmation that a nation cannot only heal from the losses of war, but can become better precisely *because* of those losses. Author Joe Klein claims, "A new kind of war meant a new set of skills. Now veterans are bringing their leadership lessons home, where we need them most" (Klein 2011, 26). Klein characterizes Iraq and Afghanistan combat veterans as more practical, more likely to problem solve, less "whiney," and more inclined to public service than the average civilian. While "The

New Greatest Generation" is compelling and features the stories of extraordinary individuals and veterans' advocacy organizations, it also tends to romanticize warfare, military training, and the hero combat veteran. It is such idealized representations that this collection attempts to challenge; repeatedly, the authors in this collection insist that, while all veterans, including noncombat veterans, have earned our gratitude and deserve the respect conferred by GI Bill benefits, idealizing veterans is, at best, irresponsible. To that end, our title, *Generation Vet*, also references Evan Wright's 2011 book, *Generation Kill: Devil Dogs, Iceman, Captain America, and the New Face of American War*. "For the past decade," Wright explains in an interview,

> We've been steeped in the lore of *The Greatest Generation* . . . and a lot of people have developed this romanticism about that war. They tend to remember it from the *Life* magazine images of the sailor coming home and kissing his fiancé. They've forgotten that war is about killing. I really think it's important as a society to be reminded of this, because you now have a generation of baby boomers, a lot of whom didn't serve in Viet Nam. Many of them protested it. But now they're grown up, and as they've gotten older I think many of them have grown tired of the ambiguities and the lack of moral clarity of Viet Nam, and they've started to cling to this myth of World War II, the good war. (Matera 2008)

Although *Generation Kill* has been criticized for glorifying violence and hypermasculinity, and for compromising journalistic integrity by venerating the practice of embedded reporting (Wright was embedded with the 1st Reconnaissance Battalion of the US Marine Corps during the 2003 invasion of Iraq), it does challenge sanitized versions of Operation Iraqi Freedom (OIF) and Operation Enduring Freedom (OEF), particularly in a period of changing combat terrain and strategies. Our title, *Generation Vet*, thus reflects a desire to acknowledge the contributions of all veterans, combat and noncombat, and to resist idealizing or homogenizing veterans who enter and contribute to scenes of writing in the university and beyond. The term *Generation Vet* also references the profound ways in which this generation of GI Bill students will influence college curricula, writing programs, and pedagogical practice. Exemplifying the leadership skills garnered in their military experience, veterans have actively promoted changes, at both national and local levels, in postsecondary policies and politics. The Student Veterans of America (SVA), for example, has deployed its political sway to spark investigations about unethical and predatory recruiting practices in the for-profit education sector, where over one-third of GI Bill funds are allocated (Sander 2013). SVA recently revoked chapter status to over forty for-profit colleges that claimed "veteran friendly" standing but that offered insufficient veterans' services and whose SVA membership included only administrative staff (Sander 2013). At Colorado State University, where we teach, our local chapter of the SVA campaigned to revise university enrollment procedures; since the GI Bill affords only thirty-six months of financial support for undergraduates, this chapter of the SVA successfully promoted an expedited enrollment process that allows student-veterans to register for core, required courses earlier in their studies. This generation of student-veteran, in other words, is generally well organized and vocal about educational aims and, as the Pat Tillman Foundation (2012) report on veterans' progress toward degree completion puts it, ready to "complete the mission" by earning their degrees.

THE GI BILL(S) AND VETERANS IN COLLEGES AND UNIVERSITIES

White's and McDonagh's comments, which open this introduction, are very much of their historical moment. Yet their remarks resonate in our contemporary scene insofar as they convey a sense of ongoing cultural obligation to the young people who have fought in the United States' wars. Paula Caplan, former head of the American Psychological Association and outspoken veterans' advocate, argues in her book *When Johnny and Jane Come Marching Home* that this work need not be left to professional psychologists but can involve everyday citizens who are willing to listen and resist comment (Caplan 2011). Many contemporary colleges and universities echo an apparent responsiveness to veterans' needs today as they seek "veteran-friendly status" and attempt to address the needs of student-veterans, including those experiencing "signature wounds"—posttraumatic stress disorder (PTSD) and traumatic brain injury (TBI) of Gulf War II service. Also mingled in White's and McDonagh's sixty-year-old comments are concerns about the tolls of war and apprehension about the "dangerous repercussions" and collective power of the huge population of returning WWII veterans in 1947. Of course, Adelbert and McDonagh were justified in voicing apprehension. As a number of scholars have noted, the original GI Bill was an overt effort to quell a potential repeat performance of the 1932 Bonus March, in which World War I veterans mobbed the capital to demand the unpaid military benefits they had been promised (Mettler 2005; Murray 2008). Given the multiple deployments demanded of the post-9/11 military due to the absence of a draft and low enlistment percentages, today's veterans certainly have ample reason to be disgruntled.

Add to this the fact that daunting economic hardships face today's veterans, especially given recent challenges to the national economy, sequestration, and a growing demand on veteran resources as a result of the aging population ("Budget Battles and a Stagnant Economy Greet America's Soldiers as They Return from Iraq and Afghanistan" 2011). As of June 2014, Syracuse University (reporting Bureau of Labor Statistics) recorded that the unemployment rate for veterans of all ages and eras was comparable to that of the general public. Among post-9/11 veterans ages eighteen to twenty-four, the numbers were substantially higher for veterans: 17.7 percent compared to 13.4 percent in May 2013, but the gap closed by January 2014 to 12.2 percent (veterans) to 12.9 percent (civilians) ("Employment Situation of Veterans" 2013). These numbers, while lower than those reported in 2011, when the unemployment rate for this veteran demographic was 30 percent (Beucke 2011), suggest not so much an improvement in veteran unemployment as the volatility of these numbers, the danger of drawing conclusions based on statistics over short periods of time. Female veteran unemployment represents its own particular set of issues as documented by Syracuse University's May 2013 National Summit on Women Veteran Homelessness. The Summit named four major factors affecting female veteran employment: (1) the long-term effects of military sexual trauma, (2) for a shortage of peer support (3) childcare needs, and (4) the availability of safe and affordable housing ("Employment Situation of Veterans" 2013). While a college education certainly doesn't guarantee economic security, there are good reasons, and among them is employability, for veterans to enroll in colleges and universities in record-breaking numbers. Only time will tell whether the Post-9/11 GI bill will have as profound an impact on social needs such as employment as the original GI Bill, which historian Dennis Johnson has included among the fifteen most influential pieces of legislation in United States history (Johnson 2009).

While the original GI Bill initiated significant changes in postsecondary instruction generally and composition pedagogy specifically, it is astonishing to note how little scholarship has explored these issues. Betty Pytlik noted, "None of the dozen or so book-length accounts I have read mention the effects that the Bill had on curriculum and pedagogy" (Pytlik 1993, 2). On the other hand, we do have several invaluable accounts that peripherally link an influx of student-veterans to transformations in writing instruction. Robert Connors (1997), for instance, pointed out in his book *Composition-Rhetoric: Backgrounds, Theory, and Pedagogy* that the postwar (WWII) "communications" movement brought together speech and English in ways that helped establish the rhetorical turn in composition. He also noted that the Conference on College Composition and Communication sprang from this period, and that the journal *College Composition and Communication* helped professionalize the discipline by publishing the work of established scholars on debates relating to "the purposes of the composition course" (Connors 1997, 205). Reflecting an expanded notion of higher education that emerged post-WWII, the work of these composition scholars was "democratizing" and "populist," Connors argued (Connors 1991, 52). Mike Edwards also notes that we would do well to remember that Donald Murray was a veteran, and that early in his career, Peter Elbow helped young men opposed to the Vietnam War craft statements required for conscientious objector status. Mike Rose (1983) offered insights into the academic experience of Vietnam veterans, particularly as this group influenced basic or remedial writing instruction. His work with veterans became part of his larger project relating to the underprepared, "remedial" writers, whose causes and instruction he has championed throughout his career. In particular, although Rose, subject to the stereotypes about veterans that permeate our culture, clumped returning Vietnam veterans alongside "parolees and newly released convicts" (Rose 1983, 110), his instructional approaches helped subsequent generations of writing teachers recognize that developmental students, among them veterans, needed not impoverished skill and drill instruction but opportunities to exercise critical thinking in rhetorically grounded writing contexts. In his 1993 autoethnography, *Bootstraps: From an American Academic of Color*, Victor Villanueva offered insight from the perspective of both veteran-student and veteran-faculty whose world view has been shaped by having "finished his tour of duty in Vietnam, left the Army, and made his way through the progression of experiences, schools, and degrees" (Villanueva 1993, 340). Among recent accounts, Liam Corley, a professor of English at California State Polytechnic, Pomona, and a national reservist who was deployed to Afghanistan, explained that, upon returning stateside, he struggled with hypervigilance, became brusque in conversations with colleagues and students, struggled with feeling that academic tasks were less meaningful than his work in Afghanistan, and had considerable difficulty concentrating and writing (Corley 2012). Such testimonies have paved the way for additional research on veterans and writing.

It is important to remember that the original GI Bill led to much greater diversity in student populations, which challenged and permanently altered previous paradigms of curricular theory and delivery. In fact, the influx of veterans changed how colleges and universities operated: the number of postsecondary schools with more than 20,000 students increased from eight in 1948 to fifty-five in 1967 (DiRamio and Jarvis 2011, ix), and growing enrollments necessitated changes in approach, including wider reliance on graduate teaching assistants. Keith Olson claims that larger classes and the increased use of graduate students as teachers "accomplished educational wonders for the veterans" (Olson 1974, 103). "Wonder" or not, the labor landscape was permanently changed since, as Pytlik points out, a job market was created for anyone with a master's degree (Pytlik 1993, 5) and teaching-methods courses slowly developed for the graduate teaching assistants upon whom so much instruction increasingly relied (7–8). Jackson Toby (2010) draws a direct link between the increased access afforded by the original GI Bill and a trend in higher education in which standards for admission and subsequent college performance have eroded. In contrast, Deborah Brandt's (1995) "Accumulation of Literacy" suggests that the post-WWII era was part of an important and rapid evolution of new literacy expectations—one that was directly influenced by the development of war-motivated literacies. Discussing the case study of Sam May and his "piling up" (Brandt 1995, 652) or accumulation of literacies, particularly from the 1920s to the 1940s, Brandt argues that May's increasingly complex language use had become expected of literate persons during and after WWII. May's childhood understanding of literacy had involved a belief in the importance of correctness, but as an enlisted soldier he was compelled to go beyond correctness produce highly complex and technical reports. Then, using the GI Bill to go to college, May became part of a significant shift involving "the emerging power of a highly educated, technocratic elite" for whom, "the meaning of education and educated language had begun to change by mid-century—shifting from the cultivated talk of the well-bred to the efficient professional prose of the technocrat—thereby altering the paths of upward mobility" (Brandt 1995, 659).

The GI Bill, because it afforded new opportunities for upward mobility, is often credited with having created the modern American middle class. It certainly afforded opportunities for a whole generation of high-achieving professionals, including more than 60,000 GI Bill-educated doctors, who would develop a vast array of new treatments and technologies (Humes 2006, 146). In addition, the wives of veterans, accompanying their spouses to campus, were also newly exposed to college education, influencing middle-class women's pursuit of higher education (Olson 1974, 102). Prior to WWII, college had primarily been the domain of the upper middle class, but the GI Bill opened college to a much larger population. The story of the historic GI Bill of Rights is thus central to the story of access to higher education in the United States. This story, in turn, is closely tied to the story of college composition. Like the GI Bill of Rights, composition pedagogy is associated with the democratizing impulse of the American university—a trend that began with the establishment of land-grant universities, continued on through the GI Bill, found new expression with the open admissions initiatives of the late 1960s and 1970s, and continues today. This democratizing effect influenced the course of higher education and the development of the teaching of writing as it is currently understood. Among other things, the social contract that emerged held that as an increasingly diverse group of people became eligible to pursue a college degree and develop the kinds of literacies demanded of citizens like Sam May, services supporting their success would follow.

Of course, the original GI Bill was no panacea, and the processes by which it was dispersed contributed to some forms of social injustice. Beth Bailey argues that over the past few decades historians have "used the GI Bill as a kind of shorthand—almost a deus ex machina—explanation for the emergence of a rapidly growing middle class in the years following WWII" (Bailey 2011, 198), but recent research argues that the GI Bill of 1944 institutionalized, consolidated, and reinforced race, gender, and sexual orientation biases and inequalities (Bérubé 1990; Canaday 2003; Cohen 2003; Frydl 2009; Onkst 1998; Rosales 2011). Exclusions were standard with the GI Bill, which "filtered benefits to male heads of households to the overwhelming exclusion of women" and "left veterans who had been discharged 'undesirably' [code for queerness] . . . without benefits" (Rosales 2011, 598). Kathleen Frydl (2009) notes that, although African Americans, Latinos, and other racial and ethnic groups had, on paper, equal access to GI Bill benefits, racial segregation and the prejudices of VA officials who determined the allocation of benefits actually enforced inequities. In addition, because writing instruction traditionally served an acculturation agenda, it was complicit in the hegemonic reinforcement of white, male privilege. Indeed, educational access continued to reflect a largely white, heterosexual, male population. In time, the services that a student-veteran like Sam May needed slowly began to be understood as more broadly needed by a diverse demographic. This shift may have helped usher in a new type of "critical and self-reflective form of acculturation" that was informed by an increasingly diverse student audience and that, in turn, informed pedagogy and curriculum (Bawarshi and Pelkowski 1999, 42).

Today, over sixty years after the first GI Bill, the 2009 Post-9/11 GI Bill, widely hailed as equivalent in generosity to the 1944 law, is the next great hope for opening the doors of access, particularly by serving a new kind of student-veteran. Certainly, intervening laws between GI Bills one and two extended GI Bill benefits after the Korean and Vietnam wars as well. However, these bills received little public attention and tepid reviews from affected veterans, although some scholars have argued that the post-Korea and Vietnam legislation went some distance toward addressing the racial and gender shortcomings of the original GI Bill (Boulton 2005). The Post-9/11 GI Bill offers tuition coverage at any in-state public university, an annual book and fee stipend, and a monthly living allowance. In addition, with the 2012 repeal of the Don't Ask, Don't Tell policy, GLBTQ veterans are making strides toward public, equal access to post-9/11 benefits. The 2013 Supreme Court decision to strike down the Defense of Marriage Act (DOMA) promises to expand the number of eligible family members to whom GI Bill benefits might be transferred. The question remains, however, as to how successful the advancement of those opportunities will be.

The Post-9/11 GI Bill may also embody affective politics that shape our interactions with student-veterans. Drawing from Frydl's (2009) *The GI Bill*, Bailey (2011) argues that the original 1944 GI Bill fostered a (primarily male) sense of citizenship, national pride, and optimism about social mobility. Suzanne Mettler (2005) similarly suggests that the original GI Bill helped to create a "civic generation" by implicitly and explicitly telling veterans that *they mattered* to the state. A number of scholars, including Mettler, have suggested that the Post-9/11 GI Bill, in contrast, is focused less on citizen's intrinsic value to the state and more on "paying soldiers back" for what they have sacrificed in OEF and OIF. Concerns about the ethics of the US "war on terrorism" and American citizens' responses to the faulty intelligence about Iraq's WMD stock-pile, generally used as the rationale for OIF, permeate discussions of the Post-9/11 GI Bill ("CIA's Report: No WMDs Found in Iraq" 2005). Thus, while we can certainly look to the 1944 GI Bill to understand major changes in the academy, we also must recognize that the Post-9/11 GI Bill represents different values born of a dramatically different cultural and economic landscape.

ETHICAL EDUCATION AND MILITARY-FRIENDLY COLLEGES AND UNIVERSITIES

Colleges and universities have had to prepare very quickly for the growth in student-veteran enrollment. In an American Council on Education (2009) survey, only half of all colleges and universities were prepared to provide services for vets, and less than half offered faculty training for working with vets. In the years since, college campuses have increasingly sought to become "veteran friendly" ("Military-Friendly Schools" 2013). For instance, in addition to designating a certifying official who verifies GI Bill eligibility and manages paperwork relating to the GI Bill (a service required of campuses that wish to obtain federal funds through the VA, which administers the program), veteran-friendly campuses generally offer some combination of support services. These often include special admissions assistance, registration help, designated financial-aid officers, housing arrangements, special academic support services, career counseling, and access to mental and physical healthcare tailored to the needs of veterans. Standout programs might also include specialized orientations, designated study areas, student-veteran organizations, award and scholarship committees, honor societies, veteran-cohort classes, faculty development workshops, preferential enrollment/registration policies, academic workshops, career counseling and professional networking opportunities, and "veteran village" living and learning communities. As this list suggests, many colleges and universities are developing multifaceted support networks that reorganize or even redefine standard university services. The clamor to obtain student-veteran enrollments has also led to the critique of institutions and their associated ratings and rankings. For instance, in a 2010 testimony to the House Committee on Veteran Affairs, Kathryn Snead, president of Servicemembers Opportunity Colleges Consortium, lamented the ways in which many universities and colleges were targeting what she calls the "new veteran market." She explained, "Many of our service members and veterans are first generation college applicants who lack general knowledge about the college search, selection, and admission process. They rely heavily upon the guidance and assistance of college admissions personnel as their primary source of reliable information."

Of course, federal dollars associated with the GI Bill are significant and come at a time when higher education, particularly in the public sector, is desperate for new forms of financial support. Sander (2012a) notes, in the *Chronicle of Higher Education*, that as the number of GI Bill recipients rose from 34,393 in 2009 to just over half a million (555,329) in 2011, the University of Phoenix, a private for-profit institution, enrolled twice as many veterans as the next-highest enrolling institution. Of the $4.43 billion in GI Bill benefits paid in 2011, $1.68 billion went to public nonprofit institutions, $1.65 billion to private for-profit institutions, and $1.02 billion went to private non-profit institutions (Sander 2012a). Critics of today's Post-9/11 GI Bill point out that tuition assistance may unfairly obligate public institutions, which charge less than private counterparts yet must absorb the cost of support services without compensatory monies. Also, private and for-profit colleges can charge more and can cover the gap between GI Bill benefits and the cost of tuition by participating in Yellow Ribbon Programs, which can result in some universities and colleges "bring[ing] in more in federal dollars than it actually costs them to educate a student" (Eckstein 2009). This phenomenon led F. King Alexander, president of California State University at Long Beach, to declare that "when the smoke clears, you'll see half the veterans at public institutions but 80 percent of the money at the for-profit institutions [in California]" (Eckstein 2009).

STUDENT-VETERAN DEMOGRAPHICS AND ACADEMIC PREPAREDNESS

Student-veterans are a heterogeneous population. They share a primary characteristic insofar as they have served in one of the five branches of the military—the US Army, Navy, Air Force, Marines, Coast Guard—or in the Reserve component of one of those branches. They also include the Army National Guard and Air National Guard, which typically serve needs such as Homeland Security and relief programs during times of national and international disaster. The National Center for Veterans Analysis and Statistics (NCVAS), an arm of the Department of Veterans Affairs (VA) that maintains a perpetually updated Veteran Population Model based on actuarial projections, reports that among other factors, the total veteran population will fall substantially by 2040, but the female veteran population will grow (NCVAS 2013). According to the National Priorities Project, a nonprofit research organization that analyzes federal data, the US Armed Forces as of March 2012 employed 1,458,219 active and 1,552,000 reserve/National Guard, with 90,000 in Afghanistan, 22,000 afloat, and 50,000 in Europe. They report a military that is 75 percent Caucasian and approximately 12 percent Hispanic. African Americans are overrepresented, comprising 19 percent of the military, compared to just 11 percent of the population overall. Women are underrepresented in the military, at just over 14 percent of the active-duty force compared to over 50 percent of the population. Servicemembers tend to come from both highly urban and highly rural origins; among US counties, Los Angeles and Orange Counties (of the greater Los Angeles metropolitan area) and Cook County (Chicago), for instance, report some of the highest levels of enlistment, but Wyoming, Alaska, and Maine also report consistently high percentages.

Regionally, southern states, such as Georgia and South Carolina, rank at the top for enlistments, perhaps reflecting the southern tradition of military service. The South is followed by the West, the Midwest, and the Northeast. Both the poorest and wealthiest zip codes in the United States are underrepresented among enlistments (National Priorities Project 2011).

By 2010 statistics, roughly 97 percent of enlistees in today's military had at least a high-school diploma (National Priorities Project 2011). Dan Berrett (2011), drawing from the 2009 American Freshman Survey, estimates that "11.5 percent of the students who later entered the military had A or A+ averages, which was less than half the percentage of nonveteran students who had earned those grades. Nearly 1 in 5 students who later joined the military had a C+ average or lower in high school, or more than quadruple the rate of their non-military peers." As a student demographic, student-veterans are both adult and nontraditional learners, who are characterized as being generally older than traditional college students and financially independent; they are thus responsible for themselves and oftentimes other family members. Student-veterans, like other adult learners, have generally been away from the classroom for several years but possess often-unacknowledged workplace knowledge. Like many other adult-learner groups, student-veterans are often concerned about the relationship between a college education and an occupational future. Unlike other adult learners, however, student-veterans' former military workplace is generally less well understood by faculty and traditional students alike; hence, making pedagogical connections between the experiences of the military and the civilian sector as well as connections between social groups (across the veteran and nonveteran divide) can be challenging for faculty. Also, while a student-veteran who has GI Bill support may enjoy better material resources than other nontraditional and adult learners, the student-veteran may also suffer from a range of lasting effects from military service, including physical and psychological wounds, and thus may need specific forms of support. Student-veteran eligibility and use of educational resources may also influence veteran homelessness, which the National Coalition for Homeless Veterans has established as an ongoing problem: While 7 percent of the general population can claim veteran status, veterans make up 13 percent of the homeless adult population, and while young veterans between the ages eighteen and thirty represent only 5 percent of the total veteran population, they constitute 9 percent of the homeless veteran population (National Coalition for Homeless Veterans 2013).

Comprehensive efforts to support student-veterans are suggested by Nancy K. Schlossberg, Ann Q. Lynch, and Arthur W. Chickering's (1989) model of adult transition, which argues that the adult learner moves in, moves through, and moves on. David DiRamio, Robert Ackerman, and Regina L. Mitchell (2008, 80) adapt this model to the student-veteran who first "moves in" to military service, then "moves through" it, gaining experience and sometimes formal education along the way. Finally the servicemember "moves out," going through a period of transition that may include returning home or heading to college. At that point the cycle starts over as the veteran moves in to the campus setting, moves through college classes, and then moves out to function in the civilian world. Using the DiRamio, Ackerman, and Mitchell modified model, we can see the college experience as a key bridge, linking transitioning veterans from one world (military) to another (civilian). The period of "moving in" to the college community involves choices such as choosing to blend in or to identify peers who have shared the military experience. It may involve directly addressing new disabilities and wounds, whether physical, psychological, or emotional. It often involves a renegotiation of personal finances and daily habits as well as dislocation from community support as offered on bases and posts, including ready access to competent medical care. Many student-veterans are thus engaged in a profound transition that is at once exciting and disorienting. Former chairman of the Joint Chiefs of Staff, Admiral Mike Mullen (2011), has argued that veterans need the full services of a support triangle comprised of educational, workplace, and healthcare support. Most student-veterans understand obtaining a college degree as a necessity and an opportunity, not an entitlement. According to the Pew Research Center's (2011, 3) report, "War and Sacrifice," nearly half of today's all-volunteer force joined the military for the educational benefits, which often begin, particularly via online courses, while the servicemember is on active duty.

Many veterans classify the process of obtaining a college degree as another "mission." Indeed, General Erik Shinseki, head of the Veterans Administration and former chief of staff of the army, in a speech before the national conference of the Student Veterans of America in the fall of 2011, reminded student-veterans that they are themselves responsible for seeing through the "mission" of college. In his remarks, Shinseki urged, "If you think this country owes you an education, you have an attitude problem. They didn't do this for any generation since World War II—until yours . . . The mission is clear, defeat is not an option, no one quits, and no one gets left behind" (US Department of Veteran Affairs. "Remarks by Secretary Erik K. Shinseki" 2011).

TEACHING IN THE CONTEXT OF THE MILITARY-CIVILIAN GAP

To many academics, Shinseki's comparison of earning a college degree and strategies for engaging in battle seem aggressive at best. Indeed, perhaps one of the most vexing issues in working with veterans is the military-civilian divide. When less than one-half of one percent of the population has been involved in military service during the decade of war encompassing OIF and OEF (Pew Research Center 2011, 2), compared to approximately 10 percent of the population involved during World War II, it is likely that neither faculty nor traditional students have sufficient understanding of their military students and classmates. The Pew Research Center (2011) bears this out. Investigating the "military-civilian gap," the report suggests that the differences between military and civilian populations are not only experiential but ideological; for instance, while 36 percent of veterans describe themselves as Republicans, a nearly equal percentage (34 percent) of civilians view themselves as Democrats. Perhaps more tellingly, 61 percent of veterans, compared to 37 percent of US citizens in general, describe themselves as patriotic (Pew Research Center 2011, 3). The Pew study also reports that veterans believe civilians do not understand what they and their families have been through, and their concerns seem borne out by statements made by civilians. While 83 percent of civilians recognize that servicemembers and their families have made sacrifices during a decade of war, only one-quarter of them describe this as unfair while 70 percent describe it as a natural outcome of having chosen the military as an occupation. Furthermore, only 25 percent of polled civilians say they have followed the wars closely, and only 50 percent report that the wars have affected them in any way. Interpreting the Pew data, *Time* reporter Mark Thompson explains,

> Never has the U.S. public been so separate, so removed, so isolated from the people it pays to protect it . . . Over the past generation, the world's lone superpower has created—and grown accustomed to—a permanent military cast, increasingly disconnected from U.S. society, waging decade-long wars in its name, no longer representative of or drawn from the citizenry as a whole. Think of the U.S. military as the Other 1%—some 2.4 million troops have fought in and around Afghanistan and Iraq since 9/11, exactly 1% of the 240 million Americans over 18. (Thompson 2011)

The implications of the military-civilian gap are profound, and the disconnect leads to some acute contradictions about how the US public—including faculty—understand veterans. Such contradictions certainly influence faculty's interactions with veterans. In "A Barbarian in the Ivory Tower," Alex Vernon, English professor at Hendrix College and US Army veteran who served in combat during the Persian Gulf War, explains:

> We [faculty] want to sympathize with individual soldiers, to hear their voices, to recognize the value of their lives beyond their military function, but to sympathize with them individually is to risk sympathizing with and supporting them collectively, which is to risk patriotism, which is to risk imperialism, which is to consort with, if not the devil, at least the devilish. (Vernon 2002)

The ambivalence many academics feel about the military and, yes, veterans, is a profoundly difficult—and profoundly important—subject to address, and the distrust goes both ways. Consider that much of the popular literature intended to advise veterans about obtaining college degrees emphasizes the dangers of a military-academic ideological divide. "Culture Shock: Five Tips to Help You Acclimate to Academia," published in the *Military Times* in 2011, typifies the tenor of the advice given to student-veterans. Among some valuable suggestions, such as "avoid split-second decision-making" and "talk like a student, not a warrior," author Jessica Lawson advises, "Don't take the bait." Lawson cites a Washington state VA director who says, "Academic freedom gives some instructors the sense that they can say whatever they want to say . . . There is a certain amount of baiting going on . . . We really try to train professors to suspend some of the rhetoric" (*Military Times*, March 31 2011, 34). Lawson recommends that student-veterans tap into the grapevine, learn about professors known for antiwar rhetoric, and "try to avoid their courses" (*Military Times*, Marc 31, 2011, 34). Even Lighthall's (2012) otherwise reasonable list of "things you should know about student veterans" is punctuated by the suggestion that faculty not discuss war or their political positions on it. It may be important for faculty to recognize that these cultural clashes can easily become litigious. Student-services researchers Persky and Oliver (2010, 118) suggest that colleges need to address "antimilitary bias" as a potential "liability issue," noting that "several states have pending legislation that specifies veterans as a protected class."

This climate shapes faculty concerns about the risk of offending student-veterans and their family members. We who teach in "veteran-friendly" institutions are often given contradictory advice about how to address these issues. On the one hand, the MLA and NCTE position statements stress the importance of promoting critical perspectives about the language and literature of war. MLA Resolution 2003–1, ratified in December 2004, takes a very clear stance:

Whereas in wartime, governments commonly shape language to legitimate aggression, misrepresent policies, conceal aims, stigmatize dissent, and block critical thought; and

Whereas distortions of this sort proliferate now, as in the use of the phrase "war on terrorism" to underwrite military action anywhere in the world; and

Whereas we are professionals committed to scrupulous inquiry into language and culture;

Be it resolved that the MLA support[s] the right of its members to conduct critical analysis of war talk in public forums and, as appropriate, in classrooms. (MLA 2003)

On the other hand, student-services literature on student-veterans and veteran-friendly colleges and universities has recommended that the topic of war be avoided unless absolutely necessary. This includes a statement from the American Council on Education (ACE 2009):

Most importantly, avoid expressing personal sentiments related to war or military personnel that could alienate or embarrass student veterans. All veterans deserve recognition and appreciation for their service regardless of our personal opinions.

Negotiating these conflicting viewpoints is always difficult, as two recent Op-Ed pieces exemplify. Historian Joyce S. Goldberg's (2011) "Why I Can No Longer Teach U.S. Military History," published in the *Chronicle*, explains that in recent years, students have enrolled in her US Military History course not to explore military history up to the Vietnam War but to "work through personal issues originating in more recent conflicts" and to find solace, seek closure, or gain personal understanding of their own or a loved one's post-9/11 military experience. Goldberg laments universities' lack of preparation and academics' lack of professional training to address such emotional needs, "but a course in military history," she insists, "is not an appropriate place for a therapy session." Literature professor Elizabeth Samet's (2011) "On War, Guilt and 'Thank You for Your Service,'" which was initially published in the *New York Times*, discusses the discomfiting phenomenon of strangers approaching uniformed servicemembers at airports and other public places with the broad comment, "Thank you for your service." Samet argues that the specter of guilt about Vietnam vets' homecomings animates this "mantra of atonement," sanitizes the reality of service during wartime, and inhibits, rather than fosters, mutual understanding between soldiers and civilians. "Today's dominant narrative," Samet (2011) insists, "favors sentimentality over scrutiny, [and] embodies a fantasy that everything will be okay if we only display enough flag-waving enthusiasm." These "bizarre, fleeting" interactions are "a poor substitute for something more difficult and painful—a conversation about what war does to people who serve and the people who don't" (Samet 2011). Samet's insights reaffirm claims by rhetoricians such as Roger Stahl (2009, 533), who argues that "support the troops" rhetoric functions primarily to deflect questions of just policy and dissociate civilians from questions of ethical military action by "manufacturing distance between civilian and soldier."

However, civilians' and military servicemembers' values do overlap in significant ways. According to the Pew Research Center's (2011) report, for instance, an equal number of both groups (35 percent) identify as Independents, rather than Republicans or Democrats. Also, civilians and veterans share nearly identical views on the connections between violence and patterns of cultural conflict: 51 percent of veterans and 52 percent of civilians say the connection between war and lasting hatred is real while 40 percent of veterans and 38 percent of civilians believe that overwhelming force is the best way to defeat terrorism.

Taking these complicated factors into consideration, the contributors to this collection convincingly establish that there's more to being "veteran friendly" than having flexible attendance policies. They explore what it means not only to be "veteran friendly" but to be real advocates of veterans *and* critical education. Writing-intensive classes might offer a location for addressing ideological differences, but doing so will require thoughtful curricula and pedagogy. The presence of veterans in composition classrooms presents both opportunity and challenge.

GENERATION VET: ENTERING THE CONVERSATION

In "Serving Those Who Have Served," a plenary speech at the Council of Writing Program Administrators conference, Marilyn Valentino (2012) named a number of issues that composition faculty and administrators must address if we are to enhance veterans' academic success. She stressed the importance of community writing groups and extracurricular writing opportunities for veterans; the potential of cohort courses composed exclusively of veterans; the need for faculty training in retention assistance and understanding military culture; and, in keeping with the CCCC 2003 resolution, fostering all students' critical thinking and reading skills regarding issues of war and concomitantly fostering faculty abilities to negotiate difficult conversations about war in our classrooms. Valentino (2012, 165) was careful to avoid characterizing veterans in light of deficit: above all, she remarked, "They don't need us to 'fix them.'"

The nascent and innovative research in *Generation Vet* shares Valentino's objectives for faculty development and innovative programs with and for veterans. This collection brings together work by scholar-teachers with diverse voices, experiences, and perspectives: some contributors are veterans, while others' family members have served or currently serve in the military. Some have found themselves in the midst of difficult situations with student-veterans in composition courses, while others facilitate community writing workshops for veterans or coordinate innovative programs, such as learning communities. Some of the essays in this collection are personal narratives, some entail original empirical research, and some forge new connections between critical theory and composition studies. All address a wide range of issues concerning veterans, pedagogy, rhetoric, and writing-program administration, and all promise to enhance our understanding of student-veterans, composition, and the post-9/11 university. As editors, our own personal histories in regard to military service have driven our interest and sustained our commitment to the issues that have emerged in this collection and in our larger research agenda. Lisa is the daughter of a career army warrant officer. Sue is the wife of a career Corps of Engineers Army officer. Among other interests, and given our histories, we believe there is a need for more research on the transition challenges faced not only by returning veterans but by their family members, to whom many veterans pass their GI Bill benefits. Very little research about this population and their educational needs is available, though we hope *Generation Vet* will spark greater awareness of our students who, as military dependents, bring particular experiences (e.g., educational disruption as military families are frequently transferred and required to move far more often than civilian families; the combat-related death of a loved one; the demands of being caregivers to one of the 3.5 million veterans with service-related disabilities [US Department of Veterans Affairs: "VA Issues New Report on Suicide Data" 2013]).

Part 1, "Beyond the Military-Civilian Divide: Understanding Veterans," addresses the potentially challenging rhetorical and cultural clashes that can arise as veterans transition from military cultures to academic cultures. Obviously, student-veterans are a diverse group with wide-ranging perspectives and experiences. However, according to a 2009 American Association of State Colleges report, student-veterans often report a sense of isolation on campus and frustration with traditional students: they express concern about entering a potentially liberal college culture that may conflate antiwar sentiment with antimilitary sentiment, and they can face difficulty finding mentors among faculty whose values may differ significantly from their own (Cook and Young 2009). In faculty-development workshops we have conducted, a common thread arises: how, particularly given many colleges' interest in attracting GI Bill funding and maintaining a "veteran-friendly" moniker, do we address difficult topics productively without creating an epistemic shutdown or discussion that some students will interpret as anti-American or antiveteran? The articles in Part I offer insights into the contact zone between military culture and academic culture, and they trouble common constructions of "the veteran."

In "Veterans in College Writing Classes: Understanding and Embracing the Mutual Benefit," Sean Morrow (US Army and formerly of the United States Military Academy, West Point) and D. Alexis Hart (Allegheny College) work to explain to writing instructors the culture shock and sense of dislocation veterans often experience in their first college courses, and they suggest that faculty, given a solid understanding of military values, can assist with veteran reintegration. In "Uniform Meets Rhetoric: Excellence through Interaction," student-veteran Angie Mallory (Montana State University) and faculty member Doug Downs discuss their differing expectations for classroom leadership; they conclude that, although sometimes difficult and unfamiliar to veterans, open-ended forms of rhetorical inquiry common to writing courses are vital if student-veterans are to make a successful transition to the civilian sector. Countering Downs and Mallory's sense of the constraints of military genres in "Not Just 'Yes Sir, No Sir': How Genres and Agency Interact in Student-Veterans' Writing," Erin Hadlock (MAJ, US Army, United States Military Academy, West Point) and Sue Doe (Colorado State University) suggest that military genres are more plentiful and their service-member users more rhetorically agentive than most faculty understand.

Military/academic cultural clashes took a very public form in 2011 when Baltimore County Community College drew nationwide attention after Charles Wittington, a student-veteran, was suspended for psychological review after publishing, in the campus newspaper, an essay from his composition class about his "addiction to killing." National response and debate were immediate, and Linda De La Ysla, the student-veteran's composition instructor, calls for an ethics of response as she recounts the events at BCCC that spurred her to develop community forums about and for veterans in "Faculty as First Responders: Willing but Unprepared."

Part 2, "Veterans and Public Audiences," explores the potential of nonacademic settings for the support and development of veterans' literacies and challenges cultural constructions of disability in and out-side the academy. In "'I Have To Speak Out': Writing with Veterans in a Community Writing Group," Eileen E. Schell and Ivy Kleinbart (Syracuse University) suggest the importance of veteran writing groups to encour-age and support veterans as they gain insight through writing about their experiences in the military and as they bring their writing to civil-ian audiences. Similarly, Karen L. Springsteen (Wayne State University), in "Closer to Home: Veterans' Workshops and the Materiality of Writing," reports on her work with the Warrior Writers Project, which brings together veterans and civilians through the materiality of writ-ing. She argues that community writing helps civilian participants in particular as they gain increased understanding of shared responsibility for war and its aftermath. Challenging common cultural constructions of the wounded warrior in academic communities and beyond, Tara Wood and Ashly Bender explore resistant forms of writing and repre-sentation of disabled veterans. In "Signature Wounds: Marking, and Medicalizing Post-9/11 Veterans," Wood (University of Oklahoma) calls for an overtly politicized approach to addressing disability that would challenge many institutional definitions of and approaches to PTSD and TBI. In "Exploring Student-Veteran Expectations about Composing: Motivations, Purposes, and the Influence of Trauma on Composing Practices," Bender (University of Louisville) suggests the importance of web environments for a generation of veterans accustomed to recording their experiences on YouTube. This new generation of student-veterans, she suggests, may embrace multimodal composition as a means of artic-ulating trauma and carving out a powerful narrative space to engage critical audiences.

Generation Vet next turns to the programmatic and pedagogical strate-gies that might best meet the needs of student-veterans. Part 3, "Veteran-Friendly Composition Practices," offers concrete strategies for writing teachers and administrators. In "Recognizing Silence: Composition, Writing, and the Ethical Space for War," Roger Thompson (Stony Brook University) considers the implications of Resolution 3 of the Conference on College Composition and Communication (which called upon writing classrooms to engage in rigorous debate about "wars perpetrated by the United States"). In light of the influx of stu-dent-veterans into our classrooms from the very wars that spurred the C's statement, Thompson argues that silence offers student-veterans a "powerful way of coping." Turning to specific locations and responding to regional differences at colleges and universities, Ann Shivers-McNair (University of Washington) reports on an innovative developmental writing program at the University of Southern Mississippi, which is located near Camp Shelby, the largest US Army Reserve base in the country. "A New Mission: Veteran-Led Learning Communities in the Basic Writing Classroom" provides insights into the successes and challenges of veteran-initiated academic programs. In "The Value of Service Learning for Student Veterans: Transitioning to Academic Cultures through Writing and Experiential Learning," Bonnie Selting (University of Missouri, Columbia) explores the service ethic often associated with veterans and discusses veteran-students' responses to service-learning programs that bridge the university and the community. Finally, in "Front and Center: Marine Student-Veterans, Collaboration, and the Writing Center," Corrine Hinton (Texas A&M, Texarkana) offers concrete strategies for writing center administrators and tutors who are working with student-veterans in record numbers.

Of course, like every collection, *Generation Vet* reveals gaps in current scholarship and implicitly calls for additional research on critical issues. As previously mentioned, we need research about the needs of military spouses and dependents who are beneficiaries of the GI Bill. Also, very little scholarship is available about military personnel's ethnic and racial affiliations in connection to literacy practices, degree attainment, and employment opportunities. Similarly, Generation 1.5 veterans, as well as those who participate in the Military Accessions Vital to National Interest (MAVNI) program, will be of particular interest to ESL and literacy researchers. MANVI provides expedited US citizenship for immigrants who (1) have legally been in the United States for two or more years and (2) have specialized linguistic skills or medical experience, both of which are in critical demand in all branches of the military. MANVI thus creates a unique literacy sponsor/recipient relationship that demands close and ethical attention.

Although many of the authors in this collection address issues of trauma and writing to heal, additional research about various aspects of trauma and the writing practices of post-9/11 veterans is of paramount importance. How does TBI affect information processing, problem solving, and the physicality of writing? What is best practice when veterans and their families disclose traumatic war experiences in our courses, particularly since Hart and Thompson (2012, 37) report that 71 percent of the writing faculty they surveyed require a personal writing assignment? Since the Veterans Administration estimates that 22 percent (and this number is likely higher due to report discrimination) of women veterans and in active military service have experienced military sexual trauma (MST), how can we meet the needs of female veterans in our classes and beyond? What educational and cultural roadblocks still exist for GLBT veterans, even post-Don't Ask, Don't Tell policies? Since the Department of Veterans Affairs reports that a veteran or active military member commits suicide every sixty-five minutes, and that over one-third of those suicides are by young men and women under the age of thirty (US Department of Veterans Affairs 2012: "Suicide Data Report"; Haiken 2013; ; US Department of Veterans Affairs: "VA Issues New Report on Suicide Data" 2013s), can community writing programs and therapeutic writing practices help address the high rate of veteran suicides and ameliorate depression?

These questions—and others that are difficult to anticipate at this time—will become more pressing in the years to come. Today, however, *Generation Vet* joins the emerging conversation and invites the development and expansion of the many lines of research and scholarship still needed. Our sense is that we will learn alongside veterans. Consider, for instance, the insights of one veteran in a longitudinal study that the editors of this volume are conducting; he told us about his premilitary literacy skills, what he took from his military experience, and his current hopes for his college experience. He said,

> When I was growing up we didn't have TV . . . because we lived fifteen miles out in the sticks in the middle of nowhere . . . So basically, I read a lot of books. My mom, she was a big reader, so I was a big reader. I was reading on a twelfth-grade reading level when I was in sixth and seventh grade."
>
> [In the military] I learned a lot about responsibility, you know. Even if you make a bad decision, still take responsibility for it just to learn something from that experience. And, the good experiences? Even you have to go over them sometimes too, ask why did I do this, instead of this? Why did that turn out so good? How can I kind of get the same results from this totally different problem?
>
> [In college] I don't need a handout or for anyone to feel sorry for me, but more of just an understanding that I'm not an eighteen-year-old coming out of high school. No, it's like I've got to relearn all of this and try and remember, so I'm trying to relearn all of this and still remember things from ten years ago along with all the new material.

As these insights suggest, we oversimplify and homogenize veterans' identities, values, and literacy experiences at our own peril. *Generation Vet* offers pedagogical, administrative, and theoretical insights about this generation of student-veterans, insights we hope will spur additional, nuanced research with and about student-veterans.

References

American Council on Education (ACE). Center for Policy Analysis and Center for Lifelong Learning. 2009. *Military Service Members and Veterans in Higher Education: What the New GI Bill May Mean for Postsecondary Institutions.* http://www.acenet.edu/news-room/Documents/Military-Service-Members-and-Veterans-in-Higher-Education.pdf.

American Council on Education (ACE). 2013. "Toolkit for Veteran Friendly Institutions: Opening Lines of Communication." http://www.vetfriendlytoolkit.org/academic/communication.cfm.

Bailey, Beth. 2011. "Losing the War." *Reviews in American History* 39 (1): 196–204. http://dx.doi.org/10.1353/rah.2011.0046.

Berrett, Dan. 2011. "Words from Wartime." *Inside Higher Ed.*, April 19. http://www.insidehighered.com/news/2011/04/08/veterans_in_college_have_vexed_relationship_to_writing_assignments.

Bawarshi, Anis, and Stephanie Pelkowski. 1999. "Postcolonialism and the Idea of a Writing Center." *Writing Center Journal* 19 (2): 41–59.

Bérubé, Allan. 1990. *Coming Out Under Fire: The History of Gay Men And Women in World War Two.* New York: Free Press.

Beucke, Dan. 2011. "Unemployment for Young Vets: 30%, and Rising." *Bloomberg Business News*, Nov. 11. http://www.businessweek.com/finance/occupy-wall-street/archives/2011/11/the_vets_job_crisis_is_worse_than_you_think.html.

Boulton, Mark. 2005. "A Price on Freedom: The Problems and Promise of the Vietnam-Era G. I. Bills." PhD diss., University of Tennessee. ProQuest.

Brandt, Deborah. 1995. "Accumulating Literacy: Writing and Learning to Write in the Twentieth Century." *College English* 57 (6): 649–68. http://dx.doi.org/10.2307/378570.

Brokaw, Tom. 1998. *The Greatest Generation.* New York: Random House.

"Budget Battles and a Stagnant Economy Greet America's Soldiers as They Return from Iraq and Afghanistan." 2011. *Economist*, December 17.

Canaday, Margot. 2003. "Building a Straight State: Sexuality and Social Citizenship under the 1944 G. I. Bill." *Journal of American History* 90 (3): 935–57. http://dx.doi.org/10.2307/3660882.

Caplan, Paula J. 2011. *When Johnny and Jane Come Marching Home: How All of Us Can Help Veterans.* Cambridge, MA: MIT Press.

CIA's Report: No WMDs Found in Iraq." 2005. *NBCNews.com*, April 25. http://www.nbcnews.com/id/7634313/ns/world_news-mideast_n_africa/t/cias-final-report-no-wmd-found-iraq/.

Cohen, Lizabeth. 2003. *A Consumers' Republic: The Politics of Mass Consumption in Postwar America.* New York: Knopf.

Connors, Robert J. 1997. *Composition-Rhetoric: Backgrounds, Theory, and Pedagogy.* Pittsburgh, PA: University of Pittsburgh Press.

Connors, Robert J. 1991. "Writing the History of Our Discipline." In *Introduction to Composition Studies*, edited by Erika Lindemann and Gary Tate, 49–71. New York: Oxford University Press.

Cook, Brian, and Young Kim. 2009. "From Soldier to Student: Easing the Transition of Service Members on Campus." ERIC Document ED505982.

Corley, Liam. 2012. "'Brave Words': Rehabilitating the Veteran-Writer." *College English* 74 (4): 351–63.

DiRamio, David, and Kathryn Jarvis. 2011. *Veterans in Higher Education: When Johnny and Jane Come Marching to Campus.* San Francisco: Wiley.

DiRamio, David, Robert Ackerman, and Regina L. Mitchell. 2008. "From Combat to Campus: Voices of Student-Veterans." *NASPA Journal* 45 (1): 73–102.

Eckstein, Megan. 2009. "Colleges Cite Inequities in New Benefits for Veterans."
  Chronicle of Higher Education 55 (22). http://cpe.ky.gov/NR/rdonlyres/DF34F5BF
  -387F-4F2C-8F0E-DDFFF1CB8AEB/0/CollegesCiteInequitiesinNewBenefitsfor
  Veterans.pdf.
"The Employment Situation of Veterans. 2013. Syracuse University. Institute for Veterans
  and Military Families.. http://vets.syr.edu/wp-content/uploads/2014/01/Employment
  -Situation-Jan20141.pdf.
Frydl, Kathleen J. 2009. *The GI Bill.* New York: Cambridge University Press.
Goldberg, Joyce S. 2011. "Why I Can No Longer Teach U.S. Military History." *Chronicle of
  Higher Education.* http://chronicle.com/article/Why-I-Can-No-Longer-Teach-US
  /129054/.
Haiken, Melanie. 2013. "Suicide Rate Among Vets and Active Duty Military Jumps—Now
  22 A Day." *Forbes*, February 5. http://www.forbes.com/sites/melaniehaiken/2013/02
  /05/22-the-number-of-veterans-who-now-commit-suicide-every-day/.
Hart, Alexis. 2013. "War, Trauma, and the Writing Classroom: A Response to Travis
  Martin's 'Combat in the Classroom.'" *Writing on the Edge.* 23 (2):37–47.
Hart, D. Alexis, and Roger Thompson. 2013. "'An Ethical Obligation': Promising Practices
  for Student Veterans in College Writing Classrooms." 4Cs Research Grant White Paper.
  http://www.ncte.org/library/NCTEFiles/Groups/CCCC/AnEthicalObligation.pdf.
Humes, Edward. 2006. *Over Here: How the G.I. Bill Transformed the American Dream.* Orlando,
  FL: Harcourt.
Johnson, Dennis W. 2009. *The Laws That Shaped America: Fifteen Acts of Congress and Their
  Lasting Impact.* Hoboken: Routledge.
Klein, Joe. 2011. "The Next Greatest Generation." *Time*, August 18, 26–34.
Lighthall, A. 2012. "Ten Things You Should Know about Today's Student Veteran." *NEA
  Higher Education Journal: Thought & Action* 28:81–84.
Martin, Travis. 2012. "Combat in the Classroom: A Writing and Healing Approach to
  Teaching Student Veterans." *Writing on the Edge* 22 (1). Spring.
Matera, Angelo. 2008. "*Into Iraq with* Generation Kill: *An Interview with Evan Wright.*"
  Godspy: Faith at the Edge. http://oldarchive.godspy.com/reviews/Into-Iraq-With
  -Generation-Kill-An-Interview-with-Evan-Wright-by-Angelo-Matera.cfm.html.
McDonagh, Edward C. 1947. "Veterans Challenge Higher Education." *Journal of Higher
  Education* 18 (3): 149–52. http://dx.doi.org/10.2307/1975213.
Mettler, Suzanne. 2005. *Soldiers to Citizens: The G.I. Bill and the Making of the Greatest
  Generation.* Oxford: Oxford University Press.
"Military-Friendly Schools." 2013. *Military Friendly.* http://www.militaryfriendlyschools.com/.
Modern Language Association (MLA). 2003. "Resolution 2003–1." http://www.mla.org
  /governance/mla_resolutions/2003_resolutions.
Mullen, Michael. 2011. "Sea of Goodwill." http://www.cof.org/files/Bamboo/programs
  andservices/professionaldev/documents/Sea-of-Goodwill-01-11-webinar.pdf.
Murray, Melissa. 2008. "When War is Work: The G.I. Bill, Citizenship and the Civic
  Generation." *California Law Review* 96 (4): 967–98.
National Center for Veterans Analysis and Statistics (NCVAS). 2013. http://www.va.gov
  /vetdata/Veteran_Population.asp.
National Coalition for Homeless Veterans. 2013. "FAQ about Homeless Veterans." http://
  nchv.org/index.php/news/media/background_and_statistics/.
National Priorities Project. 2011. "Military Recruitment 2010." http://nationalpriorities
  .org/analysis/2011/military-recruitment-2010/.
Olson, Keith W. 1974. *The G.I. Bill, the Veterans, and the Colleges.* Lexington: University
  Press of Kentucky.
Onkst, David H. 1998. "'First a Negro . . . Incidentally a Veteran': Black World War Two
  Veterans and the G.I. Bill of Rights in the Deep South, 1944–1948." *Journal of Social
  History* 31 (3): 517–43. http://dx.doi.org/10.1353/jsh/31.3.517.

Pat Tillman Foundation. 2013. "Completing the Mission: A Pilot Study of Veterans' Progress toward Degree Attainment." http://inpathways.net/Completing-the-Mission.pdf.

Persky, K. R., and D. E. Oliver. 2010. "Veterans Coming Home to the Community College: Linking Research to Practice." Paper presented at the annual meeting of the Council for the Study of Community Colleges, Seattle, WA. http://dx.doi.org/10.1080/10668926.2011.525184.

Pew Research Center. 2011. "War and Sacrifice in the Post-9/11 Era." http://www.pewsocialtrends.org/2011/10/05/war-and-sacrifice-in-the-post-911-era/.

Pytlik, Betty. 1993. "Teaching the Teacher of Writing: Whence and Whither?" Paper presented at the annual meeting of the Conference on College Composition and Communication, San Diego. ERIC document ED355541.

Rosales, Steven. 2011. "Fighting the Peace at Home: Mexican American Veterans and the 1944 GI Bill of Rights." *Pacific Historical Review* 80 (4): 597–627. http://dx.doi.org/10.1525/phr.2011.80.4.597.

Rose, Mike. 1983. "Remedial Writing Courses: A Critique and a Proposal" *College English* 45 (2): 109–28. http://dx.doi.org/10.2307/377219.

Samet, Elizabeth. 2011. "On War, Guilt, and 'Thank You for Your Service." *Bloomberg.* http://www.bloomberg.com/news/2011-08-02/war-guilt-and-thank-you-for-your-service-commentary-by-elizabeth-samet.html.

Sander, Libby. 2012a. "At Half a Million and Counting, Veterans Cash In on Post-9/11 GI Bill. *Chronicle of Higher Education* 58 (28): A1–A11.

Sander, Libby. 2012b. "Congress Looks to Safeguard Veterans' Education." *Chronicle of Higher Education* 58 (28). http://chronicle.com/article/Congress-Looks-to-Safeguard/131722/.

Sander, Libby. 2013. "National Group for Student Veterans Kicks Out 40 Chapters at For-Profit Colleges." *Chronicle of Higher Education.* http://chronicle.com/article/National-Group-for-Student/131446/.

Schlossberg, Nancy K., Ann Q. Lynch, and Arthur W. Chickering. 1989. *Improving Higher Education Environments for Adults: Responsive Programs and Services from Entry to Departure.* San Francisco: Jossey-Bass.

Snead, Katherine. Testimony. http://archives.democrats.veterans.house.gov/hearings/Testimony.aspx?TID=59709&Newsid=444&Name=%20Kathryn%20M.%20Snead,%20Ed.D.

Stahl, Roger. 2009. "Why We 'Support the Troops': Rhetorical Evolutions." *Rhetoric & Public Affairs* 12 (4): 533–70. http://dx.doi.org/10.1353/rap.0.0121.

Teaching English in the Two-Year College. 2009. Special issue 36 (4).

Thompson, Mark. 2011. "The Other 1%." *Time*, November 21. http://www.thesandgram.com/2011/11/11/the-other-1-by-mark-thompson/.

Toby, Jackson. 2010. "Using Carrots and Sticks to Improve American Colleges." *Social Science and Public Policy* 47:42–7.

US Department of Veteran Affairs. Education and Training. 2013. "History and Timeline," http://www.benefits.va.gov/gibill/history.asp.

US Department of Veterans Affairs. Mental Health Services. 2012. "Suicide Data Report," by Janet Kemp and Robert Bossarte. http://www.va.gov/opa/docs/Suicide-Data-Report-2012-final.pdf.

US Department of Veteran Affairs. Office of Public and Intergovernmental Affairs. 2011. "Remarks by Secretary Erik K. Shinseki." http://www.va.gov/opa/speeches/2011/12_09_2011.asp.

US Department of Veterans Affairs. National Center for Analysis and Statistics (NCVAS). 2013. "Veteran Population."

US Department of Veterans Affairs. Office of Public and Intergovernmental Affairs. 2013. "VA Issues New Report on Suicide Data." http://www.va.gov/opa/pressrel/pressrelease.cfm?id=2427.

Valentino, Marilyn J. 2012, "Serving Those Who Have Served: Preparing for Student Veterans in Our Writing Programs, Classes and Writing Centers." *Writing Program Administrator* 36 (1): 164–78.

Vernon, Alex. 2002. "A Barbarian in the Ivory Tower." *Chronicle of Higher Education.*

Villanueva, Victor. 1993. *Bootstraps: From an American Academic of Color.* Urbana, IL: National Council on the Teaching of English.

White, H. Adelbert. 1944. "Clear Thinking for Army Trainees." *College English* 5 (8): 444–46. http://dx.doi.org/10.2307/371458.

"Who Benefits from the Post-9/11 GI Bill?" 2012. *Chronicle of Higher Education.* https://chronicle.com/article/Who-Benefits-From-the/131132/.

Wright, Evan. 2004. *Generation Kill: Devil Dogs, Iceman, Captain America, and the New Face of American War.* New York: Putnam Adult.

PART I

Beyond the Military-Civilian Divide

Understanding Veterans

1

VETERANS IN COLLEGE WRITING CLASSES
Understanding and Embracing the Mutual Benefit

Sean Morrow and Alexis Hart

> *There is a gulf between those of us in the services and those of us who have remained civilians. We have only heard about each other second hand, and in the press. This is not good enough. We must get together. We must understand each other. Otherwise, the gulf will grow wider, bitterness and distrust will increase, and this period of demobilization will be all the more difficult.*
>
> —CPT Robert Maugham, HMS (Bolte 1945, 145)

This "gulf" between civilians and their military counterparts to which Captain Maugham drew attention at the end of the Second World War is perhaps even more evident today in an era during which only 1 percent of the US population serves in the active military and only 7 percent are military veterans (Elliott, Gonzalez, and Larsen 2011, 282). Yet, as more veterans take advantage of the post-9/11 GI Bill and matriculate on college campuses in numbers not seen since the 1940s, we college writing instructors are increasingly likely to encounter opportunities to engage with student-veterans and to facilitate their transition into the academy, opportunities that may seem both intimidating and appealing.

On the one hand, as veterans enter our writing classrooms with experiences neither more traditional students nor we are likely to have encountered, we college writing professionals may find ourselves wondering if we need to reevaluate our approaches to writing instruction. On the other hand, we may find ourselves sharing an appreciation for the mutual benefit to be had when teaching student-veterans. As community college writing professor and Marine Corps veteran Galen Leonhardy remarks, "Composition instructors must first recognize that

DOI: 10.7330/9780874219425.c001

we have much to learn from veterans, just as we have much more to do for them." He goes on to suggest that since veterans are likely to "make up a fair number of potential students. . . It is important to understand them" (Leonhardy 2009, 340).[1] Drawing upon Morrow's experiences during the recent wars as an active-duty military officer, a graduate-student veteran, and a composition instructor of both veterans and nonveterans, and on Hart's experiences as an active-duty military officer serving during the relative peace between the First Gulf War and the more recent combat operations in Iraq and Afghanistan, and as a professor of writing at a public military college, this essay brings together the insights of a relatively new initiate to academe and a more seasoned academic, of a post-9/11 and a pre-9/11 veteran, to offer an insider perspective meant to provide college writing faculty with some understanding of military culture and to offer some suggestions about personal and pedagogical approaches that may serve to assist this new generation of student-veterans in college writing classes.

First, the essay examines the range of experiences of contemporary military personnel, discusses how these varied experiences result in similarities as well as profound differences among veterans, and considers how recognizing and acknowledging these varied experiences might help writing teachers productively interact with student-veterans and more effectively incorporate these students into the broader classroom structure. Next, Morrow relates some of his personal experiences as a veteran in graduate school and then as an instructor of both veterans and future soldiers in the freshman writing program at West Point. The nature of some of his experiences may have a slightly different resonance since Morrow's postcombat experience as a student was in a graduate classroom and his college teaching experience has been limited to students who have made the commitment to serve in the military; nevertheless, the insights provided by these narratives are transferrable. Finally, the essay discusses some approaches writing instructors can cultivate in the classroom to find points of connection that can serve to bridge the civilian/military gulf mentioned above and increase the likelihood that the experiences writing instructors share with student-veterans will result in enhanced learning and increased understanding for all.

UNDERSTANDING THE SCOPE OF VETERAN EXPERIENCES

As is the case with other minority student populations, the scope of veteran experiences is substantial.[2] What makes veterans different from other minority-student populations is that even though their experiences vary widely, the context of those experiences retains a high degree of similarity. This shared context affords teachers of writing the opportunity to gain insight and understanding about their student-veterans by asking a few general questions likely to resonate with most (but, admittedly, not all) student-veterans.

> Why did you join the service?
> Was your military-service experience what you expected?
> What did you learn from your time in the service?
> Why did you choose to come to this college/university?
> What do you want to get out of and/or contribute to this class?

Of course, these questions are not all inclusive, nor do they represent a checklist to be administered to each veteran who walks through a writing teacher's classroom or office door. They do, however, enable us as instructors to gain some insight into the type and scope of experiences student-veterans may have and can provide an early indicator of veterans' willingness or desire to be open about their status as veterans within the context of the classroom and the campus. As Morrow observes,

> *These are the types of questions that give veterans a chance to decide and to convey to their instructors how they prefer to navigate their college experience relative to their experiences as veterans. As opposed to later in this essay when Professor Hart and I offer suggestions about ways for writing teachers to strive to cultivate productive learning environments for student-veterans , these questions are really designed to help veterans understand themselves as they transition from military members to college students. I imagine many student-veterans, especially in the undergraduate realm, have not stopped to ask themselves these questions yet. Most veterans I know get so busy living from experience to experience that they don't take the time to reflect on the significance of their military service as it applies to their own understanding of themselves and to their expectations for their future.*
>
> *The experiences and insights I share in this essay come from a nuanced perspective acquired by serving as an infantryman during the invasion of Iraq and then returning for a fifteen-month deployment during the Surge in 2007–2008. Shortly after my return, I entered graduate school. Although I was still on active duty, I attended class in civilian clothes and rarely mentioned my profession unless certain questions or conversations naturally led to that disclosure. After graduate school, I served as a teacher of both veterans and nonveterans in the composition and literature classroom at the United States Military Academy. While the dynamic of teaching at West Point may render my experiences different from those of writing instructors at civilian colleges and universities in the sense that all of my students chose to potentially go to war and therefore tended to maintain a different appreciation for their veteran peers, the reality was that the fears, curiosities, and apprehensions of these future officers in the presence of their classmates who had already served in combat were scarcely different from the interest, indifference, appreciation, questions,*

and assumptions of my classmates and faculty at a civilian graduate university exhibited in relation to me. In a sense, I lived this essay on both sides of the equation. While my experience may seem esoteric at first, I hope you will quickly find that being asked the questions above and being given the opportunity to reflect on the answers will resonate with the eighteen-year-old private who never finished high school, the twenty-five-year-old married mother of two who signed up to receive healthcare, the forty-year-old sergeant who joined because patriotism runs deep in her family. The experiences of these military members are undoubtedly vastly different, as discussed in the ensuing paragraphs, yet all veterans share a common bond no matter what their level of education, socioeconomic background, branch of service, or rank; all are part of the community of veterans. How that status affects veterans as students varies from veteran to veteran, and how veterans choose to publicly represent their veteran status (or not) is impossible to predict from one veteran to the next. Yet I contend that striving to understand the reasons student-veterans joined the military, how their military service affected and continues to affect them, what they hope to gain from attending college, and even what they hope to gain from any particular course, is central to making the most of any veteran's higher education experience.

It is important to recognize that the decision to enlist in the military is prompted by many factors. Some enlistees crave the challenge; others hope to travel.[3] Some are motivated by patriotism;[4] others just want their first steady paycheck.[5] Some follow a family tradition of military service.[6] Some are running toward war; others are running away from trouble. Some hope the military can provide a greater sense of identity, and some are deliberately seeking a pathway to college.[7] Some are not quite sure how or why they ended up in a recruiter's office but leave with a signed contract. Yet whatever their motivations or recruitment experiences, all enlistees eventually end up in a fairly common basic-training course.

During basic training, successful recruits learn to adapt to the strict regimen of military life. They are awakened early each morning to conduct physical-fitness training, and every moment of the remainder of their day is scheduled: they are told where to be and when to be there. If they fail to comply or to show up in the right place at the right time, not only does someone with authority track them down and bring them to where they are expected to be, but other memorable consequences result as well. Having left their loved ones and all that is familiar, many feel alone and afraid, so they must quickly learn to rely on each other to get through those trying times. They eventually learn how to function as an operational unit, how to become members of a team who can depend upon each other not only to complete a mission but also to help each other return safely. As a result, no matter where they go after the service, when they meet other veterans, they experience an instant bond of shared ethos.

After basic training, these men and women join new, but equally cohesive, units. Once they are in a unit, however, their experiences often differ vastly. Many post-9/11 veterans have never had a rocket screech over their tent to wake them up, nor have they seen first hand the spilled blood of a fellow human being. These veterans may have wished to be at war, or they may be grateful that they never experienced combat. For those deployed in Afghanistan and Iraq—even those who do not serve in "official" combat roles—combat is a daily experience. Logisticians face attacks from improvised explosive devices (IEDs), rockets, and small-arms fire to ensure the infantry gets supplies. Knowing they might find or perhaps even be blown up by an IED, engineers keep the roads safe for others. Some have seen friends die. Others have made split-second decisions they later regret. In fact, Morrow notes that a common trait among veterans is guilt.

> *All veterans tend to harbor some form of guilt, often framed as, "I didn't do enough." Veterans nearly always underestimate their contributions to the fight. Those who remained stateside may feel as if they shirked their duty. Those who deployed but lived in relative comfort may feel guilty that they didn't face the same deprivations and dangers as others. Some who were on the front lines may be dismayed they never engaged in a firefight. Those who exchanged fire with the enemy may be quick to say that what they did "was nothing." Most who acted heroically may humbly note that "anyone else would have done the same." You may even encounter veterans who seem to thrive on the notion of war and want to live out the video games they grew up on, but most veterans I know are peaceful in nature and aren't out looking for a fight. Once the fighting begins, however, they feel a commitment and a duty to contribute as much as possible, not so much for the thrill or for notions of honor or glory but out of a commitment to protecting the soldiers or civilians near them who may be in harm's way. I tend to believe that, in a broad sense, most soldiers see themselves as caretakers and problem solvers. Therefore, as long as war continues, there is a subconscious notion that we have failed to solve the problem or to provide sufficient safety to those entrusted to our care.*

Being aware of the broad range of veterans' experiences is a vital first step toward engaging productively with them as students. Indeed, today's student-veterans have been giving researchers "a consistent message . . . that they [hope] faculty members [will] acknowledge their veteran status and attempt to understand them as a student population" (DiRamio, Ackerman, and Mitchell 2008, 89). How professors attempt to honor this wish, however, will require careful consideration. The military training and mindset of humbly downplaying personal contributions affect student-veterans' decisions about whether or not and to whom to disclose their veteran status, which can make it difficult for professors to identify student-veterans because "they often [do] not want to be seen." In addition, "Student veterans [are] not inclined to announce and use their veteran status to receive preferential treatment" (Livingston et al. 2011, 322).[8] Student-veterans may also "have difficulty in their relations with college faculty [particularly] when faculty disrupt their efforts at anonymity and unveil their military experience in class" (Radford 2009, 18).

In Morrow's experience, some veterans want to keep their status private because they feel as if they have spent enough time being defined by their uniforms, and the chance to (re)enter a college classroom simply as another student is a welcome relief. For these students, the desire to receive external acknowledgment or attention is minimized by the fact that they either do not want to relive what they have been through, or they are sufficiently confident about what they achieved during their service and consider college to be their next challenge, their next mission, with no need to dwell on their past experiences.

On the other hand, Morrow has found that some veterans want to ensure that professors, classmates, and everyone else within earshot knows they served in a military uniform. These young veterans often seek recognition and validation and expect those around them to acknowledge and honor them openly.[9]

The following section presents some additional considerations for professors when encountering these seemingly contradictory positions—student-veterans' personal desire for acknowledgment and understanding of their veteran status coupled with their public reluctance to disclose that status.[10]

NEGOTIATING DISCLOSURE, CULTIVATING TRUST

Recent studies of post-9/11 veteran enrollment demonstrate that "military veterans are in many ways more prepared to flood onto college campuses than most institutions are to receive them" (Lederman 2008). However, as teachers of writing we must also recognize that many returning veterans are still likely to "experience culture shock resulting from the stark contrast between the military world and civilian institutions such as higher education" (Zinger and Cohen 2010, 39). As they transition from their military commands to college campuses, student-veterans are leaving a world (as described earlier) in which "authority is absolute, responsibility for actions lies in the hands of superiors and . . . the rules are clear" (Zinger and Cohen 2010, 39–40). Therefore, for many veterans, the relative autonomy of life as a college student requires significant adjustments. As Rosalind Loring and Edward Anderson discovered when developing a program in the 1970s to prepare Vietnam veterans for college courses at UCLA, student-veterans tend to be highly motivated, seek respect for their experiences, and want their opinions to be recognized, but they also tend to feel anxiety about their age and have "a low self-concept regarding academic matters" (Loring and Anderson 1971, 100–2). Consequently, they often request that their professors provide them with "specific assignments, explicit standards, and stated expectations for behavior" (Starr 1973, 246). In addition, due in part to the individualistic nature of most college coursework, many veterans report feeling "painfully alone, without the camaraderie of their military brethren" (Zinger and Cohen 2010, 47). Today's veterans also report that they often have difficulty relating to classmates "who tend to be younger, less respectful of authority, ignorant of what military service entails,[11] and even critical of the very conflicts in which the veterans have just risked their lives" (Elliott, Gonzalez, and Larsen 2011, 281). Not surprisingly, therefore, student-veterans are most likely to relate best to individuals who share their military background, thus they tend to seek both academic and social support from "military colleagues whom they already [know] or faculty members to whom they [are] introduced," that is, people with whom they feel "more comfortable associating . . . because of the common military experience and challenges they [share]" (Livingston et al. 2011, 323).[12] Morrow experienced such connections and sought support from veteran faculty members he met early in his graduate-student career.

> *Shortly after I entered college, I received an invitation to lunch from a faculty member I had met briefly at a reading group. During lunch, we talked of literature and future plans. He told me about his family and about some of his undergraduate students who were interested in the military. "You know," he said, "there aren't too many of us here." I didn't have to ask because I immediately knew. He was a veteran. He related his experiences from serving in the military in the 1950s and asked me about my more recent experiences. We talked about what service meant to us and about how people at the college perceived the military and the veterans on campus. It was a meaningful moment to have him reach out to me, and we still remain in touch today.*

This story features a professor who was not afraid to reach out to Morrow, ask him questions, and forge a relationship with him. Perhaps to those readers who have not served in the military, this professor's veteran status may seem to confer on him an unfair "advantage" that empowered him to take that first step to connect with Morrow. Certainly, their shared veteran status forged an immediate link, but it also obviated an understandable reluctance held by professors who have no prior military experience themselves to try to relate to a student-veteran.

In general, veterans say "it is easier to focus on school when surrounded by those who can understand what they've gone through and offer advice" (Hemmerly-Brown 2010, 12), and they frequently enter college with "a very personal bias that 'to talk-the-talk, you must have walked-the-walk'" (Shackelford 2009, 39). As a result, "if veterans are not well represented among campus faculty members and administrators, and if these individuals have little firsthand or systematic knowledge of military culture and the potential impact of wartime service on servicemembers, it may complicate campus efforts to serve student veterans and facilitate successful transitions" (Rumann and Hamrick 2009, 30). While this fear of conflicting ideologies certainly won't prevent a veteran from enrolling in college, it is a realistic concern that many veterans harbor and about which faculty should be aware.

Fortunately, today's student-veterans haven't been met with the overt hostility that Vietnam veterans on campuses in the 1960s and 1970s experienced but instead have "largely been met with polite acceptance" (Boodman, *Washington Post*, November 28, 2011). Even so, as professors we must be attuned to the fact that the policies we extol or criticize in our classrooms, even in off-handed remarks, are often policies that have resulted in the operational missions student-veterans have spent years of their lives executing, whether they agreed with the policies or not. We must be aware that what may be regarded by those of us "in command" of a classroom as a punch line to a political joke or an "unofficial" personal remark may create an uncomfortable situation for a student-veteran. While this observation is not meant to stifle debate, criticism, or even expressions of personal displeasure, it is important to ensure that as academics we present such comments within the context of critical pedagogy. In interviews with researchers, student-veterans have said they can typically discern a "distinction between professors presenting their political views as opinions versus presenting their political views within the context of the rest of the lecture material" but have also found that other students tend to accept "the professors' views regarding US policy in toto," which means it takes "a lot of courage to challenge them" (Glasser, Powers, and Zywiak 2009, 33).[13] Here, Morrow shares an example of how he felt and reacted when he found himself disagreeing with the comments of another student.

> During one of my classes, we discussed inaccuracies in after-action reports during the fight between the IRA and the British army. A fellow student started to describe the fog of war. He talked about what people feel when they are under fire and how that affects their ability to remember details. I felt the stares of my two closest friends in the class as they tried to gauge my reaction. I hope I gave none. Other than the

two women to my left and right, nobody in the classroom knew what I did for a living. Nobody else knew that if they really wanted to know what it feels like to be shot at, they could have asked. The only problem was, they did not know. I found myself willing, almost eager, to share my experiences while simultaneously not wanting to come across as a braggart, or "the guy with war stories." My regard for this other student kept me silent, and his insight was thoughtful, even though I found it to be inaccurate based upon my experience.

In another instance, Morrow found himself face to face with a published author who presented a political opinion he found to be uninformed.

I attended an evening lecture by a novelist who read from her latest book. The author spoke about growing up in a country full of conflict and then read a scene from her novel. One of the characters engaged in an extended monologue comparing George Bush to Adolf Hitler. As I sat there, I couldn't help but wonder, "If she compares George Bush to Adolf Hitler, then what would she think of me and of my soldiers?" Could this author, I wondered, really think my soldiers and I were no better than the villains who committed unspeakable atrocities sixty years ago?

I had already heard worse—from strangers, from friends, on television, and in print. These opinions made me sad: sad that those who espoused those views would likely never know the care and concern 145 rough-hewn infantrymen had shown to those civilians in Iraq whom we viewed as entrusted to our care. They would never know, as I did, that my soldiers had given their own possessions to Iraqis, or that I had soldiers badger me about ordering comfort items only to discover the intended recipients did not live within the guarded walls of our patrol base but rather in the mud huts of Fetoah. These were my thoughts as I listened to my way of life being compared to the greatest evil humanity has ever known.

While his own professors in graduate school did not make such appalling comparisons, Morrow did feel most were merely obliquely interested in and respectful of his military service and were not particularly interested in discussing it with him in any depth. To his disappointment, few of his professors even asked him about where he served, what his service meant to him, how his military experiences affected him, or what he thought about anything connected to foreign policy. While he accepts the fact that college professors are experts in their academic fields whose direct obligations to their students end when they have enabled those students to attain a greater understanding of the material being studied, he nevertheless feels that the high regard veterans ascribe to the positions of influence and trust held by professors at institutions of higher education can provide faculty members with a rich opportunity to lead and mentor student-veterans. Academics may not realize that student-veterans frequently have an idealized conception of college educators: they regard their professors as authority figures whose power comes not only from their esteemed positions and extensive knowledge but also from their presumed commitment to serving those students who have been entrusted to their care. As former marine Kelly Dalton argues, professors *can* attempt to manifest certain principles of military leadership in their classrooms: "One of the essential components of leadership is stewardship—a sense of personal responsibility and care toward those being led" (Dalton 2010, 42). Therefore, while all college students are likely to appreciate personal, human interactions with their professors outside the classroom, it is likely that veterans in particular will respond positively to personal attention and a willingness to listen nonjudgmentally. Perhaps the best way for professors to ascertain whether veterans are interested in sharing their experiences is simply to ask. If the professor gets a clear or abrupt answer that student-veterans don't wish to discuss their past military experience, then the educator should respect that response. Often, though, professors may find that these veterans simply are waiting to be asked. Morrow offers the following example from his personal experience as a graduate student as a case in point.

> The professor whom I most admire and whose talent as an educator and scholar is unparalleled never talked to me about my experiences. He was aware of them, but we never just sat down and talked about what I experienced as a combat veteran serving in a politically volatile region overseas. I am certain, given my area of academic interest, that the topics of politics, intervention, unilateral military action, terrorism, and counterterrorism could have been integrated into such a discussion. I wanted him to ask me. I wanted him to challenge me and push back on my opinions. That was why I was in graduate school—to sort out my real-world experiences in new and challenging contexts. I wanted to reexamine what I believed through lenses I had never been exposed to. In short, I wanted to be forced outside of my comfort zone.
>
> One day this professor mentioned that he had been teaching an early twentieth-century text on revolution on the day after September 11, 2001, and commented that the students reacted in a way they never had before or since. They had a different perspective on the text that day, he told me, "One which you surely understand." In hindsight, I realize that at that moment he was reaching out. I missed the opportunity to seize the moment and to engage in that personal conversation I was so eager to share with him.

Morrow's conflicting desires both to be regarded as a serious graduate student by this professor he so admired and yet to have that professor acknowledge and seek to know more about his military experiences and personal life is not uncommon among student-veterans. Just as some faculty members may have to look past stereotypes of "wounded warriors" or may have internalized the conventional view of the military as being "steeped in the traditions and practices of aggressive masculinity" (Burnett and Segoria 2009, 54), student-veterans may have to overcome "the stereotype of the adversarial roles of the liberal professor and conservative veteran" (DiRamio, Ackerman, and Mitchell 2008, 89). In addition, some veterans who have "become accustomed to strict organizational discipline and high accountability" may find "the laissez-faire culture of the academy [to be] frustrating" (Lokken et al. 2009, 74) and may therefore find it difficult to relate to faculty who may seem to be indifferent to institutional or positional authority. As a result, like Morrow, most student-veterans are unlikely to approach their professors directly and say, "I'd really like to talk to you about my experiences, and I'd like your help sorting them out and deciding what they mean to me in my civilian life."

Even so, veterans' previous lives makes up much of their practical experience and contribute significantly to their intellectual development. Thus, they will impact the veterans' academic experience and development as well. Professors have the power to help veterans come to understand "that by virtue of their personal experiences they have an important contribution to make to scholarship about real, public, political, and moral issues" (Dalton 2010, 30). Therefore, professors should seriously consider engaging veterans in personal discussions of their military service if they become aware of it. As mentioned earlier, if a professor takes the time to reach out to a student-veteran , that student will often respond enthusiastically, as Morrow did in the following example:

> *One evening, I met a professor from the college at a lecture. She asked me about my background, and when I told her I was in the military, she invited me for coffee. We met and talked for a few hours. She was a fascinating woman who was very interested in US culture and the role the US military plays in creating and disseminating culture. Her questions started out easy, casual, and not at all probing. Once I was comfortable, she began to ask harder questions, which I happily answered. Ultimately, she invited me to speak to her class in the freshmen honors college. I gladly accepted.*
>
> *As I spoke before the class, the professor asked how many students knew someone in the military. Not a single hand went up. I was stunned. For the last fourteen years I had been immersed in the military. I had never paused to think that some students may have never encountered a veteran or a servicemember.*

Had this professor not initiated a conversation with Morrow, she and her students would have missed out on the opportunity to be enriched by hearing about his experiences as a leader and as a US servicemember deployed overseas. As this example demonstrates, even academics who have no prior military experience themselves can benefit from enabling student-veterans to leverage their experiences in the service into rich academic discussions.

Fortunately, many college professors have begun to realize the pedagogical value of reaching out to student-veterans and asking them to share their stories either privately or publicly, as Morrow did. As Elizabeth O'Herrin, former associate director of the American Council on Education (ACE), points out, "Veterans can bring with them a wealth of knowledge about living abroad, as well as deep personal experience with innovation, accountability, and responsibility. The influx of veterans into our institutions provides new opportunities for the enrichment of classroom discussions and the enhancement of campus diversity" (O'Herrin 2011, 15). Other researchers have suggested that "the educational quality of military students can be improved through the development of socio-educational relationships. . . such as recognizing a student's knowledge by having them provide spontaneous accounts, presenting alternative versions of arguments, engaging various participants holding contradictory opinions, building arguments collectively through work in small groups" (Morreale 2011, 138). Leonhardy has found this to be true when teaching veterans in his writing classes: "In terms of making the private public, most veterans understand collaboration well and can involve themselves in small group interactions. . . Small groups seem to facilitate class discussions, which allow vets to establish in-group relationships and non-veterans to ask questions—questions that some students deeply long to have answered" (Leonhardy 2009, 346). The following section contains some additional pedagogical advice specifically related to working with student-veterans in college writing classes.

ENGAGING STUDENT-VETERANS IN WRITING CLASSES

Regarding classroom techniques for understanding and embracing the mutual benefit (for ourselves and for other students) of having veterans in our writing classes, we won't recommend specific exercises but will rather try to shed light on some common mindsets and attitudes held by veterans that may assist writing professors as we consider how best to engage with this student demographic. When considering student-veterans, a case might be made that they represent an "Other" whom we need to engage and try to understand for the very reason that they may seem difficult for us to comprehend. In order to help the student-veterans who enroll in our writing courses, we should seek to challenge them and to respect them in order to develop the trust and mutual respect so valued among military members.

Capitalize on Teamwork and Leadership Training

The value of leadership and teamwork is ingrained in veterans from their first day of basic training. Consequently, student-veterans may often take the lead in class discussions and help other students tap into their own experiences to find meaning through the expression of their ideas.

> *In one of my classes were two combat veterans. Both men were clearly more confident than their peers, but they could not have been more different. One student's leadership was polished, his questions probing, and his intellect acute. He projected confidence in his work and empowered his peers in class. Although his experiences in combat had been difficult, they left him feeling self-assured and ready to take on the role of a student, preparing himself for the future. The second student had a harder time adjusting to life outside a military unit. His questions, while also intelligent, always seemed defiant, with a hint of anger in them. I am certain his vibe intimidated most of the nonveteran students. When I asked, this young man confided to me that he was struggling with situations he had experienced and that he still did not feel quite comfortable outside a combat zone, where he'd had many formative experiences in the few short years since his eighteenth birthday.*

Other writing teachers may encounter one or both of these types of veterans. Some veterans will be more like the second student Morrow describes: they will feel entitled, they will be angry, they will act superior to other students, and they may even act superior to us. They may think, "There they stand now and propose to teach us again. But we expect them to set aside some of their dignity. For, after all, what can they teach us? We know life better than they; we have gained knowledge—harsh, bloody, cruel, inexorable" (Remarque 1921, 120). When we encounter such student-veterans, we should try to be responsive, just as we are when we encounter annoyed civilian students. It is likely to be more effective to ask them privately if they are having problems with the class rather than accusing them of being troublesome or asking them to leave the class immediately. We should try to discover what is causing difficulty for them and offer to help them get through those frustrations. We might even try to alleviate their frustration by giving them specific guidance about how to contribute positively to the class, concrete strategies for how to move forward in the class in productive ways that may also help such students control and direct their frustration. Morrow provides one such example.

> *I met with one veteran in my office and told him I would like him to participate more in class. I told him I would give him very specific guidance—a "heads up"—about what I would expect him to remark upon during class. While it may seem as if I provided this student with an unfair advantage, it had the intended effect. Rather*

than arriving at class bitter because he was feeling inadequate and less capable than his peers, he started coming to class feeling sufficiently prepared to engage in the discussion and then did so productively.

Provide Feedback

Because they have come from a culture in which mistakes can cost lives or destroy expensive equipment, most student-veterans crave clear directions and candid feedback from someone they trust. As Dalton explains, "Military personnel are accustomed to feedback that is 'candid and accurate'. . . even when it is negative" (Dalton 2010, 14). She goes on to explain that "student-veterans who are accustomed to (sometimes brutally) honest evaluations of their military performance will gain little from feedback that doesn't seem engaged and sincere. By giving student-veterans frequent feedback, [writing instructors can] convey a sense that they are invested in the student-veteran's progress, that they believe in the student-veteran's ability to succeed, and that positive feedback is genuinely earned" (Dalton 2010, 49–50). Leonhardy also urges writing teachers to "be aware of the power of comments on vets' papers" (Leonhardy 2009, 349–50). He recounts that what he wanted "as a younger vet-scholar, were comments that would allow [him] to gain authority, comments pointing to errors in [his] reasoning as well as in [his] spelling, comments that let [him] tell others about [his] experiences in the military" (Leonhardy 2009, 350).[14] We can aid student-veterans by giving them space to write and to speak about their experiences (or to choose not to) even as we retain professional confidence as experts in the field of writing studies; regardless of our familiarity or lack thereof with military culture or combat missions, we can respond to their texts with honesty and candor and a critical eye for the qualities of effective and appropriate discourse for a given rhetorical situation.

Provide Clear Rationales

We should also retain an awareness of the apprehension student-veterans may harbor about producing writing for a college-level course, a university professor, and a letter grade. Like other adult learners, for student-veterans "anxiety about the unknowns of academic writing [may contribute] to behaviors like repeated questions about assignments and excessive concern with grading. This anxiety can be kept to a minimum," relates Michelle Navarre Cleary, "by providing rationales for and explanations of assignments and assessment criteria and by giving plenty of low-stakes opportunities for students to practice what they are learning" (Cleary 2008, 116). In addition, many adult learners feel they "need to know how the learning will be conducted, what will be learned, and why it will be valuable" (Knowles quoted in Cleary 2008, 116). Student-veterans, who are coming from a highly mission-oriented culture, will likely also expect instructors to provide them with clear end goals and rationales for assignments as well as detailed grading criteria.

Encourage Critical Consciousness

Composition professors who take a critical-consciousness approach to teaching reading and writing often try to engage students in investigations of "the ways social formations and practices shape consciousness, and [how] this shaping is mediated by language and situated in concrete historical conditions" (Berlin 1998, 391). By taking this approach, these instructors strive to offer students a multicultural, global awareness and appreciation of various world-views. These instructors can reap great benefits from student-veterans—especially combat veterans—since they have already developed much of this critical consciousness through their real-world experiences, often overseas. As Willard Waller points out, "The veteran has a greater sophistication and a wider experience of people, especially outside of his [*sic*] own social class . . . If the veteran returns to school or college, some way must be found to capitalize on his experience" (Waller 1944, 152). If professors make the time to interact with student-veterans and attempt to learn more about their previous experiences, they may be able to help veterans begin to feel comfortable sharing these experiences in the public forum of the class, thus enriching the discussion. As Dalton remarks, "Finding ways to demonstrate to student-veterans that their personal experiences may connect directly to larger societal concerns, as well as issues with which the academy is directly engaged, may help student-veterans feel less like outsiders in the academic community" (Dalton 2010, 47). Having spent significant time engaging with members of other cultures during their overseas deployments, and having been frequently forced to reevaluate simple categories of "us" and "them," veterans can add depth to such discussions, but can also learn much from other students who are willing to challenge some of the veterans' own ingrained assumptions. Morrow relates a story of engaging a student-veteran in this way.

> *A combat veteran was struggling in my class. I offered him and another traditional student a very detailed plan for additional instruction outside of class hours. They*

responded positively, but only the veteran showed up regularly. While his diligence was impressive, his patience for his fellow struggling classmate was minimal. This veteran's resentment and immaturity manifested most memorably on one particular occasion. The other student arrived late and began to talk about her morning beauty regimen. The veteran lost his cool and said, rather calmly, "Will you please shut the f**k up and pay attention to what we need to be doing?" The veteran had little patience for a student he viewed as lazy, undisciplined, and disrespectful. The veteran failed to realize that underneath the scatterbrained appearance of a student who needed to work on her writing and her ability to follow instructions was an intelligent and poetic woman who had a lot to offer him.

Use Repetition and Imitation

Veterans often learn well by repetition and imitation. Military training is grounded in the accomplishment of individual and collective tasks. Every major maneuver is broken down into its parts (individual tasks), and those tasks are practiced over and over again until they become second nature. Only when the individual tasks are mastered are the parts made whole again in the collective task. Student-veterans therefore respond positively to writing instruction that follows a similar pattern. Phrases and sentences can be broken down, revised, and edited over and over again until a strong sentence is habitually within reach. Paragraphs can likewise be revised repeatedly. Veterans are accustomed to the idea of constant work and revision to get the little things right before moving on to the bigger things. When the parts work well independently, they can be synthesized into a collective task, which for writing teachers is a complete draft.

Morrow has also found when student-veterans are shown examples of good writing to emulate, their writing improves. In military training, an expert is put in charge and shows the novices "what right looks like." The novices watch the expert and then attempt the task just as she did it, copying her every movement. Tasks are demonstrated and then practiced until they can be executed perfectly. While Morrow was initially hesitant to employ this type of imitative teaching in a writing classroom because he feared that all sixty papers would have the same "bones" as the example paper and differ only in subject matter, he has found these fears to be unfounded. Instead, he has found that providing successful student papers as models gives student-veterans a better understanding not only of what good writing looks like but also of what makes it good writing. The examples, he has found, provide a known standard the students then strive to achieve on their own.

Get Expert Help When Necessary

While we can attempt to help student-veterans in a number of ways through our pedagogies and personal interactions, there are a few things we can't do. We can never allow our extended efforts as we seek to help a veteran to inhibit our teaching and mentorship of other students. We can't let a veteran take over our class; we cannot allow a veteran to feel entitled to anything. We especially cannot hesitate to bring veterans who may need help beyond the scope of our professional expertise on writing to the attention of someone in the administration or on the staff who is qualified to care for them.

CONCLUSION

If we know of a student who has trekked across the Appalachian Trail, or who gets up at 6 AM to help homeless families, or who has undergone physical or emotional trauma, we have encountered a psyche similar to that of the student-veteran. The raw emotions grounded in personal experience are vital to each of those students' understanding of themselves. Veterans bring formative experiences to the classroom in droves, and not only through narratives of combat. Even if we are not teaching memoir or personal narrative, these experiences shape who student-veterans are and how they write. The opportunity for us to meet the educational needs of the veterans while enhancing the overall writing experience of traditional students has not been so potentially fruitful in over sixty years. One veteran at a time, college writing professors can maximize this opportunity for both the veterans and their classrooms at large. By acquiring an understanding of military culture and experiences through the development of an open and professional relationship with student-veterans , faculty will be able to leverage the maturity and life experiences of these students to benefit all of the students in the classroom while providing veterans with an appropriate outlet for their own development as writers, as students, and as individuals.

Notes

1. Department of Education researcher Alexandria Walton Radford concurs: "As these veterans and military service members [who have fought in the Afghanistan and Iraq wars] use their new benefits to seek postsecondary education, it is important to understand their backgrounds and characteristics" (Radford 2009, vii).

2. Research on current student-veterans has revealed that many veterans feel as if college professors lack an understanding of the diversity of the student-veteran population. As one young veteran remarked, "Most professors would claim to embrace

diversity among the student population, but some would like to exclude veterans from the multiplicity list due to our war service" (quoted in Elliott, Gonzalez, and Larsen 2011, 287). Daniel Byman, Senior Fellow for Foreign Policy at the Saban Center for Middle East Policy, has also observed that "many professors harbor stereotypes about the military, not recognizing the diversity of opinion within military circles on many issues and the remarkable minds of many young soldiers" (Byman 2007). However, as Mark Bauman explains, "Learning about the military, war and combat, and servicemembers' experiences [can actually] complement a campus's broader commitment to diversity and social understanding" (Bauman 2009, 31).

3.   More than half of recent veterans (65 percent) claimed that they enlisted "to see more of the world" (Taylor 2011, 33).

4.   The 2011 Pew poll revealed that "nearly nine-in-ten post-9/11 veterans (88%) and a slightly larger share of those who served before the terrorist attacks (93%) say that serving their country was an important reason they joined the military" (Taylor 2011, 33).

5.   Somewhat surprisingly, perhaps, "only about a quarter of pre- and post-9/11 veterans say an important reason they enlisted was that jobs were scarce" (Taylor 2011, 33).

6.   As Meredith Kleykamp discovered, "Decisions to join the military are not just strategic economic calculations. Families and communities are a major source of transmission of information and norms and values regarding military service" (Kleykamp 2006, 275).

7.   Of those veterans responding to the 2011 Pew poll, 75 percent "say they joined to get educational benefits" (Taylor 2011, 33), a significant increase from previous eras. This increase may be due to the fact that military recruiters faced difficulties in the 1990s competing with colleges for "high-quality" recruits. As the rate of college tuition has risen faster than most family incomes and federal grants have concurrently failed to keep pace with rising college costs, students who may harbor "high college aspirations" may also "fear taking on a great debt burden" and therefore "may seek alternative means of paying for college" such as the GI Bill (Kleykamp 2006, 274–75). In other words, military service currently may provide "a means for members of the noncollege population with high educational aspirations to attain their goals" (Kleykamp 2006, 286).

8.   The following comment by a veteran serves as a case in point: "I wrote about my experiences as a marine in a journal assignment given by an English professor. The professor shared her admiration but I didn't want it. She put me on a pedestal, which made me feel uncomfortable. She seemed to be happy around me. I am not special; I did what I had to do. It was a job that needed to get done. The breaks my English professor gave me by letting me hand in assignments late felt unfair" (Zinger and Cohen 2010, 45). This student clearly wanted his professor to know about his service, but he did not want to receive special "breaks" not available to other students because of his military experience.

9.   These two characterizations of veterans do not tell the full story, of course. As retired army captain Shannon Meehan points out, "The stories we tell consistently portray veterans in extremes—either emphasizing vets' heroism beyond comprehension or their propensity for erratic violence . . . Because of the unreal, formulaic depictions of vets in our culture, [veterans] remain distanced from society, leaving little chance that anyone will actually see [vets] as real people with both strengths and struggles" (*NYDailyNews.com*, March 15, 2012).

10.   Paul Tschudi, a Vietnam veteran and faculty adviser to student-veterans at George Washington University, has found that the students he advises frequently "want it both ways: [They] don't want to be singled out, but want respect, and for people to know what they've been through" (Boodman, *Washington Post*, November 28, 2011).

11. When describing their sense of culture shock as they transitioned from the military to college, some veterans mentioned being "surprised at their classmates' lack of attention, text messaging, giggling and complaining . . . and a few were asked questions like 'how many people did you kill,' which they found highly uncomfortable" (Glasser, Powers, and Zywiak 2009, 33).

12. Student-veterans report that they often prefer to interact with other veterans because, unlike their more traditional undergraduate classmates, other student-veterans "[understand] the complexities of military or combat experiences, [laugh] at their jokes, [affirm] their service, and [know] the sets of challenges that may accompany return to civilian life" (Rumann and Hamrick 2009, 453).

13. Dalton also points out that "professors may unwittingly contribute to a student-veteran's feelings of difference—not only by expressing negative opinions about war or the military, but also by asking a student-veteran to function as a kind of military spokesperson by discussing his [sic] first-hand experiences of war in front of his classmates" (Dalton 2010, 11).

14. The desire for honest feedback is not unique to student-veterans . Adult students in general understand that "they need to improve [as writers] and are eager for concrete, actionable advice on how to do so. When they do not get it, they feel that the instructor is not doing his or her job" (Cleary 2008, 19).

References

Anderson, Edward, and Rosalind Loring. 1971. "The Considerations in Planning a College Prep Program for Veterans." *Adult Leadership* 20 (3): 100–2.

Bauman, Mark. 2009. "The Mobilization and Return of Undergraduate Students Serving in the National Guard and Reserves." In *Creating a Veteran-Friendly Campus: Strategies for Transition and Success*, edited by Robert Ackerman and David DiRamio, 15–23. San Francisco: Wiley Periodicals. http://dx.doi.org/10.1002/ss.312.

Berlin, James A. 1998. "Composition Studies and Cultural Studies: Collapsing Boundaries." In *Rhetoric in an Antifoundational World: Language, Culture, and Pedagogy*, edited by Michael Bernard-Donals and Richard R. Glejzer, 389–410. New Haven: Yale University Press.

Bolte, Charles. 1945. *The New Veteran*. New York: Reynal and Hitchcock.

Burnett, Sandra E., and John Segoria. 2009. "Collaboration for Military Transition Students from Combat to College: It Takes a Community." *Journal of Postsecondary Education and Disability* 22 (1): 53–58.

Byman, Daniel L. 2007. "Veterans and Colleges Have a Lot to Offer Each Other." *Chronicle Review*, December 14. http://chronicle.com/article/VeteransColleges-Have-a/10596.

Cleary, Michelle Navarre. 2008. "What WPAs Need to Know to Prepare New Teachers to Work with Adult Students." *WPA: Writing Program Administration* 32 (1): 113–28. http://wpacouncil.org/archives/32n1/32n1cleary.pdf.

Dalton, Kelly Singleton. 2010. "From Combat to Composition: Meeting the Needs of Military Veterans through Postsecondary Writing Pedagogy." Thesis, Georgetown University.

DiRamio, David, Robert Ackerman, and Regina L. Garza Mitchell. 2008. "From Combat to Campus: Voices of Student-Veterans." *NASPA Journal* 45 (1): 73–102.

Elliott, Marta, Carlene Gonzalez, and Barbara Larsen. 2011. "U.S. Military Veterans Transition to College: Combat, PTSD, and Alienation on Campus." *Journal of Student Affairs Research and Practice* 48 (3): 279–96. http://dx.doi.org/10.2202/1949-6605.6293.

Glasser, Irene, John T. Powers, and William H. Zywiak. 2009. "Military Veterans at Universities: A Case of Culture Clash." *Anthropology News* 50 (5): 33.

Hemmerly-Brown, Alexandra. 2010. "From Combat to Classroom: Soldiers Face Challenges Returning to Studies." *Soldiers Magazine* 65 (9): 9–12.

Kleykamp, Meredith A. 2006. "College, Jobs, or the Military? Enlistment during a Time of War." *Social Science Quarterly* 87 (2): 272–90. http://dx.doi.org/10.1111/j.1540 -6237.2006.00380.x.

Lederman, Doug. 2008. "Preparing for an Influx." *Inside Higher Ed.* http://www.inside-highered.com/news/2008/06/06/vets.

Leonhardy, Galen. 2009. "Transformations: Working with Veterans in the Composition Classroom." *Teaching English in the Two-Year College* 36 (4): 339–52.

Livingston, Wade G., Pamela A. Havice, Tony W. Cawthon, and David S. Fleming. 2011. "Coming Home: Student Veterans' Articulation of College Re-enrollment." *Journal of Student Affairs Research and Practice* 48 (3): 315–31. http://dx.doi.org/10.2202/1949 -6605.6292.

Lokken, Jayne M., Donald S. Pfeffer, James McAuley, and Christopher Strong. 2009. "A Statewide Approach to Creating Veteran-Friendly Campuses." In *Creating a Veteran Friendly Campus: Strategies for Transition and Success*, edited by Robert Ackerman and David DiRamio, 45–54. San Francisco: Wiley Periodicals. http://dx.doi.org/10.1002 /ss.315.

Loring, Rosalind and Edward Anderson. 1971. "The Considerations in Planning a College Prep Program for Veterans." *Adult Leadership* 20 (3): 100–2, 110–12.

Morreale, Cathleen. 2011. "Academic Motivation and Academic Self-Concept: Military Veteran Students in Higher Education." PhD diss., State University of New York at Buffalo.

O'Herrin, Elizabeth. 2011. "Enhancing Veteran Success in Higher Education." *Peer Review* 13(1). http://www.aacu.org/peerreview/pr-wi11/prwi11_oherrin.cfm.

Radford, Alexandria Walton. 2009. *Military Members and Veterans in Higher Education: What the New GI Bill May Mean for Postsecondary Institutions.* Washington, DC: American Council on Education.

Remarque, Erich Maria. 1921. *The Road Back.* New York: Little, Brown.

Rumann, Corey B., and Florence A. Hamrick. 2009. "Supporting Student Veterans in Transition." In *Creating a Veteran Friendly-Campus: Strategies for Transition and Success*, edited by Robert Ackerman and David DiRamio, 25–34. San Francisco: Wiley Periodicals.

Shackelford, Allan L. 2009. "Documenting the Needs of Student Veterans with Disabilities: Intersection Roadblocks, Solutions, and Legal Realities." *Journal of Postsecondary Education and Disability* 22 (1): 36–42.

Starr, Paul J. 1973. *The Discarded Army.* New York: Charterhouse.

Taylor, Paul, ed. 2011. *The Military-Civilian Gap: War and Sacrifice in the Post-9/11 Era.* Washington, DC: Pew Research Center.

Waller, Willard. 1944. *The Veteran Comes Back.* New York: Dryden Press.

Zinger, Lana, and Andrea Cohen. 2010. "Veterans Returning from War into the Classroom: How Can Colleges Be Better Prepared to Meet Their Needs." *Contemporary Issues in Education Research* 3 (1): 39–51.

2
UNIFORM MEETS RHETORIC
Excellence through Interaction

Angie Mallory and Doug Downs

We first crossed paths in a first-year composition (FYC) course. Angie, four months out of the navy and in her first university classes; Doug, a specialist in FYC pedagogy whose courses emphasized self-directed inquiry. On the first day, Doug asked the class what as writers they wanted to learn. Angie thought, "You don't *know* what we're supposed to learn? Just *tell* us." When asked a question, Doug often turned it back to the class with a "what do *you* think?" In discussions of scholarly readings, Angie waited for definitive "here's-what-this-text-says" explanations that rarely came. Writing assignments were given as relatively open ended: "Tell me what you think about X," with procedures, steps, or outlines rarely offered. Doug gave extensive feedback on writing but did not grade it. He sometimes arrived late to class, sometimes haphazardly dressed. He was so clearly a flake, Angie nearly dropped. She stayed only because she knew she had to take comp sometime, and she figured she could tough it out—accept the course as a waste of time, give the instructor what he wanted (though he would not be clear about what that was), and "finish the mission."

In a happier ending, a couple of weeks in, Angie began to value Doug's approach, and the course ended up being a major- and life-changing one. Here, we focus on why it almost was not: the dramatic shift in interaction with "superiors" that accompanies a veteran's addition of *college student* to her range of what James Paul Gee (1989, 1999) has called "Discourses," language-based identity "toolkits" (which we describe in detail later in this chapter). Angie's experience in FYC, along with that of the four other military veterans we interviewed, was of becoming *valued interlocutors* after years of unquestioning performance of scripts that rarely called for their intellectual input. Our interviews

DOI: 10.7330/9780874219425.c002

with veterans suggest that for many, military service bifurcates critical thinking and doing, valuing the latter. Yet in college, critical thinking *is* doing, and FYC means to teach students ways of credibly making their voices heard. Our research suggests the need for veterans and instructors to begin negotiating this shift quickly and openly—far more than literature on veterans in college has noted to date.

As in Angie's case, we found no actual failures stemming from lack of accommodation: veterans in FYC who encounter self-directed learning and new interaction with superiors don't drop the course in vast numbers or earn low grades. They adjust and usually perform among the best in the class. What interests us, instead, is how FYC instructors may be unaware of the disjunct between what they seek in their classes and the far different rules for contribution and interaction with superiors in the military. There has been almost no attention to what additions (not just *transitions*) veterans are making to their cultural knowledge as they begin college, particularly in classes that nondirectively seek student contributions to intellectual projects shared with faculty. Similarly, little attention is paid to pedagogy's assisting acquisition of the new Discourses veterans encounter. Instructors seeking to foster inquiry need better awareness of veterans' different expectations for what constitutes appropriate student-faculty interaction and teaching. Such awareness influences pedagogy, particularly in terms of feedback supporting such interaction.

We arrive at this conclusion by first discussing two weaknesses in veteran-education research—lack of attention to veterans' learning outcomes and the dominant metaphor for veterans' arrival at college, *transition*. We then consider the learning, classroom interaction, and inquiry fostered in effective composition courses: what can FYC ask of students, and where can it take them? From this baseline, we recount interviews with veterans, analyzing how military enculturation predisposes veterans to encounter leadership, expectations for contribution, and nonhierarchical interaction in FYC, and how these veterans negotiated differences between their expectations and reality. From these accounts, we derive strategies for feedback and interaction that helped veterans begin adopting Discourses of inquiry.

FRAMING THE PROBLEM: VETERANS ACQUIRING NEW DISCOURSES

Our review of research on veterans in college shows little attention paid to actual vet learning outcomes. The preponderance is actually administrative: what support structures ensure that veterans encounter the fewest headwinds moving from barracks to campus? Chief among such studies is Cook and Kim's (2009, iii) *From Soldier to Student: Easing the Transition of Service Members on Campus.* Surveying 723 institutions, the sixty-four-page report is "a first-of-its-kind national snapshot of the programs, services, and policies that campuses have in place to serve veterans." Yet it does not consider student learning; amid discussions of financial-aid, counseling, disabilities services, credit counting, and transfer, academics don't come up. We would hardly know that veterans take classes. Looking beyond student-affairs reports, there is no parallel reporting on veteran learning; conversation simply vanishes. In the ERIC database, *student learning* yielded 10,989 hits; adding in *veteran* and *military* dropped the count—to zero. Broadening the search to *student learning* and *military* generated twenty-four hits—all on job-related instruction for active-duty servicemembers. In Academic Search Complete, adding *military* and *veteran* to *student learning* reduced hits from 5,559 to 1.

The same trend dominates industry commentary (e.g., *Chronicle of Higher Education*): extensive discussion of structural challenges and opportunities, little attention to student learning (see Byman 2007; Glasser, Powers, and Zywiak 2009; Lipka 2010; O'Herrin 2011). For example, Herrmann et al.'s (2008) *CHE* article "College Is for Veterans, Too" discusses "financial aid, transfer credits, educational programs, health care, and classroom dynamics." But "educational programs" means scheduling around veterans' full lives, and "classroom dynamics" means preventing instructor politics from silencing veterans.

To us, then, the majority of research on veterans in college actually *overlooks the very point:* student learning.

That is not to say that no attention is paid to classroom experiences. There is significant conversation on what can be addressed in classes with veterans, and what veterans contribute, along two main lines: how to talk about traumatic incidents without "setting off" ex-soldiers—often cast as damaged, broken, abnormal, sometimes dysfunctional—and how to handle the professorate's left-leaning, antiwar, antimilitary, politically critical bent. Some work, like Leonhardy's (2009) article in the special veterans issue of *Teaching English in the Two-Year College*, explores how veterans create productive classroom energy based on the wealth of lived experience they have to draw on. (No other articles in that issue, and none in the 2010 "dot mil" issue of *Kairos*, considered student-veteran learning in FYC.) But there's no real discussion of veterans' learning processes and outcomes.

Given such silence, and especially since much of veterans' learning as they enter college is about how to be college students, we see a great need to explore how veterans learn and how their learning relates to effective composition instruction. One example of the cost of poor attention to how veterans learn is our second major critique of literature on veterans in college: the widespread deployment of a *transition* metaphor in describing veterans' evolution "from" military "to" academic life. While in some ways accurate, *transition* is insufficient to account for the learning necessary for veterans to acculturate to the academy.

Much veteran scholarship, particularly by Rumann and Hamrick (2010) and by DiRamio, Ackerman, and Mitchell (2008), is explicitly grounded in transition theory, particularly Nancy Schlossberg's. She characterizes transition as "moving in, moving through, moving on" (Schlossberg, Lynch, and Chickering 1989). From a cultural perspective, *transition* makes sense. The major life changes of joining up, being deployed, surviving deployment, separation from the military, and entering college are life altering (Ackerman, DiRamio, and Mitchell 2009, 6–8), and transition theory helps name the characteristics of these changes and plumb their impacts.

But scholars of written communication recognize that it is not only veterans' *positions* that change in entering college, but their *language* and discursive knowledge. These changes must also be understood as Discourse acquisition. According to James Gee (1999, 19), Discourses are "ways with words, feelings, values, beliefs, emotions, people, action, things, tools, and places that allow us to display and recognize characteristic *whos* doing characteristic *whats*." A Discourse is "a sort of 'identity kit' which comes with costume and instructions on how to think, act, talk, and write, so as to take on a social role that others will recognize"— the "saying-doing-being-valuing-believing combinations" that tell people how to *be* in given situations (Gee 1989, 7). When we recognize a performance of a Discourse, we identify the performer as a "real" X (e.g., doctor, bachelor, soldier, student) (Gee 1999, 18). Later we'll detail some of the key elements that constitute a military saying-doing-being-valuing-believing Discourse, but for now, think *uniforms*.

Gee understands Discourses as malleable, dynamic, and fuzzy. Each of us embodies multiple Discourses concurrently, each inflecting the others (Gee 1989, 7–8). For example, a soldier Discourse would be modulated by hobby, family, and faith Discourses (say, a Jewish soldier who is also a father and sails). This interplay of Discourses means that even as veterans "move" to college, they *maintain* their military Discourse, along with Discourses they acquire in college. In showing how we embody different

Discourses to different degrees in different circumstances, Gee's (1989, 9–10) theory is essentially rhetorical: failure to "shift" our "natures" (Discourses) as appropriate to a given moment may create social embarrassment and failed communication. He finds that the only way to *become* a "real" X is to "mushfake" the Discourse: use tools from one's existing Discourses to try to emulate the new Discourse. In other words, being a wannabe is how we actually acquire a Discourse. But mushfaking takes time as one gradually comes to embody the new Discourse.

In these ways, Gee's Discourse theory explains how veterans acquire Discourses of the academy, and why FYC is a central site for the beginning of that acquisition. Discourse theory lets us see the changes veterans encounter not as *transitional* but as *accretional*: veterans are not *replacing* a Discourse but *adding* one—not moving *from* a military Discourse *to* the Discourses of the academy, but rather mushfaking new academic Discourses by modulating their existing military Discourse. In ways that are centrally important to student learning in FYC, then, "transition" is simply an inaccurate metaphor for what veterans actually experience. There's a transition of *place*, but only *addition* of Discourse—re-place-ment but not replacement. Understanding this difference, and understanding the resulting inadequacy of the transition metaphor in addressing veteran learning, are crucial for investigating that learning, particularly when it concerns human interaction and discourse to begin with.

ACADEMIC DISCOURSES OF INQUIRY AS EMBODIED IN COMPOSITION COURSES

If we wish to study veteran learning in FYC as related to Discourse acquisition, we need to consider what Discourse is meant to be acquired—and what learning environments compositionists have developed to foster that acquisition. Among the best summaries of what cutting-edge FYC does is the CWPA's "Effective Teaching Practices in General Studies Writing Classes" (Rhodes, Downs, and Bowden 2011), which includes these statements:

- Pedagogically effective student writing arises out of inquiry into questions that students can find to be compelling.
- Effective instruction approaches writing as a whole and varied activity, by its nature including feedback from peers and experts, that aims to create authentically communicative results.
- Effective writing instruction encourages students to reflect on their writings.

- Effective writing instruction uses writing as a means of exploration, critical thinking and disciplinary learning.

CWPA intends this document to gather settled knowledge on writing pedagogy: stable, widely accepted practices characteristic of what well-trained teachers would implement, ideas to which well-trained college writing instructors would rarely have serious philosophical objections. To understand how different veterans' expectations of writing instruction are from these principles, we need to consider the nature of writing as an inquiry-based and interactional activity that leads experts to advocate the above practices.

We take it as axiomatic that writing is a *rhetorical* activity: it is always *situated* in time and space; always *motivated* by some authorial goal; *contingent* on its situation and motivation; materially *embodied* in some combination of modality and genre; fundamentally *interactional*, depending on a collaboration of writers and readers; and fundamentally *epistemic*, generating new knowledge rather than simply transmitting existing knowledge. Further, we understand writing as activity based: texts are tools that help groups of people accomplish a specific activity (Russell 2010), and thus writing cannot be understood or taught outside the context of any given activity because the nature of the activity helps shape the writing both directly and by shaping the rhetorical situation that shapes the writing (Geisler et al. 2001).

The first point made in the "Effective Teaching Practices" document is on inquiry because the activity or Discourse that all college education participates in, and is situated by, *is* inquiry. For this chapter, we'll describe the Discourse of inquiry in much the same way Doug has elsewhere: "Ways of behaving, habits of mind, values and beliefs, epistemologies, and dispositions that favor questioning, pursuit of new knowledge and understanding, desire to analyze and synthesize, curiosity, and 'negative capability' (Keats's term for deliberate tolerance of long-term cognitive dissonance stemming from not having one's mind made up)" (Downs 2005, 42). Such investigation via questioning requires several characteristics. First, scholarly inquiry requires a skeptical stance toward hierarchy, order, authority, and power. It tends to resist hierarchy by demanding autonomy and self-direction, which is one reason that, more than most other bureaucracies, universities favor decentralization and individual agency. Second, inquiry demands a tolerance for change, instability, and dynamic emergence—a lack of fixity and a permanent unsettledness of knowledge. Third, it demands doubt about and challenge of dogma, established doctrine, and procedure. The very purpose of inquiry is to *ask again*, to reexamine knowledge, assumptions, received wisdom, and common sense. To advance knowledge, we question and challenge it. And inquiry, fourth, requires subjective management of complexity and multiplicity—because big problems (flying to the moon, reducing poverty, understanding the gut biome) do not resolve to one simple answer but rather demand interweaving multiple systems, explanations, and solutions driven by the situated perspectives of those inventing them. Lastly, then, inquiry is voiced and unscripted: conducted in the voices of individual participants, the result of willed expression.

Now, if we are to teach Discourses of inquiry, activity theory and situated learning theory (Artemeva 2008) suggest we do so in a setting of inquiry itself (Downs 2010). Especially given that writing is situated and contingent, unscripted and voiced, it's no surprise that writing instruction has evolved to accommodate these characteristics. It uses what Jay Lemke calls an "interactive learning paradigm" as opposed to a traditional "curricular" learning paradigm. In a curricular paradigm, Lemke (1998) states, "someone else will decide what you need to know, and will arrange for you to learn it all in a fixed order and on a fixed schedule." This paradigm dominates schooled learning. (And according to education critic Ken Robinson [2010], significantly stifles student creativity.) Education's future, Lemke (1998) argues, is the interactive paradigm, "access to information, rather than imposition of learning." It "assumes that people determine what they need to know based on their participation in activities where such needs arise, and in consultation with knowledgeable specialists; that they learn in the order that suits them, at a comfortable pace, and just in time."

The development of college writing instruction since the 1970s clearly reflects the interactive paradigm, which is well suited to the expressive, interactional, developmental nature of writing itself. The expressive and process movements shifted writing instruction from a curricular paradigm of mimetic study of literature (Fulkerson 2005) to a rhetorically based interactional paradigm, turning classes into sites for reading students' own writing, reflection, and engagement with social issues from students' perspectives. College writing instruction now positions students as fully voiced *contributors* to conversations rather than as silent bodies to be acted upon by others' texts. One example is writing-about-writing (WAW) pedagogy, which makes students' contributive inquiry on writing the subject of FYC (Downs and Wardle 2007). It was in a WAW-based course that Doug and Angie's dialogue began, and it was the dual calls to inquire and to contribute that discomfited and then engaged Angie as a veteran.

This, then, is a common form of writing instruction that veterans will encounter. It

- shifts initiative from the instructor to the students;
- values questions more than answers;
- expects writing to create knowledge rather than simply transmit it;
- seeks contributions from students in their own voices;
- works via genuine interaction among students and teacher rather than in a one-way transmission of instructions from teacher to students;
- demonstrates the rhetorical nature of writing—its nonuniform, non-formulaic, unscripted aspects; and
- expects students to develop as writers in a self-directed manner varying from student to student.

This is the scene of our study: a rhetorical, interactional world encountered by students who, as our interviews show, instead expected a uniform, curricular world.

MILITARY ENCULTURATION ENCOUNTERING COMPOSITION CLASSROOMS

We want to know how veterans encounter FYC in all its nondirective, inquiry-driven, interactional glory. How do veterans map the course onto their military backgrounds, how do they mediate military and inquiry Discourses, and how do they use military Discourse to mushfake inquiry? Addressing these requires describing key elements of military Discourse—which we call *scripts*—that shape veterans' expectations of college. We then consider how inquiry-driven FYC compares to these scripts in the areas of instructor leadership, faculty-student interaction, and student contributions. This comparison demonstrates how radical veterans' learning is as they excel in college writing courses.

Our data come from interviews with five veterans (including Angie) from a range of public institutions, selected via convenience sample. Most have attended several schools, including community colleges and four-year institutions (three were actually attending MSU when they were interviewed). One is now a graduate student. All are in their twenties and thirties, and only one (currently in the reserves) plans to return to active duty. Two are male, three female; four are navy veterans, one air force. Angie conducted IRB-approved interviews of about an hour using a set primary-question list and free-form follow-up questions. Angie and Doug transcribed interview recordings together, establishing coding categories. We then coded transcripts separately and found our primary codes were reliable for analysis. We also frequently corroborated our interpretations with three older veterans from other branches (including the army and the marines).

MILITARY DISCOURSE AS SCRIPTS

Unlike Discourses of inquiry that build knowledge via collaborative argument, military Discourse makes many minds think as one to accomplish an ordered mission. The military intakes tens of thousands of recruits of varying backgrounds and mindsets and quickly trains them to respond uniformly and automatically in intense life-or-death situations. While reading researchers find that "little meaning is literally on a page and that much meaning must be contributed by the reader" (Geisler et al. 2001, 272), the military strives for the opposite: texts must be read exactingly and literally by all so that all take the same meaning; nonuniform interpretation can be fatal. What is the nature of the training that conditions individuals to uniform reading and thinking, allowing an uncommonly symmetrical response in the face of life-threatening chaos? We call it *scripting*: universal procedures delineated by nearly nonmisunderstandable texts in a rigidly hierarchical culture of unwavering deference to those texts.

Scripts include any written and trained procedure covering servicemember activities, behavior, and mission. In military Discourse, *everything* is scripted: how beds are made, pots are cleaned, missiles are loaded on airplanes; what an off-duty enlisted soldier does when meeting an off-duty officer in an off-base supermarket. Scripts include not only the how-to instructions for job training but rules of conduct governing every thinkable human behavior and interaction. From the time a recruit steps onto the bus for boot camp until the moment they're discharged or retire, every moment of their life complies with scripts developed to depersonalize and make uniform their thoughts and actions.

Take human interaction. The Naval Education and Training Professional Development and Technology Center offers a *Basic Military Requirements* course, chapter 9 of which covers "Customs and Courtesies":

> A custom is a way of acting—a way that has continued consistently over such a long period that it has become like law. A courtesy is a form of polite behavior and excellence of manners. You will find that Navy life creates many situations, not found in civilian life, that require special behavior on your part. Customs and courtesies help make life orderly and are a way of showing respect. (Naval Education and Training Professional Development and Technology Center 2002, 9–10).

"Courtesies" include saluting (ten pages of the twenty-page chapter: how to, when to, when not to), ceremonies (including colors and boarding and leaving vessels), and military etiquette (behavior in contexts such as eating and passing in halls, and "addressing and introducing Naval personnel"). The manual teaches, for example, the script for responding to an order from a superior: "The only proper response to an oral order is 'Aye, aye, sir/ma'am.' This reply means more than yes. It indicates 'I understand and will obey.' Such responses to an order as 'O.K., sir' or 'All right, sir' are taboo. 'Very well' is proper when spoken by a senior in acknowledgment of a report made by a junior, but a junior never says 'Very well' to a senior" (Naval Education and Training Professional Development and Technology Center 2002, 9–17).

Soldiers have a written rule, then—a detailed, specific, set-by-step instruction—for every action, scripts that invite neither critical thinking nor initiative in rewriting. There are serious penalties for not following scripts—in the case of high-risk jobs like ejection seat technician, the results of thinking for oneself by detouring from a written instruction can be the death of an aircrew member and the jailing of the seat tech. Even in cases where less weighty scripts (e.g., when to salute) are not followed, a script-consciousness still calls attention to the unfollowed script. The only space military culture provides for critical thinking is when it falls within the confines of a script. Nor may scripts themselves be questioned except in circumstances (such as policy reviews) that include scripts for how a script is questioned.

With this description, we don't mean to insinuate that soldiers are mindless robots—military Discourse demands uniformity *in spite of* their free-thinking autonomy. The proof of this—and the proof of the rule of uniformity—is in times of need when lives and battles are on the line and individuals abandon scripts and disregard orders, sometimes receiving honors for doing so (e.g., the recent case of Medal of Honor recipient Sgt. Dakota Meyer). Because of the severe consequences of disobeying orders, such moments tend to come in the heat of battle with nothing left to lose and the greater mission (or conscience) demanding autonomous action. (And if the disobedience doesn't work, the alternative to a medal is a court martial.)

In part because of the rigor of training required to ensure adherence to scripts, and given the necessity of uniformity to the military's mission and purpose, excellence is determined by who best embodies scripts. Servicemembers understand that one way to be excellent is to follow scripts for appearance, obedience, timeliness, knowing-without-learning, and script following.

SCRIPTS VERSUS PEDAGOGY

Given the deeply enculturated military tendency to script, we might expect veterans to try to script college. And it was in fact the appearance of expectations about classroom excellence in our interviews that first showed us the role scripts seem to be playing for veterans. We saw scripts in the main areas of expectations for instructor leadership, for student interaction with instructors, and for student contributions. However, our research demonstrates not simply the persistence of scripting; it also suggests that the scripts veterans try to deploy often work directly against the pedagogy described earlier. Where instructors seek self-directed learning, veterans judge excellence by strong instructor leadership. Where instructors are creating an inquiry-driven environment in which students contribute questions, input, and knowledge, veterans bring scripts that deny their right or ability to question or to go beyond following instructions. Where instructors seek unranked interaction toward inquiry, veterans have scripts that render talking with superiors and taking initiative taboo. In what follows, we examine these areas in detail, showing what our interviewees' scripts looked like and how they conflicted with the classroom experiences instructors are often trying to create.

LEADERSHIP SCRIPTS VERSUS SELF-DIRECTED CLASSROOMS

The military's rigid hierarchical structure puts a premium on outstanding leadership. Since servicemembers must obey orders unquestioningly, leader ethos is often a sign of whether a mission will be survivable. In a scripting culture, measures of leader ethos and quality are clear and fixed. Excellence for all servicemembers is determined in part by timeliness, appearance, and comportment—and for leaders, by decisiveness and judgment. Leaders lead by example, so whatever scripts servicemembers must follow, leaders are expected to perform to even higher standards.

Our interviews routinely showed that veterans do not cast these scripts aside. For example, every veteran we interviewed reported following the military script of showing up to a scheduled event (class) fifteen minutes early—to find no one else there. Each thought something was wrong; one even asked at an office if class had been cancelled. Another, even as she begins grad school, still shows up to class fifteen minutes early because, as she said, "that is the way to be excellent." These habits remain despite the fact that no one else is following such scripts.

Our veterans also reported being attentive to neatness and precision in dress and appearance. They see *values* in appearance—evidence of the military scripts in which excellence is evidenced by sharp creases and spit-shined boots. One veteran recounted, "At first, I was very judgmental. Because, when [an instructor] did walk in, he was wearing sandals and a T-shirt, and I think it was . . . a pair of jeans. I don't remember, but I just remember thinking, 'Wow.'" Three veterans told of being distracted for nearly entire class periods by wrinkled shirts, skewed giglines (shirt buttons should form a precise vertical line with a pants button), and sloppily rolled shirtsleeves. Said one veteran as she became aware of her own preoccupation with the instructor's gig-line being off, "I was just appalled that I wanted out of that rule-driven military environment so much, but that it was so much inside my head that I was still using it to judge other people." As veterans learn this new Discourse, they come to realize that the academy rarely locates excellence in such appearances. Instructors vary in dress, comportment, and timeliness, but few polish their shoes. Since their work is intellectual, physical appearances are often not a reliable indicator of its quality. Many instructors consider time spent fetishizing neatness to be wasted, whereas in military culture neatness *is* the work demanded by many scripts.

Veterans seem to start out unaware of this shift in values, still measuring ethos by military scripts. One veteran confessed, "I didn't know I was that conditioned." Thus, in the opening hours of class, when instructors and students are building rapport, an instructor may already be failing important tests of leadership in a veteran's mind. Angie herself had such an experience with Doug: when he hurried into class three minutes late, holding a haphazard armload of supplies, her heart sank: he didn't care about his students, or he would've taken the time to be there early and set up. Students were obviously a blip in his day. That assessment snowballed as she eyed his casual dress and his relaxed demeanor—sitting against the front of a table to talk, whereas in the military relaxing and slouching are signs of disrespect. An instructor who respected his students and was serious about teaching them would stand up tall and straight. Doug also failed to show knowledge, authority, and decisiveness by asking students what they wanted to learn and often deflected questions by evasively asking questions back. The preponderance of our data was similar: in the beginning of class, instructors may already be developing ethos problems with veterans.

And it will only go downhill because writing instructors are often not trying to be strong leaders to begin with. Per the pedagogy described earlier, instructors negotiate control and authority with students so students are able to set their own learning agendas, work at their own paces, and pose and follow their own questions. A writing class in which students learned only to follow strict instructions would be an abject failure. The one sense in which instructors might want to lead by example is in being active, vocal writers and readers. But even this "leading" looks, through transparency, like vulnerability. Students see an instructor acknowledging when writing is difficult, "shitty first drafts," rejections by editors, and frustrations when words won't come. They see a reader who makes mistakes and misinterprets, as readers will. The instructor is demonstrating the rhetorical, contingent, unsettled nature of textuality and inquiry, and that will *never* look like the strong, decisive leadership a veteran may be seeking.

CONTRIBUTIVE INQUIRY VERSUS FOLLOWING ORDERS

Military enculturation makes servicemembers mission oriented, and missions are accomplished through the generation and implementation of orders, which limit initiative taking. When servicemembers arrive at a site full of unknowns, they find the person in charge and figure out rank structure—where they fit, to whom they report, what's expected of them, and who reports to them. Risks, ground rules, and perimeter are established, and work is carried on within them. Showing initiative by disorderly scurrying around on one's own is not acceptable. As one veteran said in comparing veterans' attitudes to other students', "We're a little more used to that hierarchy—that this is the person in front of us, so respect them and do what they say." Our interviews suggest that when soldiers become students, their need for clearly defined missions, areas of responsibility, and orders linking the two does not abate. A vet in FYC is immediately figuring out her area of responsibility so that she knows *how* to take initiative. Veterans are fine readers of rhetorical situations, and from the opening moments of class, they are inspecting cues amidst syllabi and instructor demeanor, language, and responses to see where they fit and what is expected and allowed.

Without exception, our veterans first assumed the mission of FYC was skills instruction, a one-way transmission of knowledge from instructor to students via extensive skills practice: "We're so used to 'Tell me what I need to do and I'll do it,' and then the instructor's like 'No, here's your assignment, figure it out,' it's like what the hell?" Veterans don't expect to have to give input because students who *could* would already have the skills the course should teach. Furthermore, completing this mission requires clear instructions on what students are expected to produce with stepwise procedures explaining how. Repeatedly, veterans reported a desire for, satisfaction with, or frustration at the lack of such instructions. For example, "It made the writing harder . . . we're used to having [steps] A, B, C, D. That ability to be free in your writing and not be constricted to a set standard . . . that freedom just to write on a topic . . . ooh, I can write whatever I want? . . . that was frustrating . . . breaking my brain out of that mold . . . I don't have to wait for somebody to dictate to me what to write or what to think . . . that was the hard part." When freshmen just out of high school complain about a lack of directions, it usually means they want to be told what to do so they don't have to come up with it themselves. A veteran's similar complaint— "the instructor isn't clear about what she wants!"—has a different source: without a mission and orders, a servicemember is not *allowed* to move.

So, for best-practices writing instruction, an impasse forms. For the instructor, the mission is *not* skills instruction as writing is too rhetorical to reduce to skills. Rather, the mission is to help students experience writing rhetorically: organic, emerging from particular contexts, shaped by readers' needs and uses for the text. Detailed instructions and procedures aren't how writing works: how could an instructor predict what a student will want to say, and how could there be a procedure for writing independent of the writer's own process, motivation, and material? Furthermore, the mission is *teaching inquiry*, inculcating students into a *way of being* (Discourse) that questions via writing. Students must direct their own learning goals and questioning; the instructor's role is to help them expose and consider unexamined assumptions.

In this light, an expectation of clear orders and directions is a problem. An instructor's desire might be "I order you not to follow orders"; when rhetoric's answer to writing questions is "it depends," saying anything else is simply untruthful. But when a vet seeks decisive leadership and directions in order to accomplish the mission of skills acquisition, that response is, in military vernacular, "a clear sign not to proceed." For veterans who have experienced the frustration of vague military leadership, it's imperative to know precisely what is expected before moving on. So when Doug asked students what they wanted to learn, Angie wrote that she wanted to get better at right ways of writing. Doug's feedback read, "What if there isn't just one right way, and why would we want there to be?" Angie perceived this response as stonewalling, refusing to be pinned down to concrete answers, or even worse, failing to acknowledge the possibility *of* clear answers. She also felt slightly rebuffed: she had asked what she thought was the right question, and in return had basically been asked, "Why would you want that?"

Even as veterans better understand the FYC mission and thus the difficulties with issuing specific directions, the invitation for input, contribution, and true inquiry can be hard to believe. For some of our veterans, such an expectation was never part of their service, so they tended to believe the call for student opinion was itself a script—"that's just what the instructor is *supposed* to say, they don't really mean it." Or, "I was just thinking it was kinda like his initial spiel that he gives every one of his classes [sarcastic tone]: 'Well, what are *you* expecting to learn? 'Cause we're gonna be learning *this!*'" Such skepticism can be understood through recourse to "cog-in-a-machine" clichés. In such clichés, the military is portrayed as a machine, servicemembers are cogs, and everyone knows what cog they are. In contrast, inquiry-driven FYC is no machine, but it takes veterans some time to realize this and to recalculate their place in this space—to learn that questions truly are invited in college. Said one, "In class, the instructors actually value your feedback . . . a question that is not directly related to whatever the instructor is talking about, you can get away with asking it in college . . . in the navy they're like, 'that's off the subject . . . we're not talking about that.'" A further incompatibility between inquiry-driven FYC and veteran expectations for scripting is that in the military, you're not so much supposed to *learn* things as you're supposed to already *know* them: "You don't ask questions. You know, you're supposed to know it," one vet said. Admitting lack of knowledge marks failure. Another vet said directly what most others implied: "It's hard for me to admit I don't know something," and the preferred route to covering a knowledge gap is to find out on one's own. This stance toward not-knowing opposes that of inquiry-driven FYC, which understands knowledge as constructed *through* writing, not known beforehand. Writing classes force students to not-know and collaborate in search of answers. In FYC, veterans are not measured by what they know, but by what they're learning—not-knowing isn't a sign of brokenness but rather the point of showing up.

The veterans pointed out one saving grace to such disjuncts of expectations: feedback. Positive, constructive, approving feedback—which our interviewees say is often lacking in military culture—made adopting this new Discourse possible. In the absence of clear directions, veterans use peer and instructor feedback to clarify mission and procedure. In the absence of concrete, decisive answers to questions, feedback gives students confidence that if one answer to a question doesn't work, they will not be shot down but guided in another attempt. Feedback helps confirm that veterans didn't hear wrong when their instructor asked for their opinion. Crucially, though, feedback in these cases wasn't one-time, teacher-to-student communication but rather a series of loops, an *extended conversation among equals.* Extended feedback became so central to veterans' success in inquiry-based FYC that it is the key feature of the third major script conflict between military culture and writing courses: the nature and role of interaction between teachers and students.

INTERACTION VERSUS HIERARCHY

Effective writing instruction requires interaction among writers and readers: instructors create interaction among students and the instructor that makes writers readers and readers writers and students and teachers both learners. The notion is that writing instruction is a *collaboration* between students and teacher, all of them readers and writers allatonce. What is immediately difficult for veterans in this approach is scripts that establish hierarchies and ranks, strictly regulate interaction and "familiarity" across ranks, and quell the initiative talking and questioning that faculty-student interaction thrives on. The veterans we interviewed, therefore, reported a significant period of adjustment in learning what kinds of interaction with their writing instructors were permissible and desirable—as well as initial discomfort with the kinds of interaction that accompany best-practice writing courses.

One source of that discomfort is scripts that regulate interaction by rank. As we've noted, the missions the military is tasked with demand uniformity, iron will, and absolute adherence to incredibly difficult orders. The military must therefore take the notion of "nothing personal, just business" to extremes—it must create a social structure in which a ranking officer can order a soldier in their command to sacrifice lives. Proscriptions against overfamiliarity with higher-ranking officers, and scripts establishing precise and limited channels of communication and authorized verbal expression, are the only workable solution to helping thousands of people act uniformly and appropriately when lives are threatened.

The shift in stakes when soldiers become students—from lives to letter grades—significantly impacts veterans. Erin Hadlock (2011, 5), an army major and graduate student, reports one interview with a veteran: "He said that the hardest thing to get over was constantly asking himself, 'Why does it matter? If no one is going to die, why do I care? How can it be important?'" Yet even when lives are no longer at stake, the scripts don't fade. When instructors invite open discussion that questions and exposes the instructor to criticism, veterans report that their first response is to reject the invitation. Veterans treat instructors as superiors requiring deference, especially in public conversation. Divergence from these scripts—offering ideas in opposition to or questioning the leader—is disrespectful and unwelcome. Divergence from these scripts—offering ideas in opposition to or questioning the leader—is disrespectful and unwelcome. Thus, by these scripts veterans are effectively frozen, prevented from interacting with their instructors.

Part of this difficulty is that veterans don't realize how different the organizational structures of universities and the military actually are. While a "chain of command" can be extracted from a university organizational chart, shared governance, tenure, and functional organization can quickly muddy who gives and takes orders—not that the academy is terribly comfortable with orders to begin with. Intellectual work rewards not direction followers but whoever is thought to have the brightest solution to a given problem. Often the university itself can't readily identify which office should work on a given problem, or which of several authorities to take a problem to. Does academic misconduct go to the department head or the dean of students? The answer is often "it depends." *Not* a military hierarchical structure. But veterans are enculturated to a script of rank identification as a condition of interaction. Even the entrance of someone into a military classroom requires that their rank be identified and an appropriate response rendered. If the commanding officer makes an impromptu visit, whoever sees her first must call out "officer on deck!" at which the entire class stands rigidly at attention until she passes through, or puts them "at ease" (standing rigidly in a different position), or sets them back to their business with an "as you were." With this background, veterans can be troubled and disconcerted by a lack of organizational knowledge and no way to gain it.

We find, then, great initial reserve among veterans in interaction with instructors, despite the fact that this interaction would help veterans build fluency in their new Discourse. Despite being excellent students, not one veteran we interviewed made the first move in establishing contact with an instructor. In four cases, instructor feedback and mentoring eventually broke the ice, and in one case, a veteran's consultation with a retired servicemember helped her understand that, and why, college was asking her to think for herself—and then it became okay for her to talk to the instructor.

Another kind of interaction new to our veterans was praise. One vet recounted saving lives in Afghanistan, receiving no official thanks, and being denied treatment for a resulting disability until he could be discharged: "That's one reason I got out . . . and then to come here and get compliments from the professor . . . the world isn't really [so] crappy." Another vet reported that in his military instruction, praise was rarely heard. "If . . . a chief, or one of my instructors from A-school and C-school . . . were the ones grading . . . they would just say, 'You did this wrong and this wrong, this wrong, this wrong. Next time work on this.' They would never say, 'You did this well, but not this' . . . you just did this bad." When FYC seeks formerly proscribed contributions from veterans, then, it is formerly proscribed interaction with and feedback from the instructor that makes it safe to take that proscribed initiative, assert to the "superior" instructor what's important, and ask "stupid" questions. One vet told a story about an instructor's positive feedback: they "told me where I could improve, and when I first read . . . the comments it was like, 'You nailed this one.' And I was like, 'Aw, it's about time, yeah!' It's great, it just boosts you more." Even when the feedback is not completely approving, it helps make the overall request for contribution believable. The frankness of pointing out what *isn't* working is as important as the approval because it lets veterans see that in Discourses of inquiry, *thinking* and contributing are rewarded even when the resulting ideas don't work.

For all the difficulties veterans report in warming to interaction and contribution, our final assurance is that once veterans understand what they're being asked and allowed to do, *they love it.* It's not as if service-members on active duty are opinionless, don't think for themselves, don't see better ways of solving problems than their superiors do—that they don't think critically. They do: each veteran regaled us with stories of bad leadership, problems they wished they could have fixed, and situations for which their politest description was "crappy." All but one expressed true pleasure in their college writing courses once it became clear that it really was okay to *say what they thought.* What veterans learned was parameters: new, scary, initially undefined but tempting principles about mission, purpose, interaction, and what counts in academic environments as excellent participation, thinking, arguing, writing, and reading. Through spiraling loops of gradually freeing interaction—including copious feedback and modeling by instructors and increasingly fearless questioning and feedback from students—veterans came to understand what their writing instructors were looking for: the veterans' own ideas, concerns, and expression.

EXCHANGING THE SCRIPT FOR INTERACTION: HOW TO MOVE FORWARD

It takes a huge leap of faith for *any* student to believe that their contributions matter and have value, but even more so for veterans, who have also been conditioned to forget that their personhood itself matters. Our final turn here is to what veterans said builds such trust for them.

Given the disjunct between what FYC attempts to teach and the scripts veterans tend to bring, why do we not see more failure in veteran learning? How did veterans who began FYC in frustration—in Angie's case, so severe she considered dropping—end up giving glowing reviews, saying the world is a better place, changing their majors and their lives? The veterans report initial frustration followed by a turning point one veteran described as "getting to know the instructor," "figuring out what he was about." What facilitated this "knowing," and why did it shape learning outcomes so dramatically? The common thread woven through our veterans' stories is *feedback*.

Although we initially understood feedback in the traditional one-way sense of teachers and other students helping a writer see how readers experience their writing, this study suggests that feedback as *an extended conversation among equals* serves another purpose: conveying instructor ethos. Despite classroom moments that, against military scripts, might erode veterans' confidence in their instructors, written and oral feedback brings second chances for all parties as it embodies qualities veterans deem trustworthy and supports learning without scripted thinking-interacting-being. We believe that scripts and spontaneous human interaction are, in this context, mostly mutually exclusive: script consciousness does not allow the interaction that thrives in the FYC learning environment. It takes a vulnerable daring beyond what scripting is capable of to interact spontaneously. For a veteran, maybe more so than for others, spontaneous interaction requires trust built over time as instructors, day after day, show consistency. But beyond consistency, veterans seem to build trust by feeling and responding positively to innate needs met by the feedback experience: being listened to, being asked for input, having time invested in them, and being offered transparency. In short, feedback demonstrates to veterans how their instructors value them, which helps build the trust that transforms interaction to learning.

We close, then, by discussing these needs in greater detail, underlining some of the practical ways these ways of feeling valued look from a veteran perspective.

Being listened to

Veterans noted when they felt heard in their writing courses. While the veterans in our study spent between four and twelve years being listened to enough to carry out missions, their writing courses introduced a whole other kind of being heard. It's an interactive listening: instructors seek the intent behind their students' words. Veterans feel heard when their ideas seem to genuinely interest instructors. Their journey toward contributive interaction turned on phrases like, "That's interesting; could you say more about that?" Such listening bestows value veterans rarely encounter from military leaders, and it is, they say, a big deal. "The moment you realize that it's not an act—that the professor is actually curious about your thoughts and questions," one vet said, "that's the moment where everything changes."

Being asked for input.
Instructors should seek input that requires students to draw out their own opinions, values and thoughts—not necessarily about war or anything veteran related but about writing, the assignment, *how they see anything*, especially context. Veterans know they have a different view on life—they just don't expect to find it valued.

Having time invested in them.
Initially, many veterans feel asking questions wastes the instructor's time: "I just got in a habit of doing a lot of my own research because that's pretty much how they train us . . . I'll take the initiative and look it up on my own rather than waste [their] time with one of my questions." When an instructor spends time on veterans, it builds their sense of self-worth and belonging in the university. Veterans know how to read actions rather than words; mere assurances that "students are my priority" mean nothing next to actions. Investing time brings action to promises.

Being offered radical transparency.
The literature focusing on horrors veterans have seen is not wrong; sitting by the sheltered eighteen-year-old student may be one who held a dying child on a street turned battlefield, was unable to stop rapes due to mission-first requirements, or had best friends incinerated at their sides. They inhabit a place where reality is hard and sugar coating is see through and unappealing. Inquiry-driven instructor and war-tempered student often share a value for seeing and saying things as they are. An instructor's radical transparency—self-revelation and straightforwardness—builds trust like nothing else, especially in the nature of the work being embarked on. Soldiers know that a prebattle brief presented in

rosy terms is BS, and veterans still think so. For them, writing classes are battlefields and instructors are laying the battle plan. The reality that writing is hard, even for instructors, not only earns them credibility, it imbues value to veterans' struggles, shows by example that learning is acceptable and knowledge making is a process of struggle, and makes the instructor part of the team.

References

Ackerman, Robert, David DiRamio, and Regina L. Garza Mitchell. 2009. "Transitions: Combat Veterans as College Students." Special issue, *New Directions for Student Services* 2009 (126): 5–14. http://dx.doi.org/10.1002/ss.311.

Artemeva, Natasha. 2008. "Toward a Unified Social Theory of Genre Learning." *Journal of Business and Technical Communication* 22 (2): 160–85. http://dx.doi.org/10.1177/1050651907311925.

Byman, Daniel. 2007. "Veterans and Colleges Have a Lot to Offer Each Other." *Chronicle of Higher Education* 54 (16) : B5.

Cook, Bryan, and Young Kim. 2009. *From Soldier to Student: Easing the Transition of Service Members on Campus.* Washington, DC: American Council on Education.

DiRamio, David, Robert Ackerman, and Regina Mitchell. 2008. "From Combat to Campus: Voices of Student Veterans." *NASPA Journal* 45 (1): 73–102.

Downs, Doug. 2005. "True Believers, Real Scholars, and Real True Believing Scholars: Discourses of Inquiry and Affirmation in the Writing Classroom." In *Negotiating Religious Faith in the Writing Classroom,* edited by Elizabeth VanderLei and Bonnie Kyburz, 39–55. Portsmouth, NH: Heinemann.

Downs, Doug. 2010. "Teaching First Year Writers to *Use* Texts: Scholarly Readings in Writing-About-Writing in First-Year Comp." *Reader: Essays in Reader-Oriented Theory, Criticism, and Pedagogy* 60 (Fall): 19–50.

Downs, Doug, and Elizabeth Wardle. 2007. "Teaching about Writing, Righting Misconceptions: (Re)Envisioning 'First Year Composition' as 'Introduction to Writing Studies.'" *College Composition and Communication* 58 (4): 552–84.

Fulkerson, Richard. 2005. "Composition at the Turn of the Twenty-First Century." *College Composition and Communication* 56:654–87.

Gee, James Paul. 1989. "Literacy, Discourse, and Linguistics: Introduction." *Journal of Education* 171 (1): 5–17.

Gee, James Paul. 1999. *An Introduction to Discourse Analysis: Theory and Method.* London: Routledge.

Geisler, Cheryl, Charles Bazerman, Stephen Doheny-Farina, Laura Gurak, Christina Haas, Johndan Johnson-Eilola, David S. Kaufer, Andrea Lunsford, Carolyn R. Miller, Dorothy Winsor, and Joanne Yates. 2001. "IText: Future Directions for Research on the Relationship between Information Technology and Writing." *Journal of Business and Technical Communication* 15 (3): 269–308. http://dx.doi.org/10.1177/105065190101500302.

Glasser, Irene, John Powers, and William Zywiak. 2009. "Military Veterans at Universities: A Case of Culture Crash." *Anthropology News* 50 (5): 33.

Herrmann, Douglas, et al. 2008. "College Is for Veterans, Too." *Chronicle of Higher Education* 55 (13): A33.

Hadlock, Erin. 2011. "WPA Conference Paper." Paper presented at the CWPA Annual Conference, Baton Rouge, LA.

Leonhardy, Galen. 2009. "Transformation: Working with Veteran Students in the Composition Classroom." *Teaching English in the Two-Year College* 36 (4): 339–52.

Lemke, J. L. 1998. "Metamedia Literacy: Transforming Meanings and Media." In *Handbook of Literacy and Technology: Transformations in a Post-Typographic World*, edited by D. Reinking et al., 283–301. Hillsdale, NJ: Erlbaum.

Lipka, Sara. 2010. "Students' Status as Veterans and Choice of Major Play Big Parts in Shaping College Experiences." *Chronicle of Higher Education* 57 (12): A24–25.

Naval Education and Training Professional Development and Technology Center. 2002. *Basic Military Requirements (NAVEDTRA 14325)*. Washington, DC: United States Navy.

O'Herrin, Elizabeth. 2011. "Enhancing Veteran Success in Higher Education." *Peer Review* 13 (1): 15–18.

Rhodes, Keith, Doug Downs, and Darsie Bowden. 2011. "Newest Message Framework: Effective Teaching Practices in General Studies Writing Classes." *Council of Writing Program Administrators*. http://wpacouncil.org/nma.

Robinson, Ken. 2006. "Schools Kill Creativity." TED Talk video, 19:25. http://www.ted.com/talks/ken_robinson_says_schools_kill_creativity.html.

Robinson, Ken. 2010. "Bring On the Learning Revolution!" TED talk video, 17:58. http://www.ted.com/talks/sir_ken_robinson_bring_on_the_revolution.html.

Rumann, Corey, and Florence Hamrick. 2010. "Student Veterans in Transition: Re-Enrolling After War Zone Deployments." *Journal of Higher Education* 81 (4): 431–58. http://dx.doi.org/10.1353/jhe.0.0103.

Russell, David. 2010. "Writing in Multiple Contexts: Vygotskian CHAT Meets the Phenomenology of Genre." In *Traditions of Writing Research*, edited by Charles Bazerman, Robert Krut, Karen Lunsford, Susan McLeod, Suzie Null, Paul Rogers, and Amanda Stansell, 353–64. London: Routledge.

Schlossberg, Nancy, Ann Lynch, and Arthur Chickering. 1989. *Improving Higher Education Environments for Adults*. San Francisco: Jossey-Bass.

3

NOT JUST "YES SIR, NO SIR"
How Genre and Agency Interact in Student-Veteran Writing

Erin Hadlock and Sue Doe

Few things leave as powerful an impression as hundreds of soldiers, sailors, airmen, or marines in formation. Their thunderous "hooahs" create a flash bomb of sound, and their crisp rifle movements are identical and precise. The very nature of a member of the uniformed services in formation—the forward stare and rigid back at attention, the replication of exact angles of boots and the cupping of hands, and the way he or she sloped height of the formation—completely reflects this organization of discipline, rigidity, and uniformity. Over our respective careers, we have had many opportunities to be filled with equal parts awe and gloom at the power of military formations. As a former instructor at the United States Military Academy (USMA), Sue saw recent high-school graduates shorn into cadets on Reception Day, the first day of a larger, indeed comprehensive, grooming that is transformative and profound. As an active-duty officer, current USMA instructor, and army aviator, Erin has taken part in these very formations for well over a decade. Both of us, however, have also had the privilege of going deeper than the formations. We have come to know the soldiers—as well as sailors, airmen, and marines. They are far from the automatons they may first seem to be, and their training does not preclude them from acting responsibly and individually. These servicemembers may shout "Yes, Sir!" and "No, Ma'am!" until they are hoarse, but those are hardly the only phrases they know.

This essay addresses the idea that a deepened understanding of the range and limits of servicemembers' rhetorical abilities is important to our teaching of veterans as they transition onto college campuses. Moreover, we argue for increased research and analysis of student-veteran literacies rather than simplifications of them. Our own research with student-veterans on the campus of Colorado State University, a

DOI: 10.7330/9780874219425.c003

medium-sized research institution, suggests that past military experience can assist, rather than detract from, student-veterans' efforts in higher education, particularly in terms of their early college experiences with writing. In this essay, we report on our interviews with a very small sample of eleven student-veterans representing all four services and addressing their writing histories in both school and the military. We hope to uncover new connections and disconnections between the two contexts. Findings from the interviews reported here are part of a larger longitudinal study that is following student-veterans over the course of their college years in order to chronicle their transitional literacies.

We consider ourselves well positioned to speak to the relationship between student-veterans' past military experiences and current college experiences. First, in working closely with and living alongside military servicemembers, we have witnessed their aptitude, agency, and critical thinking, all of which situate them to thrive in higher-education settings. At the same time, as teachers of writing, we understand the skepticism and frustration faculty experience when working with students who are former military and feel a strong allegiance to military convention. Indeed, the very idea of a formation as invoked in our opening paragraph provides a case in point. Formations show how military might is signaled and reinforced through rigid discipline and strict uniformity. They also represent the hierarchical organization of the military more generally, a context in which commanders give orders to legions of followers who, more often than not, crisply follow orders without question. Such approaches are utterly alien to a higher-education setting. Moreover, the willingness to comply, to adhere unquestioningly to orders, worries us as rhetoricians since it appears that a military person learns not to question but to execute, not to author but to be authored. In turn, we worry that soldiers, airmen, sailors, and marines having internalized an order-following approach and will be unable to shake it, unable to take on new identities in civilian environments, including the composition classroom. Hence we acknowledge that as we ask student-veterans to understand mentorship in a new way, seeing ourselves as classroom guides and facilitators rather than leaders, we struggle with how to manage their skepticism about us and wonder if we must explain our approaches, which purposefully eschew the mission orientation associated with precise objectives and top-down military orders. At the same time, we also worry that student-veterans will be subjected to treatment based on stereotypes; they may be seen, for instance, to be fully trained followers, conditioned to say and write few things other than "Yes, Sir," "No, Sir," and "No Excuses, Sir."

In this article, we address these concerns by reporting on our research with student-veterans, the findings of which have challenged our own assumptions. Among other things, our research suggests that while rhetorical agency may seem to lie outside the experience of the largely enlisted student-veteran demographic, and while student-veterans may themselves discount their military text production, in fact they have not only produced but subverted highly stable military genres while on active duty, mastering genres and finding ways to inject signature strategies into stable forms.

We first acknowledge, however, the importance of military units—groups of individuals unified by focus and mission—that comprise all branches of the military. Military units function as units largely because they place more importance on the team dynamic rather than the individual. As stated by one student-veteran in our study,

> That's the thing about the military—that reality comes at you quick that you're not special. You do not stand out, you come in there and you start all over. You know, they say the military strips you of your individuality; that's not true. They strip you of the concept that your achievements mean anything as far as, when it comes to life and death situations. It doesn't matter if you were the valedictorian, if you were the star quarterback; what matters is what you do then and there. What matters is how you took your training and apply it to your job. That's what matters.

Nevertheless, the team dynamic is not the whole story since individuals are required to produce and circulate a variety of communications. Moreover, while units must act in concert with one another, as a unified entity, the orders that dictate those actions and the decisions about how best to disseminate and execute them are a matter of individual choice. How does the military resolve this tension between the collective mission and individual agentive behavior? In a word, *genre*. Military genres are, in fact, stable, powerful, time honored, and functionally imperative for the purposes of preparing military personnel for combat/war. Genre provides what Ken Hyland calls "cultural capital," a way to gain automatic footing and credibility in an environment where people's names may not be as important or recognizable as the medium through which they communicate. The individual, in the case of military and other genres, is not the origin of importance since in no way is an "explanation of a work . . . sought in the man or woman who produced it" (Barthes 1977). Rather, the value is placed in the mode of correspondence. It is in its classification as an official memorandum, for example, that the text becomes culturally recognizable and worthwhile, elevated to an importance exceeding the importance associated with anything an individual might create or write. Military genres hence conform to Bawarshi's (2003, 20) notion of the power of genre more generally, which "[endows] a work with certain cultural status and value." As a result, in the military environment, as with other environments, a central tension is that the individual's interest in being recognized is thrust against the demands of group conformity. Paradoxically, however, given the tools of genre, an individual soldier without the prestige of Foucault's (1984c, 105) "proper name" can garner instantaneous credibility using a document behind which the full weight of the United States military stands and can claim "given legitimacy" without necessarily ever having been "given," awarded, or anointed with such legitimacy. That is, the role of authorship in military discourse precisely demonstrates that the authority associated with authorship can prevail even in the absence of a particular, identifiable author. In using the conventions and performances of military discourse, a military person becomes the embodiment of military authority broadly defined.

Bawarshi's explanation of genre helps inform our explanation of authorship activity within the military.

> The function of a genre only seems like nothing when we, through practice and socialization, have internalized its ideology in the form of rhetorical conventions to such an extent that our invention of a text seems to emanate independently and introspectively, even almost intuitively, from us. (Bawarshi 2003, 8)

As this description helps explain, institutional buy-in within the military may lead the individual servicemember to react with a genre without even realizing the power of that genre. In such ways, military genres transcend the individual and are exerted as a structure of power/knowledge to which (military) members conform. For instance, memoranda, counseling reports, after-action reports, and operation orders all require individual authorship, but context and mission exceed and subsume the individual servicemember, and documents exist to reflect and represent the mission. In other words, individuals may utilize genres individually, but the genre is meaningful only to the degree that it is used in support of the activity, or to use military terms, the mission. Several premises about genre and the activities with which genre is associated are thus exposed. Genre is both a constraining and a liberating force, with the servicemember limited to using certain genres for corresponding activities. For instance, a servicemember would not use an operations order when a warning order or a fragmentary order is demanded by context. For instance a service member would not use an operation order when a warning order or a fragmentary order was demanded by context.[1]

Hence, genres are bound up with activities, and, consistent with activity theory, a mission-specific behavior, or activity, is determined by context, joint responsibility, role, and communication. Leontiev explains activity theory this way:

> Labor is a process, as we have seen, that is realized not by a lone being, in ways peculiar to himself alone, but under conditions of people's joint activity, under conditions of a human collective, and, as I will try to especially emphasize, in a social, that is, collectively expressed way. Through this process, people enter into communication with one another. It is not so much a matter of communication that is primarily verbal, of course, but of communication in the sense of participation in a joint action, in the sense of participation in the process of labor, first and foremost. (Leontiev 2005, 60)

As such, an E-5 in some contexts may be unlikely to generate certain types of genres, such as the operations order, which requires access to information about the objectives of the mission and the commander's intent underlying the approach. In such contexts, decisions about the production and circulation of genres are undertaken above the E-5 at a role-appropriate level. This is not to say, however, that decision making is restricted to the officer ranks. Rather, another E-5 might well be involved in the development of an operations order or integral to the construction of counseling (evaluation) reports on the soldiers serving under the E-5. Genre is thus clarified as a manifestation of the delimited activity to which it is bound and the role and responsibility that has been vested in that person.

The identities of military servicemembers are themselves constructed by military contexts and in a sense are also genres. The process of military identity formation begins with induction through boot camp, which is structured so the servicemember rather quickly sheds a past identity of individuality and embraces the identity of the team unit. This new team-oriented identity need not be exclusive of other identities but is likely to have a formative and robust effect. By design, the individual is made to feel lost. Drill sergeants are unusually aggressive, mornings are unusually early, and friends are made unusually quickly. The first few days of boot camp specifically highlight the vulnerability of the individual body and, underscoring the mutual dependence of one person upon another, work to solidify natural bonds among the recruits. Eventually, successful new recruits earn tokens of cultural capital in the forms of physical-fitness scores, ribbons and patches, and recognition from senior officers, all signaling the "natural signs of . . . strength and . . . courage" (Foucault 1984a, 179) one needs in order to adopt and be adopted by structures of power/knowledge—in this case military power and authority.

During this period of induction, veterans describe a certain ease they develop at surrendering to military authority, an ease that does not end at the conclusion of the induction period. One student-veteran in our study explained it this way:

> Being in the army is so frickin' easy. Especially like at war. You get up, go to get something to eat, you go to the trucks, go out on patrol—for God knows how long—come back, get something to eat, take a shower, and go to bed. Maybe send an email to your family or sneak in a phone call.

This ease of not having to discipline one's own time is something many student-veterans point to as different from their college experience and a significant challenge of their transition back to being civilians. Another of our student-veterans explained his surprise at having to learn how to self-regulate his time.

> I think mostly like getting back into the months of studying. Dedicating like, okay I did class, I did my homework, but then you actually have to have the extra three of four hours a week to study, to keep on top it . . . Basically just kind of look ahead down the road to see what's coming and try and react beforehand instead of acting after the fact. Then you're up until like three in the morning writing a paper.

As these quotes perhaps suggest, student-veterans can experience a sudden increase in the range and number of even low-stakes choices as a burden rather than emancipation. This phenomenon can be understood as reflecting the idea that choice itself involves responsibility, and that choices in the military involve particularly high stakes. Understandably, most people would prefer not to be saddled with such responsibility and, moreover, distributing such responsibility evenly would be impractical in military settings. As a result, in the military, internalized genres function like authority itself to become a simplifying force. The institutional buy-in the military requires causes servicemembers to react to generic commands and actions, perhaps even without recognizing the power of the genres that command such a high level of compliance. The military may thus reflect quintessential assumptions about genre, demonstrating how genre transcends the individual to become a structure of power and knowledge for which conformity is demanded, assumed, and also welcomed. Thus, if a senior officer enters the room, servicemembers immediately rise to attention. If a senior officer asks a question, an airman responds, "Yes, Sir/Ma'am, No, Sir/Ma'am," or "No excuses, Sir/

Ma'am." If a senior officer issues a lawful order, a sailor or marine obeys without asking for explanation. Such power is situated in a hierarchy of rank. When coupled with the logistical necessity of disseminating a message to all, it may be somewhat easier to understand why actions authorized in the genre of the face-to-face meeting also hold sway in the genres associated with written forms, such as memoranda or operations orders.

Why are such generic commands and responses necessary in the military? Military readiness—for war or for the call to service in any form—is founded upon standardization in order that processes might work systematically and with uniform purpose for the extreme purposes (of war and preparedness for war) deserving of such allegiance. In the military, the legitimacy of an idea can even be linked to the manner in which it is presented in that the presentation of an idea must conform to cultural norms in order for it to garner respect. The important "packaging" is consistent with theories of genre in which genre also "frames what its users generally imagine as possible within a given situation, predisposing them to act in certain ways by rhetorically framing how they come to know and respond to certain situations" (Bawarshi 2003, 22). In the military, a rhetorical frame keeps actions within a recognizable standard necessary for efficiency in an organization of more than two million people who must be instantly prepared to act in completely reliable ways in the context of life-and-death situations.

However powerful the rule of genre may be, military servicemembers have identities that precede and exceed the military, and our research suggests that they make subtle yet substantial language choices through which they inscribe their identities onto military contexts. Having said that, we realize our belief in the agency of soldiers, sailors, airmen, or marines will be greeted by skepticism, given that agency for people at war or preparing to go to war seems more or less antithetical to rhetorical context. Nonetheless, even in the highly routine, even ritualized, contexts of war and preparation for war, there is the potential and even the necessity for agentive action. For instance, while the indoctrination of new recruits is very successful at turning individuals into reliable team members, in the current nonlinear warfare environment, the military has put more focus on decision making and agency at the individual and team level than ever before, and responsibility resides less and less exclusively in the senior leader. One student-veteran in our study pointed out that the Medal of Honor has been won by those who defied not only their own self-interest but also the orders they were given. Another put it this way: "If we only did what we were told, there would be a lot more body bags."

In this spirit, we turn now to our research with student-veterans, which suggests the range of ways in which student-veterans demonstrate rhetorical agency even as, paradoxically, they often disavow it. This latter tendency toward rejecting the self as agent may occur because taking personal credit for achievement is against the basic premise of military collective (unit) action and its associated ethos. Military servicemembers learn to be self-effacing, to hold the mission's accomplishment and the team's participation above the individual's contribution. If this surprises us, perhaps we have another indicator of how far apart military and civilian culture really are.

DISRUPTION OF STEREOTYPES ABOUT NONAGENTIVE ROLES OF STUDENT-VETERANS

Our preliminary research involving surveys, interviews, and document analysis with approximately one dozen student-veterans thus far suggests three categories of agentive communication recalled by student-veterans from their active-duty days. These categories disrupt stereotypical views of the veteran and go some distance toward destabilizing claims about the rhetorical constraint determined by time in the service. Our first category, military writing, suggests that student-veterans—in our case, all enlisted—master professional forms of writing within their units. Our second category, advocacy, suggests that student-veterans undertake individual agentive writing behaviors on behalf of their peers. Our third category, assertion, suggests that student-veterans, when on active duty, engage in writing behaviors that demonstrate intentional, although often subtle, forms of subversion through their writing.

Military Writing

Student-veterans from our study provided substantial evidence of professional writing and communication ability. For instance, Jacob, a US Navy veteran who served for over eight years, contrasted his writing experiences in military schools and training contexts to his writing in professional settings within the military.

> The training where I was going through the formal school was more kind of note taking . . . They'd be like, "Explain how such and such piece of equipment works." And so you'd have to kind of regurgitate what the notes said to a point where you could make it function.

However, once he graduated from his schooling and was transferred to a ship, Jacob noted that beyond functional literacy, he was now expected to enact literacies that served important rhetorical purposes:

> The common form that I did was writing formal maintenance procedures. So, if you needed to replace some piece of equipment, there's a lot of times you would have to shuffle through various manuals, making it so that you didn't violate any procedure and making sure the maintenance was done correctly, with the correct parts . . . and sometimes these packages would be twenty pages long.

The stark contrast in Jacob's assessment of the writing from these two settings may help explain the stigma student-veterans associate with school writing generally. Jacob clearly felt that in a school setting, simply rewriting the information in his notes was enough to be recognized as proficient. It wasn't until Jacob reached his actual job, where he was able to use his skills, that he realized the importance of audience (writing procedures for others to follow), research (accounting for other "various manuals"), and critical thinking (ensuring his procedures or "packages" didn't violate other procedures). His example suggests the degree to which student-veterans, including those from the enlisted ranks, successfully write for professional military contexts. His example suggests something else as well: writing done in a school setting is often dismissed by student-veterans as "empty" while writing done in work settings is considered meaningful. In a military classroom, writing is merely a vehicle with which to pass a technical proficiency test, a way by which to be judged on skills that often actively eschew writing. However, as our student-veterans attested to, they came to see writing as an indispensable part of their technical mastery. Unfortunately, because many of them already had set definitions of "schoolhouse writing" and "professional writing," they kept the two types of writing separate.

Another student-veteran, Anita, a flight nurse, reported that medical recording (charting) was a significant part of her job, and her example establishes the power of genre within military contexts such as medical care.

> That was the main writing. Patient histories . . . Patients' medical records, that was all writing, and then memos and stuff that needed to go to the doctors, what they needed to know about. It was more like a memo printed out . . . saying, "This patient was in this section, in this place for deployment, and this theater or whatever . . . is getting sent here, type of condition." We would minimize it a lot, so we would just say "this is his condition stable." So, it was formal writing but short and concise just so they can know the idea of what's going on with that patient.

Anita also reported taking increasing levels of ownership of her memoranda as a result of feedback on her writing, which helped her to become a successful professional communicator within the medical corps.

> Every time I would write something, doctors would always revise it really quick, so sometimes they'd come up and they'd be like, "Hey, we did an intubation; just remember to put that down." When I first started, that was important, and I'd be like, "That's right! That was important." So just little stuff like that, things that I may have forgotten . . . or like, "Hey, make sure you're more, um, pay attention to detail." Like [I had to learn] every single little detail was to go in.

Functioning within the fast-paced, high-stakes world of medical triage, Anita had to learn not only how to care for the wounded but what to include in the record, the "details" that documentation of care through medical charting required. She demonstrated that she was responsive to professional guidance and feedback.

As these examples suggest, enlisted soldiers, sailors, airmen, and marines not only develop communication skills while in the service, they also get feedback on their writing that they are able to utilize. Student-veterans are also aware that they are being asked to perform complex functions and produce complex texts while in the service. However, given their often unsatisfactory experiences in military training classrooms, they may see the college writing classroom as a probable new case of going through the motions, or an obstacle to be endured on their way to real work, including that which involves writing.

These examples also reinforce the importance of genre in the military. While a civilian medical memorandum may circulate among doctors, nurses, and insurance companies, those reading and writing in that medical genre have agreed to use the same discursive schema. In Anita's case, however, the information that goes into a military medical report must speak to a wide range of activities and their agents, including combat-arms units, medical professionals, commanders who may not be involved in combat operations, and civilians working with casualty-assistance operations, to name just a few. Hence, while the military genre of the medical report certainly conforms to a discursive schema, just as it would in civilian contexts, it goes beyond that to *direct* action by a myriad actors. It must therefore speak effectively and consistently across multiple audiences and across rank hierarchies. As such, the genre of the medical report and its writing by an enlisted nurse rises to a very high level of genre expectation and performance. The medical report suggests the far reach of genre itself, and Anita's mastery of the form demonstrates the high level of professional writing that is expected and can be achieved by relatively low-ranking military personnel.

Advocacy

As Anita's example suggests, organizationally accepted genres have allowed some of the student-veterans in our study to be recognized for their individual competence and leadership authority. In some other cases, student-veterans also reported using genre as a site of advocacy and action on behalf of others. Consistent with the team orientation of military service, student-veterans in our study indicated a particular sense of exigency around the idea of writing to help peers or fellow members of their units.

Writing for the purpose of advocacy provides an example of genre being used to integrate and subvert elements of rank and role, writing, and communication requirements/expectations. For instance, Kirk, a six-year veteran of the air force, used his understanding of audience to become a mentor, demonstrating care and concern in the counseling or evaluation report.

> I had one troop that I was a supervisor for, for a matter of months, and I wrote him his initial performance review, which I actually wrote in pencil, to make it more personal. I didn't want to sit there and type it up and put it on a Formflow form . . . I just wanted to make it personal for him, because what other way should it be? You know, those things were such a joke that it was all about the number you got. You could . . . everybody was, "Don't give him a five, because it'll hurt their career later." I wanted to try and take the joke out of it and make it really personal. It was a review of what I thought of my troop, or what I thought he could improve upon, and I think when it comes from your own hand—you literally had to sit there and write it.

Here we see Kirk thinking of his peer audience and using his peer-leadership role to influence and encourage a fellow troop. In contrast, several student-veterans reported that they communicated quite differently with their commanders and senior officers. In the following example we see one such effort to negotiate the complex terrain of representing a buddy's mishap to the chain of command, which required complex understanding of audience or what Will described as "lawyering."

> The thing with accident reports or the mishap report is knowing how to . . . do the lawyering with it. How to properly present that . . . this piece of equipment failed and not the guy operating it. So you can give the guy some slack . . . So you write technicalities, you write a lot of facts, and you take those facts and you know how to tweak them a little bit.

Will's action represents agentive activity and a disruption of expectation, perhaps even a slight level of distortion for the sake of saving a peer's reputation. Will further elaborated to address writing as a function of performance evaluations.

> When you write performance reports, you know, and you know a kid's a good kid, he deserves a promotion, he deserves a medal. I'm gonna write to get that person that medal. I'm gonna write to get the guy a promotion. And even if he's not that good, or someone struggles in an area, I can sit there and lessen the impact of the areas he struggles in and heighten his strengths.

This quote suggests that Will accepts his agentive authority as a military leader through the vehicle of writing. Quite unusually for the student-veterans in this study, Will specifically stated that his writing affected promotions and awards for his soldiers, yet at the same time, he readily stated that the agency he exercised stemmed from his rank and role as supervisor and leader, dismissing his writing as nothing more than a job-related requirement.

Assertion

Some of the student-veterans in our study reported the use of language to reclaim a narrative in order to reclaim pride and assert a perspective on the record that differed from the official one. In Scotty's case, he inscribed himself and his effectiveness upon a scene that, in the official record, characterized him as having fouled up. To accomplish his self-assertion, Scotty had to subvert a standard military genre in order to reclaim his story.

Specifically, Scotty spoke with some degree of pride around completing a difficult maintenance procedure and the way he represented it in writing. After being challenged on his ability to repair a part on an airplane, he made sure to show in his writing the obstacles he had overcome and the satisfactory nature of the final result.

> I . . . wrote that in the pass down [record], very professionally . . . I said, "Despite ordnance's gesture to the contrary, I redeemed myself." I wrote it all out so people read it; it was definitely professional, but they could tell. I didn't back down.

Interestingly, Scotty remembered exactly how he explained himself. What made the account memorable for him and meaningful for us was the agency he asserted; he took pride in the fact that he did not back down and, with ever-so-much subtlety and courtesy, set the record straight in an enduring written record.

As these examples suggest, writing in the military is rarely done without a purpose, an active prompt. In response to missions, be they administrative or operational, soldiers, sailors, airmen, and marines know to turn to a certain genre in order to communicate a mission requirement. The "habitual language practices" used in military writing are born from on-the-job experience, and explicit guidance from regulations "[enacts and reproduces] situated relations, commitments, and actions" (Bawarshi 2003, 18). Indeed, all military writing is done as a cultured, social response to a requirement. Yet every genre is a "dynamic site for production and regulation of textured, ideological activities" (Bawarshi 2003, 18). This is true also for genres used in the military. We see such dynamics in the approaches each of these student-veterans took with genres they were required to use. These student-veterans also demonstrate that genres are not merely holding tanks in which to put words laden with hidden meanings. Instead, "Genres are dynamic discursive formations in which ideology is naturalized and realized in specific social actions, relations, and subjectivities" (Bawarshi 2003, 7). Military genres thus are not simply forms. They are, like nonmilitary genres, "sites of action" that "do not just help us define and organize kinds of texts" (Bawarshi 2003, 17) but are "reciprocal and dynamic" (Devitt 2004, 21). They are less "a response to recurring situation [than a] nexus between an individual's actions and a socially defined context" (Devitt 2004, 31). They are "regulated and regularized strategies that social agents use to negotiate their way through time and space" (Schryer, Mian, Spafford, and Lingard 2009, 220).

Moreover, as Marilyn Cooper (2011, 437) has argued, genres are spaces of communication, of action and reaction, of "ongoing perturbation and response." Indeed, to use Cooper's terms, and in spite of the constraints associated with military contexts, which impose real and necessary limits on individuality, the student-veterans in our study have acted as "responsible agentive rhetors." Cooper (2011, 442) argues, "Agency is inescapable; rhetors are agents by virtue of their addressing an audience. They become responsible rhetors by recognizing the audience not only as agents, but as concrete others who have opinions and beliefs grounded in the experiences and perceptions and meanings constructed in their brains." Student-veterans seem to have carefully gauged the audiences of their military genres, locating the boundaries of acceptability. In turn it seems that when military servicemembers greet form with improvisation, feedback with accessance and invitation, and insult with respectful self-assertion, those student-veterans are demonstrating that they are always and already in possession of forms of rhetorical agency.

DISTANCING THE SELF FROM WRITING

Despite overwhelming evidence of their agentive rhetorical behavior, however, participants in our study universally and categorically distanced themselves from any claim to having written while in the service. Their disavowals often seemed to be swift, nearly reflexive reactions to a question that to us seemed to have an obvious and quite different answer. We asked, "What kinds of writing did you do in the military?" They uniformly said, "None." Their responses, particularly in their consistency, caused us to probe further, and it was in doing so that we learned about the operations orders, the memoranda, the counseling and evaluation reports, the pass-down reports, the after-actions reports, the medical charting, and so forth. These examples confounded their self-reports. When we pointed out that each of their examples counted as writing, the student-veterans nodded but then quickly dismissed their efforts, saying something like "well, not long stuff," or "not papers," or "nothing that mattered." It was as if the only possible writing of value, perhaps because they were talking to university interviewers, was the academic paper. But it began to seem to us that it was also more than this. They were reluctant to lay claim to their achievements. Once assured we would not inflate their skills or embarrass them, they bathed us in details, explaining the use of the G-Force Tracker for sending nighttime reports, the details doctors wanted in patient charting, the manipulation of language to get a subordinate a promotion or reduce a troop's chances of getting in trouble, the imaginative strategies, such as using a pencil, to inscribe oneself onto a military form. The denial of writing, of personal agency in regard to writing, seemed to be a patterned performance of self in which the self did not much matter. Instead, belief in the greater importance of the unit remained intact.

The shift from a *we* focus in the military to an *I* focus in the civilian university is only part of the explanation, however. Some of their difficulty seemed also to involve their moving from an always-working-never-thinking frame of mind to an always-thinking-never-working approach (Hadlock 2012, 6), the latter of which provoked disdain and seemed in their minds to be associated with the academic enterprise and perhaps writing in particular. Anita told us that the transition to civilian life had been more difficult than she had imagined.

> I never realized it would be such a hard transition. It was an easy transition to go from civilian to military . . . I never thought it was going to be such a hard transition coming out of the military. My life in the military was . . . I would work anywhere between a minimum eight hours in the clinic to

up to sixteen hours a day when I was down range. So, it was one of those things. It was fast paced, always on top of your stuff, in and out, doing . . . I was always *doing* something. When I got out, it was like my world stopped. Um, I, it was, "What am I doing with myself?" I felt like I wasn't doing anything, I was like, "I want to do something, but I don't know what" . . . I was still kind of in shock this entire semester, and I really didn't realize it till it was the last two weeks. I was still in shock.

As Anita's example suggests, identities continue to be constituted by the discourse of the military, and student-veterans are in a state of flux between recently performing as part of a unit to figuring out how they will perform as students with a lot of free time on their hands. Leading identity theorists see the "establishment of identity as the core developmental issue with which students grapple during the college years" (Evans, Forney, and Guido-DiBrito 2010, 65), and the transition from an identity associated with a recognizable unit (for instance, the 82nd Airborne) to one as obscure as college student must surely be a significant challenge. Moreover, when servicemembers move from military discourse to discourses of their multiple new communities—civilian student, daughter, husband, veteran, worker—they may struggle, for a time, to establish an identity that feels right to them as they stand apart from their military identity. Hence, it is almost certainly as Gee (2012, 159–60) has said of identity construction: parts of persons' past identities shall always remain with them, and their identities act as the "meeting point of many, sometimes conflicting, and socially and historically defined discourses." The student-veterans in our study made the conscious decision to leave the military and pursue a path of higher education, but their experiences in college may cause them to hold on tight to a veteran lens and to resist identifying as student. One student-veteran put it this way at the end of the first semester in college:

> As a veteran, those values and beliefs are always going to be with me. I can't sit there and take those out, and schools and colleges, you know, it's predominantly liberal. It's idealistic thinking—it should be—you know, these kids should be thinking about how to solve problems without violence, how to relate with people . . . these are the things you should be learning in college. But you know, when I hear a lot of sentiment, a lot of antiwar sentiment and antimilitary sentiment, from either faculty or students, I shrug. I'm not that sensitive. I'm not going to cry about it . . . I have the linguistic skills to show that I'm more than just a grizzled vet. I'm a learner in academia as well. I have a different perspective. Unfortunately, you know, I don't think it's a bad thing that you have the capability of going to college . . . But you don't have the secondary perspective of millions of Americans who didn't go into college and went into the service. So, your ideas and values are going to be a little bit different.

And another participant described his first semester in college, in which he took first-year composition.

> I think everything I wrote had something to do with the transition because it was either dealing with my status as a veteran or not dealing with it; and when I was not dealing with it, it was sort of in an effort to get away from it . . . because you know, my military experience has taken up over a third of my life. It's very much a part of who I am, but then at the same time, you know, I guess just like any other group, whether it's women, minorities, religion, veterans, you know, you kind of want to be like, "Yeah, I'm a veteran . . . but I'm also all these other things."

Anita summed up the difficulty of the move away from writing as a flight nurse to writing as a college student.

> I already knew what I needed to write. I already knew what kind of form, the way I had to write it. But when it comes to school, they give you a topic, or you choose a topic, and you have to write it, and you have to research it. It's like, it's totally different. I already knew that I had to put all this medication, whatever we put in this patient, I had to write it down, while in this paper that I have to write down, I have to go research and I have to try to find what exactly should I put in the essay, like what's gonna go in that essay . . . It's up to me, not the form that tells me exactly what . . . to do, I'm just like, you know, there's so much that I can write about!

These examples suggest that one of the difficult transitions student-veterans must make is that while knowledge authority in college classrooms may be said to reside with the professor, responsibility for learning lies with the student and hence, success is "based on individual learning and experiences" (Baechtold and DeSawal 2009, 38). Foucault has argued that knowledge never actually comes from the self but instead is constituted from the discourse and structures of power/knowledge surrounding the body. Foucault adds that the process by which a body transforms is rather "discontinuous," quickly breaking "with the ways of speaking and seeing" as an individual, young adult, or civilian and entering into "a whole new 'regime' in discourse and forms of knowledge" (Foucault 1984b, 54). However, since most military recruits are successful, it is reasonable to expect that the transition to new illusions of knowledge construction are bound to be difficult.

The life-changing nature of military service and the distance many student-veterans feel from those with whom they share classroom space (both faculty and students) may contribute to the reasons student-veterans, who have clearly exerted writerly agency within the constraints of their military service, are reluctant to admit they have done so. The student-veterans in our study offered a number of disclaimers about their writing in the military:

(1) I didn't really think about it as writing too much . . . I did a lot of this writing, you know, and a lot of times it was more like direct steps to perform. Torque, bolt this, you know. At the time I didn't really think about it as writing, but now that I think about it, it was, because you have to write to make sure that everybody understands it and performs it correctly.

(2) It was official logbook stuff, so we had what we called a pass-down record book, and we had one for each aircraft, and that was literally all the writing I did. That, and MAFs (Maintenance Action Forms) . . . MAFs are work orders. So a pilot would come back and write up an MAF; I have to go fix it and write down in the MAF so there's an official record. And also in the shop, like let's say it was "aircraft three, landing gear blow down." I had to go out there and figure out what was wrong with it. I would then write, 'cause it is more or less if anything happens to the bird, if it ends up crashing, or anything like that . . . I'd write full detail in the pass down what I did, what we did, what we checked, and it's also there because, like most jobs, you don't finish in one shift, so the next guy can come in and see what you did. So you have to be able to write clearly for anyone else to read it and know what you did.

Interviewer: That sounds like pretty important writing.

Well . . . but it was mostly like one page, like just one front of the page, like that was mostly what it was.

These examples suggest that another factor leading to self-denial of writing agency may involve defining what counts as writing. Student-veterans may be passing off their workplace writing as simply a facet of their professional work, while by their definitions, Writing (with a capital W) performs some finer functions, such as the novel at one end and papers for teachers at the other. In addition, their tendency to distance themselves from having engaged in writerly behaviors, even when confronted by evidence to the contrary, suggests that writing is too reflective and sedentary to be considered agentive work by student-veterans. Within a context that ideologically and materially connects meaningful behavior to physical doing and that connects meaningful behavior to that which involves the unit, writing done by the individual servicemember may be seen quite simply as self-indulgent.

PEDAGOGICAL RECOMMENDATIONS

Our job as faculty working with transitioning student-veterans may therefore revolve around *direct explanation* of the ideological differences between two worlds: the one the student-veterans inhabit and the one they recently inhabited. Student-veterans may need to identify and unpack the kinds of action agency that were valued in the military and compare these to the kinds of learning and writing agency that will be needed in college classrooms and beyond. It may be important that we quickly clarify the purposes of writing as they are taught in the composition classroom, making our approaches clear and expecting neither resistance nor acceptance. We offer two concrete ideas for how this might be done.

We might begin with directly addressing the values of the university and a discussion of how the values of college differ from values held in other facets of society, including but not limited to the military. Rather than naturalizing the values of the university, we might name and critique our own values as a long list of scholars have argued for some time that we do (see Berkenkotter 1984; Bizzell 1997; Graff and Birkenstein 2009; Rose 2009), and by doing so establish that we understand, as student-veterans do immediately upon arriving, that the university is not value neutral. Among university values we might address are the interest in critiquing the status quo, locations of power, and hegemonic adoption of mainstream values along with the naming and valuing of varied and marginalized perspectives. We might also address seemingly contradictory features of academic writing that demonstrate the complexity of university values, asking student-veterans to interrogate the differing values and inherent contradictions apparent in each. One lesson might involve the use of qualifiers as academic convention and symbols of scholarly restraint, and the second might involve its converse, the writing of thesis statements for which students demonstrate mastery of the gesture of authority long before they can claim actual expertise.

Student-veterans often recognize the use of qualifiers in academic settings as conflicting with what they have known in the military: One student-veteran put the values conflict this way: "Yeah, I mean, qualifiers are a sign of indecision and uh, you cannot have indecision in the military. For better or worse." Here we see the deeply held beliefs about the importance of conveying strength, certainty, and reliability in military settings. The use of qualifiers is understood as weakness by many student-veterans, or as one student-veteran put it, "Equivocation will get someone killed." Hence, the very idea that servicemembers might admit that their understanding was partial or tentative is anathema to military bearing, yet such admission is precisely what is required of student-veterans in academic settings. One approach would involve showing examples of equivocation as a sign of strength in written arguments. Here it might be possible to talk directly about the rhetorical differences between written argument and preparation for combat. Argumentation might thus be posed as an alternative to certainty, one that requires a different skill set that also requires practice—a kind of basic training in the representation and valuing of multiple perspectives, the strategies of moderation, and the modulation of tone.

A second, complementary lesson might involve addressing the contradictory (to the notion of modulation and moderation addressed above) need to summon a pretense of authority in one's writing through use of the thesis statement. We would directly state that in learning the strategies of claim and thesis in the academic argument, the student-writer is taking on the voice of certainty and conviction and, however improbably, stating a *thesis* long before having full knowledge of the topic. Addressing this approach directly with student-veterans may be helpful since creating an argumentative claim may seem a completely unearned privilege to them, an approach they would rarely take in the military. We invoke the example of "Sergeant's Time Training" to explain what we mean here. Military units are constantly undergoing refresher training for varying skill-level tasks that are not used daily and for which it is important to maintain required levels of proficiency (i.e., calling for medevac help is only an easy task to those who are well trained in the endeavor). Sergeant's time training thus establishes a regular time for units to engage in such training, an approach that accounts for units being in various locations and hence not able to participate in instruction conducted at formal training sites.

With such training, only subject-matter experts are able to run the refresher, and servicemembers do not become subject-matter experts until they have demonstrated a consistent proficiency in performing the task. In contrast, not only are students generally not subject-matter experts in many of the subjects about which we ask them to write, but we insist that they make an individualized claim—an argument, no less—about a topic long before they can claim expertise in the subject. Directly addressing the purpose and value of this practice might help student-veterans understand and accept the differences in pedagogy they recognize at some level as being inconsistent with their experience.

Together, these two lessons—or others like them—would ask student-veterans to observe and critically analyze differing beliefs about authority and genres of "delivery" of information between the military and academe. Since academic culture simultaneously demands that students make claims for which they are largely unqualified yet also embrace an attitude of humility that admits knowledge is tentative, student-veterans might gain insight and appreciation for the complicated values bound up in such practices.

The tougher nut to crack may be student-veterans' belief about the importance of their current and future efforts, in college and beyond.

Many veterans believe the most meaningful and agentive time of their lives is now behind them. The challenge, therefore, may be to help student-veterans see legitimacy in reclaiming agency as "just a student" when previously they may have been in charge of million-dollar tanks, the refueling of billion-dollar aircraft, arranging supply logistics for thousands of troops, or tending the lives of wounded servicemembers on an aircraft bound for Walter Reed Army Hospital. To put it quite simply, the power of prior experience with the military may at least initially confound student-veteran's sense of the relevance of most civilian endeavors, and college pursuits in particular, perhaps best symbolized by the abstract notion of college writing. One of our central tasks may be to assist them with seeing the relevance of a civilian livelihood, to help them believe there are worthy endeavors short of preparation for and engagement in war, and to help them see the value and power of language—to argue, to instruct, to deepen one's understanding, even to heal. To make the initial bridge, student-veterans may need to see both the importance and the applicability of their prior experience and the relevance of their current education to the significant civilian challenges that lie ahead. Two of our study's student-veterans began to take such steps in the first year of college. Anita, the former flight nurse, reported,

> I can sit down and write the essay. I had, you know, the discipline was there. Honestly, me writing an essay and me writing a report was completely different and when I first started writing, I was like, I don't know how to get this set up. But the thing is, I had the discipline of doing it because I wrote in the military. Writing in the military . . . you had to get the report done or you couldn't leave. And when it came to writing the essay or whatever assignment I had, I had to sit down and write, so I could get a good grade.

Adam, an Airborne Ranger, reported the value that army writing was having for his efforts in school.

> All writing I had done prior to the Army was school based and often a collection of other people's ideas. But counseling statements forced me to create my own opinions on soldiers' actions and get them onto paper. This was not easy at first, but the more practice I had, the better I became. By the time my five-year contract was over, writing a monthly evaluation was about as easy as talking. The military forced me to write and I am better because of it. I apply this to all of my writing now. I learned how to organize my own thoughts and get them on paper . . . Before counseling statements, I knew what I was trying to say but I just couldn't get it written down . . . My experience in the army has made me a better writer.

These student-veterans turned college writers have convinced us that the first-year composition course can be an important site for transition and reintegration. They also suggest to us that the student-veteran can educate the academy about the skills they have developed in the military. In our university settings, we should explore the contradictions contained within our constructions of veterans' powers of critical thinking, educating ourselves about the complex problem-solving skills required not only for combat roles but for the myriad forms of work and skill developed through military service. We need to continue to explore the literacy habits of student-veterans and develop a richer understanding of them.

Note

1. An Operations Order, or OPORD, is a prescribed five-paragraph (Situation, Mission, Execution, Service Support, Command and Signal) field order used to inform military units of the details of a forthcoming operation. The OPORD is the primary order that is given for a mission.

    A Warning Order, or WARNO, is given in advance of the OPORD to let military members under the command know that they may be receiving an Operations Order. The WARNO contains a few basic details of the situation and what the mission may entail. However, much of the pertinent information for a proper Operations Order is still forthcoming.

    Once an OPORD is given, the situation may change before the mission is actually begun or, during the operation the situation may change so that the Operations Order must be modified. In these cases the commander will issue a Fragmentary Order, or FRAGO. The FRAGO will state exactly how the situation or mission has been changed and what must be done to make up for the change.

References

Baechtold, Margaret, and Danielle M. De Sawal. 2009. "Meeting the Needs of Women Veterans." Special issue, *New Directions for Student Services* 2009 (126): 35–43. http://dx.doi.org/10.1002/ss.314.

Barthes, Roland. 1977. "The Death of the Author." In *Image-Music-Text*, edited and translated by Stephen Heath, 142–48. New York: Hill and Wang.

Bawarshi, Anis. 2003. *Genre and the Invention of the Writer*. Logan: Utah State University Press.

Berkenkotter, Carol. 1984. "Student Writers and Their Sense of Authority over Texts." *College Composition and Communication* 35 (3): 312–9. http://dx.doi.org/10.2307/357459.

Bizzell, Patricia. 1997. "The Prospect of Rhetorical Agency." In *Making and Unmaking the Prospects for Rhetoric*, edited by Theresa Enos and Richard McNabb, 37–42. Mahwah, NJ: Erlbaum.

Cooper, Marilyn M. 2011. "Rhetorical Agency as Emergent and Enacted." *College Composition and Communication* 62 (3): 420–49.

Devitt, Amy J. 2004. "A Theory of Genre." In *Writing Genres*, 1–32. Carbondale: Southern Illinois University Press.

Evans, Nancy J., Deanna S. Forney, Florence M. Guido, Lori D. Patton, and Kristen A. Renn. 2010. *Student Development in College: Theory, Research, and Practice*. 2nd ed. San Francisco: Jossey-Bass .

Foucault, Michel. 1984a. "Docile Bodies." In *The Foucault Reader*, edited by Paul Rabinow, 179–87. New York: Pantheon.

Foucault, Michel. 1984b. "Truth and Power." In *The Foucault Reader*, edited by Paul Rabinow, 51–75. New York: Pantheon.

Foucault, Michel. 1984c. "What is an Author?" In *The Foucault Reader*, edited by Paul Rabinow, 101–20. New York: Pantheon .

Gee, James. 1989. "What Is Literacy?" *Journal of Education* 171 (1): 18–25.

Gee, James. 2012. *Social Linguistics and Literacies: Ideology in Discources*. New York: Rutledge.

Graff, Gerald, and Cathy Birkenstein. 2009. *They Say/I Say: The Moves That Matter in Academic Writing—With Readings*. New York: W. W. Norton.

Hadlock, Erin. 2012. *The Role of Genre, Identity, and Rhetorical Agency in the Military Writings of Post-9/11 Student-Veterans*. Thesis, Colorado State University.

Hyland, Ken. 2012. *Disciplinary Identities: Individuality and Community in Academic Discourse*. Cambridge: Cambridge University Press.

Leontiev, A. N. 2005. "The Genesis of Activity." *Journal of Russian & East European Psychology* 43 (4): 58–71.

Rose, Mike. 2009. *Why School? Reclaiming Education for All of Us*. New York: New Press.

Schryer, Catherine, Marcellina Mian, Marlee Spafford, and Lorelei Lingard. 2009. "The Trial of the Expert Witness: Negotiating Credibility in Child Abuse Correspondence." *Written Communication* 26 (3): 215–46. http://dx.doi.org/10.1177/0741088308330767.

4

FACULTY AS FIRST RESPONDERS
Willing but Unprepared

Linda S. De La Ysla

In twenty-five years of teaching college writing at both four- and two-year institutions, I have encountered students—traditional age and nontraditional—whose life issues, singly or combined, impeded their success at school: academic unpreparedness, diagnosed and undiagnosed learning disabilities, unemployment and its attendant financial difficulties, substance abuse, family demands, a history of physical or mental abuse, and homelessness. However, over the past four years of teaching at the Community College of Baltimore County (CCBC), I have seen the influx of individuals from a distinct demographic: US military veterans whose deployment to Iraq and Afghanistan has often left them with psychological, physical, and emotional challenges. In 2010, CCBC had approximately 800 student-veterans enrolled full or part time. That year, those student-veterans joined the more than 22,000 veterans who resided in Maryland and who had recently returned from either Operation Enduring Freedom (OEF) in Afghanistan or Operation Iraqi Freedom (OIF) in Iraq (Brown and Kurtinitis, *Baltimore Sun*, January 31, 2011). Since 2010, the number of returning Maryland veterans has increased by the thousands, and not surprisingly, our community college has—within one year—experienced a 25 percent increase in student-veterans eager to take advantage of the post-9/11 GI benefits.

The appeal of the two-year community college to veterans may likely be due to the fact that—like the majority of their classmates (57 percent in 2011 according to a 2011 fact sheet; Community College of Baltimore County, n.d.)—many student-veterans at CCBC work outside of school. In addition, many student-veterans who were underprepared in high school or who have been out of school for a number of years need to

DOI: 10.7330/9780874219425.c004

take non-credit-bearing courses in basic math, reading, and writing; two-year colleges are well positioned to meet those needs.

But it is not only skills that some student-veterans lack; it is peace of mind. According to a recent RAND report, nearly one in five student-veterans suffers from posttraumatic stress disorder (PTSD), traumatic brain injury (TBI), or depression (O'Herrin 2011, 16). Furthermore, active-duty veterans younger than twenty-five are most at risk for PTSD (Seal et al. 2009, 1651). In addition, for those student-veterans who may have entered military service with some of the life challenges mentioned earlier, the potential for stress and distress rises exponentially. We in higher education should be deeply concerned about meeting the needs of student-veterans, but it is important to emphasize that only some of our student-veterans struggle with the aforementioned conditions. Elizabeth O'Herrin (2011) contends, "Because veterans (have) . . . an incredibly wide range of experiences, it is impossible to take a one-size-fits-all approach to serving them" . . . [they] are a diverse population with an incredibly wide range of experiences" (16). Therefore, tailoring our programs to serve all student-veterans is key; whether we are administrators, staff, or faculty, such diversification presents a huge challenge.

A CASE FOR NARRATIVE

Many of us who teach writing assign a personal narrative essay early in the semester about a significant event. Most of the student-veterans in my composition classes—as well as those in the classes of CCBC colleagues—frequently choose to write about service-related experiences. If the student-veteran has seen combat and perhaps suffers from post-deployment trauma, the essay may center on that trauma, which is not surprising. Certainly, for student-veterans whose military training values stoicism and toughness in the face of adversity, the personal narrative provides an opportunity to write about events or share observations that may have been previously silenced. I have also observed that for students lacking military experience, such narratives can provide insights into the unique and valuable experiences of those who have served. At CCBC, students from Cameroon, Nepal, Jordan, Ecuador, China, and Moldavia sit alongside students from primarily African American communities or counties to the north with rural, Caucasian populations. Bring into the mix student-veterans with their unique perspectives and the writing classroom becomes a site where "dialogue, diversity, and hybridity" flourish (Tobin 2004, 6).

Having said this, I recognize that the social-epistemic trend in composition studies has turned away from personal narrative; as Lad Tobin (2004, 3) writes, "It is the autobiographical essay that has become the shibboleth in the contemporary English department." Nevertheless, there is a radical need for such writing among student-veterans. Narratives of a confessional nature enable student-veterans to write about the significance of experiences and achieve insight into the origin of prevailing values and feelings. And despite ongoing criticism from some composition studies circles, stories of military experience are *not* disconnected or solipsistic but instead arise from a "larger political and historical reality" (Tobin 2004, 106). It is in the writing classroom that the implications of this reality can be explicitly addressed. Indeed, one teacher of writing who has worked with gang members and prisoners contends that confessional narrative may permit a student to "tell his [sic] stories and heal himself [sic] so that he [sic] might not have to kill himself [sic] or others" (Nelson 2000, 44). For some student-veterans whose military experiences have left wounds, both seen and unseen, personal narrative will prove to have a cathartic effect while providing a compassionate adult reader, the professor. At minimum, however, it "raises all the usual and rhetorical questions about audience, purpose, point of view, ethos, pathos, logic" (Tobin 2004, 111).

ETHICAL CONCERNS

If and when a student-veteran suffering from combat-induced PTSD or depression chooses to write about these topics, how do we respond? Many teachers of writing lack a clear sense of what to do or what to say when meeting those wounded warriors in person and on the page. Supportive and pedagogically sound response (and in some cases referral) is needed. G. Lynn Nelson (200, 45) argues that the first "call" is to listen. Indeed, real listening implies the creation of an open space in which we acknowledge students' stories as reflective of how their distinct sociopolitical and cultural contexts have shaped identity. With an increasing number of individuals returning from military deployment, we may expect to encounter more narratives of a disturbing nature. In addition, not only might we find ourselves unprepared to deal with those stories, but we may even be "traumatized" by them, as one author suggests in her recent book on women veterans (Holmstedt 2009). By drawing from an experience that transpired in 2010 with a student-veteran in my composition class, an experience that gained national media attention,[1] I will lay out the dilemma in which I found myself. In addition, I will share my own brand of what has been called "secondary trauma," a condition that "affects people who experience trauma secondhand . . . it can seriously affect mental-health counselors, first responders, critical-care nurses, and others . . . involved in treating those exposed to traumatic events" (Holmstedt 2009, 312). The incident showed me how poorly prepared I was to deal with the student-veteran's trauma-induced issues. In addition, I discovered I was unaware of resources that existed on my campus to support student-veterans. Finally, I will explain how good arose from that period of turmoil.

A CHILLING NARRATIVE

I teach in the English department of the Community College of Baltimore County (CCBC), an ethnically diverse community college in Baltimore, Maryland. CCBC has three campuses plus three satellites geographically dispersed around the Baltimore Beltway. In 2011, our college had 34,000 credit students, 18 percent full time and 82 percent part time. Continuing-education enrollment topped 35,000 students. Demographically, the average student is twenty-six years old; 44 percent are minority students, primarily African American. Over 50 percent of CCBC students work twenty or more hours per week, and 45 percent receive some form of financial aid (Community College of Baltimore County n.d.).

At the time of this incident, I had just begun my second year of teaching at CCBC. In the fall of 2010, I was teaching two paired sections in the Accelerated Learning Program, or ALP. In this model, eight developmental writing students are mainstreamed into a credit-bearing introductory composition class with twelve other students. The eight are concurrently enrolled in a workshop section that takes place the hour after the composition course, with the same professor teaching both sections. Crucial to student success in the ALP is the small group, where individual attention can be given in skills building and feedback on drafts. In addition, professor-to-student and student-to-student relationships can be nurtured. ALP professors also intentionally address affective and life issues as they relate to students' academic progress. Research data from the past six years has shown that students enrolled in the ALP basic writing courses at CCBC are both retained and complete the English sequence at a higher rate than students enrolled in traditional developmental writing courses of twenty students. The class format is relevant to this discussion of student-veterans because as a faculty member, I become well acquainted with my students and the fabric of their lives outside the classroom. After all, we meet for six hours per week.

One of the students in this cohort, I will call him C. J., identified himself as a veteran. While FERPA guidelines constrain me from commenting on the details beyond what has been written and televised in the media, I will do my best to navigate through this often-tricky terrain. Furthermore, at the risk of sounding defensive, it is true that my role as the student-veteran's writing professor was not accurately reported. That is, the media was given the impression—perhaps from the student-veteran himself—that I had assigned the disturbing essay in question, assessed it as excellent, and encouraged the student to submit it to the school newspaper. As the following details will show, these were misrepresentations of the actual events.

From the start C. J. stood out in a quiet way. As the photos in the *Baltimore Sun* article show, he was a good-looking man in his mid-twenties with sandy hair in a buzz cut. Colorful tattoos spanned the length of both arms. The photo shows him wearing the clothes he often had on: a dark T-shirt, pressed jeans, and a heavy medallion on a long gold chain. His expression was serious and he rarely smiled (Walker, *Baltimore Sun*, November 21, 2010). In class, he always sat nearest the door in the very last row of seats, whether we were in the larger comp class or in the more intimate class of eight. He was invariably soft spoken and polite, "Ma'amming" me whenever we had a conversation. Within the first week of classes, and as later reported in the *Sun* article, C. J. revealed that he was an ex-infantryman who had served and been injured multiple times in Iraq. In addition, he suffered from PTSD, traumatic brain injury, and physical pains due to shrapnel still embedded in his body. He also reported having insomnia (Walker, *Baltimore Sun*, November 21, 2010). Once in a while, C. J. stood up discreetly to stretch. Just as discreetly, he sought me out for extra help with some assignments. Naturally, I was glad our increased time together each week in the paired ALP classes would give me ample opportunity to help him succeed. True to his word, C. J. made a habit of showing me his notes, many of which he had highlighted in yellow, or turning work in early for my feedback. To my mind, C. J. was a conscientious student-veteran who, despite many challenges, was trying his best to do well in college. Also, we were developing a comfortable relationship, as I often do with the "ALP-ers"; he would linger after class to discuss his other classes, especially his favorites.

By the third week of the semester, students were writing first drafts of their narrative essays about a significant event. Before handing in the essay, students shared their drafts in writing groups. As I moved from group to group, I observed C. J. reading aloud to a group of three attentive students. Although I did not hear the entire essay, it was obvious that he had written about his military experiences. A few days later, I collected students' revised essays to give them preliminary response. C. J.'s essay was six pages, three pages beyond the required length. In his essay, he recounted in some detail the circumstances surrounding his multiple injuries, mentioning the difficult recuperation he endured both in Germany and in the States (Walker, *Baltimore Sun*, November 21, 2010). The essay also recounted battle scenes. As is often my practice when conferencing with students whose papers have a solid narrative flare, I encouraged revision and even suggested that he might submit a revised paper to the school newspaper. I commented, as I often do, that a strong revision would work to his benefit in earning a high grade by semester's end. C. J.'s face broke into a rare smile, and he promised to pare down the essay and follow my suggestions for revision.

However, as soon as we parted, I felt wary. How out of my element I was in the face of C. J.'s combat-related experiences! As a result, I decided to send an email to our campus psychologist in order to get a general idea about what resources existed on campus for veterans. His response indicated that he had "once run" a support group for veterans on campus, but that it had more or less fizzled out due to nonattendance. He emphasized that he was always available to students and student-veterans and that furthermore, he was trained in treating PTSD. I thanked him, wondering how one might approach an adult male combat veteran, especially one as private as C. J., and suggest he seek psychological counseling. It seemed presumptuous to do so, especially since it was highly possible that C. J. was —as are many other veterans—already in the care of a therapist.

Two weeks later, C. J. came up to me after our Friday class: "Ma'am," he said, "*this* is the piece I want to submit to the paper." Since I was rushing to a meeting, I only had time to read the title: "War Is a Drug." *Uh-oh*, I thought. Unbidden, scenes tumbled into memory from the recent film, *The Hurt Locker*. As I struggled to keep my face composed, I asked C. J. whether he would like me to read and comment on his piece before he submitted it. Yes, he would. Hurrying across campus, I began to worry. If the title of this piece accurately previewed its content, then what? At home later that evening, my fears were realized. As published several weeks later in a front-page article in the *Baltimore Sun*, the essay was C. J.'s revelation that being a soldier in wartime had changed him forever. Now, he had an addiction to killing. Most appalling was his graphic description of how much he enjoyed sticking a knife into a man and watching the life drain out of his enemy. C. J. wrote that he wanted to rejoin his comrades in combat and continue to kill more "rag-heads" (Walker, *Baltimore Sun*, November 21, 2010).

That evening, in the privacy of my own home, before what would be extensive national media coverage, I was C. J.'s first audience, his first responder. The content of his essay repelled me as I struggled to reconcile my impressions of C. J. as a quiet, hardworking student-veteran with this self-portrait of someone who loved to kill. I was saddened at the enormity of the unseen burden he was carrying around. While I wanted to help, I wondered at the same time, who *is* C. J.? How had my instincts about him as a person been so off mark? My thoughts replicated those of one college teacher who was confronted with a disturbing essay written by one of his students: "His behavior during the first three weeks of class had been neither hostile nor sullen nor otherwise out of place . . . Why, then, had he chosen to respond with a shocking narrative of drunken attacks on gay men and homeless people in nearby San Francisco?" (Lankford n.d., 1). I felt similarly stymied and confused as a different kind of war began inside me, one that culminated in *what am I dealing with here? What should I do?*

Indeed, that and related questions would plague me throughout the days and weeks that followed: what *are* the ground rules when a student-veteran writes such a troubling narrative? I wanted to do whatever was in C. J.'s best interest, but did I truly know what that was? Of course there was the campus psychologist, but I remained unsure about referring C. J. Perhaps he was already under someone's care. And if he were not, would it not be overstepping my bounds to tell an adult male that *I* thought he needed counseling? Mulling over these concerns, I did feel a brief wave of trepidation as I struggled with the disconnect between C. J. the student and C. J. the obviously traumatized veteran. And later, after the Behavior Intervention Team suspended C. J., alluding to the young man's history in other places, I also worried for a short time about my safety. But mainly, after reading his essay, I was afraid—not of C. J., but of my unpreparedness to deal with the situation. My dilemma was not unique. In the introduction to *Trauma and the Teaching of Writing*, Shane Borrowman (2005, 2–3) describes his own reaction on the morning of 9/11: without engaging his students in conversation over the attack, he cancelled classes. He writes: "My failure that September morning, on the simplest possible level, came about because of lack of preparation . . . I was at a loss . . . because it had never entered my mind that I might have to be prepared for such an occurrence." Perhaps like Borrowman, I did not do more because I did not know what to do, never imagining that I would be in such a situation.

I needed to communicate with C. J. Since it was the weekend, I left a voicemail message and sent an email as well. Although the weekend passed without word, I fully expected to see him on Monday when we could speak privately. But Monday came and went. Once more, I attempted to contact C. J., but it did no good. In all honesty, I cannot recall the rest of that week. Teaching six courses that semester (four of them were the paired ALP sections), I was inundated with papers and preparation, and the thought of the disturbing essay was pushed to the back of my mind, for which I was grateful. And since C. J. had asked for my input on his essay, it never occurred to me that he might send it in to the campus newspaper without conferring with me. Eventually, he returned to class. Before I could broach the subject, C. J. announced that he had electronically submitted "War Is a Drug" to the faculty advisor of the newspaper. Beyond a feeble "you did?" I was speechless. When he wondered out loud when his piece might be published, I replied that it would most likely be reviewed by the editors.

My first thought was to speak with the faculty advisor of the newspaper and give her some context for the essay. Because I felt that anyone reading "War Is a Drug" would assume—perhaps rightly—the worst about C. J., it seemed important to advocate for him. Certainly, I hoped against hope that he was *not* as disturbed as the essay implied. At the same time, I told the faculty advisor how violent and offensive the piece was and worried aloud over its being published. She listened to my concerns and reassured me that both she and the student editorial board would review the submission. While not suggesting outright that the piece *not* be published, I left with the distinct impression that it *would* be carefully scrutinized and that she would make a careful, final decision. In fact, I assumed that the essay would be rejected out of hand, or—if accepted—heavily edited for typos as well as its pejorative term for Muslims.

Interestingly, it never crossed my mind that the thoughts, feelings, and experiences C. J. shared were anything but genuine. I mention this point because some campus veterans immediately questioned his credibility once the essay was published. They pointed to C. J.'s choice of weapon, a knife, as one rarely used by infantrymen in combat. They suggested that perhaps he had never served at all, that the entire essay was a fiction. I, however, accepted the essay as C. J.'s own account. As I struggled with my feelings, I wondered whether one of the reasons C. J. went MIA for a week after he gave me "War Is a Drug" was because the writing of the piece had reopened the traumas he had experienced. Authors Goggin and Goggin (2005, 32) observe, "Individuals are both compelled to and repelled by discoursing on the trauma—some respond with an outpouring of oral and written discourses while others are silent." Had C. J. felt so "repelled" by what he had disclosed in "War Is a Drug" that he was unable to come back to class?

Again, classes and papers descended on me. For the next couple of weeks, I once more put aside any conversation with C. J. related to the content of the essay, as well as any attempt to refer him for services. Today, like Borrowman, I wonder at my inaction. In part, I was operating on the assumption that C. J.'s essay would end up on the cutting floor. In part, I hoped (naïvely) that by not publishing the essay, the "problem" would recede until I figured out how to follow up with C. J. Of course, C. J. asked me more than once whether or not the paper was going to publish his piece, to which I replied that I did not know (of course, true), despite my concealed preference. Finally, at the end of two weeks, the answer came: when I walked into my ALP class, C. J. was reading a copy of the October 10 edition of our campus newspaper. "They published it!" he announced, looking pleased. Dismayed, I took the paper, glanced at the essay, and saw that it had been printed typos and all, completely uncensored. I was truly shocked.

Events moved quickly after that. Suddenly, I found myself thrust into an unwanted spotlight. Within forty-eight hours, I had a phone message plus a personal note left on my desk while I was in class: "Call Dean Black." When I reached the dean of the School of Liberal Arts, he explained that the next day my presence was requested at a specially convened meeting of the college's Behavior Intervention Team (BIT). They would like to ask me questions in reference to the student-veteran who had written the essay. I put down the receiver and immediately called the English department chair, a friend and colleague. She filled me in: over the past seventy-two hours, everyone from the faculty newspaper advisor to the college president herself was being inundated with emails from CCBC faculty, staff, and student-veterans, the majority expressing outrage and concern over C. J.'s essay. A very small number were sympathetic to his plight. According to my chair, the greatest outcry was coming from student-veterans who objected to the essay's portrayal of veterans as killers. They felt that C. J.'s essay did an injustice to the vast majority of veterans who had served proudly and who were now lawabiding citizens and good students. As mentioned before, some accused him of fabricating the incident. A few implied that "someone" should "do something." I felt torn because it seemed to me that others were condemning him without knowing him. At the same time, I was now becoming insecure about my own powers of judgment when it came to C. J. Nevertheless, I was anxious to give the BIT team my perspective.

Since I was a relative newcomer, and untenured, I asked my department chair to accompany me, a request to which she readily agreed.

A dozen campus representatives attended the BIT meeting: campus deans, the head of security, the campus psychologist, the judicial affairs officer, and others. At their request, I shared my impressions of C. J. and told them how the essay in question had come to be written. The team members listened attentively, asked questions for clarification, and at the end of an hour and a half, thanked me. When I inquired about next steps, they explained that their procedure was to interview the student himself as soon as possible. The following day I was in Washington, DC, presenting at a conference with colleagues. At the midmorning break, I checked my cell phone and saw that C. J. had left multiple messages. When I reached him, he explained that he was meeting with the BIT later that afternoon. We discussed his concerns, and although I tried to be reassuring, at that point I had no idea what the BIT would decide. By that evening, I was still waiting to hear the outcome of C. J.'s interview. When we finally connected again, he announced, "They've kicked me off campus." This was an erroneous impression that C. J. would subsequently report to the media (Walker, *Baltimore Sun*, November 21, 2010). Several weeks after the essay had been made public, the *Baltimore Sun* article, "A Fight for Freedom," appeared on the front page of the Sunday edition. "War Is a Drug" was reprinted in its entirety and included a full-page, color photo of C. J. as well as additional photos and background information that took up an entire inside page. While the *Sun* did concede that CCBC was attempting to obtain documentation about C. J.'s psychological health, it implied that the college was treating this student-veteran unfairly (Walker, *Baltimore Sun*, November 21, 2010). Some members of the media took a less partisan view; the *Chronicle of Higher Education* reported, "The college, expressing concerns about safety, said he could return to the campus if he provided a psychological evaluation" ("Community College in Maryland Suspends Veteran Who Wrote about Addiction to Combat" 2010).

From that moment on, I began receiving multiple emails and phone messages from reporters asking for my "side of the story." How had I, as a person and a professor, *felt* when I read "War Is a Drug?" Since the media had been led to believe I had not only assigned the essay but had given C. J. an *A*, it seemed as if my ethics and judgment were in question (Walker, *Baltimore Sun*, November 21, 2010). As a professional, I would have liked to set the record straight. However, ego was less important than following FERPA guidelines and presenting a unified front to the media. So—as requested—I "turfed" all media inquiries to the college's public relations officer. Throughout those weeks of nearly constant inner turmoil, I was wracked with ambivalence over the affair, still unable to reconcile my image of the quiet young man who had worked so hard in the two English courses with the details of his past and current struggles as revealed in the *Sun* article (Walker, *Baltimore Sun*, November 21, 2010). Karen Holmstedt (2009, 310), who interviewed women combat veterans for *The Girls Come Marching Home*, makes a comment that resonates with me: "I was humbled by their candor but also felt helpless at the end of the interview . . . I knew I had helped them by listening, but I didn't have any tools to make them better." Neither, I felt, did I.

As for the college administration and public-safety officers, I know they must have been haunted by past incidents of shootings at schools and colleges around the nation. While concerned for C. J., their overriding concern was for the safety of the campus community. They encouraged all his professors to do their best to help C. J. keep up with the coursework during that interim period. For my part, I communicated with C. J. through texting and occasional phone calls. Whenever we spoke, he sounded disheartened and frustrated. Why was the college "kicking him out," he asked? In fact, C. J. was confused by the word *suspension*, having equated it with *expulsion*. Although I explained to C. J. more than once the difference between the two terms, and that he might still be able to return to classes if he produced the necessary documentation from his VA psychologist, I am unsure whether he heard me. He insisted that he could not get an appointment at the VA for weeks. Unfortunately, I do not know if this was true. I urged C. J. to keep up with his studies so he would not lose the credits. Towards that end, I sent him all his graded papers with instructions for revision, as well as his new assignments. However, sadly, if predictably, C. J. did not submit any papers to me: after all, here was a young man with TBI who needed face-to-face clarification on just about every assignment, and that wasn't going to happen under the circumstances.

In the end, although C. J. submitted some documentation, it was not the documentation that CCBC had requested (Mytelka 2011). Our college's position was criticized vociferously by some who felt we were taking too hard a line; in fact, according to one highly placed CCBC administrator, it was not until three months later, after the Tucson shootings of a member of Congress and others by a disturbed former student at Pima Community College (PCC), that CCBC's position was bolstered. After the Tucson incident, the CCBC administrator's counterparts, both in the state of Maryland and nationally, endorsed the way CCBC handled the situation. Ironically, PCC was lambasted in the media for not dealing more proactively with the shooter, Mr. Loughner. As the *New York Times* reported, "The focus has turned to whether it (the college) did all it could to prevent his apparent descent into explosive violence" (Sulzberger and Gabriel, January 14, 2011). Surely, it was to avoid the "explosive violence" of past campus shootings that CCBC endeavored to weigh all the information available. The college sought to safeguard the campus community and still leave the door ajar for C. J. should he produce the requested documentation. Unfortunately, as reported elsewhere, that documentation was not submitted by semester's end (Mytelka 2011).

FIRST RESPONDERS

Referring to Mary Louise Pratt's question, "'What is the place of unsolicited oppositional discourse . . . in the imagined classroom community?'" Richard Miller (1994, 393–94) proposes three possible responses: (1) comment on the essay's "surface features and formal qualities"; (2) refer the student to a psychologist; or (3) use the content as an opportunity to bring to light important issues. He strongly favors the latter course of action. And yet, when a student writes about his love of killing, as C. J. did in his essay or as poet Nikki Giovanni's student at Virginia Tech did regarding his own disturbing impulses—then what? Indeed, although Giovanni reported her concerns about student Cho to college officials and the young man was removed from her class and tutored privately, he nevertheless returned to wreak havoc at Virginia Tech (*Valley Morning Star*, April 19, 2007). When a student writes about violent tendencies, it seems inappropriate to conduct a classroom discussion of mental illness or PTSD. However, as discussed later in this essay, we at CCBC found that it proved beneficial to publicize the difficult issue of PTSD to the campus community, thus ultimately supporting the previous suggestion that "oppositional discourse" might prove to create a site for discussion.

As writing teachers, we are expected to give feedback on written work. When that work is a troubling personal narrative, our role as responders becomes even more complex. In that case, we are *responsible* to address not only faulty transitions and awkward syntax, but also laden content. Indeed, to be "response-able" suggests that we have *the ability to respond* to the content of the narrative. When powerful writing is shared, such as the emotionally laden narrative C. J. wrote, we are transformed— whether we are aware of it or not—into the role of what in emergency medicine is called a "first responder." That is, we find ourselves literally first on the scene and, in many cases, alone as the first, and possibly only, audience for a student's story. There is, however, one major difference between those of us who labor on the page with our students and those who work at the site of medical emergencies: our medical counterparts have had training and possess certification to provide care in the field. They are able to stabilize an injured person until the latter reaches the hospital. In a real sense, such first responders have the potential to make the difference. Yet what are the possible responses to the essay that disturbs, unsettles, even shocks? Do we silence the writer or refer them to a psychologist, thus labeling as socially and ethically repugnant the ideas expressed therein? Do we respond, as Scott Lankford did, by treating and responding to the gay-bashing essay "Bums, Queers, and Magic" as if were a fictional account? Or, do we bring into open discussion the issues expressed in the essay, interrogating those ideas as manifestations of larger cultural/societal tensions? (Miller 1994, 395).

At the time of this incident, however, the only option for which I felt prepared at all was to direct C. J. for psychological support. And even then, I didn't know what the boundaries were, or even how to broach the topic. For if C. J. was as plagued with violent thoughts as he'd written in his essay, then a visit to the campus psychologist might not be sufficient to deal with his issues. At any rate, while I clearly felt the need to respond, I did not have the "ability" to do so in an effective or timely manner because his issues as a combat student-veteran were beyond anything I had ever encountered. In short, I was a first responder "at the scene," but one who lacked the skills and was unaware of resources. Ultimately, our classrooms become sites where we can help, hinder, or ignore the issues that confront some of our student-veterans.

HOW "GOOD" CAME FROM "BAD": MAKING IT PUBLIC

From my first conversation with C. J. on the day when he believed he had been expelled from campus, I was fortunate to have the tremendous support of three colleagues in the English department. Like me, they were disturbed about increasing incidents of combat trauma among student-veterans, sharing my concerns about our unpreparedness to meet those needs. In addition, they lent me a sympathetic ear whenever I was feeling beleaguered by yet another call from the media, or by self-doubts. Without exception, all of us had taught student-veterans; we found the majority of those individuals to be among the most disciplined and hardworking members of the class. As others have noted, student-veterans returning from Iraq and Afghanistan "are pursuing vocational and educational interests to build a secure future" and college is now "the new front line" for those individuals (Zinger and Cohen 2010, 2). Furthermore, many student-veterans view college as a bridge to a civilian identity that is still evolving. We also found that all of us had encountered student-veterans reporting PTSD, TBI, depression, or all three. As we discussed the apparent gaps between knowledge, needs, and resources at CCBC, we tallied what we did know about student-veteran resources on campus as well as about learning opportunities for faculty and staff to better understand the distinct needs of this population. We knew that each of our three campuses had an Office of Veterans Affairs as well as a VA Certifying Official (VACO) whose primary job was to facilitate paperwork for student-veterans using the Post-9/11 GI bill. I recalled our campus psychologist's comment that although he had once offered a support group for student-veterans, the group had languished due to nonattendance, lack of interest, or both. Curious, I searched the college homepage for student-veteran support mechanisms. On the Student Clubs site, there was a Veterans Association hyperlink that took me back to the Financial Aid Office. Beyond that, it was unclear to us as faculty what—if any—support mechanisms, either formal or informal, existed on our campuses. In fact, O'Herrin (2011, 16) notes that "fewer than half of all schools with military and/or veterans programs offer opportunities for faculty and administrators to acquire information about the unique needs of military student populations." In fall 2010, that was certainly the case at CCBC.

It was only a matter of time before we began to visualize an educational forum that would take place in the spring of 2011. We formed an ad hoc committee of one adjunct and four full-time faculty members, all in the English department. Initially, our intended audience was the faculty, but soon it expanded to staff, student-veterans, and nonveteran students—in other words, the entire campus community! Meeting either on campus or at a local coffee shop, our group represented all three campuses. We felt it was important to hold not one but three consecutive fora to take place on each campus so as many people as possible could attend. Our goals were (1) increasing awareness and appreciation of student-veterans at CCBC as a distinct population with diverse needs; (2) disseminating information about resources available to student-veterans or to those who come into contact with student-veterans; and (3) bringing to the attention of the campus community the growing prevalence of PTSD/TBI/depression among student-veterans. The vehicle for doing this would be a film (yet to be selected) most likely dealing with combat-related trauma and a panel of student-veterans and other experts who could represent unique perspectives. What we would *not do* was explicitly refer to the incident involving C. J., due to FERPA constraints, or rehash the public controversy involving the college's handling of the affair, which we all felt would be counterproductive. We dubbed ourselves Project 101: The Veteran's Educational Initiative. Despite this encouraging start, I was concerned about operating in a vacuum. As a grassroots faculty committee, we did not yet have the institutional nod. Our chair, pleased about our work, urged us to "work with Student Life," but so far I had not yet had success connecting with that office. "Build it and they will come"? What if we did, but no one showed up? Having worked for over a decade in university program planning and administration, I realized the importance of college-wide coordination. For example, what had already been done for student-veterans, what was currently taking place, and what was being planned? New to CCBC, I lacked knowledge of the institutional history so vital when launching an initiative; in addition, only one in our group had been there longer than five years. Nevertheless, pending further discussions with Student Life, we energetically planned and divvied up responsibilities. I volunteered to seek out the VACO on my home campus as well as follow up with student life support services.

Within the Financial Aid Office on each campus was an area designated for student-veterans. When I visited what was then a cramped corner in that office, the only evidence of student-veteran-related concerns was a large American flag draped on the wall behind a desk and the presence of a clean-cut young man wearing a green uniform shirt and working at the computer. The VACO was friendly and enthusiastically supported the concept of an educational forum, mentioning the huge need for additional support for student-veterans. With over 300 student-veterans on our campus alone, she had to guide them through the GI Bill paperwork maze. In addition, she frequently served as a listening ear for their many concerns related to the transition from the military to civilian and student life. There was an informal network of student-veterans who mentored incoming peers, yet that network shifted on a regular basis due to graduation or attrition. As she talked about "my vets," it was apparent to me that it would be difficult for any faculty member to access that informal network of mentors. Although there did not exist at that time a student-veterans' database, she gave me the names of some student-veterans on campus whom she thought would be excellent presenters for the fora, recommending in particular the current student-body president, an ex-marine. She was also excited because the college planned to expand her office to accommodate the growing numbers of student-veterans expected in the near future.

Walking back to my office, I once more reflected about the problematic nature of increasing faculty understanding of veteran issues and awareness of resources. First, faculty needed to recognize the existence of student-veterans as a distinct yet heterogeneous group on our campus and realize that within that diversity were individuals suffering from combat-related disorders. Next, faculty had to be aware of whatever resources existed on campus as well as off. In addition, faculty had to know *how* to connect student-veterans to those resources. Surely if I, as an interested faculty member, met with difficulty in determining what to do and where to turn, it was probable that other faculty—and surely student-veterans themselves—would meet similar obstacles as well. As one adjunct CCBC faculty member observed about our campus: "[Veteran] resources are hidden in plain sight."

As mentioned before, the format that most appealed to us was a panel comprised of experts in veteran issues, questions handled by a moderator, and a provocative film excerpt to be used as a springboard for discussion. We planned to offer the three fora in May 2011. The *Frontline* documentary we previewed and chose was *A Soldier's Story*, which highlights returning veterans suffering from combat-related stresses such as PTSD and TBI. The ten-minute clip features a young Iraq veteran with PTSD who had been ordered to shoot an Iraqi woman apparently concealing an explosive device beneath her *burka*. Once she fell, nothing was found. Our group's consensus was to focus on postdeployment PTSD and related issues because we felt that many nonmilitary members of the campus community were underinformed or undersensitized to the unique challenges that an increasing number of student-veterans might be facing. We invited as moderators faculty or staff who had served in—or currently were serving in—the military (in fact, our first choice for my home campus was a faculty member in the Army Reserves who was called up before he could participate). After the film, the moderator would pose prepared questions to various panel members before we opened up the Q & A session of the two-hour forum. For each panel (there were three, one at each main campus location) we invited two to three student-veterans from that campus, our thoughts being that they might be known to members of the audience and could put a face to the forum. Next, we invited two individuals from official veteran organizations: a sergeant from the local National Guard armory as well as an outreach representative from the state Department of Veterans Affairs. It was fortuitous that the latter person was also a woman whose extensive army service could bring a female perspective to the forum. Next, the chief campus psychologist with training in PTSD treatment was present at each forum in order to demonstrate the presence of on-campus counseling support for student-veterans and also to serve as a resource in the event of any emotional responses from the audience or panelists. Last, we invited a Vietnam-era veteran who often served as advocate and mentor to veterans in the community; he was not, however, affiliated with a particular veteran activist group because we were concerned about the forum's being used as a platform for a specific issue that might not serve CCBC student-veterans.

All told, nearly 150 members of the campus community attended the three fora. At each event, the format included a welcome from a faculty or staff moderator with military experience, followed by the ten-minute excerpt from *A Soldier's Story*. The moderator posed prepared questions to the panelists and then the audience was invited to participate. In the lively Q & A that ensued, student-veterans received most of the questions. While they acknowledged the fact that a number of combat veterans experience PTSD as depicted in the film, not all of them do, and they expressed deep pride in the positive contributions they themselves had made during the recent conflicts through the building of roads, schools, clinics, or otherwise through the provision of humanitarian aid. They described the fellowship developed in the military, a fellowship clearly in evidence as they interacted on the panel. Throughout, I was struck with the attentiveness of the audience, most of whom were students. Again, the diversity of student-veterans must always be kept in mind, for while we may have to respond to narratives that describe disturbing combat-related events, we cannot overlook the larger population of student-veterans whose discipline and leadership serve them well as they reinvent life postdeployment.

Ultimately, this initial campus-wide educational event represented another response to the needs of student-veterans, not to mention those of faculty, staff, and other students. We succeeded in opening up dialogue about PTSD and gave both veterans and student-veterans an opportunity to "publish" their experiences and be *responded to*, not only by professors but by their fellow students lacking military backgrounds. We realized that, for any future events, we should broaden the scope of the sessions so as not to focus only on combat-related illness. The student-veterans on campus were vocal in their desire to be viewed as individuals—individuals with a unique experience, but with a diversity of backgrounds and needs. This first event might well be regarded as our campus community's attempt to make public those issues so often difficult to broach in our classrooms. Previously, I had observed that in-class discussion about posttraumatic challenges such as C. J.'s might prove problematic and inappropriate at the time those challenges are disclosed; however, I see in retrospect that CCBC ultimately *did* acknowledge "the elephant in the room" and help break down barriers of communication between student-veterans and others.

THE MARYLAND CAMPUS COMPACT FOR STUDENT-VETERANS

While plans for the educational fora were underway, an important document was being forged by higher-education leaders and veteran advocates: the Maryland Campus Compact for Student-Veterans. Endorsed by its chief proponent, the lieutenant governor of the state of Maryland ("the nation's highest-ranking elected official to serve a tour of duty in Iraq"), the compact was signed by twenty-one community and public four-year institutions in January 2011 (Maryland Campus Compact for Student-Veterans 2011). The CCBC college president, whose own son is an army reservist, heartily supported the compact. In identifying the impetus for the compact, one article said: "A troubling essay published in the student newspaper at Community College of Baltimore County . . . (was) one of several catalysts . . . (Brown and Kurtinitis, *Baltimore Sun,* January 31, 2011). On the same day, a press release from the lieutenant governor's office stated that the compact's commitment would "do more for the men and women who have served in the US Armed Forces and seeks to ensure the educational success of veterans" (*Targeted News Service,* January 31, 2011). Specifically, the institutions would designate a go-to person for all student-veterans, as well as "provide training for faculty, staff, and student leadership to promote greater awareness of veteran issues" (*Targeted News Service,* January 31, 2011). While the signing of the compact represented official commitment to student-veterans, I wondered about the ongoing challenge to coordinate future educational efforts campus-wide.

ENTER V.I.T.A.L.

Although our ad hoc committee of English faculty hoped to launch a similar round of fora the following year, other teaching and committee responsibilities prevented the necessary planning. It seemed to me that we still had inconsistent coordination with student-support services, contributing to the sense that we faculty were operating in the dark. Also contributing to that sense was the discovery that an adjunct English instructor—whose veteran status was unknown to any of us on the ad hoc committee—had independently obtained funds from Student Life to bring to campus a female journalist who had recently published a memoir on her experiences with a combat unit in Iraq. While that talk took place in the spring of 2011, it was attended only by the students of the adjunct instructor and a few others, which to my mind represented a squandered opportunity for effective campus education.

Such lack of cohesion on the part of campus entities planning events for student-veterans was a reminder of the inherent difficulties we were experiencing at CCBC, despite our president having signed the statewide compact. Since we lacked an overall Coordinator of Veterans Affairs, or another means by which to share ongoing efforts/communication with the campus-life division, I was feeling very discouraged and even considered stepping down as titular head of the ad hoc committee. My colleagues convinced me not to and rallied around to begin planning an event for November 2011. Less ambitious than the previous fora, it would be the same week as the Veterans Day memorial service organized by Student Life. We felt it was important to try to build student-veteran events around what already existed on campus in terms of honoring vets.

However, before that event took place, the dean of campus life casually mentioned in passing that CCBC had just been awarded a two-year grant to collaborate with the Maryland Veterans Administration to increase VA mental-health support on our campus and assist with campus-wide coordination of services for student-veterans. By the fall of 2012, the Veterans Integration to Academic Leadership (VITAL) psychologist would have an office on the Catonsville campus, where she would provide counseling to student-veterans, point them to community services, and assist with campus-wide educational initiatives. Indeed, obtaining that grant was a turning point for several reasons: it served as an impetus for acquisition of a comfortable space for a Veterans Service Center (on the Catonsville campus, the VACO's cluttered desk within the Financial Aid Office was, in essence, the only veteran-friendly space on campus); it spurred the reassignment of an administrative assistant to work in the Catonsville VSC as an office manager; and it allowed interested faculty to work in tandem with the VITAL psychologist as she familiarized herself with CCBC. Once I connected with her and we had a meeting with the dean of campus life, it made sense to coordinate (!) and plan for a big event for spring 2013.

STUDENT-VETERANS SYMPOSIUM, BOOTS TO SUITS

As of this writing, many positive developments have unfolded at CCBC related to student-veterans. Indeed, with the VITAL psychologist as a key ally—and the person who had the ear of the division dean who obtained the grant—many of us interested in student-veteran issues convened to

plan a large-scale symposium. Much to my (our) relief, we were no longer just four or five eager faculty members in the English department.
Our group, which we call the Veterans Success Committee, is comprised
of members of the Student-Veterans Association; their faculty advisor;
VA Certifying Officials from all three campuses; the VITAL psychologist; the CCBC head psychologist; the administrative assistant assigned
to the Veterans Service Center; the assistant director of Student Life; the
dean of Campus Life; and other faculty across campus. I took the lead
and was designated as chair of the committee. This enthusiastic group
began meeting in winter 2012 to plan the Boots to Suits symposium that
took place in April 2013. A Student Life cocurricular grant of $4,000
bolstered our efforts.

   In our discussions, it became clear that the academic success of
student-veterans had to be the focus of our efforts, given the retention and completion agendas of community colleges nationwide.
Furthermore, we decided that the transition from military to civilian/
academic life had to be addressed in symposium workshops. The college
president gave her wholehearted support and offered to invite the lieutenant governor, a veteran and chief political backer of the compact, as
our keynote. At the symposium, after the presentation of the colors by a
local VFW branch, Lt. Governor Brown gave an inspiring keynote, which
was followed by two concurrent sessions of three workshops each: one, a
panel of student-veterans discussing their concerns; two, a panel targeted
at faculty issues in the classroom; and three, a personal testimonial from
an ex-marine, a former CCBC student, who shared his story of trauma,
addiction, homelessness, and successful transition to civilian life. Over
185 students, vets and nonvets, CCBC faculty and staff, plus community
members, attended Boots to Suits. Afterwards, some of my students who
had heard the student-veteran panel reported that it was a moving experience to hear the vets speak and expressed the wish that they could continue the conversations with student-veterans in the future.

REFLECTIONS AND QUESTIONS

The ongoing meetings with the Veterans Success Committee members
opened my eyes to the concerns of student-veterans and deepened my
admiration for them and for others on our campus whose efforts support student-veterans. While our perspectives vary, we are united in our
purpose. One of the VA Certifying Officials recently commented, "I am
so happy because I'm not alone anymore. It feels as if I've finally found
my own planet!"

In addition to this successful symposium and our commitment to offer another next year, plus shorter educational workshops targeted at faculty, we were able to obtain funds from the college's President's Innovation Grant program in order to purchase TV/DVRs, printers, and military history books for the Veterans Service Centers on all three campus sites. I am also piloting a veterans-only section of English composition in the fall of 2013. One CCBC advisor who works with student-veterans reassured me, "You won't have any problem getting enrollment; veterans continue to ask for courses with only-veteran cohorts." I hope this is true because I am looking forward to working with, and supporting, student-veteran writers. Last, and of great importance, our group has formally requested that the Veterans Success Committee become an official college-wide committee. Such recognition has been sought by other higher-education institutions that place a high priority on student-veteran academic success. In addition, another session on veteran issues and military culture will be offered at the end-of-semester faculty professional development day.

As of this writing (May 2013), CCBC has over 1,000 student-veterans. There is no doubt that our campus has made important inroads and deserves the designation of veteran friendly. Nevertheless, the VITAL grant will soon come to an end. Although CCBC has reapplied for continued grant funding, we do not yet know if such funding will be awarded. In the absence of grant support, how will CCBC sustain its continued efforts and expand its offerings to student-veterans? There is still much to do. In the meantime, faculty members contact me about struggling student-veterans in their classrooms: "What do I do?" "Where do I go?" "Who can help?" Now, I can direct them to the VITAL psychologist, to the VACO for benefits clarification, or to the Veterans Service Centers, where student-veterans socialize and study together. Still, I cannot help but wonder how the incident with C. J. might have turned out differently had these resources been in place three years ago. What became of him? Did he return to school, receive treatment for his PTSD? I wish I had done more, known more because then, as now, we faculty must respond, on multiple levels. In the meantime, we remain willing . . . but unprepared.

Note

1. I was the professor whose student, Charles (C. J.) Whittington, a former combat veteran, published the graphic essay "War Is a Drug" in the campus newspaper. This incident, in fall 2010, created turmoil at CCBC and sparked national debate

over how colleges should respond when student-veterans reveal psychological disturbances. CCBC's actions have been both criticized and defended.

References

Borrowman, Shane. 2005. Introduction to *Trauma and the Teaching of Writing*, edited by Shane Borrowman, 1–10. Albany: SUNY Press.

"Community College in Maryland Suspends Veteran Who Wrote about Addiction to Combat." 2010. *The Ticker* (blog). http://chronicle.com/blogs/ticker/a-maryland-college-suspends-a-veteran-who-wrote-about-addiction-to-combat/28517.

Goggin, Peter N., and Maureen D. Goggin. 2005. "Presence in Absence: Discourses and Teaching (In, On, and About) Trauma." In *Trauma and the Teaching of Writing*, edited by Shane Borrowman, 29–51.. Albany: SUNY Press.

Holmstedt, Karen. 2009. *The Girls Come Marching Home: Stories of Women Warriors Returning from the War in Iraq*. Mechanicsburg, PA: Stackpole Books.

Community College of Baltimore County. n.d. "Key Facts FY 2011." Planning, Research, and Evaluation. Catonsville, MD: Community College of Baltimore County.

Lankford, Scott. n.d. *"Queers, Bums, and Magic": How Would You Grade a Gay-Bashing?* Paper presented at a meeting. Los Altos Hills, CA.

Maryland Campus Compact for Student-Veterans: Memorandum of Understanding between the State and Maryland Institutions of Higher Education. 2011. Annapolis, MD: State of Maryland Office of the Lieutenant Governor.

Miller, Richard E. 1994. "Fault Lines in the Contact Zone." *College English* 56 (4): 389–408. http://dx.doi.org/10.2307/378334.

Mytelka, Andrew. 2011. "Military Veteran Balks at Request by Community College in Maryland." *The Ticker* (blog). http://chronicle.com/blogs/ticker/military-veteran-balks-at-request-by-community-college-in-maryland.

Nelson, G. Lynn. 2000. "Warriors with Words: Toward a Post-Columbine Writing Curriculum." *English Journal* 89 (5): 42–6. http://dx.doi.org/10.2307/822294.

O'Herrin, Elizabeth. 2011. "Enhancing Veteran Success in Higher Education." *Peer Review* 13 (1): 15–18. http://library.ccbcmd.edu:80/validate?url=http%3A%2F%2F0-search.proquest.com.library.ccbcmd.edu%3A80%2Fdocview%2F1081785540%3Faccountid%3D3784.

Seal, Karen, Thomas J. Metzler, Kristian S. Gima, Daniel Bertenthal, Shira Maguen, and Charles R. Marmar. 2009. "Trends and Risk Factors for Mental Health Diagnoses among Iraq and Afghanistan Veterans Using Department of Veterans Affairs Health Care, 2002–2008." *American Journal of Public Health* 99 (9): 1651–58. http://library.ccbcmd.edu:80/validate?url=http%3A%2F%2F0-search.proquest.com.library.ccbcmd.edu%3A80%2Fdocview%2F215091985%3Faccountid%3D3784.

Tobin, Lad. 2004. *Reading Student Writing: Confessions, Meditations, and Rants*. Portsmouth, NH: Heinemann.

Zinger, Lana, and Andrea Cohen. 2010. "Veterans Returning from War into the Classroom: How can Colleges Be Better Prepared to Meet their Needs." *Contemporary Issues in Education Research* 3 (1): 39–51. http://library.ccbcmd.edu:80/validate?url=http%3A%2F%2F0-search.proquest.com.library.ccbcmd.edu%3A80%2Fdocview%2F196350958%3Faccountid%3D3784.

PART II

Veterans and Public Audiences

5

"I HAVE TO SPEAK OUT"
Writing with Veterans in a Community Writing Group[1]

Eileen E. Schell and Ivy Kleinbart

There is a deep necessity for veterans to create when so much has been shattered and stolen. A profound sense of hope comes from the ability to rebuild and transform.

—"Welcome to Warrior Writers" 2009

As colleges and universities establish composition courses comprised of cohorts of student-veterans, a parallel movement of "self-sponsored" community writing groups led by and for military veterans is forming across the country. Such groups serve as "sponsors of literacy," what Brandt (2001, 19) refers to as "agents, local or distant, concrete or abstract, who enable, support, teach, and model, as well as recruit, regulate, suppress, or withhold literacy—and gain advantage by it in some way." These writing groups actively sponsor veterans by encouraging and supporting their efforts to write about and process their experiences in the military. Examples include Warrior Writers, a group of Iraq/Afghanistan veterans who write and make art about their combat experiences; Veterans of War/Veterans of Peace, a group of Vietnam veterans and peace activists led by acclaimed writer Maxine Hong Kingston; and Operation Homecoming, the National Endowment for the Arts-funded writing classes for recently returned troops on military bases, to name only a few. These writing groups have produced a wealth of publications, performances, and documentaries; they also maintain web and social-media presences and publish anthologies that attract other veterans and veterans' service providers for online networking and exchange. In addition, writers like Marine Corps veteran Sergio Santos (2011) have set out to create a national consortium of veteran writing groups, seeking to share writing assignments and group activities. Efforts to involve

DOI: 10.7330/9780874219425.c005

veterans in writing about their military experiences have proliferated in response to the upsurge in United States military activity since 9/11 and the subsequent need to reintegrate veterans into civilian society. The emergence of these groups also suggests an increased cultural readiness among civilians to hear veterans' stories and to learn from them in ways that allow us to begin facing the realities of war.

Inspired by a burgeoning national movement of veteran writers, we, Eileen Schell, a writing professor, and Ivy Kleinbart, a writing instructor, at Syracuse University started the Syracuse Veterans' Writing Group in March 2010 for veterans of all ages and branches of the military and for their supporters. Participants have included veterans ranging from the Korean War to Vietnam to Desert Storm to more current conflicts, including Operation Iraqi Freedom (OIF) and Operation Enduring Freedom (OEF). We meet once a month to work on writing accounts of life in and out of the military. Our meetings center on instruction in techniques of nonfiction writing (character development, dialogue, scene construction, and reflection), drafting new work, sharing stories, exchanging feedback, and polishing and preparing work for publication on our group website or in other venues.

Syracuse University (SU) has a long history of welcoming veterans, dating back to WWII. The university has recently invested in a Veterans' Resource Center and targeted academic programs for OIF and OEF veterans. It is also home to the Entrepreneurship Bootcamp for Veterans with Disabilities (EBV), which assists post-9/11 veterans with disabilities in establishing their own businesses, founded at SU's Whitman School of Management in 2007. In addition, SU's Institute for Veterans and Military Families (IVMF), founded in June 2011, focuses on educational programming, employment opportunities for veterans, and research that improves the lives of veterans and their families.

This chapter addresses our motivation and processes in setting up a community writing group for military veterans, as well as some of the challenges we've encountered and the outcomes we have been able to assess thus far. We address how self-sponsored writing about military service provides veterans with an outlet for self-exploration of military service (to make sense of it, to put it into perspective, to testify to and confront it) as well as an opportunity to write in ways that educate the public about military life, including speaking out about the realities and costs of war.

Early in the group's formation, several discussions arose regarding the risks of writing about military service. Depending on the subject matter, writing may be perceived as subversive to the military's culture of secrecy. One member of the group voiced concern that his writing could jeopardize his top-security military clearance. Others have expressed fears about betraying their comrades or uncovering repressed memories they aren't prepared to deal with. Sharing one's writing with others invariably entails exposure; the feelings of vulnerability that surface may be uncomfortable for veterans who have grown accustomed to presenting a strong, controlled façade. One Iraq War veteran attended several meetings and decided he couldn't continue participating in the group because the writing process was too intense. However, despite the fears and risks associated with writing, those who persist often achieve some measure of reconciliation, healing, or catharsis. As one of the veterans in our group, Derek Davey, put it in an e-mail to Eileen about his military service in the eighties and his son's death as a marine in Iraq: "I have realized since my son died that I *have to* speak out—write out may be more appropriate. It is not necessarily a story about him or me, but the experience must be told. I firmly believe the old adage: 'those who know nothing of history are doomed to repeat it.'"

The importance of veterans' narratives regarding the personal, collective, historical, and economic costs associated with military service and warfare is reflected in the psychological literature of posttraumatic stress disorder (PTSD), also known as posttraumatic stress injury (PTSI), and in recent veteran-authored memoirs in which topics such as civilian death or so-called "collateral damage," traumatic brain injury, and PTSD are addressed honestly and unflinchingly (see Meehan with Thompson 2009). Through the work of veterans' writing groups and public art projects, writing teachers have the opportunity to work with veterans to produce writing that describes and makes sense of their experiences. These groups help veteran writers to see themselves as societal witnesses to warfare. The role of societal "witness" is one that PTSD specialist Dr. Edward Tick, founder of the nonprofit organization Soldier's Heart, says must come with a society taking responsibility for the "soul wounds," the psychological and spiritual costs, that war exacts:

> Instead of having a parade and going shopping, we could use our veterans' holidays as an occasion for storytelling. Open the churches and temples and synagogues and mosques and community centers and libraries across the country, and invite the veterans in to tell their stories. Purification ceremonies and storytelling events are also opportunities for the community to speak to veterans and take some of the burden of guilt off them and declare our oneness with them: "You killed in our name, because we ordered you to, so we take responsibility for it, too." (Kupfer 2008)

Tick (2005, 237) argues that veterans' stories implicate us all: "Our society must accept responsibility for its war-making. To the returning veteran, our leaders and people must say, 'You did this in our name and because you were subject to our orders. We lift the burden of actions from you and take it onto our shoulders. We are responsible for you, for what you did, and for the consequences.'" This acknowledgment of civilian complicity stands in stark contrast to a culture of denial and forgetting in which citizens blame leaders for initiating wars and veterans for fighting them and then completely disavow the consequences, or glorify those whom they believe to be heroes.

As we have started the Syracuse Veterans' Writing Group, both of us have come to understand how our own experiences with writing, with veterans, with war, and with antiwar work drew us to establish the group. By sharing our stories, we situate ourselves as civilians who answered a call to be responsive to veterans' stories and to create a space for interaction and exchange about those stories.

STARTING UP: EILEEN'S STORY

For much of my life, I have felt connected to military veterans and their stories. Growing up on an apple and pear orchard in Washington state, I frequently heard the stories of WWII and Korean War veterans who did seasonal work on our farm. Their stories of service and combat emerged in fragments, bits and pieces I eagerly grabbed onto as an antidote and reality check to the afternoon reruns of the popular comic WWII television saga, *Hogan's Heroes*. Later in life, I started working with veterans as an editor and writing instructor. At age twenty-two, I helped Colonel Jack Swayze (1993), a WWII B-24 bomber pilot, edit his harrowing and heroic wartime memoir, eventually published under the title *Sporty Course*. In 1999, I established a memoir-writing group at a senior-living community that is still in session today; the group includes several WWII and Korean War veterans who have written about their wartime experiences.

The stories that influenced and haunted me the most, though, were the ones I heard at home, those told by my father, who emerged untarnished from peacetime military service, and by my uncle, a Vietnam vet, who was visibly traumatized by his combat experiences. Unlike my father, who entered military service under the dictates of the draft and who never faced combat, my maternal uncle Brady Smith, an avid pilot, signed up and served two tours in Vietnam as a helicopter pilot, flying two missions every day at the end of the war: one to drop off troops, the other to pick up the wounded and the dead. As a young child during this time period, I learned bits and pieces of his story through eavesdropping on my parents' after-dinner conversations. Indeed, I often felt compelled to share what I knew of his story as if to unburden myself of its weight. Much to my kindergarten teacher's alarm during sharing time one day, I raised my hand and stood up by her chair to report the following news:

> "My uncle," I said haltingly. "My uncle Brady was shot at by a sniper in Vietnam."
>
> My teacher Mrs. Beck looked on, her mouth a tight line; she leaned forward in her chair slightly.
>
> "He's okay," I reassured with a glance at her. "He flies helicopters in Vietnam. He has a bulletproof vest."
>
> My classmates looked up at me blankly. I wondered for a moment if they knew what or where Vietnam was—I didn't really know myself; it was somewhere across the ocean where the army had sent my uncle to fly helicopters. Vietnam was a story on the news every night at dinner, my parents watching with rapt attention for news of Saigon or other parts of Vietnam. I searched the screen for my uncle in his flight suit lifting off over the jungle.
>
> Mrs. Beck thanked me and I returned to my seat on the carpet. Her eyes rested on my face as the next child shared. She talked to me a little more than usual that day, stopping by my desk as I wrote out my ABCs.

Like many civilians whose loved ones go to war, I would only come to know and understand the full weight and impact of my uncle's story later in life and only through bits and pieces; it is a story that haunts me still, especially after Brady's death a few years ago.

> Two years after I shared the sniper story, I saw Uncle Brady for the first time since he had been deployed. I was seven years old. He came to my grandmother's funeral in his army dress uniform, decorations on his chest, black shoes so shiny they looked like polished obsidian. I saw him across the room at the funeral reception, drink in hand. He was a splendid sight—neatly cut brown hair, a handsome face, and sharp blue eyes with pouches and dark circles under them, the famous "family bags," as my mother called them. I walked toward him.
>
> "Hi, Uncle Brady," I said, looking up at his looming figure, gold buttons, and stiff uniform fabric.
>
> "Hi," he said, looking down and smiling the distracted smile of an adult caught up in adult conversation.
>
> And then a second later: "Who are you?"
>
> "I'm Neva's daughter. Your sister Neva," I added.
>
> His smile widened. "Oh, yeah. Eileen." He put his warm hand on my shoulder for a second, and then he turned away as someone called to him from across the room. He walked away, his broad uniformed back moving across the room. I wouldn't see him again for five years.

As I look back, I can only imagine how horrible it must have been for Brady to come home to his mother's funeral. A trip home, rather than being a respite from death on the battlefield, was the occasion for yet another death.

Brady would return to flying, weighed down every day with grunts to be unloaded in rice paddies and on jungled hillsides. His chopper was the biggest low-flying object in the sky—a black bird hovering over the landscape in contrast to the silver jets streaking across the sky, dropping napalm or bombs. His chopper was a satisfying target for the NVA, who didn't want what he was delivering—the steady stream of soldiers (FNGs)[2] sent to wade around in the paddies, blow tunnels, and search and burn villages. Sometimes when he landed back at the airfield after unloading troops, his chopper was so filled with bullet holes that the guys on the base would stick bamboo slivers into the holes so his helicopter would look like a porcupine.

The next time I saw Brady was Christmas Day 1977. Five years had passed, the war was over, but the real war, the war within, was still underway. I had overheard my parents discussing Brady on a number of occasions—how he lived in Panama City, Florida, drinking and hanging out until dawn with other veterans before he finally came home at the insistence of his younger brother.

But the party life was far from evident in Brady's face that cold winter afternoon when I saw him at my aunt's log cabin in eastern Washington state. The Christmas tree was laden with beautiful ornaments, glowing with twinkling lights, rising two stories in the high-ceilinged cabin. Stockings hung over the fireplace, and the smell of roasting turkey was in the air.

The festive atmosphere seemed lost on Brady. Unlike the tall, broad soldier I remembered when I was seven, the man I saw before me in civilian clothes was thin, worn, and closed inward, his fingers yellowed from cigarettes and his face drawn; he had deep bags under his eyes. He told my mother as I sat nearby that he often could not sleep at night, that he had flashbacks to scenes of Vietnam. His voice was muted, measuring what he would say and not say. My mother asked gentle questions, prodding him. She had not seen him in a long time. She wanted to know what he had been through and she wanted to know how he was doing. I was a bystander, an onlooker, the only child in the room. I felt awkward looking on, but I was interested. I had heard stories about Brady, I felt drawn to him and his pain, but I was also aware that my cousins were upstairs shouting and laughing. It was Christmas Day, and the war was over . . . or was it? The war would never be over for Brady or for many he served with.

When Brady died years later from complications associated with chronic obstructive pulmonary disease (COPD) and associated wartime injuries, I was flooded with remorse that I would never know his stories. I also was deeply angry, as were many of us, about the war in Iraq. Once again, we were sending troops off to fight yet another war without a clear rationale, mission, objective, and exit strategy. As I participated in antiwar protests, I imagined yet another generation of veterans like my uncle coming home to a country deeply out of touch with what they had seen, done, and experienced. After hearing veterans from Maxine

Hong Kingston's writing group read their work and discuss their writing group at the Conference on College Composition and Communication in San Francisco in 2008, I decided to cofound a veterans' writing group in my own community.

To inaugurate the Syracuse Veterans' Writing Group, I invited Captain Shannon Meehan and Roger Thompson (2009), authors of *Beyond Duty*, a searingly honest Iraq War memoir, to participate in the writing program's Nonfiction Reading Series. Their February 2010 reading at Syracuse University drew a variety of veterans and employees of the local Veterans Administration Hospital, as well as faculty and students. Ivy attended the reading, and we ended up in a dialogue about the writing group, which ultimately convinced her to take part, as she notes below.

STARTING UP: IVY'S STORY

Unlike Eileen, none of my immediate family members served in the military, and I had little exposure to veterans' stories prior to my work with the writing group. When I attended Shannon Meehan's reading at Syracuse University in February 2010 (mentioned above), I found myself reacting to his stories about the war in Iraq with a strange mix of sympathy for the trauma he'd suffered, respect for his honesty and openness, and anger over the civilian deaths he claimed responsibility for in his book. His reading stirred up intense emotions I had evidently been suppressing.

After 9/11, although deeply saddened by the loss of American lives, I felt alienated by the president's rhetoric of vengeance and such polarizing warnings as "Either you are with us, or you are with the terrorists" (Bush 2001). I was strongly opposed to the war in Iraq and troubled at how easily the public was misled into interpreting the events of September 11 as a viable cause of the war. Even more upsetting were Bush's reelection and the abuses of power that accumulated as the Iraq and Afghanistan Wars continued: the devastating force used in Fallujah, the abuse of prisoners at Abu Ghraib, the use of torture and indefinite detention at Guantanamo, and the practice of extraordinary rendition. Meanwhile, daily losses of life and infrastructure were reported on the radio as dispassionately as the weather. In response, I became involved in several antiwar demonstrations.

Having actively opposed the wars in Iraq and Afghanistan, I struggled with the decision to participate in a veterans' writing group. While enthusiastic about the idea of teaching creative writing in the community, I was concerned that my antiwar politics made me a poor choice to colead the group. I had no experience working with veterans and worried that my responses to their writing would prove inadequate—or worse, insensitive. I thought about how I had reacted to Meehan's story and wondered: am I compassionate enough to work with veteran writers? Can I respect their choice to serve? Do I blame them for the bloodshed? I had no idea what I would encounter in listening to veterans' stories, and I was afraid of the unknown. In retrospect, I think I was hiding behind my objections to war as a way of avoiding the brutal realities of its impact on veteran and civilian lives, and as a way of denying my own complicity.

Eileen emailed me about her uncle and explained how rewarding her work with veteran writers had been over the years. Ultimately, she convinced me that the experience had much to teach me, and she was right. Working with the Veterans' Writing Group has been an incredible journey in coming to understand and value the diverse experiences, insights, and powers of endurance of our group members. Their stories, struggles, and perspectives have awakened me to the realities of how the military operates and the reasons people agree to serve. Over the past three years, I have developed a deep respect and admiration for the members of our group, and I look forward to seeing and working with them at group meetings. I feel a connection to them as writers and as human beings.

As I've come to know the writers and their individual as well as collective stories, I've realized that no matter an individual's reason for joining the military—whether they volunteered, were drafted, or joined because they felt they had no other choice—the terror and devastation of combat cannot be foreseen; there is no sufficient form of emotional preparation for war. Most soldiers who face combat will return traumatized, and their trauma must be heard, and, as Tick argues, witnessed. Writing is one way to begin that process.

STARTING UP THE SYRACUSE VETERANS' WRITING GROUP

For our first Veterans' Writing Group meeting in March 2010, only a small number—four veterans—showed up, even though a dozen or more had expressed interest in joining the group via e-mail and phone calls. Our numbers included one white female OIF veteran, one white male OEF veteran (also the local president of the Student Veterans' Club), an African American male veteran of the navy and of the Gulf War, and a white male Vietnam-era veteran. Initially, we spent time simply getting acquainted; Eileen handed out a general overview of plans for the group, and we brainstormed and discussed what members would like to write. We set aside twenty minutes for group members to make lists of stories or ideas they might want to write about at some point and invited them to share some of the items on their lists. Two local Veterans' Administration representatives stopped in at the end of the meeting to hand out information about enrolling in VA benefits.

After that first meeting, we decided to meet monthly on Saturday mornings for two hours. This schedule would maximize opportunities to participate for those who worked or attended classes during the week We also planned to work around the schedules of those with National Guard weekend duty. The group was designed loosely around classic creative-writing workshop methods, with members reading their writing aloud and their peers responding with comments, questions, and suggestions. We decided to provide some basic instruction in the craft of nonfiction and to hand out two or three writing prompts per month, many of them inspired by writing-workshop discussions, other veteran writers such as Tim O'Brien, or current events.

Early on, we agreed that what was written in the group would remain in the group unless members wanted to go public via posting their stories on our website or sending materials out for publication. Members could choose to listen until they felt comfortable sharing their work in a group setting; they could also share their writing with us privately. As the group leaders, we agreed that our focus would not be on enforcing a certain standard or aesthetic of writing; rather, we would focus on eliciting stories and encouraging experimentation while still making some suggestions to improve the work or make it more effective for a writer's specified audience. Then, if veterans wanted to take their writing further, we would work with them on editing and polishing their pieces.

As civilians leading a writing group comprised of military veterans, we initially struggled with feelings of inadequacy even though we brought years of experience as writing teachers. What authority did we have to be leading a veterans' writing group? What entitled us to invite these stories and listen to them? Would veterans be better off with a fellow veteran leading the group? These questions gnawed at us during our first few months of group meetings. Gradually, however, we realized we could act as the kind of audience many of the veterans wanted to reach out to— civilians who have an interest in the lives and experiences of military veterans. We could listen, empathize, generate dialogue, and offer our expertise as writing instructors.

To minimize emphasis on grammar, spelling, and usage, we established a group structure from the beginning in which veterans typically read their writing aloud without distributing copies to the group. Thus, *listening carefully* is crucial to the success of the exchange. Not only does listening require serious concentration and note taking, but we have also found that it helps to listen *for* certain types of gestures or occurrences in the narrative. In addition to listening for content, flow, patterns, and themes in the work, we also listen for absences, ways in which the writing comes up short on detail and provides moments of emotional understatement. We strive to mirror back our strongest impressions of the piece, provide feedback on a notable strength of the writing, and ask questions that spark more writing. Occasionally, one of us suggests to a group member that they write about something specific. At a recent meeting, for example, Eileen suggested to a newcomer that he write about his tattoos; he returned the following month with a fully formed essay on the subject, containing anecdotes of military and familial bonding, research on his ancestry, and meditations on loss and survival.

To continually publicize the group and attract new members, we place flyers in branches of the local public library and send them to an e-mail listserv including veterans' organizations and the VA Hospital, located just minutes from campus. We maintain an active Facebook presence and a website where we post meeting agendas and writing prompts; we also post and share group members' writing. Our social-media presence has allowed other veteran writing-group leaders and project coordinators to network with our group. Our writing group has been the subject of feature stories in two local publications, a weekly newsletter called *The Eagle* (Liptak, August 15, 2011), and *Syracuse University Magazine* (Ready 2012). The group was also briefly mentioned in a recent *New York Times* article (Simon, February 1, 2013). These mentions each attracted the attention of veterans who saw the coverage.

Now in its third year of operation, as our group continues to meet and draw new members, we have begun to expand our reach to include other activities related to writing. In the fall of 2012, three of our group members collaborated with an undergraduate film student to produce a series of video narratives, and the group has recently agreed to work with an undergraduate student in photography on a photo-essay project that involves making a series of portraits of veterans. Recently, we added a thirty-minute meditation session prior to our monthly Saturday morning meetings, led by Dr. Diane Grimes, a mindful communication expert and Syracuse University professor. In her sessions, Dr. Grimes emphasizes that meditation is a daily practice that gives group members a chance to improve their focus as writers, manage anxieties and reactions associated with PTSD, and deal with the stresses and pressures of everyday life. In addition, one of the OEF veterans in our group now sponsors an evening social group for writers that meets once or twice a month at a local American Legion post. Over beer and soft drinks, group members informally share their writing without the structure of a formal critique/feedback process. Plans are also in the works for a weekend writing retreat that we envision as a space for both writing and verbal storytelling. Finally, later this year we intend to begin the process of compiling an edited anthology of group members' writing in an attempt to disseminate their work to a wider audience.

MOTIVATIONS AND PROMPTINGS

Maxine Hong Kingston (2006), acclaimed writer and founder of the long-running Veterans' Writing Group in northern California's Bay Area and editor of the anthology *Veterans of War, Veterans of Peace,*[3] contends that writing allows veterans to speak truths, to "write the unspeakable": "Writing, [veterans] keep track of their thinking; they leave a permanent record. Processing chaos through story and poem, the writer shapes and forms experience, and thereby, I believe, changes the past and remakes the existing world. The writer becomes a new person after every story, every poem; and if the art is very good, perhaps the reader is changed, too." Kingston further explains the motivation for veterans to write:

> As Odysseus, the archetypical warrior, made his way home, he narrated his journey—setting off to war, waging the long war, coming home—to listener after listener. The story grew until, finally home, he could tell the whole tale and become whole. We tell stories and we listen to stories in order to live. To stay conscious. To connect one with another. To understand consequences. To keep history. To rebuild civilization. (Kingston 2006)

The tale of Odysseus has inspired not only Kingston and her writing group, but also a whole generation of Vietnam veterans who have worked with Dr. Jonathan Shay (1995; 2003), a psychotherapist who has used the epic war story to narrate his two books on Vietnam veterans, *Achilles in Vietnam* and *Odysseus in America,* to explain the effects of PTSD/I, and to undergird his therapeutic practice.

In conducting the group, we have seen veterans write for all of these reasons as well as define their own purposes for writing. One of the Vietnam veterans in our group, Peter (Pete) McShane, sees his writing as a way to understand the chaos of war and its aftereffects. In an e-mail he addressed to Eileen shortly after he joined the group, he referenced Shay, noting, "Our culture doesn't know how to help its warriors

reacclimatize to civilian life. The military is only beginning to understand the problem, but there are still significant institutional barriers,
and the military may never be able to fully embrace the changes that
are necessary to help soldiers leave the battlefield behind." Writing,
Pete notes, has become a way to address and process his experiences
and give meaning and shape to his memories. However, he acknowledges that confronting the past is not easy for many veterans, including him.

> Vets have difficulty sharing their deepest, most painful memories. If we
> don't feel comfortable with a group, and especially the group leaders,
> we're not going to open ourselves up. It's a trust thing. When I first read
> my material in workshops in 2006, I was embarrassed and self-conscious,
> because I was the protagonist and there wasn't a single Vet in any of the
> groups. That's what really pushed me to create the manuscript as a novel,
> so I could assign my character to someone else. It made it easier to tell
> my story, but I've had this gnawing feeling in my gut ever since that the
> real story hasn't come out. As I mentioned in our meeting, it was the two
> creative non-fiction DWC [Downtown Writers' Center] workshops I took
> earlier this year that pushed me over the edge, [and gave] me the courage
> to present my material as memoir.

Pete, who served as a Special Forces medic in the Vietnam War, is still
asking questions about his service and how it affected him. He continues
to develop his materials and is currently polishing a two-hundred-plus-
page memoir manuscript and getting ready to submit for publication. In
a prose poem entitled "Why I Write," published originally on our website
and then by the *New York Times* along with several other veterans' pieces
under the heading "Warrior Voices," he asserts his need to know "why":

> I write because I want to know why.
>   I was a money changer with the empty suits and charlatans, the social
> and economic elite, the pinky rings and silver spoons; we had nothing
> in common. They never served. Their sons and daughters never served.
> They went to the Country Club, flew to Monaco and St. Moritz, man-
> aged their investments, traveled to homes in the mountains and on the
> seacoast. They'd court a customer in good times and kick them out when
> times were tough. I held them in contempt for turning their backs and
> was fired for insubordination. If not for my VA pension, I'd be travelling
> from park bench to cardboard box. I want to know why; why didn't I play
> the game?
>   When I left the service, I put my military memorabilia in a box and
> stored it away, out of sight. I wanted no part of that memory to cloud my
> future. I would see the box every time we moved and try to leave it behind,
> but the box followed me everywhere, and the memories caught up with
> me. They came to me in nightmares; they came to me while having dinner

with my wife; they came to me while in the passing lane on the Interstate; they came to me while walking in the forest. I want to know why; why I felt remorse, fear, anger?

I want to know why our CO [commanding officer] grandstanded and got us shot; why I saved his life, but couldn't save others more worthy; why they napalmed the camp while Tommy was still there; why I chose not to return to my team; why I trusted no one; why I pushed the people away who cared for me; why I compromised my humanity; why we had to pay the price for others' cowardice; why the bullet merely grazed my heart and why I'm still alive? I want to know why, so I parried with the memory fragments.

I wrote, and I parried. I wrote, and it hurt. I wrote, and I cried. I wrote, and soon the pain diminished. (McShane, *New York Times*, February 1, 2013)

Clearly, writing is helping Pete to figure out why he volunteered to go to Vietnam in the first place. Moreover, in his efforts to make sense of his military experiences, he is discovering a great deal more about some of the other enigmas of his personal past.

In parallel fashion, Ginger Gunnip (now Peterman), one of the few women in the group, sees writing as a release from the stress she experienced in the military and in her upbringing. As a single mother and full-time student at the university, Ginger finds writing to be cathartic and has opted to take several courses in creative nonfiction as a way of balancing the demands of her rigorous engineering studies and personal life (she plans to graduate from SU in the fall of 2013 with a writing minor). This catharsis may come from achieving some degree of clarity in dealing with the complicated and often confusing emotions associated with traumatic memory. In Maxine Hong Kingston's (2006) words, writing enables many veterans the chance "to gain a measure of control over their feelings and unravel tangled knots of emotions."

Even as writing has the potential to help order the chaos of war and untangle tight knots of emotion and memory, it also reveals the ambiguities of war and military service. As Vietnam veteran and acclaimed author Tim O'Brien notes, ambiguity is at the heart of a war story.

For the common soldier, at least, war has the feel—the spiritual texture—of a great ghostly fog, thick and permanent. There is no clarity. Everything swirls. The old rules are no longer binding, the old truths no longer true. Right spills over into wrong. Order blends into chaos, love into hate, ugliness into beauty, law into anarchy, civility into savagery. The vapors suck you in. You can't tell where you are, or why you're there, and the only certainty is absolute ambiguity. (O'Brien 2009, 78)

One of the veterans in our group, Robert (Bob) Marcuson, has made grappling with the ambiguity of warfare, military service, and language itself a signature theme of his writing. After surviving six weeks in the infantry in a combat zone in Vietnam, Bob was resting in his bunk back in a safe zone when he was shot by a soldier who mistakenly discharged his rifle in the barracks below. Gravely wounded, he was rushed to the hospital and survived. Eventually, he was mustered back to the United States to finish out his duty stateside. Surviving "friendly fire," the great oxymoron of warfare, had, ironically, pulled him away from the war zone and ensured his survival. This experience of being wounded while at rest and by a comrade rather than an enemy has inspired much introspection around the ironies and ambiguities of war and life in general. What are the chances of getting wounded by friendly fire while lying in one's bunk? What is a safe zone? Who is the enemy? How does language sometimes misdirect the listener from the meanings we intend? In a piece entitled "Eagles and Ambiguity," Bob describes a visit with General Westmoreland: "A few years later, standing at attention at the foot of an army hospital bed in San Francisco, I met General Westmoreland. He asked me where I was hit, meaning, of course, where in Vietnam. I answered, 'In my side.' The General shot me a very peculiar look" (Marcuson 2011c, 1). Bob realized when he saw the general's puzzled expression that General Westmoreland wanted to know the literal geographic location or battle where he was wounded, not the site on his body.

In another piece entitled "Catch 17—Inspection," Bob explores the simultaneous arbitrariness and scripted nature of military weapons inspections: "Catch 17 is the military doctrine that says you will not pass inspection if they don't want you to, nor is it easy to fail when they want you to pass" (Marcuson 2011b, 1). Yet another of his pieces, "August Revolution 1968," chronicles a time when he and other soldiers were asked to impersonate "hippies" on their military base so soldiers could conduct a drill about how to control "hippie protestors" at the upcoming 1968 Democratic National Convention. He writes, ironically, "My orders were to exchange my uniform for civies, then go out and skirmish, riot, be a hippie, go places I was not allowed to go and do things I was not allowed to do. So that's what I did. I traded my dog tags for the love beads hanging in my locker, talisman from another time, and I went out to riot. (Marcuson 2011a, 1). The piece narrates a hilarious and ironic story of the simulated "riot" drill, for which Bob was conveniently prepared, love beads and all. In grappling with his role in the drill, he explores the thin line that sometimes existed between Vietnam-era troops and "hippies." Through explorations of ambiguity, Bob has brought into view the deep contradictions and incongruities of military service as well as the ambiguities of language in trying to convey such experiences. As he puts it in "Eagles and Ambiguity," "I can't say when I became obsessed with ambiguity, but its intimacy with language suggests it goes way back. There's no sense defining the word. Your sense of ambiguity will still be at least slightly different from mine, and maybe a lot. That is, of course, my point" (Marcuson 2011c, 1).

Another specific motivation we have seen in our group is the desire to use writing to speak out about the costs of war: the loss and grief associated with it and the politics of warfare. Derek Davey, mentioned earlier in this piece, served as a pilot in the marines and is the father of a fallen marine, Seamus Davey, killed in Iraq. Derek is a member of Gold Star Families Speak Out, a branch of Military Families Speak Out, an organization for those whose loved ones have been killed or have died since the Iraq and Afghanistan Wars began. The organization's motto is that the best way to support the troops is to bring them home and take care of them when they get here. Derek has written several pieces for the group that chronicle his military experiences and also his son's story, all the while participating in protests and other public-speaking events that highlight the need to bring the troops home and stop fighting these wars. In a poignant piece about grief and loss, he writes about daily walks with the family dog, Shadow, whom he refers to as his "therapy dog."

> I had been told, and I had read myself, that physical training is the best way to relieve post-trauma and grief. Natural endorphins flowing through your body are the best medicine. Shadow and I leave the house every day, very early, 5 a.m. sometimes, and walk to the park. I let her off her leash after I have scanned the area to be sure no other 2 or 4 legged walkers are nearby. I do my steady walk and daydream of better things. Walking and viewing trees, open spaces, corn fields, cows behind their fences and deer in the hills in the distance ease my soul, and I can forget the troubles for a while. Shadow runs and runs. She is a natural sprinter and rodent chaser. A few whistles guide her back my way when her hunting leads her too far. . . . We return home, and I leave for work, coming home at lunch for another quick romp. Later in the day she receives extended belly and jowl rubbing and goes on more squirrel chasing. I will talk to her at length about nothing at all really. I ignore the teasing that my daughters and wife give me for loving a dog. (Davey 2011)

Not only is this piece about Shadow the "therapy" dog, but it is also about the shadow of war and the grief surrounding Seamus's death. Other pieces he is writing and speeches he has delivered at peace events are calls to end war making. Thus, Derek uses writing and public speaking to serve as an impassioned advocate for addressing the costs and causalities of war and to call for an end to wars.

Finally, some of the veterans present their writing to foster a greater understanding of military life among civilians. Ginger Gunnip, wrote a short piece to testify to difficult truths of military suicide.

> It would be much too real to talk about death in the military. Suicide watch begins in basic training. We aren't even in the real army yet. We are safe at home. Take the man's shoelaces and belt (which are part of his uniform) and assign him a buddy. He is never left alone; 24/7 surveillance even in the bathroom. Take his word for it; he is thinking about hurting himself and others. Put him in a bright orange road guard vest and allow him to direct traffic at our graduation, but do not allow him to graduate. Keep him in the stressful situation that has led him into pondering taking his own life. After surviving a year-long deployment, would a soldier come home safely just to kill himself within a few days of their arrival? Yes.
>
> Talk about the men and women who have lost their lives serving their country. Can we hear about them as much as celebrities like Charlie Sheen and Brittany Spears? (Gunnip 2011, 1)

Ginger's short but provocative piece challenges the complacency and lack of awareness the general public demonstrates toward the stresses and pressures of military service. While soldiers are fighting, dying, and committing suicide at alarming rates, the general public is tuning into celebrity news updates, often forgetting our nation is even at war.

As the group provides members a space to do the work of narrating, processing, witnessing, and critiquing, it also provides opportunities for community building. Veterans need a safe space in which to tell their stories, and they seem to find it among other veterans who can understand and relate to them. Often just as powerful as their writing in forging a sense of community and shared experience are the stories that emerge spontaneously in response to a writing prompt, a story someone has read, or simply the act of reintroducing themselves when a new member arrives for the first time. We allow ample time for members to respond to one another and to reflect on how one person's story resonates with their own experience. We usually take a fifteen-minute break halfway through our sessions and are often surprised at the kinds of stories that emerge during this time. Such verbal exchanges are crucial to the bonding process and culture of openness and trust that galvanizes and sustains group participation.[4]

TENSIONS AND DIFFERENCES

As different generations of veterans interact, there are bound to be differences in their understandings of the military based on demographics and whether they volunteered or were drafted, were officers or enlisted personnel, experienced combat, or served during peace time. Every writing group experiences tensions and moments of difference, and such moments can be productive if they are not suppressed but become instead a subject of exploration, questioning, and analysis. One such moment of difference arose early in the group when a writing assignment sparked group members to consider their motivations for serving in the military. One OIF veteran wrote a piece about joining the military that featured an army recruiter sitting at her parents' dinner table. Having come to recruit her brother, the recruiter turned to her and asked if she had considered a military career. She noted that the idea to serve attracted her because her brother and other friends were joining. She hadn't needed to join for economic or educational reasons—she was a college graduate and did not need the GI Bill. One of the Vietnam veterans in the group wondered why anyone would let a recruiter into their home, let alone allow the recruiter to sit at a dinner table with family members. This remark highlighted the difference between a draft and an all-volunteer force and led to a discussion about the reasons the all-volunteer-force (AVF) veterans in our group had volunteered in the first place—their reasons, motivations, and sometimes ambivalent and tangled feelings about what military service had done for and to them. One Gulf War veteran admitted that he and a friend had decided to sign up after watching the comic movie *Stripes*, which chronicles the mishaps of a group of men joining the army. He joined to see the world and serve, but he also joined for deeper reasons—to honor a family legacy of male relatives who had served. Yet another member noted that military service had run in his family for the last three generations—family members had served in WWI, WWII, and Vietnam—thus making him the fourth generation to serve (in OEF). For him, it was a tradition and a legacy decision.

Even with these explanations, it was clear that there were distinct generational differences. In some cohorts, such as WWII-era veterans, most men and some women served, making serving a rite of passage, while during the Vietnam era only some individuals served while others were deferred, went to Canada, became conscientious objectors, or had their numbers come up in the draft lottery. In today's all-volunteer force, to serve is to carry the burden and responsibility of military service for all who do not serve. Many serve because the military is a way out of a troubled neighborhood, out of poverty, and into college via the GI Bill.

In addition to addressing generational differences in who served and why, our group has been challenged to address what military service looks and feels like for women veterans. Initially, our group had only one and sometimes no female veterans present at monthly meetings. Over time, our group numbers have grown from one female veteran to three who attend on a regular basis. With women veterans taking part in the group, conversations and writing topics have expanded to address the specific challenges female troops face in the military's male-dominated command structure and culture, including sexism, sexual harassment and military sexual trauma (MST), the challenge of guarding male detainees as a female Military Police officer (MP), and the travails of parenting and being absent from children's lives while in the military (the latter issue faced by male troops with families as well). Thinking about gender differences has provided group members an opportunity to consider and confront their own perceptions and views about women serving, especially since the official ban on women serving in combat roles has been lifted.

Both verbal bonding and occasional debates over differences in experiences and generations spawn new writing projects or cause other angles of an individual's story to become evident. Conversations sometimes go beyond writing the military experience to life decisions and stories about family, relationships, and childhood memories. We have seen regular members begin to forge identities and identifications not just as military veterans but as veteran writers in a larger writing community who actively describe and make sense of their experiences.

DEFENDING AND WRITING: COMBATTING STEREOTYPES

Peter Katopes (2009), Vietnam veteran and vice president of Academic Affairs for LaGuardia College, argues that the strife over the Vietnam War era led to an unfortunate series of stereotypes of military veterans that we haven't yet shaken in our culture. Veterans are often portrayed as societal "problems," "victims," or "ticking time bombs." Popular movies like *First Blood* (1982), depicting Rambo, a disturbed Vietnam veteran, and the more recent *Brothers* (2009), the story of a traumatized and jealous OEF veteran, do little to dispel or complicate such depictions. These constructions of veterans are based on a deficit model in which veterans are seen as damaged goods, as outsiders, "Others" who are a danger to civilian society. Worse yet, Katopes (2009) argues, is the stereotype of the veteran as a "victim," as someone "not very smart or a member of a relatively powerless and ill-defined underclass." Equally problematic for many veterans is the post-Vietnam era categorization of all veterans as saviors who deserve a hero's welcome and appreciation in airports and special discounts in local businesses. Such a hero's welcome is, in part, an attempt to make up for how abysmally Vietnam-era troops were treated. However, being constructed as a hero may cause veterans to feel ambivalence and embarrassment; some veterans may want to defer such acknowledgment and credit others they served with, especially fallen comrades.

In our writing group, we emphasize that veterans, rather than the popular press or media, can be *authors* of their own military experiences. We also emphasize, as Andrew Carroll of Operation Homecoming does, that military service is good preparation for writing.

> Good writing requires sharp attention to detail, and troops are drilled constantly on the importance of "situational awareness," of carefully observing one's surroundings and mentally noting: What's different, unique, out of place? Good writing also depends on originality and ingenuity, and service members are trained to improvise and think creatively to solve seemingly insurmountable problems. . . . For members of the armed forces, words are more than marks on a page or spoken utterances. They are one's honor. They are orders and missions. They are life and death. (Carroll 2008, 6)

Like Carroll, we encourage group members to think about how their military training is an asset—that *they*, not the popular media or press, are best poised to tell their stories and define their understandings of war and military service. The act of writing, then, becomes a way for veterans to reclaim their stories in a society all too willing to turn away when veterans' stories do not fit well-worn grooves and narratives.

CONCLUSION

While the federal government and various veterans' organizations extend economic, educational, and social-service benefits, we see ourselves as part of a national movement to create spaces for veterans to speak out and represent their experiences rather than being silenced or used as tools of patriotism or pawns of war. This work is especially important as thousands of veterans are returning to our campuses and our communities after repeated deployments to Iraq and Afghanistan. While the war in Iraq may have been declared "over," the struggle for military veterans to be recognized, heard, and reintegrated into society is far from over.

In doing this work of encouraging veterans' stories and creative expression, we also see ourselves as working against the silence, denial, and forgetting our society exercises about the real human costs of war.

We see ourselves as part of the wave of both civilians and veterans who are trying to testify to the consequences and experiences of war—consequences and experiences that we and others bear responsibility for as citizens of a nation that sent them to war.

Notes

1. Many thanks to the Syracuse Veterans' Writing Group members who generously agreed to allow us to cite their writings and emails connected to the group: Derek Davey, Ginger Gunnip (now Peterman), Robert (Bob) Marcuson, and Peter (Pete) McShane. We also thank all current and former members of the Syracuse Veterans' Writing Group for so generously sharing their work and for creating with us a thriving veterans' writing community in the Central New York area.
2. FNG is an acronym for "Fucking New Guy," a slang term used to refer to new troops in the field in Vietnam.
3. Kingston's San Francisco Bay area Veterans' Writing Group was inspired by Buddhist monk Thich Nhat Thanh's meditation-based peace retreats in Vietnam for war veterans and their family members.
4. Copies of group members' writings can be found at http://wrt.syr.edu/syrvetwriters/ under the link Members' Writing.

References

Brandt, Deborah. 2001. *Literacy in American Lives*. Cambridge, MA: Cambridge University Press. http://dx.doi.org/10.1017/CBO9780511810237.

Brothers. 2009. Directed by Jim Sheridan. Los Angeles, CA: Lionsgate Films. Film.

Bush, George. 2001. "Address to a Joint Session of Congress and the American People." *White House: President George W. Bush*. http://georgewbush-whitehouse.archives.gov/news/releases/2001/09/20010920-8.html.

Carroll, Andrew. 2008. Introduction to *Operation Homecoming: A Guide for Writers*, edited by Andrew Carroll. http://arts.gov/sites/default/files/OperationHomecoming Workbook.pdf.

Davey, Derek. 2011. "Therapy Dog." *Writing: Syracuse Veterans' Writing Group*. Members' Writing. http://wrt.syr.edu/syrvetwriters/.

First Blood. 1982. Directed by Ted Kotcheff. Los Angeles, CA: Orion Pictures. Film.

Gunnip, Ginger. 2011. "April 2, 2011." *Writing: Syracuse Veterans' Writing Group*. Members' Writing. http://wrt.syr.edu/syrvetwriters/.

Katopes, Peter. 2009. "POV: Veterans Returning to College Aren't Victims, They're Assets." *Community College Week*, March 23. http://www.ccweek.com/news/templates/template.aspx?articleid=995&zoneid=3.

Kingston, Maxine Hong. 2006. "Tell the Truth and So Make Peace." *KOA Books: Veterans of War, Veterans of Peace*. http://www.vowvop.org/introduction.php.

Kupfer, David. 2008. "Like Wandering Ghosts: Edward Tick on How the U.S. Fails Its Returning Soldiers." *Sun Magazine* 390, June 2008. http://thesunmagazine.org/issues/390/like_wandering_ghosts?page=2.

Marcuson, Robert. 2011a. "August Revolution 1968." *Writing: Syracuse Veterans' Writing Group*. Members' Writing. http://wrt.syr.edu/syrvetwriters/.

Marcuson, Robert. 2011b. "Catch 17." *Writing: Syracuse Veterans' Writing Group*. Members' Writing. http://wrt.syr.edu/syrvetwriters/.

Marcuson, Robert. 2011c. "Eagles and Ambiguity." https://docs.google.com/document/d/1UkaDAkgVYaH5c5U8wnPH2-DZSReq_lH20CJsdm2YPiY/edit.

Meehan, Shannon, with Roger Thompson. 2009. *Beyond Duty: Life on the Frontline in Iraq.* Cambridge, MA: Polity.

O'Brien, Tim. 2009. *The Things They Carried. Reprint.* New York: Mariner.

Ready, Frank. 2012. "War Stories." *Syracuse University Magazine,* Fall/Winter. http://sumagazine.syr.edu/2012fall-winter/orangematters/Veterans%20Writing%20Group.html.

Santos, Sergio. 2011. "Military Veterans' Writing Examiner." *Examiner.com.* http://www.examiner.com/military-veterans-writing-in-national/sergio-santos.

Shay, Jonathan. 1995. *Achilles in Vietnam: Combat Trauma and the Undoing of Character.* New York: Simon and Schuster.

Shay, Jonathan. 2003. *Odysseus in America: Combat Trauma and the Trials of Homecoming.* New York: Simon and Schuster.

Swayze, Jack. 1993. *Sporty Course: Memoirs of a World War II Bomber Pilot.* Manhattan, KS: Sunflower University Press.

Tick, Edward. 2005. *War and the Soul: Healing our Nation's Veterans from Post-Traumatic Stress Disorder.* Wheaton, IL: Quest Books.

"Warrior Writers: Warrior Writers Veterans Day Veterans Speak." 2009. Warriorwriters.blogspot.com. Oct. 27, 2009. warriorwriters.blogspot.com/2009_10_01_archive.html.

6

CLOSER TO HOME
Veterans' Workshops and the Materiality of Writing

Karen Springsteen

I finished writing this essay during July 4 celebrations as hundreds of us gathered to celebrate a robust Independence Day. I was reminded of what I consider my first adult act—resigning my US Army officer's commission to protest the Vietnam War. My second adult act was to cease using my first name, Walter, which means "warrior." I was born Walter Shepherd Bliss III, carrying the military legacy from my father and his father and further back. I did not want to have this warrior legacy evoked for the rest of my life, even if those calling me "Walter" were not doing so consciously. So I decided to use my given middle name, which is my great-grandmother's last name, as my first name. I wanted to honor my matrilineal legacy. I think this has made a great difference in my life . . . Deciding what to entitle this essay has not been easy, nor has writing it been easy. This essay is more personal than most of my writing—closer to home. (Bliss 2006, 22)

In the passage above, "closer to home" seems to denote, for Shepherd Bliss, writing that is personal, intimate, and tied to his very sense of self. Bliss notes an almost visceral connection in hearing one's name spoken aloud, some imprint left upon the conscious body by such a label. In changing this label, Bliss changed his life, granting himself "the peace of a shepherd, rather than the trauma of being called a warrior. I appreciate having a warrior inside and available, but I do not want it to be always leading me" (Bliss 2006, 22).

The ability to see bits of language as ever present, personal, visceral, and embodied is an ability to consider language as a material force. According to David Bleich, language may be material "in the sense that it has tangible effects and that it matters all the time" (Bleich 2003, 469). If an image of a wrecked Humvee, for example, saved for years on a cell phone, is used to inspire a poem, then one may come to see that thoughts and ideas represented by language are, in fact, derived from

DOI: 10.7330/9780874219425.c006

the material world. Language in the abstract (the immaterial) gives way when the dates of an IED explosion, for example, are tattooed on a soldier's forearm, creating a physical mark for all who see them: *never forget.*

Images like these are burned in my brain as, for over three years, I have helped organize and conduct veterans' writing workshops as a civilian contributor to the national Warrior Writers project.

Founded in 2007, Warrior Writers (warriorwriters.org) is a nonprofit organization that aims to create a culture that articulates veterans' experiences, provides a creative community for artistic expression among veterans, and generates sites for veterans and civilians to bear witness to the lived experiences of warriors. In what follows, I describe how I came to be a part of Warrior Writers and use my experience to suggest that writing's materiality is a significant factor by which veterans bring their experiences of war and military service "closer to home"—an expression used not only by Shepherd Bliss but by many other veterans who aim to put a finger on just what is so powerful about writing.

BEGINNINGS

When I first began to work with Warrior Writers, I had no great family history with the military or knowledge of wartime experience. Now, however, writing together with veterans, I have come to understand that there is less of a disconnection between war and home than many civilians think. At a Warrior Writers workshop I helped to organize, held on a college campus, a former marine offered the word *chains* as a writing prompt. I thought: *what do I, a civilian, having lived a life of relative safety and security, have to say about chains?* As a quiet, intense energy settled into the room, I scribbled the following in my marbled composition notebook:

> Ever since I moved to the North Country, I have been collecting bits of printed matter related to the war and its aftermath, or perhaps I should say "its ongoing-math." My collection is like one of those paper chains we made when we were kids—each person's little strip hooking onto the next. A Sesame Street-themed booklet for kids whose parents are deployed, taken from a kiosk at the Watertown mall. A newspaper from Ottawa with a front-page headline: No Peace for Vets. The card an ROTC officer gave me when I told him I took a year of Arabic. The half-ass note written by an Air Force recruiter as an excuse for Sarah to go take her ASVAB. The free Fort Drum paper I snagged at Valero while the guy in front of me bought a case of Old Mil at 7:45 in the morning. There are so many more little pieces I could add to this chain, including the pages we are all making right now. When the Veterans Taskforce tries to tie yellow ribbons around

the trees next month, I want them to tie these paper chains instead. *Some of us don't care for yellow ribbons unless they end war.*

After the last of the pens stopped moving, each of the participants read aloud what we had written, me going last, and when it was time for the next prompt, my co-organizer, an Iraq veteran, offered "Dear Veterans Taskforce" as a response to my words. *We are connected*, and it is the quality of these connections that has lead me to look more deeply into the power of veterans' writing and veterans' writing workshops.

I began to work with Warrior Writers out of a stroke of luck, having been in the right place at the right time to meet my co-organizer and another interested veteran. However, I knew even before we met that war was a part of my community. I was open to the experience of working with veterans and mindful of the sacredness of the opportunity I was being offered. In some small way, I was prepared for this work as a compositionist who had collaborated with members of historically underrepresented groups since the beginning of my career. On the other hand, I had no idea what a profound impact the work would have on me. The workshops I have helped to conduct have included combat and non-combat veterans, active-duty military personnel, and family members on a small college campus located seventy-one miles from Fort Drum, a major training site for more than 35,000 Army Reserve and National Guard troops. The workshops have been nonacademic in nature (no grades, no college credit) as the focus is placed on community building, understanding, nonjudgment, and healing.

The atmosphere of trust in our workshops and the fact that this work was never intended as "research" stop me from sharing more than my own memories, experiences, and images in this chapter. I cite veterans I know who have made their words public through performance or publication. Otherwise, the voices of people I include in this chapter are composite voices, and the stories I include are appropriately fictionalized to protect writers' identities. I work from snippets in my notebook, scraps of paper, piles of printed matter I have amassed, artwork given to me by veterans, and books by and about veterans, from all sorts of disciplines, that I collect and try to inhale at a pace never fast enough to keep up with the urgency of the messages veterans have to share. Make no mistake; this is a personal essay. But I hope it is also a communal one, demonstrating that there *can be* less of a disconnection between war and home than many think *if* we look to veterans who are already speaking, writing, and publishing and to civilians who are already listening, reading, and standing with veterans of wars past and present.

Across this nation, for example, numerous Warrior Writers workshops have been conducted, resulting in veterans' spoken word performances, art exhibits, and three published anthologies of veterans' writing: *Move, Shoot, and Communicate; Remaking Sense;* and *After Action Review,* all edited by Warrior Writers founder and director Lovella Calica.

According to Calica,

> There is a deep necessity to create when so much has been shattered and stolen—a profound sense of hope comes from the ability to rebuild. Workshops begin by discussing how we can use writing as a tool for expressing ourselves, dealing with emotions, understanding consequences, and relating to each other. Although it is often challenging and exhausting for veterans to write, relive events, reflect and try to describe their feelings, this process helps lighten the weight of their memories and thoughts (Calica 2008, 3).

That writing can carry psychic weight, that it involves the physical body, and that it is a way of building human relations all point to the notion of writing as a material practice: a practice that can effect real changes within writers and their worlds. In the section below, I outline three veterans' writing efforts that intersect closely with Warrior Writers as I further illustrate a notion of materiality in writing discussed by Bruce Horner and David Bleich.

MATERIALITY IN VETERANS' WRITING

In *Terms of Work for Composition,* Horner gives an extensive materialist critique of writing practices. Horner includes attention to the physical conditions of space and bodies within the writing setting, socioeconomic conditions and the forms of consciousness they produce, institutional and social relations, and writing technologies. With regard to technology specifically, Horner notes, "The materiality of writing might be understood to refer to networks for the distribution of writing, controls over publishing (in whatever forms), and global relations of power articulated through these" (Horner 2001, xxvii). Along this dimension, materiality becomes a question of who has the right, privilege, position, or ability to record and circulate veterans' words.

This facet of the materiality of veterans' writing is crucial to grasp. A scenario in which veterans may be unable to find an opportunity, much less a site, for producing compositions that capture their experience is a scenario directly confronted by Warrior Writers and other veterans' writing and self-publishing efforts. In the early 1970s, for example, a number of Vietnam veterans sought publication for a collection of their creative writing but were unable to find a commercial publisher willing to print their words. According to Caroline Slocock, "Their conviction that this literature both deserved and could find a substantial audience led these writers to establish their own independent press," which they named the First Casualty Press (Slocock 1982, 107). In 1972 and 1973, the press published two anthologies, *Winning Hearts and Minds* and *Free Fire Zone*, both of which were given this epigraph: in war, truth is the first casualty.

More recently, the Veterans Book Project (veteransbookproject.com) has helped those who served in Iraq and Afghanistan, their families, and others directly affected by these wars to turn their photographs, illustrations, and writings from combat into softbound books. Some forty-nine books from the Veterans Book Project are available for purchase on a self-publishing website and are also available for free on the web as downloadable digital files. Whether viewing these books on screen or holding the pages in one's hands, one cannot escape the direct, in-your-face, often stunning quality of the compositions. Images of the desert countryside show camels and sheep and sunsets mixed with missiles and tanks and trucks. Images take the reader inside barracks and operating rooms where bodies fill the page. There are scenes of friendship and scenes of fear. Written text offers coherent narratives about joining the military, deploying, and coming home. Poems and bits of prose convey the consequences and complexities of these acts. Each book is a unique visual-verbal articulation of the war, and each is a contribution to a larger body of work. Stacked up, the books represent what project leader Monica Haller calls "a framework" in which "war materials can be seen, refashioned, and analyzed by the public" (Pederson 2013, 22). Speaking to the issue of materiality directly, Haller writes, "No dust settles on these archives. [Each] book contains a powerful living collection of data, memory, and experience that is so relevant it trembles" (Lewis 2010).

A collection of writing can tremble in the sense that the exchange between its writer and reader can resonate, reverberate, and register in the physical body; it can be *felt* as what Bleich calls a "palpable aspect of social relations" (Bleich 2001, 119). "The concept of the materiality of language," he writes, "means that words, like everything else, are rooted in matter as trees are rooted in earth" (Bleich 2001, 121). The book captured in the image to the left, for example, is tactile and organic.

Its cover is composed of paper that has been formed from the threads of the author's military uniform, which was worn throughout his tour of duty in Iraq. This book was created as part of the Combat Paper Project (combatpaper.org), which joins veterans and civilians together in a

Figure 6.1

transformative process that reclaims the material of uniforms as art and broadens the traditional narrative surrounding service and the military culture (Combat Paper Project 2011). The process may be initially somewhat shocking to some audiences; combat papermakers' uniforms are cut up, beaten into a pulp, and formed into sheets of paper upon which writing and visual representations are inscribed. With a Combat Paper cover, this hand-bound book is the twelfth of 250 total copies that were produced by the Combat Paper Project's independent publishing arm. It was given to me as a gift from the writer in the context of a Warrior Writers workshop.

That relation of giving, the generous act of sharing this written material, has formed a social and moral bond. In the absence of the writer but bearing the mark of his hand and body, this book has become, for me, a form of life that lays emphasis on what Marie McGinn, following Wittgenstein, calls the "vital connection between language and the complex system of practices and activities binding a community together" (quoted in Bleich 2001, 121). Indeed, the words used as the postscript to *Free Fire Zone*, published by that First Casualty Press some forty years ago, echo every time I close the cover of this book: "Now you have heard it; what happened is part of you too" (Slocock 1982, 111).

It is hard to describe the great honor I feel in becoming a small part of Warrior Writers. When I touch the pages we have written together, I am reminded that the anxiety of civilians over how we respond to war and to veterans is subordinate to the courage of those veterans who raise their voices to speak and to write. With Nancy Sherman, I hope that "soldiers in the current generation do not view their war as a private burden banned from their families and communities" (Sherman 2010b, 7). Through the collective making of paper, through the printing of the written word, through the digital technological distribution of writing, through the collection of living memories in the body of the book, and through the workings of the human hand, veterans have kept first-person subjective experiences of war and military service before a reading public. By materializing experience in these ways, writing brings the war closer to home.

A PERMANENT RECORD

My own efforts with Warrior Writers have occurred at a grassroots level, and the projects I described above have also occurred in a ground-up, do-it-yourself manner. At the same time, however, efforts of national arts organizations, government agencies, and long-established veterans' writing communities have also aimed toward materializing war and military experience through writing. Beginning during the first Gulf War, for example, Maxine Hong Kingston assembled a community of veterans and family members in writing and meditation workshops, which have served as an inspiration for many of us who are involved in Warrior Writers.

These workshops have been ongoing since the 1990s and have gathered over 500 participants. In 2006, a 610-page collection of stories and poems from Kingston's group was published by Koa Books with the title *Veterans of War, Veterans of Peace* (vowvop.org).

In the introduction to this book, Kingston describes the vitality and humanity of the workshops she helped to create.

> The veterans needed to write. They would write the unspeakable. Writing, they keep track of their thinking; they leave a permanent record. Processing chaos through story and poem, the writer shapes and forms experience, and thereby, I believe, changes the past and remakes the existing world. The writer becomes a new person after every story, every poem; and if the art is good, perhaps the reader is changed too . . . We practiced writing in community. We would not have to write alone. We had one another to write with, and to write for. If you felt like quitting, you'd look across the table or garden or terrace or grove, and see the others bowed over their notebooks and laptops, and you kept going . . . All these years, these faithful writers have paid attention to wars past and wars ongoing. Their stories and poems are immense in scope, and in heart, and—amazingly—full of life and laughter. They carried our motto: Tell the truth. (Kingston 2006, 1–3)

Telling the truth of wars, I have learned, requires the vision of veterans on many fronts and a view of war and military service generational and transnational in scope. So much of war and military culture is glorified, yet so much is also left in the dark, undifferentiated, unfiltered, or forgotten. It is helpful, then, to gather and create material traces—some scraps of truth, one after the next—that build what Kingston calls "a permanent record," a collective composition broader than individual memory, external, physical, and capable of illumination.

Books:

> Bowden, Lisa, and Shannon Cain, eds. 2008. *Powder: Writing by Women in the Ranks from Vietnam to Iraq.* Tuscon, AZ: Kore Press.
> Phillips, Joshua E. 2010. *None of Us Were Like This Before.* Brooklyn, NY: Verso.

Documentaries:

> *Body of War.* 2008. Directed by Ellen Spiro and Phil Donahue. Los Angeles: Docurama Films. DVD.
> *The Invisible War.* 2012. Directed by Kirby Dick. Los Angeles: Docudrama Films. DVD.
> *Poster Girl.* 2011. Directed by Sara Nesson. New York: Portrayal Films. DVD.
> *Where Soldiers Come From.* 2011. Directed by Heather Courtney. Austin, TX: Quincy Hill Films. DVD.

On October 27, 2000, the US Congress made a move toward creating such a record when it unanimously passed into law the Veterans Oral History Project Act (www.loc.gov/vets), which called upon the American Folklife Center to "collect and preserve oral histories along with letters, diaries, and other firsthand materials from veterans of World War I, World War II, and the Korean, Vietnam, and [pre-9/11] Persian Gulf wars, as well as from civilians who served in support of these wars" (Sorkin 2004, 3). As these wars grow more distant, thousands upon thousands of veterans' recordings, images, and writings have been collected, comprising a national archive that may be tapped by veterans and civilians today. Similarly, at a local community level, my own St. Lawrence County Historical Association recently dedicated its quarterly publication to a project titled We Remember: Pictures and Letters of World War II Veterans. Like a smaller-scale version of the Veterans History Project, We Remember included, among many items, the following two letters, written sometime between 1941 and 1945, by Ernest E. Veio to his brother and sister-in-law in Pierrepont, New York.

June 29

This is my second letter from a prisoner of war camp. I am allowed to write three letters and four postcards per month. This time I will tell you a few things I would like to have you send me. I am allowed to receive one 10-pound package of clothing every three months. For the month of July, August and September, I would like one blanket, one half dozen toothbrushes, toothpaste, razor and razor blades, heavy underwear, socks, and army officers' shirts. If there is any weight left, send what other clothes you think I would need. Do not send any other civilian garments, only army clothes. All I have is what I was wearing when I was shot down. It will be necessary to get a license from the Red Cross and you will have to send the parcel through them.

July 3

Tomorrow is July 4 and for the first time in my life I am able to appreciate what independence means. I am well and not wounded. I parachuted to safety. All I am wondering about is how you and Frank felt when you heard I was missing. I suppose you thought that the inevitable had happened, but you see, it hadn't. I hope it wasn't too long before you were notified I was a prisoner. Again I say, don't worry about me, and before you know it I will be home. You can put a piece in the paper about my being a prisoner if you want to. It will explain why I haven't written to some people (St. Lawrence County Historical Association 2008, 35).

The focus on survival and the desire to communicate represented in Veio's World War II letters remains a motivation for veterans who put pen to paper amidst the current wars. In 2004, for example, the National Endowment for the Arts project, Operation Homecoming (nea.gov/national/homecoming), invited troops and their families to write about wartime experiences as those experiences were, in fact, still happening: Operation Homecoming offered some fifty writing workshops on twenty-five bases across five countries, on an aircraft carrier, and aboard a fleet ship in the Persian Gulf. Selections of the writing produced in these workshops were then published in an anthology of the same name, for which nearly 2,000 manuscripts—over 10,000 pages of writing—were submitted (Carroll 2006, xiv).

In the preface to this anthology, National Endowment for the Arts Chairperson Dana Goia describes the overwhelming response to this project.

> When news of *Operation Homecoming* appeared in the media . . . phones began ringing, fax machines whirred, and e-mails poured into our headquarters at the Old Post Office in Washington, DC, as military personnel and their families asked to participate. Some soldiers even called from Baghdad and Kabul on their satellite phones, eager to sign up for the workshops. For weeks, letters and manuscripts continued to arrive, including several powerful testimonies by Vietnam War veterans, who wished they had been offered a similar chance to come to terms with their difficult wartime experiences. All of this happened before the program had even begun (quoted in Carroll 2006, xiv).

Goia's testimony helps make clear that writing is a vital and desired activity for many veterans. Writing workshops are a way for veterans to find kinship, solace, and affirmation. Whether writers are lashing out, laughing at, deconstructing, or otherwise making sense of war and military experience, the workshops can allow veterans to begin talking, even if they are "only" talking to themselves.

VETERAN-CIVILIAN DIALOGUE

Outside of such workshops, however, veterans may face public audiences who are not yet willing or in a position to understand what veterans have to say, despite the kinds of efforts outlined throughout this chapter. Mike Rose recently argued, for example, that although US citizens have been "awash with support our troops rhetoric," we have not necessarily addressed "the multiple needs our troops have when they return home" (Rose 2009, 143).

Troops who return home from deployments may be greeted with displays of national flags, flowers, yellow ribbons, and military regalia. Beyond these forms of recognition, however, veterans may not always experience a deeper public understanding of what their service has entailed. In a poem titled "Charlie Battery Has Places to Go," Nathan Lewis (2009, 11–12) writes about witnessing the death of an eight-year-old Iraqi boy.

> His face is covered with a jacket.
> I stare at his dirty bare feet
> Later, back home,
> when asked by fools and children
> Did you see any action?
> I always want to tell them
> But I never saved the courage to tell
> About this sort of action

The question "did you see any action?" or even the polite offering "thank you for your service" may be evidence of a failure "back home" to engage veterans' subjective experience of war in an adequately substantive way. "Do you know what it's like to be thanked?" asked Jon Turner, a former marine who, after enlisting at the age of seventeen, served two tours in Iraq, four months in Haiti, and later testified at the Winter Soldier investigation organized by Iraq Veterans Against the War (Turner 2009). His question is deeply rhetorical, a direct address and provocation to audiences who may feel, in Sherman's words, that "war is not something to touch or probe, especially if we don't wear the uniform." In "The Untold Stories of War," Sherman claims that "what it feels like to put on a military uniform, deploy, and come home is still not really part of the public conversation about war" (Sherman 2010a, B7).

Veterans Sanctuary: http://veterans sanctuary.blogspot.ca/

Iraq Veterans Against the War, Aaron Glanz. 2008. *Winter Soldier: Iraq and Afghanistan: Eyewitness Accounts of the Occupations*. 2008. Chicago: Haymarket Books)

Perhaps it needs to be. Upon seeing an announcement for a Warrior Writers workshop that I placed in the local newspaper, an eighty-six-year-old World War II veteran called my home to ask what I thought I was doing. I told him that Warrior Writers was a support group for veterans. He remained unconvinced. Agitated, he told me *you can't do anything for vets,* deepening my sense that an intersubjective failure to communicate with and among veterans in this nation is generational. A veteran of the Korean War with whom I discussed this phone call reminded me that men of his generation were taught to *put it in a trunk and put it away.* But such denial is no longer necessary. "For so many years now," writes Iraq veteran Drew Cameron,

> the wars waged by our country have influenced our daily rituals, our morning consciousness. For some the recognition is very close to home. For all of us though, war, as it does, continues to pressure the very fabric of our culture and worldview. Have we not all become veterans of war then? It is this very question of responsibility, of openness and honesty that reveals the essence of conflict and how it shapes our collective lives. When someone says: "I cannot know what it was like over there," we want them to. When someone says: "I can't imagine how it must have been," we need them to. When someone says: "I cannot," they must. (Lewis 2009, vii–viii)

Given this invocation, some readers may feel moved to initiate or participate in veterans' writing workshops within community literacy contexts. To conclude this essay, then, I offer a discussion of three specific situations community facilitators and veteran-writers might expect to negotiate in their collaborations, including the reactions of veteran and civilian audiences. The scenarios are drawn from my experience helping to sponsor and conduct Warrior Writers workshops.

WORKSHOP SCENARIOS

1. Nobody Shows Up

One workshop participant, who came to the workshops off and on, was on active duty in the National Guard. She once had to drive five hours on a Sunday night from drill practice in order to take an exam the next morning and then go on to work. Two participants attended a workshop once, revealing unforgettable testimonies and authorial voices, but then disappeared. They stayed on our e-mail list and periodically sent messages, making references to what was going on in their lives and asking me to keep them in the loop. We stayed in touch, but they did not return. Some of the workshops we offered drew many writers; one was met with an empty room. Flyers were posted all over the community on different occasions, but turnouts varied. Some veterans in the community hate writing. Some are stoic, not wanting to seek what they may perceive as help. Some don't want to talk, or simply can't talk, about their experiences—yet. Some have injuries to their eyes and hands. Some are so happy to be out of the service that, in the words of one Vietnam veteran, *the last thing they want to do is to join something.*

At the same time, veterans who leave the service lose a community and a certain sense of identity. The sharing that takes place within veterans' writing workshops can mediate such an experience, but it certainly cannot be forced. In an address given as part of Operation Homecoming at New York's Fort Drum, Richard Bausch encouraged soldier-writers to "work harder than you have ever worked on anything else in your life, hour upon hour upon hour, with nothing in the way of encouragement, no good feeling" (National Endowment for the Arts 2001). The same advice may be given workshop facilitators. We cannot be motivated merely by a desire to validate our own good intentions, and we cannot give up if nobody shows. Such a shallow well of intention will quickly dry up.

2. Protective Instincts Arise

A civilian once came to a workshop because he was writing a drama about veterans. He said he was moved to do so when a friend's son was killed in Afghanistan. Although our advertising indicated that the workshops were for veterans, active duty, National Guard, Reserves, and family, we would not reject a peaceful outside participant. This writer clearly wanted to learn all he could. He stayed for the length of the workshop, took copious notes, and asked many questions—digging for details about such things as uniform types, MREs, and military colloquialisms. Some weeks later, I received a voicemail message telling me he had finished the piece and asking me to please call back so we could "get their [the veterans'] voices out there."

This workshop participant and I are both civilians, and we are both interested in veterans' issues. However, I did not return the voicemail. Later, when we when we ran into each other on campus, I stopped to apologize. I explained the reasons for my silence and engaged in an honest conversation about why it would be best if he didn't come back to the workshops. Perhaps because he had been there, he understood why he wouldn't come back.

I tell this story to illustrate a tension that community facilitators and veteran-writers may feel between openness and protection. This tension has pulled me, for example, between a commitment to publishing this essay and a desire to withdraw the essay in order to keep my work with Warrior Writers more private and personal. I have found that at the heart of this tension are fears about appropriation and assumptions about veterans' vulnerability that may or may not hold true. For example, given the benefits of the new GI Bill, the existence of veterans' writing workshops on campus may be used as proof that the college is "yellow ribbon friendly" and referenced in marketing efforts directed toward prospective student-veterans. Outside of the writing workshops, however, the reality for student-veterans on campus may not be so friendly.

It should be said that most who attempt to use the workshops in the favor of some goal are kind hearted rather than exploitative. Mostly, they are curious and want to "help." Nonetheless, workshop facilitators must remain vigilant, holding tight the tensions we feel because those tensions affect the context of trust within the workshops and the extent to which veteran-writers are willing to share their experiences.

3. Someone Cries

> In recent months, I've been trying to honor the lives I took by writing and speaking publicly about my experience, to show that those deaths are not tucked neatly away in a foreign land. They may seem distant, but they are not. Soldiers bring the ghosts home with them, and it's everyone else's job to hear about them, no matter how painful it may be (Meehan, *New York Times*, February 22, 2010).

Expressing pain by crying is a normal emotional, physical, and spiritual act. During the times in our workshops when writers have cried, we simply *ride it out.* We let the emotion be. Then, if the writer doesn't want to talk, we say *maybe another time.* Or, *what was it about?* This approach seems simplistic, especially in light of the clinical psychiatric model of care toward which so many veterans are pushed. Yet, I have been witness to its effectiveness.

Meehan, Shannon, and Roger Thompson. 2009. *Beyond Duty: Life on the Frontline in Iraq.* Malden, MA: Polity Press.

There is the impression among civilian audiences that one must be a certified therapist in order to work with veterans, or that writing with veterans is ill advised because it will stir up and multiply the ghosts. Rejecting this fear, the late Ray Bradbury claims that veterans' writing is, instead, "an act of health" (quoted in *Muse of Fire: Writing the Wartime Experience* 2007). Indeed, for a veteran dealing with posttraumatic stress, for example, finding a community of writers who have all "been there" in some way can provide the right audience for the composition of a logical question: *how is this a disorder?* In the sense that this question rejects stigma and speaks back to a system that insists veterans are sick, this veteran used the space of the writing workshop as a space of strength.

Tears can be part of that strength. As Paula J. Caplan (2011, 177) puts it, moving "outside a pathologizing framework" can reduce a sense of isolation among veterans that comes from their possible belief "that they are crazy or at the very least have responded weirdly to war." Caplan (2011, 177) writes that many vets have told her that "the best thing someone has ever done for them is to say something along the lines of, 'if I have been through what you just described . . . I would be feeling the same way you are. I don't think you're crazy. In fact, if you hadn't been this upset, I would have wondered why.'"

At the same time, I have met on multiple occasions with the director of counseling on the campus where our workshops were held, familiarized myself with local mental-health resources, and gathered to have on hand names, phone numbers, and brochures from the VA and other veterans' support organizations, such as a veterans' crisis hotline: 1-800-273-TALK, "Veterans press 1." I recognize the severity of the problems that veterans face in the United States today, and I resist romanticizing veterans' writing. Yet, I also refuse to represent work in veterans' writing groups as "risky"—not only because we have held workshops safely for a period of more than three years, but also because such a representation marginalizes and alienates the very people with whom I want to connect.

Crisis Line for Veterans, Active Duty/Reserve and Guard, and Family/Friends: veteranscrisisline.net; 1–800–273-TALK, "Veterans press 1"

The foregoing discussions of these three scenarios may be useful in keeping dialogue open about what happens within and around veterans' writing workshops. Many more scenarios could be written covering such topics as how to negotiate patriotism and antiwar sentiment within the workshops, what kinds of writing prompts have proven to be most useful, how to encourage writers to draw upon a full spectrum of military experience—not just combat or deployment—and how to educate civilian publics about the work accomplished by veterans' writing.

Even more scenarios could be written about the ways in which participants change as a result of this work. I, for example, am less and less inspired to return to an academic setting after seeing the relevance of community writing such as this and have altered the direction of my career in order to prioritize veterans' community literacy work. However, most important to any facilitator's education (academic or otherwise) is the understanding that the group doing the writing changes the writing; the workshops are always dynamic. There is no formula or template or set number of books one could read to nail down what is an organic and open-ended process. To conduct the workshops in a responsible way, then—to be ethical, not just benevolent—facilitators must stand ready to witness, to listen, and to respond to what is yet unknown. This is, in fact, where I would locate the risk in facilitating veterans' writing workshops.

Author's Note

I thank Nate Lewis for bringing me into Warrior Writers and for encouraging me to continue with the work. I am grateful for his example, his generosity, and his creative voice.

References

Bleich, David. 2001. "The Materiality of Language and the Pedagogy of Exchange." *Pedagogy: Critical Approaches to Teaching Literature, Language, and Composition* 1 (1): 117–41. http://dx.doi.org/10.1215/15314200-1-1-117.

Bleich, David. 2003. "Materiality, Genre, and Language Use: Introduction." *College English* 65 (5): 469–75. http://dx.doi.org/10.2307/3594247.

Bliss, Shepherd. 2006. "Sound Shy." In *Veterans of War, Veterans of Peace,* edited by Maxine Hong Kingston, 20–28. Kihei, HI: Koa Books.

Calica, Lovella. 2008. *Warrior Writers: Re-Making Sense.* Barre, VT: Iraq Veterans Against the War.

Caplan, Paula J. 2011. *When Johnny and Jane Come Marching Home: How All of Us Can Help Veterans.* Cambridge, MA: MIT Press.

Carroll, Andrew. 2006. *Operation Homecoming: Iraq, Afghanistan, and the Home Front, in the Words of U.S. Troops and Their Families.* Chicago, IL: University of Chicago Press.

Combat Paper Project. 2011. "About Combat Paper." http://www.combatpaper.org.

Horner, Bruce. 2001. *Terms of Work for Composition: A Materialist Critique.* Albany: State University of New York Press.

Kingston, Maxine Hong, ed. 2006. *Veterans of War, Veterans of Peace.* Kihei, HI: Koa Books.

Lewis, Nathan. 2009. *I Hackey Sacked in Iraq.* Burlington, VT: Combat Paper Press.

Lewis, Nathan. 2010. Objects for Deployment. N.P. Veterans Book Project.

Muse of Fire: Writing the Wartime Experience. 2007. Directed by Lawrence Bridges. New York: Red Car Films. DVD.

National Endowment for the Arts. 2001. "Richard Bausch: A Letter to a Young Writer." http://www.nea.gov/av/video/oh/bausch.html.

Pederson, Claudia Costa. 2013. "The Veterans Book Project: An Interview with Monica Haller." *Afterimage* 41 (2): 21–25.

Rose, Mike. 2009. *Why School: Reclaiming Education for All of Us.* New York: New Press.

Sherman, Nancy. 2010a. "The Untold Stories of War." *Chronicle Review,* April 16, B7–B9.

Sherman, Nancy. 2010b. *The Untold War: Inside the Hearts, Minds, and Souls of Our Soldiers.* New York: W.W. Norton.

Slocock, Caroline. 1982. "Winning Hearts and Minds: The 1st Casualty Press." *American Studies (Lawrence, Kan.)* 16 (1): 107–18.

Sorkin, Virginia. 2004. "The Veterans History Project: From Concept to Reality." *Folklife Center News* 26 (2): 3–9.

"WWII Letters." 2008. *St. Lawrence County Historical Association Quarterly* LIII (2): 30–39.

Turner, Jon. 2009. "Combat Paper Artist Talk and Reception." Fire House Gallery, Burlington, VT, February 20.

7

SIGNATURE WOUNDS
Marking and Medicalizing Post-9/11 Veterans

Tara Wood

Campuses are encouraged to meet the challenge of becoming veteran-friendly by putting in place personnel, policies, resources, and programs that reflect sensitivity to and understanding of the needs of veterans. Supporting the troops should be an action plan, not just a happy slogan. There is an urgent *need to share best practices, to exchange ideas, and to conduct research that will provide campuses with the information needed to promote the academic achievement of veterans who are students.*

—Ackerman, DiRamio, and
Mitchell 2009, 13 (emphasis added)

Much of the conversation regarding how to meet the administrative, educational, financial, and medical needs of student-veteran populations has been aimed at pointing out the gaping absence of effective policies, procedures, organizations, support systems, and institutional measures. To further complicate the task of meeting these needs, veterans returning from combat are frequently diagnosed with the "signature wounds" of Operation Enduring Freedom (OEI) and Operation Iraqi Freedom (OFI): traumatic brain injury (TBI) and posttraumatic stress disorder (PTSD). Disability studies (DS) offers significant perspectives to this conversation, perspectives that are especially attuned to the (potentially) oppressive position of "disabled." Student-veterans with "signature wounds" may not identify as "disabled," but they are subject to a medicalizing culture that will nonetheless label them as such. One benchmark of scholarship in DS is resisting the normalizing tendencies of medical models of disability, and if teachers, researchers, and writing program administrators (WPAs) aim to effectively and purposefully make classrooms veteran friendly, they must mirror this resistance.

DOI: 10.7330/9780874219425.c007

Doing so will allow student-veterans fuller participation in learning environments and will ensure that pedagogies are adapting to and respecting the unique needs of individual students rather than responding to lists of symptoms that need to be "fixed." Such attention to the implications of DS for student-veterans with TBI/PTSD[1] will serve to circumvent exclusive reliance on medical expertise to guide decision making by allowing for social and cultural considerations of disability. Social models of disability offer promising alternatives to the medical models and cognitive rhetorics that inhibit access and exacerbate the stigmas associated with disability.

MEDICAL AND SOCIAL MODELS OF DISABILITY

Medical models of disability are rooted in the rise of science and medicine in the past century and are best understood as models of bodies that position illness and abnormality as both a problem of and the responsibility of the individual afflicted. Because student-veterans with TBI/PTSD occupy both the position of veteran *and* the position of student with disability(s), thoughtful and deliberate consideration of best practices for developing programmatic and classroom strategies is required, and this consideration must be attentive to the critiques of medical models offered by DS scholars. A central methodological tactic of these scholars is to offer *social* models of disability as alternative approaches to understanding the experiences of those rendered "disabled."

Until the 1970s, disability as a subject of research had been primarily relegated to medical professionals.[2] Mike Oliver (1990), a leading researcher/campaigner for the social model, identified two main problems with the medical model: "Firstly, it locates the 'problem' of disability within the individual and second it sees the causes of this problem as stemming from the functional limitations or psychological losses which are assumed to arise from disability" (3). This critique supplied the necessary fodder to understand disability as a socially constructed ideology that placed certain individuals in a sociopolitical position of lack. Medical paradigms rely exclusively on rhetorics of cure, a return to normalcy, thus forcefully retaining the cultural logic of a "natural" body. Jay Dolmage and Cynthia Lewiecki-Wilson argue that not only were these cultural logics of the body maintained but also that the primacy of medical models "sustained historic exclusions and founded new ones on scientific grounds, through the arrangement and discipline of abjected others around the rational subject-observer" (Dolmage and Lewiecki-Wilson 2010, 29). Dolmage and Lewiecki-Wilson go on to argue that DS "holds that disability is a complex political and cultural effect of one's interaction with an environment, not simply a medical condition to be eliminated" and that the latter epistemology pathologizes disabled subjects with "dehumanizing results" (30). A social-disability perspective requires that theorists, teachers, and/or WPAs, who address the needs of individuals who identify (or are identified by others) as disabled, understand disability as both a physical, material experience *and* as a sociocultural positioning mediated by the dominant-hegemonic discourse of ableism (see Davis 1995; Dolmage 2008; Garland-Thomson 1997; Linton 1998). Engaging a social-disability perspective allows teachers and WPAs to examine the medical understandings of TBI and PTSD *and* the social contexts that give rise to such understandings.

"SIGNATURE WOUNDS": UNDERSTANDING TRAUMATIC BRAIN INJURY AND POSTTRAUMATIC STRESS DISORDER

In 2009 Army Brigadier General Loree Sutton, director of the Pentagon's Centers of Excellence for Psychological Health and Traumatic Brain Injury, estimated that approximately 20 percent of veterans returning from combat had TBI (Gilkey, *USA Today*, March 5, 2009). However, T. Christian Miller of ProPublica and Daniel Zwerdling of NPR broadcasted a report documenting the catastrophic numbers of uncounted and undiagnosed veterans suffering from TBI (Miller and Zwerdling 2010). Miller and Zwerdling relied on interviews from soldiers, experts, and military leaders, as well as government records, previously undisclosed studies, and private correspondence between senior medical officials to expose poor screening, substandard treatment, routine misdiagnosis, and lost documentation of "signature-wound" soldiers. Recent research confirms Miller and Zwerdling's report (Kato 2010; Shea 2010) and estimates that soldiers have about a 40 percent chance of cognitive injury during their times of service (Kato 2010; Milliken, Auchterlonie, and Hoge 2007; Radford 2009; Shea 2010; Tanielian and Jaycox 2008).

Traumatic brain injury is defined as "a blow or jolt to the head or a penetrating head injury that disrupts the functioning of the brain" (American Council on Education 2010, 2). Most TBIs are caused by improvised explosive devices (IEDs) with which soldiers come in contact in the field (National Council on Disability 2009). According to the Defense and Veterans Brain Injury Center (DVBIC) (2011), 90 percent of TBIs are mild, and most individuals with mild TBI (mTBI) are able to resume their normal lives. The DVBIC (2011) states,

While TBI may result in physical impairment, often the more problematic consequences involve an individual's cognition, emotional functioning, and behavior. These can impact all aspects of life including the development and maintenance of interpersonal relationships and the ability to function in social settings. Community re-integration efforts are therefore aimed at maximizing individual strengths and creating supportive environments that will allow for a return to work and family.

One of the trickiest aspects of working with student-veterans who have experienced TBI is the vast spectrum and severity of symptoms.

To further complicate the subject positions of student-veterans with TBI, faculty, researchers, and WPAs can also safely assume that many will have the compounded disabilities of both TBI and PTSD. According to the book *Invisible Wounds of War: Psychological and Cognitive Injuries, Their Consequences, and Services to Assist Recovery* (Ramchand et al. 2008, xxi), nearly 300,000 veterans experience PTSD. PTSD was not recognized officially as a disorder until 1980, although its roots are fully entrenched in the relation between military and traumatic experiences, particularly in reference to the Vietnam War (Reynolds, Mair, and Fischer 1995). The American Psychiatric Association's (1994) Diagnostic and Statistical Manual of Mental Disorders-IV posits the essential feature or criterion of PTSD to be "the development of characteristic symptoms following exposure to an extreme traumatic stressor involving direct personal experience of an event that involves actual or threatened death or serious injury, or other threat to one's physical integrity" (424) in which the "person's response involved intense fear, helplessness, or horror" (428). The individual affected by PTSD persistently reexperiences the traumatic event, avoids stimuli associated with the trauma, and persistently experiences symptoms of increased arousal such as outbursts of anger, hyperviligence, exaggerated startle response, difficulty concentrating, irritability, and difficulty falling or staying asleep (American Psychiatric Association 1994, 428).

The relationship between the Americans with Disabilities Act (ADA) (1990) and medical definitions of both TBI and PTSD is also important to note. The ADA defines disability as "a physical or mental impairment that substantially limits one or more major life activities" or "record of such an impairment" or "being regarded as having such an impairment" (Americans with Disabilities Act 1990, Section 3.1). Because the ADA Amendments Acts of 2008 "added 'concentrating' and 'thinking' to its expanded, non-inclusive list of 'major life activities,' PTSD has become an acknowledged disability" (Shackelford quoted in Weigel and Miller 2011, 30). In the world of institutionally sanctioned accommodations, however, acknowledgment only counts if the veteran has been "officially" diagnosed. The recent push for changing PTSD to posttraumatic stress *injury* (PTSI) speaks volumes in terms of the lengths the military will go to increase diagnoses through attempts to reduce stigma.[3]

The prevalence of PTSD in veterans returning from combat in Iraq and Afghanistan is difficult to assess due to the many variables that determine the most accurate percentile. PTSD is diagnosed by several different measures, each revealing different patterns of case diagnoses and prevalence, such as the Post Deployment Health Assessment questionnaire (PDHA) and the seventeen-item PTSD checklist (PCL), among others. Time of testing, instrument, and sponsoring institution play roles in determining the *demonstrable* prevalence of PTSD.

Determining the prevalence of TBI, however, is even murkier. The literature review of TBI studies provided in *Invisible Wounds* identifies only two peer-reviewed studies, both of which are aimed at determining the frequency of mTBI. Hoge et al. (2008) relied on three criteria: loss of consciousness, being dazed and/or confused, and not remembering the injury (Hoge et al. 2008; Vasterling et al. 2006). However, these tools need to be further validated (Ramchand et al. 2008, 41). *Invisible Wounds* further reveals that several themes emerged from the review of the literature concerning the prevalence of PTSD, depression, and TBI. Some of these themes include limited research on the prevalence of TBI, reliance on criteria that have not been validated for most existing studies that define cases of PTSD and depression, and a likely exclusion of a significant number of servicemembers with PTSD and depression (Ramchand et al. 2008, 47–48). That said, it is also important to note that "regardless of the sample, measurement tool, or time of assessment, combat duty and being wounded were consistently associated with positive screens for PTSD (Ramchand et al. 2008, 51). Understanding the definitional criteria for both TBI and PTSD as well as their symptom catalogues and the measures used in determining their prevalence is of great significance to WPAs. By no means does a symptom list equip instructors of composition with the means of diagnosing student-veterans in their classrooms with either TBI or PTSD. It does, however, create an awareness that might inform institutional policy, curriculum design, and classroom practice. Furthermore, administrators need to be aware of how the invisibility of these disabilities creates significant institutional problems.

For example, if student-veterans are undiagnosed for either TBI and/ or PTSD, their lack of official documentation denies their legal right to accommodations under Section 504 of the Rehabilitation Act of 1973

(Rehabilitation Act 1973; see also Russo and Osborne 2009). Consider then the student-veteran (one of the presumably thousands with mTBI that has gone undiagnosed) who returns to college. This student experiences trouble concentrating and could greatly benefit from extended time on an essay exam. Yet, because so many institutional and administrative offices are so firmly entrenched in medical models of disability that say "no accommodation without documentation," this student is denied equal access to demonstrating their abilities. If WPAs are keen to social-disability perspectives from DS that argue for teachers building strategies for access by working directly with the student-veteran (Barber-Fendley and Hamel 2004), perhaps they might provide such tools in their teacher-training programs.

In addition to being attuned to issues of cause, prevalence, and characteristic symptoms, WPAs and teachers need to be aware of the effects of TBI (and perhaps to a lesser extent PTSD) on communication. According to the National Institute of Neurological Disorders and Stroke (NINDS 2011), individuals with mild/moderate TBI "become easily confused or distracted and have problems with concentration and attention. They also have problems with higher level, so-called executive functions, such as planning, organizing, abstract reasoning, problem solving, and making judgments." In terms of language and communication, student-veterans with TBI may experience aphasia, which is defined as "difficulty with understanding and producing spoken and written language" (NINDS 2011). While researchers in speech and language pathology have devoted substantial scholarship to measuring the effects of mild to severe TBI on patients' oral speech, there remains a significant need to further investigate the effects of TBI on writing. While it might seem logical that this research rests firmly in the domain of learning-disability specialists, medical professionals, and the like—I argue that scholars in composition studies, such as Feldmeier White (2002), Barber-Fendley and Hamel (2004), and Dunn (2001), have rightly pointed to the importance of infusing this conversation with social-disability perspectives that offer alternatives to classroom and institutional practices that position difference as deficit. Barber-Fendley and Hamel (2004), for example, argue for alternative assistance programs that are housed not in student-services centers but in composition programs. While these authors do not refer to student-veterans specifically, their critique of such disabling metaphors of "leveling the playing field" is certainly relevant for student-veterans with TBI and/or PTSD.

MARKING: THE RHETORICITY OF WOUNDS

To claim TBI and/or PTSD as the "signature wound(s)" of the wars in Iraq and Afghanistan is to say these injuries "mark" a solider. Not only is it the shared experience but also the (often invisible) mark that follows the soldier back home. Etymologically, *signature wound* means "marked hurt" or "sealed injury." How university faculty, WPAs, and university officials intensify, diminish, conceal, or exacerbate these "marks" varies across campuses and across classrooms. Disability studies, with its attention to the ways in which bodies are socioculturally constructed (for better or worse), provides the most apt lens for analyzing the merits of these variations.

In the article "Posttraumatic Stress Disorder and the Returning Veteran: The Rhetorical and Narrative Challenges" by Bekah Hawrot Weigel and Lisa Detweiler Miller, the authors discuss the effects of militarized ableism[4] on returning veterans with PTSD. They cite Gregory A. Leskin, a representative from the National Center for PTSD, as stating that resilient people are less likely to develop PTSD (Weigel and Miller 2011, 30). The assumption here is that PTSD is an avoidable pathology for individuals who are strong and irrepressible, a version of ableism that appears fully couched in militarized constructions of masculinity. Weigel and Miller go on to deftly theorize the identity narratives available to returning veterans with PTSD: the Homeric hero and the ticking time bomb, a pair that prove parallel to DS conceptions of the supercrip and the invalid. Disability activists theorize the archetype of the supercrip as that individual who manages to supersede the pathology of their supposed deviant body, whereas the invalid remains the incompetent in need of piteous care. For student-veterans, occupying either of these archetypal narratives merely services the ablebodied collective, yet the denial of every component of each also proves difficult. For example, student-veterans may desire the very hypermasculinization that at once denies them, or student-veterans may very well need some serious accommodations in order to succeed in their academic careers.

John Cali (2012), blogger and veteran of OEF, writes about his struggles with identifying as someone with PTSD, stating that "the only lasting help that can be provided is through educating society on mental health in hope that the stigma changes. People feel socially uncomfortable being labeled depressed, anxious, bipolar and so on. If we can educate society we will create supportive environments for all that suffer from mental illness" ("Post Traumatic Stress Disorder To Be Renamed"). When Cali indicates that he hopes for a "supportive environment," he tacitly draws attention to the lack of support those with mental disabilities experience in social settings.

The college composition classroom as a social setting might potentially be nonsupportive if stigmatizing (or even patronizing) discourse is employed, encouraged, or allowed. Being marked as mentally disabled (as those with PTSD might be) can have significant consequences on a student's ability to be heard and valued in classroom settings. Catherine Prendergast (2001, 191) argues that a diagnosis of being mentally ill "necessarily supplants one's position as rhetor." In her recent book, *Mad at School: Rhetorics of Mental Disability and Academic Life*, Margaret Price (2011, 26) extends Prendergast's insights by stating, "We [people with mental disabilities] speak from positions that are assumed to be subhuman, even non-human; and therefore, when we speak, our words go unheeded . . . persons with mental disabilities are presumed not be competent, nor understandable, nor valuable, nor whole." Both Prendergast and Price, using social-disability perspectives, make the point that students marked mentally ill (whether institutionally or individually disclosed) have no rhetoricity; they are rhetorically disabled (Prendergast 202; Price 26). To apply this perspective to student-veterans with PTSD compels consideration of their rhetorical position in the composition classroom, perhaps in whole-class discussion, in the ways their participation is assessed, or in the ways in which they communicate with their professors.

MEDICALIZING THE STUDENT-VETERAN: DRAWING PARALLELS BETWEEN CRITIQUES OF COGNITIVE RHETORIC AND CRITIQUES OF MEDICAL PARADIGMS

Just as student-veterans with TBI/PTSD are marked in ways that stigmatize, infantilize, and/or ostracize, attempts to remediate students with disabilities are often grounded in efforts toward "normalcy," efforts fully couched in medical models of disability. As mentioned previously, Price (2011, 26) argues that "the failure to make sense, as measured against and by those with 'normal' minds means a loss of personhood." This section demonstrates that when teachers and WPAs attempt to understand student-veterans through the lens of normalcy and under the assumptions of the promise for cure, they risk the dehumanizing effects suggested earlier by Lewiecki-Wilson and Dolmage.

The American Council on Education identifies several *cognitive* difficulties that student-veterans with TBI and PTSD may experience when performing academically:

Attention and concentration difficulty;

Information and processing challenges;

Learning and memory deficits;

Sluggish abstract reasoning;

Slowed executive functions (problem solving, planning, insight/aware-
ness, sequencing).(adapted from ACE 2010, 3)

Of special interest is that the ACE report does not include the following sentence in the bulleted list but rather prints it below the list as a
rhetorical afterthought of sorts: "Other challenges often associated with
difficulty in classroom performance may include the effect of additional
stressors (home, work, unit, etc.), sleep disturbance, difficulty with time
management, and panic attacks" (ACE 2010, 3). While this choice of
arrangement may seem inconsequential, it reveals an emphasis on cognitive difficulties at the expense of more sociopolitical attentions. This
rhetorical move also manages to obfuscate the connection between academic performance and students' social-material conditions.[5] Much of
the current research aimed at "helping" to meet the needs of student-
veterans reinforces a medical model of disability that foregrounds cognitive, functional, and skill-based literacies as opposed to political, social,
and cultural challenges that administrators, teachers, and staff need to
meet. Bruce Horner (2000, 36) points to this elision of material social-
ity when he writes of the actual lacks experienced by many college students (a lack I believe especially applicable to student-veterans): "lack
of time, lack of health and health insurance, lack of child care, lack of
sleep." This is not to suggest that the cognitive realities of TBI should
not be addressed and attended to, a task itself in need of significant further research. Rather, it demonstrates that a unifocal approach to com-
pensating and/or remediating each cognitive lack associated with TBI/
PTSD only addresses one component of an incredibly complex set of
challenges, experiences, and expectations.

For example, in the PBS documentary *Where Soldiers Come From*
(2011), Matt "Bodi" Beaudoin discusses his struggles with TBI, which
resulted from an IED detonation during his service in Afghanistan. He
states, "For me, what I'm dealing with is like, sleep problems and head-
aches . . . [and] now they're not treating TBI, they're treating the symptoms that you get for it." What the ACE list reveals as only worthy of a
small byline is, in fact, Bodi's greatest struggle. Another veteran in the
film, Dom, associates extreme irritability with his TBI, stating that "it's
tough to try and tell people that I'm an antisocial nutcase that doesn't
want to go anywhere. You don't want people to know that. You want to

find out for yourself then deal with it." Bodi's and Dom's narratives indicate that information and processing challenges, while they may have biological indicators (and with such biological evidence merit medical scrutiny for treatment options), do not adequately capture their experiences living with TBI. This is all to say that when teachers and administrators seek to effectively meet the needs of their student-veteran populations, such efforts must be guided by a much more dynamic, social, and cultural portrait than medical rhetoric might allow.

A social-disability perspective asks that teachers not simply focus on the cognitive consequences of TBI on an individual writer's ability to construct sentences but rather deeply concern themselves with how the composition classroom serves as a place in which the student's rhetorical considerations are imbued with the politics of personal experience. While the disciplinary history of composition studies may indicate past endorsement of cognitive models of writing and writing processes, those who identify more with social-epistemic rhetorics would most likely agree that to relegate all cognitive issues associated with TBI to medical professionals and all psychological issues to psychiatric professionals is to reinforce medical models of disability. Furthermore, drawing on the work of socially minded scholars, we can map a vastly theorized conversation in rhetoric and composition (the ideological underpinnings of composition curricula) onto a central tenet of DS, namely the rejection of medical dominance over bodies that exhibit nonnormativity. This mapping is of great consequence to student-veterans in that it prevents WPAs from *once again* relying on cognitive models to achieve the pedagogical goals prescribed for students cast in a position of lack (see Feldmeier White 2002; Rose 1988). For example, documentation of TBI for a student-veteran may result in accommodations for extended testing time and a distraction-free testing environment. Relying on a medical/cognitive model (such as the one that informs these accommodations as a one-fits-all solution for students with TBI) ignores the fact that these accommodations don't really apply to the composition classroom. In such a situation, if a writing instructor assumes that a student-veteran with TBI is "handled" by the medicalized system of accommodations set out by disability-service centers,[6] their reliance on such models reinscribes the student as "lacking," in need of a quick fix from an outside party, a fix rendered moot in the process-based writing classroom. The instructor misses an opportunity to engage a social-disability perspective on how to increase access and promote inclusivity not only for this student but for all students in the class.

Any scholar, researcher, administrator, or teacher wary of medical models of disability will approach the automatic placement of any student with a "condition" into the hands of medical expertise as cause for concern. Medical expertise relies heavily (if not exclusively) on the ontology of cure, the Western, linear healing script. This curative-process model neatly delineates the spectrum that tirelessly pushes toward resolution, health, normality, and ablebodiedness. Indeed, it is such an epistemological commonplace to privilege the process of "health" seeking that any critique of medical aims seems an abrupt, antithetical resistance typified by those individuals who can only be described as irrational. However, as many writers, scholars, and individuals with disabilities have so aptly argued, the absolute power of medical expertise in Western culture erases the sociopolitical contexts in which so many "ill" people find themselves violently enmeshed. In his critique of both the expressivist and cognitivist models of process-based rhetorical models, Berlin's (1987) oft-cited historical account of our field reveals some telling parallels with medical-model discourse. His discussion of cognitive rhetorics critiques the normative cognitive process of writing, implicating those who research writing as a stagnant, cognitive process of invention and development. He summarizes that in cognitive rhetorics,

> the work of the writing teacher, then, is to understand these basic cognitive structures and the way they develop in order to provide experiences for students that encourage *normal* development and *prevent* structural *distortions*. The teacher intervenes in the composing process of students in order to ensure that their cognitive structures are functioning *normally*, thus enhancing their ability to arrive at *truth* in examining the external world. (Berlin 1987, 16; emphasis added)

The normalizing imperatives of cognitive approaches to writing are analogous to the normalizing imperatives of medical discourse on disability. Tom Fox's (1999) book *Defending Access: A Critique of Standards in Higher Education* is likewise suspicious of cognitive rhetoric and applies it also to conceptions of access. He writes that "we fall into the trap of imagining that language standards and social boundaries are one and the same (Fox 1999, 6). Jay Dolmage (2008), in his essay "Mapping Composition: Inviting Disability in the Front Door," builds on Fox's critique, writing that

> normalizing students with disabilities not only perpetuates the myth of typical or natural learning, it also reinforces standards that, even when mastered, do not offer greater access. Instead, the process of normalizing (making typical or natural) the process of writing is used in service of exclusion, delineating the "abnormal." (Dolmage 2008, 17)

The commonalities shared by medical models of disability and cognitive rhetorics include naturalizing or standardizing[7] conceptions and constructions of language and literacy, normalizing the structures of thought in language, and the empirically universalizing effects of mapping the linear progression of language development.[8]

Social-epistemic rhetoric, on the other hand, aims toward "enabl[ing] students to realize the diversity of world views within our society—the different ways in which language is used to organize experience" (Berlin 1987, 170). Likewise, DS resists the tendency to establish normative constructions of rhetorical fitness, seeking rather to understand and value difference among bodies rather than rank and file them according to orders of normalcy.

Tracing these parallels enables a new discussion of how student-veterans might/can/should be positioned, constructed, assisted, and valued in college composition classrooms. The inattention to difference (often mediated by a variety of ideological apparatuses) exhibited by both cognitive models and medical models may result in addressing veterans, particularly those with TBI/PTSD, as students in a position of lack. Therefore, all pedagogical (and institutional, for that matter) efforts must be aimed at filling the deficit they embody. From a social-epistemic perspective, the relegation of dysfunction to a distortion of cognitive processes ignores the ideological influences at work in each student's lived experience. From a social-disability perspective, positioning the pedagogical strategies for students with disabilities as recuperative reinforces the normate[9] student population. Rather than simply normalizing or medicalizing the veterans with TBI/PTSD who come into our composition classrooms, it is necessary to be sensitive to their political, ideological, medical, and cultural positioning and to avoid those teaching strategies that attempt to position student-veterans as disqualified, dysfunctional, and/or deviant. Again, all this is not to say that TBI and PTSD do not warrant serious medical considerations; my argument suggests that to meet the needs of student-veterans, composition instructors must be attuned to the ways in which particular medical/cognitive-based rhetorical models remain inadequate. We should look instead to social-epistemic models and toward methodological conceptions typical in DS such as of demystifying normalcy, critiquing medical models, and redefining rhetorical fitness (Dolmage and Lewiecki-Wilson 2010).

For example, in thinking of how rhetorical fitness is defined in the composition classroom, looking at potential "problems" for student-veterans with TBI is revelatory. The American Speech-Language-Hearing

Association (2013) lists several impacts on spoken and written language for individuals with TBI. These impacts include poor sentence formatting, trouble concentrating, forgetfulness, and trouble with multiple meanings. To flip these impacts in terms of rhetorical fitness is to define a "good writer" as an excellent sentence formatter, focused, nuanced, and someone with a good memory. However, resisting medical models and cognitive rhetorics requires that composition instructors be willing to adjust their expectations of fitness to make room for variant ways of communicating, evaluating, teaching, and accommodating. The adaptations called for here are not meant to erase the above criteria for rhetorical fitness; (for some) memory and focus are key to successful writing. But they're not *essential* criteria upon which to evaluate success in a composition course. The realization that some students with disabilities don't have easy access to such criteria calls for a reconceptualization of performative objectives. However, this resistance requires critical analysis of a pedagogy based on lack[10] as well as an affirmation of the composition instructor's expertise regarding pedagogical pathways for particular students with disabilities rather than simply leaving it to Veterans Affairs, disability resource centers, or medical professionals.

In an effort to humanize my critique of a pedagogy of cognitive lack, a specific example of a writer with TBI proves useful. Anthony Johnston (2011) is a veteran diagnosed with TBI who also considers himself a writer, publishing both before and after his service (and consequently, before and after his TBI diagnosis). In his essay "Not What I Had in Mind," he paints a clear portrait of the complexities of TBI's effects not only on writing but also on his relationships, work life, self-esteem, and much more. He writes:

> I used to tell stories, and some of them were even true. I used to write without any effort at all . . . I came home from work one day and told my wife that long married friends were getting divorced and the next day I told her the same story, oblivious to the fact that she already knew. And a thousand other stories, all with the same beginning and end happened to me, around me, and through me. And I couldn't see the forest for the trees. It's like being a spectator watching the movie about your life, but you are completely amazed by what happens after you think it can't get any worse. But it does. (Johnston 2011)

The above passage is not meant as exemplar of the effects of TBI on writing. In fact, it's meant to do the exact opposite. This is Anthony's experience. He identified as a writer before. He struggles with memory. Repetition. He has a wife. He remained undiagnosed until long after the injury. All of these variables contribute to the complexities of his experience with TBI. Researchers, writers, and teachers in the field of rhetoric and composition pride ourselves on tireless attention to the contexts in which individual writers find themselves. To construct a cognitive-based pedagogy aimed at filling in the gaps for TBI sufferers essentially suggests that all individuals with TBIs deserve equal treatment and that treatment shall be defined by medical expertise.

I offer this example not only to humanize but also to make clear that while Anthony is not a college composition student, his story affirms that a pedagogy aimed at strictly addressing cognitive lacks (i.e., assigning tasks and activities geared toward increasing memory skills or improving problem-solving functions) remains fundamentally inadequate due to its lack of acknowledgment of the sociocultural dynamics of TBI on any individual's approach to a given rhetorical situation. In other words, Anthony's struggles with memory were not solved cognitively per se; rather he processed these "lapses" emotionally and socially alongside those closest to him, namely his wife and his friend.

While Johnston's case involves TBI, student-veterans with PTSD are equally disserviced by cognitive-based pedagogies. While some cognitive address might be appropriate (and by cognitive address I mean something equivalent to functional-literacy-skill rehearsal), instructors better serve student-veterans by being attuned to the sociopolitical conditions that determine their classroom success. In 2008, *NeuroRehabiliation* published an empirical study that reported on the college experiences of students with TBI. In an effort to document the challenges of this student demographic, the study revealed that a majority of the study participants felt as if others did not understand the problems they faced.[11] Furthermore, a majority of the participants reported that they felt "overwhelmed" in the classroom environment and that they were (for the most part) unaware of the disability services available to them (Kennedy, Krause, and Turkstra 2008). This study makes clear that merely attempting to address the cognitive "deficits" of student-veterans with TBI does not effectively address the challenges they meet in the college classroom.[12]

This chapter argues that teachers and WPAs striving to meet the urgent need expressed by Ackerman, DiRamio, and Mitchell should inform themselves with perspectives offered by scholars in disability studies. The best practice suggested is the adoption of a social-disability perspective that allows writing programs and classrooms to be attuned and sensitive to the complex cultural experiences of student-veterans who have TBI and/or PTSD. Adopting such perspectives can keep us wary of overmedicalizing the veterans in our classrooms. It can help us better combat the oppressive and ableist stigmas so often associated with the identity marker of "disabled." And, most importantly, it can help us recognize student-veterans as human beings who deserve to be valued, not as symptoms or disorders that need to be fixed.

Notes

1. Throughout this essay, I use the combined term "TBI/PTSD." It is important to note that TBI is not always coupled with PTSD or vice versa. By no means do I mean to conflate these profoundly different experiences of disability (both in terms of short-term and/or long-term effects) and this stylistic move should not be understood in that way. When I use this slash, it is *only* to avoid the repetition of "TBI and/or PTSD" throughout the piece.
2. For more on the history of disability in the United States, see *The New Disability History: American Perspectives* edited by Paul K. Longmore and Lauri Umansky (Longmore and Umansky 2001).
3. Army General Peter Chiarelli called for this change, arguing that the term *disorder* "has the connotation of being something that is a pre-existing problem that an individual has" prior to service and "makes the person seem weak" (quoted in Fong 2012). This change is regarded as ineffective by blogger and veteran with PTSD John Cali (2012) in his post titled "Post Traumatic Stress Disorder to be Renamed in the Military." It makes me wonder about what such a change would mean for those individuals diagnosed with PTSD as a result of noncombat related trauma, such as rape. I think a strong argument could be made that General Chiarelli's efforts to reduce stigma only serve to highlight the intense aversion to weakness so intensely proselytized in military discourse.
4. Ableism is a form of social prejudice (often resulting in discriminatory practice) against people with disabilities. Weigel and Miller (2011) nuance this general understanding of ableism with a discussion of how it presents itself in military rhetoric, arguing that the military insists on privileging the able body, particularly in regards to strength, masculinity, and resilience.
5. Bruce Horner (2000) makes a compelling argument regarding particular composition pedagogies' inattention to the social-material conditions of students in his book *Terms of Work for Composition: A Materialist Critique*. See the "Students" chapter for the critical examination of cognitive lack.
6. It is important to note that many of the accommodations offered through disability-service centers (including the ones mentioned in this example) are absolutely crucial for students with disabilities, and efforts to gain these accommodations in higher education have been hard fought within the disability rights movement. That being said, my point with this example is to make it clear that an overreliance on an accommodation-based system results in missed opportunities for understanding the complexities of disability experience and of pedagogies that might increase inclusivity and access. It must not be assumed that systematized accommodation automatically means access for students with disabilities. The lack of teacher input in this assumption is likewise problematic, as Feldmeier White (2002) also argues.
7. Lennard Davis (2002) traces the linguistic history and etymology of the use of *normalcy* (as opposed to *normality*) and linguistic standardization in his book *Bending over Backwards: Disability, Dismodernism, and Other Difficult Positions*.
8. Berlin (1987) also critiques the expressivist model of process-based writing instruction for its insistence on the individual writer as the origin of Truth, an insistence

couched both in Platonic metaphysics and nineteenth-century Romanticism (11). The most telling parallel at work here is in the positioning of the individual. Just as in expressivist models of composition the individual is the terministic screen through which all knowledge about "good" writing is filtered, the nonnormative body of the individual with a disability is the lens through which all knowledge about abnormality is drawn. The disability is seen as a problem of the individual, not as the sociospatially produced symptom of a larger cultural hegemony of ablebodiedness. One glaring difference here, of course, is that in expressivist theories of writing, the individual is privileged. In medical models of disability, the individual is pathologized. That said, the erasure of sociopolitical context is the parallel of most use to my argument here.

9.   In the book *Extraordinary Bodies: Figuring Physical Disability in American Culture and Literature*, Garland-Thomson (1997) defines normate as "the constructed identity of those who, by way of the bodily configurations and cultural capital they assume, can step into a position of authority and wield the power it grants them" (8).

10. For an extended discussion of pedagogies based on lack and deficit representations of students, see Marguerite H. Helmers's (1994) book *Writing Students: Composition, Testimonials, and Representations of Students.*

11. It is important to note that this study is not necessarily veteran specific. That said, I argue that the challenges identified are not only applicable to student-veterans but also significantly more complex and/or intense.

12. In thinking through just what sociopolitical conditions to be aware of, it is also useful to note that lack of social support and increased "life stress" are two increased risk factors for PTSD (Brewin et al.2000).

References

Ackerman, Robert, David DiRamio, and Regina L. Garza Mitchell. 2009. "Transitions: Combat Veterans as College Students." Special issue, *New Directions for Student Services* 2009 (126): 5–14. http://dx.doi.org/10.1002/ss.311.

American Speech-Language-Hearing Association (2013). "Traumatic Brain Injury (TBI)." American Speech-Language-Hearing Association: Disorders and Diseases. http://www.asha.org/public/speech/disorders/tbi/.

American Council on Education. Association on Higher Education and Disability. 2010. "*Accommodating Student Veterans with Traumatic Brain Injury and Post-traumatic Stress Disorder: Tips for Campus Faculty and Staff.*" Report from the Veterans Success Jam, Washington, DC.

Americans with Disabilities Act. 1990. 42 United States Constitution Code Chapter 126.

American Psychiatric Association. 1994. "Posttraumatic Stress Disorder." In *Diagnostic and Statistical Manual of Mental Disorders IV*. Washington, DC: American Psychiatric Association.

Barber-Fendley, Kimber, and Chris Hamel. 2004. "A New Visibility: An Argument for Alternative Assistance Writing Programs for Students with Learning Disabilities." *College Composition and Communication* 55 (3):504–35.

Berlin, James. 1987. *Rhetoric and Reality: Writing Instruction in American Colleges, 1900–1985*. Carbondale: Southern Illinois University Press.

Brewin, Chris R., Bernice Andrews, and John D. Valentine. 2000. "Meta-analysis of Risk Factors for Posttraumatic Stress Disorder in Trauma Exposed Adults." *Journal of Consulting and Clinical Psychology* 68 (5): 748–66. http://dx.doi.org/10.1037/0022-006X.68.5.748.

Cali, John. 2012. *Veteran's Guide to PTSD, TBI, and Unemployment: A Blog for Veterans by a Veteran* (blog). http://veteransguide.blogspot.com/2011/11/post-traumatic-stress-disorder-to-be.html.

Davis, Lennard. 1995. *Enforcing Normalcy: Disability, Deafness and the Body*. London: Verso.
Davis, Lennard. 2002. *Bending Over Backwards: Disability, Dismodernism, and Other Difficult Positions*. New York: New York University Press.
Defense and Veterans Brain Injury Center (DVBIC). 2011. "Care Coordination." Service Members and Veterans. http://dvbic.dcoe.mil/audience/service-members-veterans.
Dolmage, Jay. 2008. "Mapping Composition: Inviting Disability in the Front Door." In *Disability and the Teaching of Writing: A Critical Sourcebook*, edited by Cynthia Lewiecki-Wilson and Brenda Jo Brueggemann, 14–27. New York: Bedford/St. Martin's.
Dolmage, Jay, and Cynthia Lewiecki-Wilson. 2010. "Refiguring Rhetorica: Linking Feminist Rhetoric and Disability Studies." In *Rhetorica in Motion: Feminist Methods and Methodologies*, edited by Eileen L. Schell and K. J. Rawson, 23–38. Pittsburgh: University of Pittsburgh Press.
Dunn, Patricia Ann. 2001. *Talking, Sketching, Moving: Multiple Literacies in the Teaching of Writing*. Portsmouth, NH: Boynton/Cook.
Feldmeier White, Linda. 2002. "Learning Disability, Pedagogies, and Public Discourse." *College Composition and Communication* 53 (4): 705–38. http://dx.doi.org/10.2307/1512122.
Fong, Kanani. 2012. "More Than Just a Name Change: PTSD to PTSI." *War Retreat.org*. http://warretreat.org/2012/01/12/more-than-just-a-name-change-ptsd-to-ptsi/.
Fox, Tom. 1999. *Defending Access: A Critique of Standards in Higher Education*. Portsmouth, NH: Boynton/Cook. http://dx.doi.org/10.2307/358972.
Garland-Thomson, Rosemarie. 1997. *Extraordinary Bodies: Figuring Physical Disability in American Culture and Literature*. New York: Columbia University Press.
Helmers, Margeurite H. 1994. "Can't Get No Satisfaction." In *Writing Students: Composition Testimonials and Representations of Students*, 19–44. Albany: State University of New York Press.
Hoge, Charles W., Dennis McGurk, Jeffrey L. Thomas, Anthony L. Cox, Charles C. Engel, and Carl A. Castro. 2008. "Mild Traumatic Brain Injury in US Soldiers Returning from Iraq." *New England Journal of Medicine* 358 (5): 453–63. http://dx.doi.org/10.1056/NEJMoa072972.
Horner, Bruce. 2000. *Terms of Work for Composition: A Materialist Critique*. New York: State University of New York Press.
Johnston, Anthony. 2011. "Not What I Had in Mind." *One Veteran's TBI Story*. http://ginacarson.com/ud/disabilities/veteran-tbi-story/.
Kato, Lorrie N. 2010. *The Psychological Adjustments of Veterans Returning from Afghanistan and Iraq*. PhD diss., Fielding Graduate University.
Kennedy, Mary R. T., Miriam O. Krause, and Lyn S. Turkstra. 2008. "An Electronic Survey About College Experiences After Traumatic Brain Injury." *NeuroRehabilitation* 23:511–20.
Linton, Simi. 1998. *Claiming Disability*. New York: New York University Press.
Longmore, Paul, and Lauri Umansky, eds. 2001. *The New Disability History: American Perspectives*. New York: New York University Press.
Miller, T. Christian, and Daniel Zwerdling. 2010. "Military Still Failing to Diagnose, Treat Brain Injuries." National Public Radio. June 8.
Milliken, C. S., J. L. Auchterlonie, and C. W. Hoge. 2007. "Longitudinal Assessment of Mental Health Problems among Active and Reserve Component Soldiers Returning from the Iraq War." *Journal of the American Medical Association* 298 (18): 2141–48. http://dx.doi.org/10.1001/jama.298.18.2141.
National Council on Disability. 2009. *Invisible Wounds: Servicing Service Members and Veterans with PTSD and TBI*. http://www.ncd.gov/publications/2009/march042009/.
NINDS. 2011. *Traumatic Brain Injury: Hope through Research*. 5:30.Bethesda, MD: National Institute of Health, National Institute of Neurological Disorders and Stroke. http://www.ninds.nih.gov/disorders/tbi/tbi_htr.pdf.

Oliver, Mike. 1990. "The Individual and Social Models of Disability." Paper presented at the Joint Workshop of the Living Options Group and the Research Unit of the Royal College of Physicians. London: United Kingdom.

Prendergast, Catherine. 2001. "Rhetorics of Mental Disability." In *Embodied Rhetorics: Disability in Language and Culture*, edited by James C. Wilson and Cynthia Lewiecki-Wilson, 45–60. Carbondale: Southern Illinois University Press.

Price, Margaret. 2011. *Mad at School: Rhetorics of Mental Disability and Academic Life.* Ann Arbor, MI: University of Michigan Press.

Radford, A. 2009. *Military Service Members and Veterans in Higher Education: What the New GI Bill May Mean for Postsecondary Institutions.* Washington, DC: American Council on Education.

Ramchand, Rajeev, Benjamin R. Karney, Karen Chan Osilla, Rachel M. Burns, and Leah Barnes Caldarone. 2008. "Prevalence of PTSD, Depression, and TBI among Returning Servicemembers." In *Invisible Wounds of War: Psychological and Cognitive Injuries, Their Consequences, and Services to Assist Recovery*, edited by Terri Tanielian and Lisa H. Jaycox, 35–85. Pittsburgh: Rand.

Rehabilitation Act. 1973. 29 United States Constitution Code Chapter 794.

Reynolds, John Frederick, David C. Mair, and Pamela C. Fischer. 1995. *Writing and Reading Mental Health Records: Issues and Analysis in Professional Writing and Scientific Rhetoric.* 2nd ed. Mahwah, NJ: Lawrence Erlbaum.

Rose, Mike. 1988. "Narrowing the Mind and Page: Remedial Writers and Cognitive Reductionism." *College Composition and Communication* 39 (3): 267–302. http://dx.doi .org/10.2307/357468.

Russo, Charles J., and Allan G. Osborne Jr. 2009. *Section 504 and the ADA.* Thousand Oaks, CA: Sage.

Shackelford, Allan L. 2009. "Documenting the Needs of Student Veterans with Disabilities: Intersection Roadblocks, Solutions, and Legal Realities." Special issue, *Journal of Postsecondary Education and Disability* 22 (1): 36–42.

Shea, Kevin Peter. 2010. *The Effects of Combat Related Stress on Learning in an Academic Environment: A Qualitative Case Study.* PhD diss., Kansas State University.

, Terri, and Lisa H. Jaycox, eds. 2008. *Invisible Wounds of War: Psychological and Cognitive Injuries, Their Consequences, and Services to Assist Recovery.* Pittsburgh: Rand. http:// dx.doi.org/10.1037/e527612010-001.

Vasterling, Jennifer J., Susan P. Proctor, Paul Amoroso, Robert Kane, Timothy Hereen, Roberta F. White. 2006. "Neuropsychological Outcomes of Army Personnel Following Deployment to the Iraq War." *Journal of the American Medical Association* 296 (5): 519–29. http://dx.doi.org/10.1001/jama.296.5.519.

Weigel, Bekah Hawrot, and Lisa Detweiler Miller. 2011. "Posttraumatic Stress Disorder and the Returning Veteran: The Rhetorical and Narrative Challenges." *Open Words: Access and English Studies*, 5 (1): 29–37.

Where Soldiers Come From. 2011. Dir. Heather Courtney. Austin, TX: Quincy Hill Films. Film.

8
EXPLORING STUDENT-VETERAN EXPECTATIONS ABOUT COMPOSING
Motivations, Purposes, and the Influence of Trauma on Composing Practices

Ashly Bender

In April 2011, from "somewhere deep in the heart of Afghanistan," came yet another viral music video remake by a group of deployed military servicepersons. The participating personnel gave their most intense gazes, worked their dance moves, and lip-synced along with Britney Spears in her hit song "Hold It against Me"—all against the backdrop of their Afghan landscape ("Hold It Against Me 266 Rein Marines Official Version" 2011). Both American and British news sources quickly latched on, commenting on and supporting the work of these military service-members. Just four days after the video was published on YouTube, the *Daily Mail Online* asserted that the video had already earned 50,000 views (Blake, *Mail Online*, April 22, 2011). Four months later, it had over four million. But this video is just one in a genre common among deployed personnel. Almost exactly one year earlier, a remake of Lady Gaga's "Telephone" had a similar moment in the spotlight, and a search of YouTube for any of these videos links to multiple versions of these songs and many others ("Telephone Remake" 2010).

It should come as little surprise that military servicepersons make use of these technologies during their deployments given the prevalence of digital and social media in our society. For many, social-networking sites in some form have been a significant part of their lives—how they connect with their friends, family, and the world in general. These technologies allow military personnel to engage a broader interactive audience that earlier forms of communication, such as letters home or editorials, did not allow. In *The Blog of War*, Matthew Currier Burden (2006) uses early blog entries from military servicepersons in Iraq and their families

DOI: 10.7330/9780874219425.c008

to demonstrate how blogs specifically allow these populations to process their experiences and communicate with one another. Beyond blogs, though, there's a clear presence of military personnel on a wide range of social-media sites, including Facebook and YouTube.

The consistent presence of these individuals on social-media sites belies a perceived need among military servicemembers for these technologies. Given that these spaces are communication spaces, there is a considerable amount of literacy practice embedded in these spaces, which in turn raises questions about the purpose and value servicemembers may imagine for the texts created there. The most obvious purpose seems to be to stay connected to friends and loved ones back home. However, other motivations may be underconsidered, such as dealing with traumatic experiences, especially in the case of digital compositions posted on social media. This motivation is increasingly likely, even if it is not a primary purpose, in light of recent research by the Pew Research Center (2011) that finds that nearly half the veterans involved in the Iraq and Afghanistan conflicts claim to have lived through a traumatic experience. The larger purpose of this essay is to consider, first, how this motivation may work in the context of composing digital texts while deployed and, second, how those prior experiences and practices may influence student-veterans' expectations in the composition classroom. In this exploration, this project considers three major aspects of composing as a therapeutic strategy, as asserted by prominent psychologists, and how those aspects may connect with composing for the classroom.

TRAUMA STUDIES AND DIGITAL SOCIAL MEDIA

In the field of trauma studies, composing is common strategy for managing traumatic experiences. This strategy is popular because scholars and psychologists in this field identify a traumatic experience as one that breaks the rules and expectations of established personal and societal narratives (Herman 1992; McFarlane and Yehuda 1996; van der Kolk 1996). In this understanding, established narratives are the expectations members of a culture hold based on the rules, guidelines, and stories that are told in that culture (Herman 1992; van der Kolk 1996). For example, it is the role of parents to protect their children, so experiences in which children perceive that their parents are harming them or allowing harm to come to them are often interpreted as traumatic events. Composing about these experiences then can be effective for coping with trauma because it offers individuals the opportunity to fit their experiences back into a comprehensible narrative (Herman 1992).

In addition, as a therapeutic strategy, composing also works to achieve three major goals, primarily developed by trauma psychologist Judith Herman (1992): develop a reliable social network, develop a language and narrative space for the experience, and engage a critical audience. Importantly, the medium for this therapeutic composing strategy is not defined, allowing individuals to select the medium most appropriate to their situations and needs. While the medium may be open, composing for and with social media is one option that fits especially well with the three major goals of therapeutic composing.

One obvious connection here is that social-media networks are often important communities for their members, and establishing a reliable social network is the first goal for managing and preventing posttraumatic stress. This reliable social network is crucial because the members of the network are able to help the individual process the experience into a comprehensible narrative and they are able to intercede if the individual seems to not be managing the effects of the experience (Herman 1992; Shalev 1996). Psychologist Arieh Y. Shalev (1996, 87) explains that in a preventative approach to traumatic stress, preparation with a reliable social network can moderate the initial reaction to the traumatic experience because "it reduces uncertainty, increases one's sense of control, and teaches automatic responses that are less readily eroded under stress." For military servicepersons, training often offers some of this preparation formally, while the bonds and relationships of organizational units and teams offer some preparation informally. In an approach similar to this preventative strategy, Herman (1992) incorporates the strong support network into her three-step recovery plan by emphasizing the importance of reconnecting after experiencing a trauma. Herman reports that trauma survivors often pull away from those around them for a variety of reasons, including shame, inability to discuss the experiences, and the belief that others wouldn't understand. This constriction from social interaction also offers them the control of their surroundings that was lost during the triggering experience. By engaging in positive and supportive relationships, the social network can help survivors combat the various reactions to the experience and reenter the world around them. Ultimately, a consistent social network provides an audience for the coping strategies of the acute stress response and the possibility for crucial feedback if coping strategies become ineffective.

Fortunately, digital-studies scholarship has shown us that one of the primary advantages of digital media and social networking is that these technologies offer users the opportunity to develop strong and supportive social networks (Davies 2006; Guzzetti 2006; Roozen 2009). Also, these sites can be freeing spaces because they seem to provide an opportunity to evade the gaze of perceived authorities, and thus, users can be more candid (Davies 2006). The sites overall are seen as safe spaces for users to interact with others in their discourse communities even though many of the sites are technically still available to the wider public. This safety is often protected by the site users through both explicit and implicit strategies for accepting new users and marking insiders and outsiders (Davies 2006). In these safe community spaces, users can feel more comfortable creating meaningful relationships because they feel connected to and invested in a reliable and responsive audience.

The reliable social network in stress management is more than just a collection of friends, however. This group also works to reaffirm and negotiate experiences and reactions, according to Herman (1992). Online social networks offer this kind of feedback. When users display their sites and other digital products, their fellow community members offer them a range of supportive and critical feedback, a process that reaffirms the users' membership in that community and the relationships therein. Bronwyn Williams (2009) illustrates this point in his study of young website designers who purposefully choose the images, music, and other features of their pages to share their identity, evoke particular reactions, and engage their viewers. In addition, they spend extensive time viewing and interacting with their friends' pages. This behavior can be seen across a variety of social platforms, not just personal web pages such as MySpace or Facebook. For example, in addition to his main argument, Kevin Roozen's (2009) study, "'Fan-Ficing English Studies': A Case Study Exploring the Interplay of Vernacular Literacies and Disciplinary Engagement," demonstrates how fan-fiction communities pride themselves on their mentoring structure, which includes critical and repeated feedback on users' work. For deployed military members, composing and communicating on social-media sites allows them to stay in contact with their reliable social network by offering a space to maintain those important connections.

Composing for social media also matches with the second major goal of preventing and treating traumatic stress: developing language and narrative space for the experience. As mentioned earlier, the reason an experience is traumatic is because the individual is not able to reconcile the experience with their societal or personal expectations for the situation (Herman 1992; van der Kolk 1996). By developing language and narrative space, individuals are able to name their experiences in the context of existing and evolving narratives. Although many strategies have been developed for this process, one common approach is the use of scriptotherapy, or writing therapy, which effectively blends both the language and narrative-space needs of the survivor. Scriptotherapy and a reliable support network can both work to facilitate the discussion of the experience and give voice to reactions resulting from managing a traumatic experience (Herman 1992).

Although writing therapy is often associated with journaling or other kinds of traditional writing, digital-media composition offers similar opportunities for creators to develop the language and narrative space for their experiences. For example, video composition, which will be considered in more depth below, is similar to traditional composing in that it includes concept development, narrative planning, collaboration, and audience awareness. The decisions made in each of these stages require the detailed and global attention to the topic that psychologists claim facilitates the management of psychological distress (Herman 1992; van der Kolk 1996).

Sometimes generating original words and descriptions of an experience can be difficult, though, especially if that experience is traumatic In their 2010 *Kairos* article, "Diogenes, Dogfaced Soldiers, and Deployment Music Videos," Geoffrey Carter and Bill Williamson hint at this possibility by demonstrating how, in multiple examples of videos posted to YouTube by deployed military personnel, the creators of the videos selected songs with lyrics that can be repurposed to apply to the deployed context (Carter and Williamson 2010). These lyrics often recall or reference very real experiences for the military servicemembers creating these remixed videos.

The popularity of remix in digital composition, in fact, offers the opportunity for a wide range of broad structures to begin from when working to develop language and narrative space for traumatic experiences. It is not just words, lyrics or otherwise, that offer this structure. Erica Rosenfeld Halverson (2010, 2361) broadens Carter and Williamson's discussion by arguing that video compositions offer even more advantages than traditional compositions because "meaning is constructed not just with individual modes, but also in the ways that the modes interact with one another and what is created as a result." Thus, the action and images in the video also work to repurpose the words and allow for a richer development of language and narrative space for the experience. Overall, digital compositions create a unique opportunity to create a robust narrative space by capitalizing on multiple modes rather than privileging a certain mode as traditional print composition often does.

In considering the previous two aspects of therapeutic composing and its connection with digital social-media composing, focus has been on the individual and the close social network of friends who are sympathetic even when critical. The third important goal of therapeutic composing involves engaging a critical public that is, in contrast to the reliable social network, not as familiar and is much more likely to disagree or respond negatively to the individual's words and work. Judith Herman (1992) explains that this third factor is not essential for all those who experience trauma, but some do feel compelled to engage a wider network than their core social network. Affecting this wider public may be particularly important when trauma survivors feel their larger societal narratives have been significantly violated in addition to their personal narratives. To reconcile this violation, they seek recognition and validation from their cultural community in a process Herman (1992, 207) labels the "survivor mission." Those who engage the survivor mission hope to affect the thoughts, beliefs, and actions of the larger community in response to the survivors' particular trauma, rather than just addressing their core social network. Often, survivors attempt to achieve this goal by joining a social-justice group or a support organization for fellow trauma survivors. In some cases, though, survivors seek to reach an even broader public audience and thus opt to publish their experiences, either through traditional literary publishing routes or using social-media venues, such as YouTube.

YouTube is an especially useful social-networking site for reaching a wide public audience because, as Julia Davies and Guy Merchant emphasize, YouTube has a more "public, 'marketplace' type of feel" in comparison to other social networks. In turn, "one is always aware of the presence of others." This more public feel is created in part by the layout of YouTube, which heightens users' awareness of the possibility of interacting with others who are both supportive of and opposed to their identity, message, and presence. Military servicepersons posting videos to YouTube are likely to understand that while YouTube offers a user-friendly way to communicate with their core networks, they can also earn a broader recognition of their experiences and responses in this network. The videos and the servicemembers are necessarily opened to public critique (Davies and Merchant 2009, 58).

This variety of users and the possibility of public critique can also create opportunities for cultural citizenship. Jean Burgess and Joshua Green develop this claim by using Joke Hermes's description of cultural citizenship, which includes "'less formal everyday practices of identity construction, representation, and ideology, and implicit moral obligations and rights'" (Burgess and Green 2010, 77). Everyday practices include, for Burgess and Green (2010, 78), the "creation, showcasing, and discussion of video content on YouTube." This mobilization of cultural citizenship matches closely with Herman's description of the survivor mission, the drive to affect the beliefs and responses of a community about and to a particular kind of experience. YouTube can thus be used by servicemembers for purposes of engaging audiences, not simply for social, performative, or therapeutic purposes.

The variety of users on YouTube creates the opportunity to engage a critical audience and affect their perspectives and worldviews. As video creators open themselves and their texts to this audience, however, they must also be willing to receive both positive and negative feedback. On a site like YouTube, with such a diverse user base, negative responses can devolve into a practice called "trolling," an intense negative response from a user whose goal is often simply to upset the creator. Burgess and Green (2010, 96) assert that "learning how to 'manage' trolls, both practically and emotionally, is one of the core competencies required for effective and enjoyable participation." YouTubers must accept both positive and negative reactions when using the site. Similarly, willingness to hear negative feedback is essential to the survivor mission because it asks that survivors recognize that their experience and reactions are their own and to activate "the most mature and adaptive coping strategies of patience, anticipation, altruism, and humor" (Herman 1992, 207). Thus, we can see another similarity in the objectives of the treatment of psychological distress and the affordances of digital composition and social-networking sites.

As demonstrated above, there are strong connections between the strategies for preventing and managing traumatic stress and many aspects of composing—especially digital composing for social-media sites. While managing traumatic stress is not always the purpose or motivation, it's clear that there is an established history for this motivation. Also, given that these strategies are equally useful in prevention and treatment situations, it's possible that these factors may be at play even when they are not explicitly acknowledged. Research exploring the social media use of military servicepersons offers some insight into the extent that managing traumatic stress or traumatic experiences may be a motivation for the works this population creates.

MILITARY PERSONNEL'S USE OF SOCIAL MEDIA

Relatively few studies have considered military personnel's use of digital and/or social-media technology. The limited amount of research on this topic may be a result not only of the relative newness of accessible digital media for active-duty and deployed personnel but also of the restrictions set by military administration against personnel's social media use. In an interview for a special issue of *Kairos* with Mike Edwards and D. Alexis Hart, Lieutenant General William B. Caldwell IV explains that social media use, such as blogs, Facebook, and Twitter, were previously banned due to concerns about such use compromising the integrity and safety of military activity. However, these restrictions have recently been lifted, with some caveats, as a way to improve the experience of military personnel and to improve military-civilian relationships (Edwards and Hart 2010). While some military servicemembers clearly made use of digital and social media even while restrictions were in place, the lifting of these restrictions has led to increased use and thus greater opportunity for research regarding the military servicepersons' use of these technologies. The research considering this topic in the contemporary conflicts suggests that these social sites may offer venues and opportunities for managing psychological distress related to war experiences.

Communications scholar Kari Andén-Papadopoulos (2009b) was one of the first to broach this topic in her article "US Soldiers Imaging the Iraq War on YouTube," which broadly discusses the grassroots journalism elements of videos posted to YouTube by deployed personnel in contrast to traditional journalism. She argues that there is a "confessional" nature to this grassroots journalism approach (Andén-Papadopoulos 2009b, 21). In her analysis, she considers different genres of videos commonly published on YouTube by deployed military personnel. In her discussion of the first genre, Combat Action videos, Andén-Papadopoulos (2009b, 22) most directly considers the display of PTSD symptoms, arguing that these videos take on the perspective of a servicemember suffering from posttraumatic stress disorder. She extends this discussion in "Body Horror on the Internet: US Soldiers Recording the War in Iraq and Afghanistan" (Andén-Papadopoulos 2009a) by analyzing graphic and violent images and the associated commentary posted by military personnel and other users of *NowThatsFuckedUp.com*. She argues that these images, and similarly the videos, are "primarily symptoms of an affective reliving of traumatic war experiences" (Andén-Papadopoulos 2009a, 921). While these considerations are certainly important, violent digital texts are only one genre published on social-media sites. She also points out three others: humorous videos made out of boredom, tribute videos, and videos documenting interaction with Iraqi civilians. Often, she claims, these videos work against the official message of the military and focus instead on what Andén-Papadopoulos calls the "reality effect" of day-to-day activities (Andén-Papadopoulos 2009b, 26). Andén-Papadopoulos's suggestion that military personnel are attempting to create a "reality effect" in digital compositions addressing their deployed experiences further suggests that managing traumatic stress is at least partially a motivation for composing these texts.

The humorous videos stand in most marked contrast to the violent-combat-experience videos and images. Andén-Papadopoulos (2009b, 23) suggests that these videos work to "offset the monotony, and also to release stress and frustration." She describes the humor in these videos as "frat-style humor" and points out that these videos "mock the grim realities of war" to abate boredom. Geoffrey Carter and Bill Williamson (2010) extend Andén-Papadopoulos's claims by arguing that this humor actively abates psychological distress by "waging humor . . . [to] deal with issues like the pressure and cynicism of war." Rather than describing it as "frat-style humor," Carter and Williamson describe the humor used in these videos as a "kynicism," or dark and mocking humor, which reclaims negative labels or experiences in an effort to assert some control over them. For Carter and Williamson (2010), these videos allow military servicepersons to comment on the degradation and discomfort of their experiences in a way that is both critical and accepting. Each of these elements is important. The *critical comment* allows them to give voice to their frustrations and other emotional reactions to their duties rather than bottling up those emotions. It is an "antidote to despair" (Carter and Williamson 2010). The *accepting commentary* offers military personnel a sense of control and agency in the face of being given orders and being deployed by superiors. Carter and Williamson (2010) suggest that this combination allows those composing these videos to obey and fulfill their orders while retaining some distance in order to critique the agenda and behavior of the military and the government as a whole.

Carter and Williamson (2010) and Andén-Papadopoulos (2009a, 2009b 2011) both enrich our understanding of military servicepersons' multimodal texts, demonstrating how the texts can be essential to the psychological well-being of those who are deployed, but their analysis focuses primarily on the text itself, leaving the composing and publishing processes largely underconsidered. An investigation of the entire composition process from creation to dissemination would offer another perspective on what student-veterans may see as the value and purpose of creating and composing in the classroom. Even though not all veterans deal with psychological distress following their service, many must find ways to deal with the realities of their experiences.

Given the strong connections between preventing and managing traumatic stress and the composing process, connections suggested in at least some of the digital social-media compositions of military service-members, this project examines the composing, circulation, and audience response of a music-video remix created by a group of deployed military personnel. This analysis suggests that experiences with creating these kinds of projects may shape student-veterans' expectations of the composing process in the classroom. As a result of this analysis, instructors can be better informed about how these students, and arguably all students, might approach different kinds of composing tasks, what value they may see in such tasks, and how they might conceptualize the process of completing those tasks.

COMPOSING WHILE DEPLOYED: PROCESSES AND MOTIVATIONS IN THE REMIXED-MUSIC-VIDEO GENRE

The digital compositions military personnel create while serving include a broad range of genres, as Andén-Papadopoulos notes in her articles. One of the most common is the humorous music video created to parody well-known songs. The amusing-music-video genre can be further divided into two main subgenres. In the first, videos seem to be less structured or premeditated. The creators record a single continuous shot, often play music from a separate device, and dance or sing along in whatever setting is most convenient. The songs in these videos are typically more recent Top-40 hits. The humor tends to be situated in the performance of the military servicemember rather than in any complex allusions. While these videos certainly offer some affordances for managing traumatic experiences, the second subgenre does so more directly.

The videos in this second subgenre are designed to follow many of the same conventions of industry music videos. Servicemembers creating these videos extensively plan the set design, the choreography, and the overall narrative of the video. In contrast to the first set of videos, these videos use a broader range of songs that seem to be selected to achieve a particular purpose or message in the video. A number of these videos use songs in which the lyrics either directly reference war experience or can be reinterpreted to do so. For example, as Carter and Williamson (2010) explain in their article, two deployed soldiers created a video for the song "This is Why I'm Hot" by rapper MIMS in which they changed the meaning of *hot* to reference the temperature in the desert rather than the performers' level of attractiveness. In other cases, deployed military personnel engage in more direct parody by completely rewriting the song, such as in the video posted by DDKemp "Somewhere in Kosovo" which parodies the Beach Boys' "Kokomo" ("Kosovo Soldiers Sing/Perform the Beach Boys Kokomo" 2007). The intentional repurposing of the original text in this genre suggests that traumatic stress management and prevention is a viable motivation for composing in the works of military personnel. The composing and publishing process for these videos offers opportunities for the creators to engage in the three strategies for preventing and managing traumatic stress discussed earlier: developing a reliable social network, developing language and narrative space for the traumatic experience, and engaging a critical public.

The overlap between the composing process and traumatic-stress-management strategies can best be seen in an analysis of a stand-out example of this genre. As mentioned above, many videos are posted by deployed military members; therefore, this project analyzes a representative YouTube video created by a group of deployed military police, the Fantastic 14, in which they perform Vanilla Ice's hit "Ice Ice Baby." This video serves as a prime example for two reasons. First, with 1,157,783 views and approximately 3,600 comments at the time of this writing, there is opportunity to consider not only the production process but also the circulation and reception aspects of the text. Second, the video suggests the incorporation of each of the traumatic-stress-management strategies to a roughly equal degree, which is essential to understanding how stress management as a motivation for composing may shape student-veterans' expectations of the composing process.

When considering the composing process, the natural place to start is the actual production process—what was produced, the conditions for production, and the purposes for composing. The genre itself, music-video remixes made by deployed personnel, indicates many of these factors of production. The Fantastic 14 are a group of military police who, at the time of the production of this video, were deployed to Iraq. Together, these men dance and lip-sync to Vanilla Ice's hit song against a variety of backdrops that display the living and working conditions of being deployed. In the video description, the uploading user lam918 ("Vanilla Ice Remix [Gotta See]" 2007) suggests that one of the primary purposes of the video is to "have fun" and reduce boredom. However, there is a suggestion in the content of the video and the supporting text lam918 ("Vanilla Ice Remix [Gotta See]" 2007) writes that this video may have also been intended to develop and reinforce the group's role as a reliable social network for its members.

The beginning of Fantastic 14's remix opens with a scrolling title naming the group as responsible for what follows. This group owner- ship and public identification establish from the outset that these indi- viduals perceive themselves as a cohesive unit. This is reinforced in the description of the video that uses the collective pronoun *we* to describe their purpose and goals. Lam918 writes, "We had a little free time while we were in iraq and took a minute to make this video for all of you back in the states to enjoy! . . . just because we are a group of mili- tary police doesn't mean we don't know how to have fun!" Although lam918 posts as an individual, he addresses viewers from the collective perspective of the group, and his investment in the group is revealed through his energetic tone and exclamation points. Based on these two examples, the Fantastic 14 appears to be a close-knit group highly invested in the success of each individual and the group as a whole.

The investment in individuals is reinforced in the final two minutes of the video, which recognizes the contribution of each individual by filming each one doing a final, solo dance move. This section of the video also functions similarly to the credits in a traditional film because during the final dance, the participant's name, nickname, and role are superimposed on the screen. These written credits offer the participating military police a variety of identity roles. First, the given name allows for the recognition of the individual as a military service- member and as a member of the military police. The nickname rein- forces membership in this particular unit of military police. Finally, the third line recognizes their loosely-interpreted roles as individual per- formers in the video and in the musical group Fantastic 14.

In these credits, the internal humor of the group is also displayed. The first individual in the credits is listed in the role of "main star," the second is listed as "lead dancer," and the third "co producer." Following traditional credits, the viewer naturally expects that this third line denotes the contribution to the video alone. For the rest of the dancers in the video, however, this third line offers seemingly random suggestions about the person's contribution, including "Shut up!" and "TinPenny" and a list of question marks. These phrases or "roles" may be interpreted by outsiders as negative, but adding two minutes of playing time to a video to recognize each group member individually suggests that each member is important for the whole group's success. This is especially true given that video editing requires a lot of time and often tedious, repetitive tweaking. Overall, the pre- sentation of this video from beginning to end reinforces the cohesion of this group.

In addition to the collaborative work of this video helping to develop a reliable social network, remixed music videos may also assist in developing language to articulate traumatic experiences and place them into a narrative for the participants. As explained above, Carter and Williamson (2010) suggest that one purpose of this genre is to use lyrics that can take on a new meaning in the context of being deployed. He uses multiple videos to demonstrate his point, one of which is the Fantastic 14's video. Carter and Williamson (2010) explain that the use of Vanilla Ice's lyrics "gunshots rang out like a bell / I grabbed my nine all I heard were shells" are likely recalling similar, real experiences for these servicemembers. For Carter and Williamson (2010), the use of this song and these lyrics in the video "show that that the soldiers refuse to take themselves and their conditions too seriously." Further, the kynicism form of humor used works as a way to cope with their position and their experiences Carter and Williamson (2010).

The idea that the repurposing of the words is important for processing the conditions of being deployed is reinforced when the actions of the participants and the settings included in the video are considered. As Halverson (2010) argues, the multimodality of video is an advantage because it allows meaning to be constructed on multiple levels. This multimodality may in turn allow the military personnel to cope with multiple aspects of the deployed experience. This can be seen in some of the scenes from the Fantastic 14's video. While some scenes include the military police doing choreographed dancing, during other verses they act out the lyrics. For example, the second scene begins with the entire group riding in or on a combat vehicle, but as Vanilla Ice sings "I'm on a roll and it's time to go solo," all but the central performer abandon the vehicle. The driver continues to act out the lyrics through this verse. When the lyrics Carter and Williamson examine are heard, the driver ducks in reaction to the "gunshots" and pulls out his gun while continuing to lip-sync with the song. This may be primarily an extension of Carter and Williamson's claim that these military police are refusing to take their situation too seriously, but the bodily reenactment of potentially stressful situations also offers opportunities for the participants to create a multifaceted language about these experiences.

As an example of its genre, this video suggests that the production process of composing in this genre creates prime opportunities for the first two strategies for preventing and managing traumatic stress: developing a reliable social network and creating language and narrative space for the traumatic event. While these two strategies are of course important to the management of traumatic stress, digital composing and publishing offer ample opportunity for the third strategy of engaging a critical public. This strategy can best be seen in the circulation and audience-response aspects of the digital composing process.

CIRCULATION ON SOCIAL MEDIA

One of the advantages of social-media sites is that they facilitate circulation of texts by making it easy to for users to upload and share their work. Some sites target narrow audiences, while others aim to attract a broader audience. As explained earlier, YouTube's high visibility in popular culture as well as its "marketplace feel" offer users potential access to a very diverse audience (Davies and Merchant 2009). Further, the interface is specifically designed for the sharing of videos and to encourage interaction between the user uploading the video and the video's viewers, as well as interaction between viewers. It also encourages circulation by providing code to embedded videos on other pages, such as personal blogs and links to share the video on other social-media sites, like Facebook. The videos created by military personnel attract a significant audience on YouTube.

Indeed, in response to the servicemembers' music videos, YouTube users make extensive use of all the feedback options made available by the site, including "likes," "dislikes," commenting, and sometimes even video responses. In terms of the Fantastic 14's Vanilla Ice remix, which is one of the most popular videos posted by deployed military serviceperson with currently 1,157,783 views. More than 5,716 have elected to click the "like" button, 134 pressed the "dislike" button, and the video has received 3,607 comments from its viewers. These numbers indicate that the Fantastic 14 have reached a significant portion of their intended audience, "those back in the states." It further suggests that this video has been widely circulated and that audience response has been extensive. Consequently, the creators of the video have been able to engage that critical public audience that serves as the third strategy for managing traumatic stress. While lam918 seems to be aiming for a sympathetic audience when he writes "hope you like it!" the public publication of the video on YouTube necessarily creates opportunity for both supportive feedback and critique.

AUDIENCE RESPONSES AND COMMENTS

Comments on the videos generally fall into three major categories: support of the video and the military, support that also recognizes the primary purpose for deployment, and, finally, negative critique—both trolling and sincere—of the servicemembers individually or the military as a whole. The majority of the approximately 3,600 comments fall into the first category, praising the video and the military servicepersons' work in the military. These comments tend to focus on the humor of the video, pointing either to specific moments or discussing the video as a whole. For example, lilbill11891 writes "hey glad to see yall havin fun . . . i like the video lol . . . thanks." This viewer and the many who post similar comments offer the creators of the video a recognition of both identities shown in the video—professional and personal—and offer encouragement for the enterprise of both identities. Through this first type of comment, the Fantastic 14 can feel confident in achieving their goals of "[having] fun" and engaging their audience in that fun. Within this first group of comments, there is similar a type that praises the group or individuals for their more subjective characteristics, such as attractiveness, bravery, dance skills, and so forth. These comments also positively reinforce the servicemembers' multiple roles and purposes in their deployment and express support from their named audience.

The second kind of supportive comment also recognizes the realities and conflicts inherent in combat experiences. Often these realities are qualitative evaluations of the location, such as in mpsmi's comment "shittiest place in the world and they can still have a laugh." Sometimes they focus on more specific aspects in the background of the video, like ktzo6991's comment, which points out the bullet holes in the wall structure in a particular shot. In these comments, the military members are able to feel empathy and understanding from their audience. Many of these viewers self-identify as part of a military branch or as having a close family member who serves. The validation in these comments then functions like support groups, in which members often share similar experiences. Herman (1992, 68) argues that trauma survivors often feel some level of guilt as they struggle to develop "a fair and reasonable assessment of their conduct" during the experience. When we hear of someone's trauma, our instinct is often to not judge their actions during the trauma, but survivors can feel that this response is inauthentic and uncritical, that it attempts to avoid the reality of the experience rather than validate it. This second group of comments offers recognition of the compromising position military personnel are sometimes in and praises these individuals for maintaining morale in their situation.

Despite the overwhelming support shown in most comments, a third set of comments offering negative critique is also present in the commentary. The percentage of these comments is admittedly small, but their existence allows for the authentic audience needed to engage cultural citizenship and/or the survivor mission, as discussed above. The most common comment of this type claims that military personnel are "wasting" tax money. In fact, this response is so common that a supportive viewer remarks, "I think it's funny how many times I see the 'tax dollars well spent' comment. That's the only thing they can think of to say." Other negative comments include abusive commentary on the validity of the war and the actions of military servicepersons. Some of the more abusive comments on these videos base their claims on broad, and sometimes uninformed, knowledge of historical events.

As with the videos, though, the comments can also be rated by other users, many of whom "dislike" these negative comments. Once a comment receives a certain number of "dislike" votes, it is removed from the Comment pages. Admittedly, the comment can be revealed by clicking a "Show" button, but users have the ability to hide it from the less persistent reader. In some cases, the user posting the video or posting the comment removes negative comments, which are then marked as removed by YouTube. These removed comments are often part of larger comment conversations that rage in the Comment pages of these videos.

Another variation on the comment is the comment conversation, which is a back-and-forth exchange between two or more viewers who generally disagree as they discuss the video and the context of the video. These comments tend to trigger the supportive viewers of these videos, who are intensely protective of the military personnel posting the videos and the military complex as a whole. They often respond aggressively to negative comments left by other users, often with personal attacks on the individual's intelligence or their overall worth as a human being. In some ways these conversations reveal to the military servicemembers posting these videos that they are sparking debate and consideration of the exigency and reality of war—their traumatic experience. These conversations can be spaces where military personnel and responders develop and use their cultural citizenship while also helping the military members composing these texts feel validated and connected, even while deployed.

STUDENT-VETERANS' EXPECTATIONS ABOUT COMPOSING FOR THE CLASSROOM

Overall, the YouTube platform, its users, and the videos in particular offer an example of how the digital composition process may be at least partially motivated by an attempt to cope with traumatic experience.

Student-veterans with experience composing these texts, and even those who are only familiar with the process, may bring expectations developed in this context into the classroom. As instructors, we should consider these expectations and how they could inform our classroom practices. Although expectations will certainly vary based on prior experience with composing as well as the conditions of the student-veteran's service, the connections between digital composing and therapeutic composing discussed above can offer insight into some of the expectations that may be brought into the classroom.

Often the composition classroom focuses on the production aspect of the composing process. The production process, as demonstrated earlier, can create opportunities for composers to develop and strengthen their reliable social network and offer opportunities to develop meaningful language about their experiences. The Fantastic 14 video, and others like it, suggest that a reliable social network is important and valuable in deployed contexts. In addition to the official work deployed personnel complete together, they also sometimes work together as a group to create creative projects, like the Fantastic 14 remix. As result of the emphasis on group networking, it is possible that student-veterans will privilege a collaborative approach to composing rather than an individualistic approach. The contexts of deployment and the classroom are obviously strikingly different, so it is unlikely that student-veterans will expect to be working on collaboratively authored assignments. Nevertheless, a collaborative approach in production stages like brainstorming, drafting, and developing may be seen as natural based on student-veterans' prior experiences. Further, if a reliable social network has been a significant aspect of the production processes of student-veterans, it may be important to their personal composing process to have a support network as they work on individual projects. Often instructors attempt to create similar networks in the classroom by incorporating group work that allows students to offer each other feedback as they develop ideas and content for their compositions. It is important to note that student-veterans are sometimes wary or resistant to working with traditional students because they sense a divide between themselves and these students. Some student-veterans attribute this distance to the fact that they are often older than other students, feel they have more experience than other students, and perceive that they are more focused on their school work than other students (Washington State 2009). Despite this, instructors should work to develop a reliable and safe social network in the classroom since classmates are one of the best resources students have when working on course projects. One option for facilitating this network can be regular group activities that encourage students to help each other work toward common goals together. The Washington State Department of Veterans Affairs (2009) notes that group activities may be frustrating at first for student-veterans who are used to quick responses as opposed to the drawn-out deliberative nature of group work; however, the VA suggests that over time student-veterans will value this teamwork approach if they perceive valuable results. Another option is to encourage student-veterans to first consider their classmates as part of the critical public that is engaged as the third strategy for managing traumatic stress. In this case, students would be encouraged to participate in critical discussion of student work, and these discussions might facilitate the development of a reliable social network for later projects in the course.

In addition to composing with the feedback and help of a reliable social network, the production aspect of the composing process can also offer opportunities to create meaningful language about the content of the composition, especially if that content is related to personal experiences. The treatment of personal experiences is specifically important when managing reactions to a traumatic event, but the strategy can also be useful when composing about a wide range of topics. It is important for instructors to note that student-veterans may not be eager to write about or even discuss in class their experiences while serving (Washington State 2009). Nevertheless, the Fantastic 14's video and others like it show that it may be important for student-veterans to be able to connect their work with their experiences.

Also, it is important to consider the fact that the creators of these remixed-music videos are drawing heavily on previously created material. In fact, as both Carter and Williamson and I demonstrate in our respective projects, the repurposing of a previous text is important to the meaning-making happening in the videos created by deployed personnel. Experience with this kind of practice may lead student-veterans to view the incorporation of others' work into their own as important to the composing process. One way to capitalize on this familiarity with repurposing already created work is to incorporate the use of templates in the course, such as ones in Gerald Graff and Cathy Berkenstein's popular text, *They Say I Say: The Moves that Matter in Academic Writing.* Graff and Berkenstein (2006) offer templates for incorporating the work of others into academic writing as a way to help students write about the research they are doing in ways that are valued in the academy. Offering templates or starting points can also benefit student-veterans, who report that the transition to campus life is often difficult because they are not familiar with the expectations of academic work and the details needed to succeed in the campus context. Student-veterans say that an explanation of how to begin a project and an outline of how to proceed are especially helpful (Cook and Kim 2009, 36). Although the rhetorical contexts for these two practices are different, each practice relies on remixing existing work to create something new and useful for the composer.

Although the production process is often emphasized in the composition classroom, the analysis of the Fantastic 14's video shows the value of the circulation and audience-response aspects of the composing process. In the classroom, circulation and audience response are often seen through peer review, which normally occurs in the drafting stage. For those who have experience with social publishing, sharing the finished version of their project may add value to the project as well. In this case, peer review during drafting could then serve as interaction with a reliable social network, and sharing the finished product could facilitate the kinds of critical conversation seen in the comments in response to the Fantastic 14's video.

Finally, if engaging a critical public is an important motivation for composing, student-veterans with this experience may find that agonistic conversation in response to their texts is an important part of the composing process. In this case, these texts serve as catalysts for discussion and ways to mediate and regulate the discussion. Therefore, there may be an expectation that if a project is meaningful it will necessarily incorporate the opportunity for audience response to the finished product. Fortunately, the comments following the Fantastic 14's video and others in this genre can serve as a model for agonistic discussion about sensitive topics. Of course, as some of the comments excerpted above demonstrate, it is possible when discussing these highly charged topics that audience response may be extreme. The comments further show, however, that extreme commentary can still offer the opportunity for response. If nothing else, the more aggressive comment conversations can serve as examples of how not to engage in productive discussion. Ultimately, participation in digital composing, especially when the motivation may be dealing with traumatic experiences, can develop an expectation that meaningful compositions are shared with a varied audience in an attempt to spark conversation.

CONCLUSION

Even though comparatively few veterans are diagnosed with posttraumatic stress disorder, the Pew Research Center (2011) reveals that nearly half of post-9/11 veterans still feel as though they must cope with some kind of psychological distress as a result of their experiences. Given this prevalence, it behooves rhetoricians and composition instructors to consider how these experiences might influence student-veterans' approaches and attitudes toward composition assignments. This project shows how the creation and sharing of remixed-music videos on YouTube, as one kind of the many digital texts out there, may be motivated by a need to manage emotional and psychological reactions to the realities of deployment. Understanding the connections between the digital composing process and the goals of therapeutic composing helps instructors to consider what expectations student-veterans may have in the classroom, especially if they have created the kinds of videos considered here.

Primarily, the expectations suggested in this chapter emphasize that student-veterans may be able to develop relationships with their fellow students that would create a social network that could offer support in the composing process, especially in the production process. The connections between the digital composing process and the goals of therapeutic composing show that this social network is important for developing the content of a text. The development of that social network may be a challenge in the classroom given the distance student-veterans often see between themselves and "traditional" students (Washington State 2009). In this case, the suggested expectation that texts serve as catalysts for discussion could function as a starting point from which to begin conversation and build classroom relationships that span the initially perceived distance. Even when student-veterans are not composing about their military-service experiences, familiarity with the kind of composing examined here may influence their expectations of and approach to composing for the classroom. The consideration of one motivation and the way it shapes expectations aims to contribute to the emerging conversation about ways composition instructors can facilitate student-veterans' transition into the academy and to spark further discussion of and investigation into students-veterans' expectations about composing.

References

Andén-Papadopoulos, Kari. 2009a. "Body Horror on the Internet: US Soldiers Recording the War in Iraq and Afghanistan." *Media, Culture and Society* 31 (6): 921–38. http://dx.doi.org/10.1177/0163443709344040.

Andén-Papadopoulos, Kari. 2009b. "US Soldiers Imaging the Iraq War on YouTube." *Popular Communication* 7 (1): 17–27. http://dx.doi.org/10.1080/15405700802584304.

Burden, Matthew Currier. 2006. *The Blog of War: Front-line Dispatches from Soldiers in Iraq and Afghanistan.* New York: Simon and Schuster Paperbacks.

Burgess, Jean, and Joshua Green. 2010. *YouTube: Online Video and Participatory Culture.* Cambridge, MA: Polity Press.

Carter, Geoffrey, and Bill Williamson. 2010. "Diogenes, Dogfaced Soldiers, and Deployment Music Videos." Special issue, *Kairos* 14 (3). http://www.technorhetoric .net/14.3/topoi/carter-williamson/2_dog.htm.

Cook, Bryan J., and Young Kim. 2009. *From Soldier to Student: Easing the Transition of Service Members on Campus.* Washington, DC: American Council on Education.

Davies, Julia. 2006. "'Hello Newbie, **big welcome hugs** hope u like it here as much as i do ': An Exploration of Teenagers' Informal Online Learning." In *Digital Generations, Children, Young People and New Media,* edited by David Buckingham and Rebecca Willett, 211–28. New York: Lawrence Ehrlbaum.

Davies, Julia, and Guy Merchant. 2009. "YouTube as Verb . . . iTube? weTube? they-Tube? . . ." In *Web 2.0 for Schools: Learning and Social Participation,* 53–69. New York: Peter Lang.

Edwards, Mike, and D. Alexis Hart. 2010. "A Soldier Interacting, without Mediation." *Kairos* 14 (3). http://www.technorhetoric.net/14.3/interviews/edwards-hart/index .html.

Graff, Gerald, and Kathy Berkenstein. 2006. *They Say I Say: The Moves that Matter in Academic Writing.* New York: W. W. Norton.

Guzzetti, Barbara. 2006. "Cybergirls: Negotiating Social Identities on Cybersites." *E-learning* 3 (2): 158–69. http://dx.doi.org/10.2304/elea.2006.3.2.158.

Halverson, Erica Rosenfeld. 2010. "Film as Identity Exploration: A Multimodal Analysis of Youth-Produced Films." *Teachers College Record* 112 (9): 2352–78.

Herman, Judith. 1992. *Trauma and Recovery: The Aftermath of Violence—from Domestic Abuse to Political Terror.* New York: Basic Books.

"Hold It against Me 266 Rein Marines Official Version." 2011. YouTube video, 3:58, posted by "atarin18," April 18. http://www.youtube.com/watch?v=rCrG6TzG-nw.

"Kosovo Soldiers Sing/Perform the Beach Boys Kokomo." 2007. YouTube video, 2:30, posted by "DDKemp," October 7. http://www.youtube.com/watch?v=UsO84nmeeSk.

McFarlane, Alexander C., and Rachel Yehuda. 1996. "Resilience, Vulnerability, and the Course of Posttraumatic Reactions." In *Traumatic Stress: The Effects of Overwhelming Experience on Mind, Body and Society,* edited by Bessel A. van der Kolk, Alexander C. McFarlane, and Lars Weisaeth, 155–81. New York: Guilford Press.

Pew Research Center. 2011. "War and Sacrifice in the Post-9/11 Era: The Military Civilian Gap." *PewSocialTrends.org.* http://www.pewsocialtrends.org/2011/10/05 /war-and-sacrifice-in-the-post-911-era/.

Roozen, K. 2009. "'Fan Fic-ing' English Studies: A Case Study Exploring the Interplay of Vernacular Literacies and Disciplinary Engagement." *Research in the Teaching of English* 44 (2): 136–69.

Shalev, Arieh Y. 1996. "Acute Posttraumatic Reactions in Soldiers and Civilians." In *Traumatic Stress: The Effects of Overwhelming Experience on Mind, Body and Society,* edited by Bessel A. van der Kolk, Alexander C. McFarlane, and Lars Weisaeth, 102–14. New York: Guilford Press.

"Telephone Remake." 2010. YouTube video, 3:45, posted by "malibumelcher," April 23. http://www.youtube.com/watch?v=haHXgFU7qNI.

van der Kolk, Bessel A. 1996. "Trauma and Memory." In *Traumatic Stress: The Effects of Overwhelming Experience on Mind, Body and Society,* edited by Bessel A. van der Kolk, Alexander C. McFarlane, and Lars Weisaeth, 279–302. New York: The Guilford Press.

"Vanilla Ice Remix (Gotta See)." 2007. YouTube video, 5:40, posted by "lam918," April 7. *YouTube.* http://www.youtube.com/watch?v=e1-5I25T7fM.

Washington State Department of Veterans Affairs. 2009. "Veteran Guidelines and Best Practices in the Classroom." Olympia, WA: WDVA Publications. http://www.dva.wa.gov/PDF%20files/Veteran%20Best%20Practices%20in%20the%20Classroom%20.pdf.

Williams, Bronwyn T. 2009. "Looking for the Right Pieces: Composing Texts in a Culture of Collage." In *Shimmering Literacies: Pop Culture and Reading and Writing Online*, 64–90. New York: Peter Lang.

PART III

Veteran-Friendly Composition Practices

9

RECOGNIZING SILENCE
Composition, Writing, and the Ethical Space for War

Roger Thompson

In a key moment in Saint Augustine's *Confessions*, Augustine reflects on the silence of one of his mentors. Though later Augustine emphasizes the power of speech when he overhears a child reading holy words and experiences a moment of conversion, his figuring of Ambrose as a silent reader is instructive to not only Ambrose's students but to us as teachers in a time of war.

> When he [Ambrose] was reading, his eyes ran over the page and his heart perceived the sense, but his voice and tongue were silent. He did not restrict access to anyone coming in, nor was it customary even for a visitor to be announced . . . We supposed that in the brief time he could find for his mind's refreshment, free from the hubbub of other people's troubles, he would not want to be invited to consider another problem. We wondered if he read silently perhaps to protect himself in case he had a hearer interested and intent on the matter, to whom he might have to expound the text being read if it contained difficulties, or who might wish to debate some difficult question . . . Whatever motive he had for his habit [of silent reading], this man had good reason for what he did. (Saint Augustine 1991, 92–93)

Implicit in Augustine's reflection on silence is his discomfort with it, his general sense that, even if it is thoughtful and with "good reason," Ambrose's silence is unapproachable, perhaps even indicative of his desire to be left out of the "hubbub" of other people's problems. While in this case Augustine is the student and Ambrose the mentor, we might recognize in Augustine's response a similar discomfort that we teachers feel with silence in a learning environment. Can we, as Augustine does, "go away" (Saint Augustine 1991, 93) when the silence lingers too long? Can we leave knowing that we "could not put the questions [we] wanted to put to him as [we] wished to do" (Saint Augustine 1991, 92)

DOI: 10.7330/9780874219425.c009

even if that silence disrupts or unsettles the ordered space of a class-room? Given that Ambrose is often cited as one of the originators of the just-war theory, I find myself wanting to lean into Augustine's reading of Ambrose's act of silence, to connect what we know about veterans and the shifting demographics of our classrooms in this time of war with our own capacities to understand silence in writing classes.

What we know about veterans in the classroom continues to evolve as our discipline becomes increasingly engaged with the effects of a culture of war on our students, whether they be student-veterans, nontraditional students, or the stereotypical four-year college student newly graduated from high school. Marilyn Valentino (2010) used her CCCC president's address to remind the college-writing community that veterans will be matriculating in increasing numbers in the coming years, and with that increased enrollment, writing instructors bear a special "ethical obliga-tion" to consider the issues that combat veterans, in particular, bring to the classroom.[1] One of the central questions in light of those numbers and Valentino's call is whether encouraging classroom debate about war is, in fact, desirable, or even ethical. In other words, *should* we encourage discussions about war in classrooms and campuses populated by veter-ans, and, more specifically, should we encourage our veterans to engage in that dialogue?

As writing instructors, we likely have an immediate impulse to declare that debate and conversation are desirable. We likely believe that dis-cussion and the exchange of ideas lead to healthy development of crit-ical-thinking skills and help students develop strategies for addressing the ambiguity and complexity of difficult decisions. What we may for-get, and what we likely need to understand ourselves in more complex ways, is that silence is, itself, a strategy, one that we ourselves deploy in various situations and that our students use to negotiate particularly difficult terrain. Indeed, as Ambrose's actions illustrate to Augustine, teachers' silences profoundly affect the classroom. Whether silence is deployed explicitly as a rhetorical strategy or not, we communicate with our silences, and our students, like Augustine, read our silences in mul-tiple ways. If we know our students inscribe multiple meanings to our silences, we might ask ourselves what meanings we are assigning to our student-veterans when they greet our questions, our assignments, or our presence with silence. We know silence is a powerful way of cop-ing with war experiences, and our obligation is to understand how that silence functions and what it might mean to ask our veterans to speak to or through it. Such consideration does not apply solely to those faculty who assign personal essays. Indeed, even those assignments purposely constructed to avoid personal writing still provide opportunity for student disclosure about the war experience, whether that disclosure be through written words or through rhetorical uses of silence.

In this essay, then, I want to explore how student silence about war may be an embodiment of power and agency in a classroom. Drawing on seminal scholarship on the rhetoric of silence and on a body of war literature from the current conflicts, I suggest that writing pedagogy during war requires us to rethink the notion that classroom engagement with the question of war can be divorced from personal experiences. At a time when student-veterans and their families are increasingly populating college campuses, and during a time when many of our students have only known the country at war, we are presented in our classrooms with a rhetorical situation that necessitates reconsideration of how we teach. During wartime, and especially on campuses with active military and/or veteran populations, discussion and writing about war may, regardless of the intentions of our assignments, be an inherently private matter. Even when we do not use an explicitly expressivist pedagogy or teach "personal writing," assigning work related to war during wartime necessitates special consideration of student lives. Part of that consideration is the acknowledgment that the wartime experience is personal, that students' connections to war may be largely invisible to us as instructors, and that imagining our pedagogy as one that circumvents those invisible connections to war fails to create space for students to shape their own responses to the war experience, whether they be civilians, military family members, or veterans. Silence is one way they may do so, and as a legitimate, complex, and powerful response to war, silence is a particularly important rhetorical strategy that can embody the personal even in those assignments that ask students to engage in nonpersonal writing. In other words, what our students are not telling us about their lives in a country at war may not be omission and failure to engage in important questions as much as it is choice and assumption of agency. Encountering war, I argue, means encountering complex personal silences that both deploy power and circumscribe student engagement with our assignments and classrooms.

WRITING, HEALING, AND LEGACIES OF SILENCE

Dave Hnida begins his memoir about the Iraq War by ruminating on his father's service in World War II. Hnida is a doctor, and his book, *Paradise General*, covers his two deployments to Iraq. He represents himself from the beginning of his story as descended from a dark heritage of war, and his text is as much an attempt to understand that heritage as it is an attempt to understand the war he is himself serving in. Hnida writes on the book's opening page that his father "was one of the main reasons I was hiding in a sandy ditch in the middle of Iraq." His father had been "a mean drunk" who "felt the need to retreat to the safety of the bottle" because as an infantryman in World War II, he had "sent a number of young men into battle and could never forgive himself for the ones who didn't return." Hnida's decision to become a doctor who would serve in war suggests a profound desire to heal not just the wounds of the warriors he was treating but also the wounds of his father. It is as though he is seeking to save those lives his father felt he had lost. His dad, a "member of the 'Greatest Generation' was silent about his war" (Hnida 2010, 1) until he quit drinking and until his son himself went to war. Hnida explicitly links generations of silence and suffering and suggests that his service is an attempt to understand (and likely repair) his father.

Hnida's positioning of himself as part of a legacy of silence is not unique in recent war memoirs. Not surprisingly, many of the memoirists come from military families. Most, including Hnida, explicitly link their service to their attempts to understand the silences surrounding war within their own households. Nathaniel Fick has said that the writing of his excellent memoir *One Bullet Away* was inspired by his grandfather, who served in World War II but whose service he did not know "a great deal about" (Fick 2005). Jeremiah Workman, in *Shadow of the Sword*, discusses the silence that surrounded his grandfather's service in World War II. On discovering that his grandfather had earned a Purple Heart, Workman questions his mother about him. His mother begins:

> "He was wounded during World War II."
> "How?"
> "Nobody knows. He never talked about it. We just know he was infantry and fought in Europe."
> "My grandfather was a hero?" Why hadn't I heard about this? My grandfather always seemed such sore subject, almost taboo. We never spoke of him. All I knew is that he died long before I was born (Workman 2009, 61).

Workman's understanding of his grandfather ultimately becomes one of the many shadows that he must confront in order to heal from his own wounds of war, and those shadows and their accompanying silences reach across generations and threaten to destroy Workman and his family.

Hnida and Workman, like many of the memoirists from OIF, self-consciously position themselves as speaking through a silence that has held them, and oftentimes their families, captive, and their texts frequently position silence as a kind of insidious power that undermines their self-confidence, their mental health, and their humanity. The act of writing, then, breaks the silence. It makes their particular war stories public, visible, and, potentially, heard. Writing, in this way, transforms into healing and a way to cope with the wounds of war.

In 2008, I experienced precisely how powerful and difficult this type of healing can be when I ghostwrote a war memoir for one of my former students at the Virginia Military Institute. VMI is a state-sponsored military college that offers the opportunity for students to either seek a commission in any of the branches of the armed services or simply move on to the civilian job market like most of today's college graduates. By 2003 and the onset of the Iraq War, the student body at VMI was fully immersed in discourse about the war. Debate about terrorism, Afghanistan, and Iraq permeated not just our classrooms but the entire culture of the institution. Roundtables were convened featuring prominent commentators and military leaders, and cadets read and discussed editorials and analyses about the roots of the conflicts. Commissioning rates skyrocketed as the idealistic student body sought an opportunity to serve and, to most of their minds, defend the United States. As a faculty member who had no military background and was still relatively new to the VMI system, I found the enthusiasm of my students for seeking out an opportunity to participate in the war both inspiring and unsettling. My students' profound idealism and belief in some core tenets of American democracy moved me, even while I recognized that for most of my students, adherence to those beliefs often represented unexamined acceptance of "American values" common in the heightened political rhetoric at the time.

Still, after September 11, 2001, most of us faculty had a new appreciation for the choices our students faced. Cadet response to the terrorist attacks was, on the one hand, determined, and on the other hand, measured. Our students were already keenly aware of the sacrifices members of the military have to make, so while there was shock and anger, there was also a tempered, silent resolve about what might happen in the years ahead. By 2008, the determination that was so keen in the immediate aftermath of the attacks had been replaced by an even more palpable understanding of the costs of war as stories from alumni filtered back and became part of the institutional culture. The idea of service was replaced with the idea of sacrifice.

One of my students, Shannon Meehan, graduated in 2005 and went on to become a tank commander for the 1st Cavalry of the US Army.

He was deployed to Iraq and while there confronted the horrific consequences of his own actions when he accidentally killed a family and eight children. In the weeks that followed, he was also injured and suffered trauma to his arm, leg, and back. Worse, he suffered a traumatic brain injury from the IED blast that struck him, and he was medically retired from the service, despite hopes of making the army a career.

While recovering from his TBI, Shannon was also diagnosed with PTSD. The war for him remained real, palpable, and almost unbearable, and at some point, Shannon felt a need to share his story. At first, he shared it with just a few family members and friends. In doing so, he found that telling his story helped make sense of his war, of his actions in the war. He also found that in telling his story, he helped others make sense of the war themselves. He decided to share his story more broadly.

When we collaborated on his memoir, my role became that of a friend trying to help him name the problems that continued to undermine his own health. I tried to offer a nonjudgmental ear to a story that, in some ways, seemed too horrible to hear, let alone tell. I was very quickly aware of how ill prepared I was for the process we were undertaking. I believed in Shannon and in his need to speak through a very powerful silence that had come to control him. I believed that telling his story had the power to help him order a ruined world. I was, though, profoundly unprepared for how that action would resonate not just with readers of his story but with me, the writer, as well.

The book, *Beyond Duty* (Meehan and Thompson 2009), went through five printings in five months, was picked up by CNN, NPR, and major newspapers and magazines, and led to speaking engagements for Shannon and me at colleges and universities around the country. We were also invited to speak at Walter Reed, the National Traumatic Brain Injury Center, and West Point, and we consulted with organizations grappling with an expanding veteran population. We continue to do so. Shannon's story about civilian casualties and the terrible costs of war hit a chord, and as we worked together to respond to readers and audiences, we both found ourselves confronting powerful silences that shaped our lives.

Ample research testifies to the therapeutic power of writing as a way of being heard. In the mental-health professions, writing has been used as a therapeutic technique for decades, and in recent years, scholarship on expressive writing as an interventional technique in the treatment of PTSD and war stress has repeatedly demonstrated its viability as a therapeutic tool. Most of the research surrounding the value of expressive writing in the treatment of PTSD uses what is commonly called the Pennebaker Protocol, which was developed by James Pennebaker

(1997) as a standardized way for researchers to deploy expressive-writing techniques. The standardization, which requires researchers to assign fifteen to thirty minutes of writing during a period of between two and four consecutive days, aims to ensure consistency in research methodology and research results.

Numerous studies have used the protocol, and those studies consistently report veterans and others with PTSD derive value from expressive writing exercises, even if Pennebaker has since suggested that the grounds for some claims remain "tenuous." The research of Matt Gray and Thomas Lombardo suggests that writing about traumatic events produces less-fragmented recollections of the event and less anxiety than oral retellings (Gray and Lombardo 2001), and work by Joshua Smyth, Jill Hockemeyer, and Heather Tulloch demonstrates that not only does expressive writing reduce some trauma symptomology but also significantly reduces actual cortisol levels, a key indicator of stress, in patients (Smyth, Hockemeyer, and Tulloch 2008). The researchers note that "although patients are still struggling with the core features of their PTSD (i.e., re-experiencing, avoidance, and hyperarousal), their capacity to regulate those responses is facilitated following expressive writing" (Smyth, Hockemeyer, and Tulloch 2008, 92). Similarly, Tim Hoyt and Elizabeth Yeater, whose work attempts to control for research subjects who have either high or low "negative trait emotion" (i.e., their work attempts to account for differences in research subjects' preexisting negative emotions), demonstrate that expressive writing has clear benefits (Hoyt and Yeater 2011). Those who had "negative emotion" traits at time of the study reported that while the writing assignment (which asked subjects to write about a traumatic experience) was very difficult and emotionally stressful, it was nonetheless helpful and beneficial to them. Even research that suggests limitations to expressive writing as a method for long-term healing typically indicates some significant benefits to the act of writing. For instance, Denise Sloan, Brian Feinstein, and Brian Marx note in their work that though expressive writing may not produce particularly "durable" effects (i.e., have demonstrable permanent healing effects), expressive writing provides short-term relief for certain symptoms of PTSD (Sloan, Feinstein, and Marx 2009). These studies are among many that consistently demonstrate that writing offers some, if not significant, benefit to those, especially veterans, who have endured trauma.

The evidence for the value of writing about war, however, does not imply that the composition classroom is the appropriate place for such writing. Indeed, the intensity of my experience working with Shannon

makes me wary of classroom exercises that might purposefully elicit disclosure of war experiences in most composition course settings. The
classroom, with all of its complexities of race, gender, socioeconomic
background, age differentials, educational backgrounds, trauma histories, and various demonstrations and embodiments of power, may in fact
be an unsafe venue for encouraging writing about war even if instructors are earnest in their desire to help students openly exchange ideas,
including those not explicitly about the war.

The history of composition studies' reception to the type of personal
writing that might lead to revelations about private matters testifies to
the profession's anxiety about personal writing in the composition classroom.[2] Scholars have typically divided personal writing in composition
into various camps, most notably the expressivist and the cultural/criti-
cal studies camps, with some scholars, like Anne Ruggles Gere (2001),
suggesting that a psychoanalytic model also plays a significant role in how
personal-writing assignments are deployed in classrooms. For expressiv-
ists, the concepts of voice and, to some degree, disclosure are central to
the act of writing. Students move toward self-knowledge, sometimes in
isolation, sometimes over and against a student's own history, politics,
and culture. The goal of the teacher is, at least in part, to help students
gain voice and articulate for themselves their own personal histories or
their place within the histories of others. As Richard Fulkerson (2005,
667) summarizes, "Writing [for the expressivists] is a means of fostering
personal development, in the great Socratean tradition of 'knowing thy-
self.'" For cultural-studies theorists who maintain an interest in reflective
writing, the role of personal writing is to help students locate themselves
within a complex web of social, political, and economic matrixes so
they can more fully express themselves within those domains. Students
respond to texts, engage in discussions about cultural controversies, and
ultimately learn to see themselves as wrapped within very specific power
structures and hegemonies that, for most teachers in this field, need to
be exposed and undone.

Such characterizations of the two schools of thought are, of course,
reductionistic. Positions fall within both camps, and indeed overlap or
escape traditional boundaries altogether. Further, many who teach personal writing from the cultural/critical-studies perspective may recoil at
the suggestion that reflective essays frequently assigned in such courses
are personal essays, in that the personal suggests to them a kind of
romanticized self that simply does not exists. Even so, both realms of
personal writing have come under considerable scrutiny, especially
from scholars who have concerns about student performance within

the academic discourses of the university. Certainly the expressivist school has borne the brunt of the criticism. Patricia Bizzell (1982), in one of the most frequently cited positions, argues that expressivist writing does students harm by failing to prepare them for both academic discourse and the types of critical thinking attendant to that discourse. Burton Hatlen (1986), in some ways building off Bizzell's claims, argues that helping students understand themselves in order to become better writers fails to recognize that many students may not have the tools for either project and thus do not have the inherent capacity to develop a voice that leads to better writing. James Berlin (1988), standing as the foundation for many cultural critics, expressed considerable concern that expressivist writing simply fails to acknowledge political structures that inform all writing. For all of these commentators and others, the idea that students who gain voice will improve their writing remains under considerable attack, and the notion of voice and how or if to teach it still has not found solid footing in the scholarship, let alone in the practices of teachers at colleges and universities. Teaching students to find a voice, then, likely needs to be considered carefully in teaching personal essays, and in those classrooms with student-veterans, in particular, asking students to share their personal voice and story might be particularly problematic. In those classrooms, a veteran may find silence to be their only rhetorical response to an assignment, and that silence may, in fact, be part of the voice the teacher is trying so hard to elicit.

For example, a veteran, who might be in their mid-twenties and who has had two combat deployments, led young soldiers in battle, and learned to negotiate the complicated hierarchy of a military career system, may feel alienated in a classroom of eighteen-year-old students, many of whom likely have not experienced life-and-death decisions or the difficulties of carving out a career path in a large organization. A veteran's silence around not just war, but ambiguous or incendiary topics, may be a strategy for coping with the dissonance they feel in the classroom, a way to negotiate the rules of a new space and setting. It may simply be a strategy to humor their peers as they learn how to adjust to college. More importantly, it may be a strategy for dealing with stress or mitigating the fear that they may replicate the violence of war, even if only in words. Silence provides, then, a tool with which some veterans approach difference in a way that we, as teachers, likely cannot fully appreciate. The potential range of reasons for a veteran, like any student, to use silence is expansive, but in the case of the veteran, as with other groups who may endure sustained significant trauma, we teachers must listen closely to that silence, to hear it and try to understand what it may mean. Our job, then, is to understand not only how writing can help heal the wounds of war but also that we need to respect silence as a legitimate response to certain assignments and even the classroom as a whole.

SILENCE, STUDENT-VETERANS, AND THE WRITING CLASSROOM

Cheryl Glenn (2004, 5), in her seminal rhetorical study of silence, *Unspoken: A Rhetoric of Silence*, argues that silence is, in fact, "a form of speech." As a form of speech and a necessary part of dialogue, it should be understood rhetorically and as inextricably linked to speech as a way of conveying meaning. It is, in other words, one strategy for communicating, for responding to circumstances, and for assuming identities. As Glenn (2004, 155) says, "Silence can deploy power." Even so, Glenn notes that silence is not always a choice. She argues that silence can be the result of being silenced, of having some aspect of our identity closed or controlled. "The question," says Glenn (2004, 13), "is not whether speech or silence is better, more effective, more appropriate. The question is whether our use of silence is our choice (whether conscious or unconscious) or that of someone else."

Glenn suggests that as writing instructors, we need to be especially aware of how our actions might be effectively silencing our students. Perhaps equally important, and regardless of our theoretical preferences or backgrounds, we must examine whether we are providing room for silence as a choice for students and whether we are helping students see the power of what is unsaid as much as the power of what is said. For teachers who employ expressivist pedagogies, providing room for silence is likely even more important because such pedagogies tend to ask students to provide details of their private lives in ways that other pedagogies do not. When we teach students the value of understanding the world rhetorically and ways of assuming control of voice and expression, we bear special responsibility to understand how our behaviors and rhetorical choices might impinge upon the choices of our students. This task, of course, is virtually impossible. Our own latent and unexamined biases and preferences emerge in the classroom regardless of our best intentions and efforts. Our best response, however, is to move in the direction we ask our students to move: toward awareness of and engagement with our own internal narratives as they respond to a given rhetorical situation. In other words, careful consideration of our rhetorical situation when doing something as mundane as crafting assignments should point us to an awareness that the surging veteran population in colleges as a result of war is an important, if not central, part of our college communities. When we ask students to make conscious choices about their writing processes, from invention to revision, we are asking them to understand their positions in the rhetorical situation that their assignments frame for them. If we are asking students to make such choices and to think hard about their own processes in light of specific rhetorical contingencies, we writing instructors can model that same ethic when framing assignments, prompting discussion, and creating classroom activities. A classroom with veterans, for example, may require us to change something as basic as where we ask our students to sit.[3] The rhetorical situation of war affects not only student voice or activity or expression, it demands that we make pedagogical choices that demonstrate awareness of war as a very real classroom contingency. Understanding that contingency in all of its complexities helps us when we ask our students to participate in dialogue about it, and as we develop more sophisticated understandings of the ways our students (both civilian and veteran) respond to war, we may gain more nuanced understandings of how our students communicate what war means to them. Silence is one of those ways.

A quarter of a century ago, James Moffett (1982) argued for integrating a meditative silence into the writing classroom. Moffett's point was that such silences (exemplified by "gazing" or "visualizing") provide a means for student reflection and connection to "inner speech." More recently, Pat Belanoff (2001) has argued that silence in the classroom offers space for student reflection that might ultimately order fragmented memory. Drawing on examples from medieval literature and religious writing, Belanoff (2001, 400) suggests that silence actually facilitates acts of literacy and argues that, despite the fact that "we're a culture fearful of silence," writing instructors must find some way to make space for silence when asking students to engage in acts of literacy. For George Kalamaras (1996–1997, 24), using silence in the classroom creates a radical space of learning that holds "dialectic suspect in favor of dialogics and conversation" because "dialectics begins with the assumption that there is, indeed, a thesis and an antithesis to resolve . . . a binary framework that leads to hierarchies of winners and losers." The result is that a classroom that embraces silence as a meditative and empowering strategy would "create continual opportunities for multi-vocality and revision" (Kalamaras 1996–1997, 25).

Scholarship on silence in the classroom tends to focus on meditative silence but it provides important insights into how a culture will, in the

words of Stuart Sim (2007, 2), "suffer if significant space is not made for
[silence]." For Sim, the increasing chatter of culture creates a need for
silence, and his "manifesto for silence" turns on the idea that silence is a
type of action over against the "noise" of our lives. That action can have
significant impact on a classroom. Suellyn Duffy (2011, 298) writes that a
student's silence "invited me into a kind of silence . . . one in which I had
to put aside any early preconceptions about [that student]." Duffy's student "enacted a kind of agency through her silence" (Duffy 2011, 300).
This suggests silence as empowerment, as negotiation of difficult circumstances. As Perry Gilmore (1985, 148) points out in a study of emotional displays in the classroom, student silences often have more than
one audience. The silence is likely a response to not only the teacher but
also to other students in the classroom.

While Duffy's study deals with her teaching students in the deep
South, it offers insight into how teachers might approach the issue of
the silence of veterans. In the case of student-veterans or even simply
those classrooms wrestling with the vestiges of war, it might suggest a way
to move beyond the "hierarchies of winners and losers" and toward a
space where widely divergent opinions are not encouraged to be voiced
as much as honored as voices in their own rights. Such an honoring of
both voice and silence is likely our best response to war in the classroom.
It provides space for war, for veterans' stories and experiences, while
simultaneously providing space for a kind of sacred silence that many
soldiers, sailors, airmen, and marines enact intuitively.

Directives for how best to negotiate war and silence in every writing
classroom are undoubtedly impossible to form if for no other reason
than the wide variety of colleges seeing surging student-veteran populations. Nonetheless, building a pedagogy that deliberately engages with a
wide range of rhetorical strategies helps communicate to students that
both diverse voices and silences will be honored in the class. The four
recommendations below, then, are hardly universally applicable; certain
colleges have very small veteran populations or, indeed, even populations who have no direct contact with the war. These recommendations
do, however, offer some concrete ways to communicate to all students
that we teachers are engaged with the effects of war on our culture and
in our classrooms.

(1) Educate yourself on common veteran issues in order to gain a literacy
    about war and the veteran experience. There is a wide range of ways
    to do this. Attend lectures by veterans. Read war memoirs. Participate
    in activities hosted by your institution's student-veteran groups. More

directly, access resources provided by veterans' services. The VA provides informational guides about veterans' issues, as does the DoD's National Traumatic Brain Injury Center. Most veterans' groups also provide information about veterans' services in the area, and the Wounded Warrior Project offers useful information for both civilians and prior military servicemembers. Writing program administrators should consider educating writing faculty by inviting representatives of an institution's veterans' programs to train faculty on veterans' issues and make them aware of veterans' resources on a campus.

(2) Seek out student-veteran services on your campus and ensure that students are aware of them. The research Alexis Hart and I have conducted under a CCCC Research Initiative Grant suggests that many, if not most, faculty are unaware that their institutions have a veterans' coordinator, a veterans' student group, or a certifying official. Indeed, very few know what a certifying official does and how important that official is in ensuring that student-veterans receive educational benefits. Learn about these folks on your campus and provide contact information for them on your syllabus. Not all veterans self-identify as veterans, and most colleges do not offer any means by which faculty can discover if a particular student in a class is a veteran. It is largely only through self-disclosure that a faculty member learns it. Nonetheless, many veterans or family members of veterans have need of veterans' services or veterans' groups on campus. Indeed, it is not enough to ensure veterans are aware. We are a country at war; we are a culture at war. A variety of students may need to know about services on campus. Make that information transparent and available. What we are doing here is acknowledging that even if a student chooses silence as a strategy in one of our classes, they can choose another strategy in other settings that may feel or be safer.

(3) Learn to recognize, understand, and appreciate military structure and organization and how it might shape veteran responses and approaches to your class. A common experience for many student-veterans is a sense of disconnect from the type of structure they experience in the military. By learning about that military structure, we gain insight into some of the challenges some student-veterans face. Indeed, we likely also gain insight into some of the strengths student-veterans bring to the classroom. Understanding how and why military hierarchies work, then, provides not simply insight into our students, but likely insight into some of our own assumptions and biases about military service, representations of war and veterans, and institutional constraints on a very specific student demographic.

(4) If you choose to engage a class in discussions about war, provide options for writing assignments that, on the one hand, invite

participation in conversations about war and, on the other hand, offer the necessary space for students to deploy silence as a strategy. This pedagogy is empowering regardless of whether you are aware of veterans in the classroom or not. It honors the real complexity of war, the range of experiences and biases we each bring to discussions of war whether we are veterans or not, and it allows students to choose how they best can enter the conversation. Silence, here, should not be read as a failure to participate. Instead, it may be a viable, safe, and most appropriate response to a difficult issue. Offer space for that silence by providing alternatives by which students may express their positions or by which students can engage in the assignment.

The final suggestion above, to learn to provide opportunities for silence, is the most important and, likely, the most challenging for us as instructors of writing. Many of us have been trained to believe that written expression leads to the strongest rhetorical statements a student can make and that silence is a kind of failure or inability or unwillingness to engage. Even if the idea that silence is an act of agency is not foreign to us, we may feel uncomfortable approaching it in a composition classroom where the demands of most institutions insist that our students produce reams of written words. That dilemma, however, is predicated on the idea that silence is the antithesis of expression instead of part of rhetorical composition. If, instead, we can shift our understanding of silence to see it as an enactment of a different kind of speech, and thus teachable and visible as rhetorical action, we can find ways to introduce it into our coursework.

Anne Ruggles Gere (2001, 200) discusses her attempts to introduce silence as a viable rhetorical tool with her students, and she notes that especially in classes where personal writing is valued, "many students need specific instruction in order to resist the pressure to write self-revealing narratives. All students deserve to know that they need not disclose things that make them uncomfortable, and it is particularly important to put the tools of silence in the hands of students from populations typically underrepresented in higher education." Though Gere does not identify veterans as one of those groups, they make up a considerable demographic minority that enjoys the same federal protections as other minority groups, and their movement from the highly codified and objectified world of military discourse likely makes the transition to a classroom that includes personal writing feel particularly uncomfortable, if not overtly hostile to their own sense of personal safety. Among the tools Gere recommends are literary readings that include very clear, rhetorical uses of silence and ensuring students understand that silence is not the antithesis to speech but a powerful part of speech—not a lie of omission but an active ethical and aesthetic choice they may deploy in their work. For instructors who demand personal writing, especially those teaching veterans, teaching rhetorical silence is likely an ethical obligation, not simply an aesthetic classroom exercise.

These suggestions, then, are a way to communicate with students. They imply commitment not simply to understanding war and veterans' issues but to understanding different strategies for coping with the war experience. Our classrooms are opportunities to provide space for understanding and negotiation, and for those of us at colleges and universities with a clear and obvious military presence, that space must include awareness of the rhetorical uses of silence. We might feel we should help in the healing from war by asking our students to write about their experiences or by asking our students to engage in debate about the war, but maybe healing is not precisely what we should be seeking. Maybe all we should be seeking is empathy and a capacity to actually recognize the costs of war. Maybe all we should be seeking is to simply bear witness both to those who choose to break the silence and to those for whom silence *is* the best strategy for understanding their war. Both strategies, ultimately, demonstrate a powerful kind of agency, and both deserve to be honored.

Notes

1. In 2010, veteran enrollment surged in colleges, with an estimated 800,000 using the Post-9/11 GI Bill to fund their education, and those numbers are increasing (Department of Education 2011).

2. Among the most surprising results of the recent research Alexis Hart and I have conducted on veterans in college writing classrooms is the finding in our national survey of writing instructors that personal essays remain a pervasive feature of many college composition classrooms. We found that more than 70 percent of instructors reported using the personal essay in their classes, and while our survey participants were self-selected, the number of respondents and the wide range of institutions they represented, both in type (community college, four year, for profit) and geographic region, suggest that personal narrative is deeply embedded in composition as, at the very least, a rhetorical tool taught by writing faculty. From our perspective as researchers investigating student-veterans, this suggests heightened possibility of disclosure of veteran status in a classroom.

3. A common suggestion for teachers who have veterans in the classroom is to allow students to seat themselves; many combat veterans, in particular, feel safer when they are seated in a place where no one is behind them and the rest of the class is in front of them, often at the back of the class. The reasons for this suggestion vary but all boil down to a sense of safety and security for the veteran. Such advice might fly in the face of traditional advice to have a student move to the front of the classroom if that student is having difficulty in the course.

References

Belanoff, Pat. 2001. "Silence: Reflection, Literacy, Learning, and Teaching." *College Composition and Communication* 52 (3): 399–428. http://dx.doi.org/10.2307/358625.

Berlin, James. 1988. "Rhetoric and Ideology in the Writing Class." *College English* 50 (5): 477–94. http://dx.doi.org/10.2307/377477.

Bizzell, Patricia. 1982. "Cognition, Convention, and Certainty: What We Need to Know about Writing." *Pre/Text* 213 (3): 243.

Department of Education. 2011. *New Programs Help Veterans Transition from the Military to College.* http://www2.ed.gov/news/newsletters/ovaeconnection/2011/04212011.html.

Duffy, Suellyn. 2011. "Student Silences in the Deep South: Hearing Unfamiliar Dialects." In *Silence and Listening as Rhetorical Arts,* edited by Cheryl Glenn and Krista Ratcliffe, 293–303. Carbondale: Southern Illinois University Press.

Fick, Nathaniel. 2005. *One Bullet Away: The Making of a Marine Officer.* New York: Houghton Mifflin.

Fulkerson, Richard. 2005. "Composition at the Turn of the Twenty-First Century." *College Composition and Communication* 56 (4): 654–87.

Gere, Anne Ruggles. 2001. "Revealing Silence: Rethinking Personal Writing." *College Composition and Communication* 53 (2): 203–23. http://dx.doi.org/10.2307/359076.

Gilmore, Perry. 1985. "Silence and Sulking: Emotional Displays in the Classroom." In *Perspectives on Silence,* edited by Deborah Tannen and Muriel Saville-Troike, 139–62. Norwood, NJ: Ablex Publishing.

Glenn, Cheryl. 2004. *Unspoken: A Rhetoric of Silence.* Carbondale: Southern Illinois University Press.

Gray, Matt, and Thomas W. Lombardo. 2001. "Complexity of Trauma Narratives as an Index of Fragmented Memory in PTSD: A Critical Analysis." *Applied Cognitive Psychology* 15 (7): S171–86. http://dx.doi.org/10.1002/acp.840.

Hatlen, Burton. 1986. "Old Wine and New Bottles." In *Only Connect: Uniting Readings and Writing,* edited by Thomas Newkirk, 59–86. Upper Montclair, NJ: Boynton/Cook.

Hnida, Dave. 2010. *Paradise General: Riding the Surge at a Combat Hospital in Iraq.* New York: Simon and Schuster.

Hoyt, Tim, and Elizabeth A. Yeater. 2011. "The Effects of Negative Emotion and Expressive Writing on Posttraumatic Stress Symptoms." *Journal of Social and Clinical Psychology* 30 (6): 549–69. http://dx.doi.org/10.1521/jscp.2011.30.6.549.

Kalamaras, George. 1996–1997. "Meditative Silence and Reciprocity: The Dialogic Implications for 'Spiritual Sites of Composing.'" *Journal of the Assembly for Expanded Perspectives on Learning* 2:18–26.

Meehan, Shannon, and Roger Thompson. 2009. *Beyond Duty: Life on the Frontline in Iraq.* Boston: Polity Press.

Moffett, James. 1982. "Writing, Inner Speech, and Meditation." *College English* 44 (3): 231–46. http://dx.doi.org/10.2307/377011.

Pennebaker, James W. 1997. "Writing about Emotional Experiences as a Therapeutic Process." *Psychological Science* 8 (3): 162–66. http://dx.doi.org/10.1111/j.1467-9280.1997.tb00403.x.

Saint Augustine. 1991. *Confessions.* Translated by Henry Chadwick. New York: Oxford University Press.

Sim, Stuart. 2007. *Manifesto for Silence: Confronting the Politics and Culture of Noise.* Edinburgh: Edinburgh University Press.

Sloan, Denise M., Brian A. Feinstein, and Brian P. Marx. 2009. "The Durability of Beneficial Health Effects Associated with Expressive Writing." *Anxiety, Stress, and Coping* 22 (5): 509–23. http://dx.doi.org/10.1080/10615800902785608.

Smyth, Joshua M., Jill R. Hockemeyer, and Heather Tulloch. 2008. "Expressive Writing and Post-traumatic Stress Disorder: Effects on Trauma Symptoms, Mood States, and

Cortisol Reactivity." *British Journal of Health Psychology* 13 (1): 85–93. http://dx.doi.org /10.1348/135910707X250866.

Valentino, Marilyn J. 2010. "CCCC's Chair's Address: Rethinking the 4th C: Call to Action."

Workman, Jeremiah, and John Bruning. 2009. *Shadow of the Sword: A Marines Journey of War, Heroism, and Redemption.* New York: Random House.

10

A NEW MISSION
Veteran-Led Learning Communities in the Basic Writing Classroom

Ann Shivers-McNair

You walk into class that first day, you look around, and your heart sinks. You want to fit in, but you don't feel like them. I would have clung to anything that said "veteran" on it because I wanted to be around more people like me.

—Joel, student-veteran peer tutor
for veterans-cohort group

Neither basic writers nor veterans are new to our colleges and universities. Indeed, as George Otte and Rebecca Mlynarczyk have observed, with steady increases in enrollment in basic writing courses and since the passage of the Post-9/11 GI Bill, both groups constitute significant and growing populations at many institutions: "Because of the demographic of the US military, many of [the veterans enrolling in colleges and universities] will be first-generation college students who have been out of school for years—a group that has historically needed basic writing or other types of remediation to succeed" (Otte and Mlynarczyk 2010, 181). But these students are often marginalized by the academic and social cultures at their institutions. My institution, a midsized regional university in the Deep South, is located just a few miles north of a large army reserve component training site, and there is a strong presence of ROTC, National Reserves, National Guard, and veterans on our campus. And yet, at the time of this study, there were no dedicated services (beyond GI Bill-benefits counseling) for veterans at the institution—though our new VA representative has been working assiduously to change that. And even though veterans and military-affiliated students were visibly present in all our first-year writing courses, our

DOI: 10.7330/9780874219425.c010

composition program did not offer formal services to address veterans' needs and interests. A 2012 report for the American Council on Education (ACE) suggests that, in fact, many college campuses still lack organized services for student-veterans, even though student-veteran enrollments have risen significantly since the ACE's first report in 2009 (McBain, Kim, Cook, and Snead 2012, 7). Moreover, we can imagine that the veterans who find themselves in our basic writing courses are doubly marginalized and therefore especially deserving of our attention; like many basic writing students, these student-veterans often come to us as "wounded writers," to borrow Stephanie Boone's (2010) phrase. Boone defines wounded writers as those who have deep-rooted feelings of inadequacy, or a lack of "belief in [their] potential and agency" as writers (Boone 2010, 229).

With these exigencies in mind, I set about to create a positive space for veterans in the redesign and implementation of my institution's basic writing curriculum: specifically, I piloted a peer-led cohort group for student-veterans in basic writing. Because developing programs for student-veterans is necessarily contingent on institutional climate and circumstances, I collected demographic data on our students in first-year writing courses and involved both student-veterans and my institution's VA representative in the development of a basic writing cohort group for self-identified veterans and military-affiliated students, led by a veteran who is also an alumnus of the basic writing program. To guide my efforts and contextualize my observations, I turned to current scholarship on the importance of a like-minded community for student-veterans, as well as scholarship on the social and pedagogical benefits of learning communities, especially for marginalized students and students in developmental courses. I also conducted a survey of and held discussions with my English department colleagues about supporting student-veterans in the classroom, and I learned that not all my colleagues saw a need for such efforts. My experiences working with student-veterans, institutional partners, and my colleagues have led me to believe that involving student-veterans in the implementation of support efforts and forming a strategic partnership with the campus VA representative are key to turning academic checkpoints into points of access.

METHODS

I decided to pilot a learning community for veterans in an Expanded Composition class after working with Joel, a student-veteran and current ROTC candidate who took my class and told me he wanted to see more veterans in the program.[1] Expanded Composition extends the traditional first-year, first-semester writing curriculum over two semesters and is modeled after the Stretch Program at Arizona State University (see Glau 1996). Our program was beginning its third pilot year, and my colleague, the director of composition, and I had procured administrative approval to move into full implementation the following year.[2] I had been considering bringing back former Expanded Composition students to work with new students as peer tutors, or mentors, and Joel's insistence on the value of the program for student-veterans prompted me to form a cohort for veterans. "My biggest fear coming back to college was writing papers," he explained. While his work as a technician in the navy did involve writing, he described the writing as "mostly jargon and chicken scratch," adding that the first assignment in our writing course, a personal essay, felt "weird." He believed that the year-long format and emphasis on developing a writing community would help student-veterans with the transition into college life. That same semester, a new VA representative was hired in the admissions department, and she was eager to change what she saw as a culture of apathy toward student-veterans at USM. Given Joel's and the new VA representative's energy for creating a more visible community for veterans, I felt the time was right to implement a cohort group for veterans. And while such a model is especially dependent on institutional climate and context, I share my observations here in the hopes that others who may be considering similar efforts can benefit from the insights of the student-veterans who shaped and participated in our cohort group.

I designed this pilot as an instrumental case study, knowing my pilot group would likely be small.[3] As such, I knew that achieving a true random or representative sample for the case study would be impossible; rather, these study participants came together because of a common interest and goal. The experiences and perspectives of the student-veterans in this study are not meant to represent all student-veterans' experiences and perspectives. In fact, this case study was deeply rooted in the exigencies and limitations of our specific context. For example, the admissions department did not have a system in place for easily contacting incoming student-veterans (indeed, it was difficult to gather data on the past enrollment of military-affiliated students). And because Expanded Composition was still in a pilot phase, we could only offer five sections. I had a ten-minute time slot to advertise Expanded Composition during our summer preview sessions for incoming first-year students, and I included an invitation for our military-cohort group. But Joel told me that student-veterans are not likely to attend the summer preview sessions, an observation corroborated (albeit anecdotally) by the VA representative.

I decided, then, to survey our entire first-year composition program to gather much-needed demographic data on student-veterans and military-affiliated students in our program and, I hoped, to recruit student-veterans for my military-cohort group. Our Expanded Composition program is designed to accommodate students who initially enroll in a traditional first-year course and decide (or are encouraged) to enroll in Expanded Composition, so I administered the survey of first-year classes in the first two weeks of classes (the student survey is included in the appendix). I was somewhat surprised to find, in that first week, there were no self-identified student-veterans in my Expanded Composition classes and only one in the program. But in the following weeks, two student-veterans joined my Expanded Composition class: John and Jeff, whose instructors had recommended the Expanded Composition course. They were eager to form the military-cohort group with Joel, who worked with them during in-class workshops and met with them informally outside of class. Because their group was so small, they welcomed Jean, a campus police officer who had begun her first semester as an undergraduate student. Over the course of the program, I observed the group in class and conducted periodic semistructured interviews with the cohort members. While I was certainly interested in the rhetorical success of their writing, I was particularly interested in studying the ways in which a veterans-cohort group within the classroom community could provide the student-veterans a place to find "people more like [them]," as Joel put it, and also ultimately connect them to a larger community of writers and peers.

STUDENT-VETERANS AT MY INSTITUTION

Creating an effective learning community for student-veterans requires an understanding not only of national discourse and best practices but also of local circumstances, atmosphere, and population. Indeed, as several scholars have noted, administering surveys to and collecting data from the student population, especially, is important to establishing effective programs and partnerships (see Ford, Northrup, and Wiley 2009; Kattner 2009; Palmer 2011). The first question to ask, then, is how many student-veterans are in the first-year writing courses.

In their 2009 report for the American Council on Education (ACE), Bryan J. Cook and Young Kim discuss programs and services for veterans at higher-education institutions categorized as having low veteran

Table 10.1 Percent Increase of GI Bill Users, 2001–2011

Academic Year(s) — All Campuses	Highest Semester Enrollment of GI Bill Users	Percent Increase From Previous Year
2010–2011	729	31.6%
2009–2010	554	24.8%
2001–2008	444	18.9% (average)

Source: USM institutional data.

enrollment (LVE), or a military/veteran population less than or equal to 1 percent of total enrollment; moderate veteran enrollment (MVE), a military/veteran population between 1 and 3 percent; and high veteran enrollment (HVE), a military/veteran population greater than 3 percent (Cook and Kim 2009, 11). Measuring student-veteran enrollment at my institution proved difficult. Although the Post-9/11 GI Bill allows veterans to transfer unused educational benefits to spouses and children, our institutional data on students using the GI Bill did not distinguish between veterans and beneficiaries of veterans. Still, we'd had a significant increase in GI Bill users since the Post-9/11 GI Bill went into effect in August 2009 (see table 10.1).

In 2011, the year this study was conducted, we had 665 undergraduate students on our main campus using the GI Bill (see table 10.2), but we were certain not all those students were veterans. In fact, in surveys of students in our first-year writing classes, we found that 40 percent of students who reported using a military/VA/GI Bill to fund their education were beneficiaries of veterans (see table 10.3). When I mentioned this to the VA representative, she pointed out that many veterans enter the university with transfer credits and may not enroll in a first-year writing class, suggesting that in upper-division courses, veterans likely constituted a larger percentage of GI Bill users. Still, even if we assumed only 60 percent of our total GI Bill users were veterans, veterans constituted more than 3 percent of our total undergraduate population (about 400 students), and we would be considered by the ACE report standards to be an HVE institution. This was not surprising given my institution's proximity to military sites. Furthermore, John Schupp of the SERV program told me (via e-mail on August 11, 2011) that some 67 percent of my state's deployed veterans have returned to the state, which is above the national average. After all, as Joel remarked, "We're in the South. People are really supportive of the military."

What was surprising, however, was how few formal services my institution offered for veterans compared to the HVE institutions in both the

Table 10.2 Undergraduates Using GI Bill

Fall 2011—Main Campus	Total population	GI Bill Users
All undergraduate	12,277	665 (5.4%)
First-year writing survey respondents	1,295	47 (3.6%)

Source: USM institutional data and surveys.

Table 10.3 First-Year Writing Survey Respondents Using GI Bill

Course	Total Respondents	Veterans*	Active Duty	Reserves	Beneficiaries	Total Using GI Bill
English 099	158	0	0	1 (0.6%)	3 (1.9%)	4 (2.5%)
English 100E	70	2 (3.1%)	0	0	1 (1.4%)	3 (4.3%)
English 101	1,067	12 (1.1%)	2 (0.2%)	8 (0.8%)	18 (1.7%)	40 (3.8%)
Total	1,295	14 (1.1%)	2 (0.2%)	9 (0.7%)	22 (1.7%)	47 (3.6%)

Respondents who marked "veteran" and another category ("reserves" or "active duty") were counted as veterans to avoid duplication of data.

Source: FYW survey, fall 2011. (See Appendix A.)

2009 and 2012 ACE studies. The 2009 ACE study measured the percentages of institutions offering the following services and programs for veterans (by veteran enrollment): VA education-benefits counseling, transition assistance, financial aid/tuition-assistance counseling, employment assistance, career planning/career services, campus social and/or cultural events, academic support/tutoring, and academic advising (Cook and Kim 2009, 14). My institution's services—or lack thereof—more closely aligned with those of LVE institutions in the ACE reports: we had not added staff or programs to support student-veterans, nor did we offer dedicated counseling services. Before July 2011, one staff person in our university registrar's office was responsible for certifying students using the GI Bill, and that was the extent of services for veterans on our main campus; that person was replaced by a staff person in the financial-aid office who became responsible for VA education benefits counseling and for financial aid/tuition-assistance counseling.

While the services offered at my institution are the most commonly offered among all types of institutions, HVE institutions typically offer

Table 10.4 Student-Veteran Interest in Proposed Services

Course	Number of Veterans	Yes to Cohort Group	Maybe to Cohort Group	No to Cohort Group	Yes to Veterans' Lounge	Maybe to Veterans' Lounge	No to Veterans' Lounge
English 101	12	9 (75.0%)	2	1	10 (83.3%)	1	1
English 099 and 100E	2	2 (100%)	0	0	2 (100%)	0	0
Total	14	11 (78.6%)	2	1	12 (85.7%)	1	1

Source: FYW survey, fall 2011. (See Appendix A.)

more services than my institution does (Cook and Kim 2009, 14). So, our current VA representative began working to increase the services on our campus: she began hiring student-veterans through the VA and has articulated a plan to create a veterans' lounge/study area on campus that would offer transition assistance and counseling as well as academic support and tutoring. As I found in my survey of students in first-year writing classes, a significant number of students could benefit from and are interested in these services.[4] Nearly all the veterans and military personnel who identified as such expressed interest in the veterans' lounge/study area and the veterans-cohort group for writing students (see table 10.4).

Nevertheless, the results of the survey challenged some of my perceptions prior to this study. I had supposed, as Ryan Kelty and Meredith Kleykamp suggest, that "because military service and higher education are typically pursued at similar points in the life course, young military veterans may have lower levels of education attainment than peers who go straight into college" (Kelty, Kleykamp, and Segal 2010, 194). I noticed more self-identified veterans in my basic writing courses than in my traditional first-year courses, but the results of the survey showed, on the contrary, that there is a lower percentage of self-identified student-veterans in our basic writing courses than in our traditional first-year course, or at least there was in this particular semester.[5] This finding proved a sensitive issue in discussions with Joel, who, on the one hand, expressed irritation with people who stereotype veterans as "dumb grunts," and, on the other hand, emphasized the importance of our Expanded Composition class and a military cohort for first-year student-veterans. "It's not singling veterans out; it's saying, hey, we understand that it's different, because it is," he explained. Although Joel did not take our non-credit-bearing English 099 course, he did take Math 099 and had this to say about the possible negative effects of veterans being forced to take non-credit-bearing developmental classes: "I wouldn't take a 099 course unless I had to because there is a stigma." Moreover, given the GI Bill's time limitation, student-veterans who spend too much time in basic courses risk seeing their benefits run out before they complete their degrees. Still, these student-veterans and military-affiliated students found in their military cohort a community of determined peers for whom, as cohort member John put it, "failure is not an option."

STUDENT-VETERANS AND COMMUNITY

Just as much of the scholarship on addressing the needs and interests of student-veterans comes from the field of student services, existing services and programs for veterans—even those services categorized as academic—tend to be based in student services (see Cook and Kim 2009). Student-affairs administrators and researchers know well the importance of community in the success of all students, especially subgroups like student-veterans (Cook and Kim 2009, 9; DiRamio, Ackerman, and Mitchell 2008, 87). And should not these opportunities for connection be made available to student-veterans in the classroom as well? Galen Leonhardy (2009, 346), a compositionist and a veteran, notes the value of peer-group work—that staple of so many first-year writing courses—for student-veterans: "In peer groups, vets get to have their work read, quite often for the first time. Small groups seem to facilitate class discussions, which allow vets to establish in-group relationships and non-veterans to ask questions—questions that some students deeply long to have answered." But not all interactions with civilian classmates are positive; DiRamio, Ackerman, and Mitchell (2008, 87) point out that "several [student-veterans] even described irritation and impatience with their less mature civilian peers."

Joel found himself in this dilemma: he wanted to connect with his classmates in Expanded Composition, but at times the differences and distance proved exasperating. He explained in an interview that taking up academic writing after years away from school was intimidating enough, and because he was required to engage in extensive interaction with peers in group workshops and discussions, he would have welcomed an opportunity to work with students with similar experiences and maturity. He admitted to feeling alternately baffled and frustrated by his predominantly eighteen-year-old classmates, whom he jokingly called "the kids," in classroom discussions and group interactions. He expressed his hope that by his returning to the Expanded Composition classroom as a peer tutor, first-year student-veterans would not only have each other but also see "I'm here, I was in the military and I had to de-mode," and even though "it was scary at first, it really does get better."

While Joel is not a combat veteran, he acknowledged that this tension between wanting to connect with peers and feeling misunderstood is even greater for combat veterans. Jeff and John are both combat veterans, and John was very frank—first with his cohort group, and eventually with the entire class—about his combat injuries and struggles to adjust to college life. Indeed, Ackerman, DiRamio, and Mitchell (2009, 8) note, in their study of combat veterans' transition to college life, that "for many with whom we spoke, [becoming a college student] was the most difficult transition of all." In addition to problems with the VA and a lack of campus support services, these veterans described the difficulties of relearning study skills and dealing with psychological and physical wounds from combat. "I was in a coma for three months," John explained one day, "and they didn't think I was going to wake up." After his recovery, John experienced short-term memory loss and anxiety, as well as chronic pain from other injuries. He told me that the beginning of the semester was almost excruciatingly nerve wracking, but he gradually became more confident in his classroom and study skills. John was eager to identify and incorporate a community of student-veterans into his network of support. He emphasized that being able to talk to Joel about what to expect in our course was reassuring, and he said he hoped to be able to offer first-year student-veterans the same support.

But while our research and student-veterans themselves have identified the importance of a like-minded community in the transition from the service to college, we must also consider that many student-veterans are reluctant to be singled out as such, and many also want to assimilate into university culture. DiRamio, Ackerman, and Mitchell (2008, 88) found, in their interviews with student-veterans, that "blending in" was a priority for veterans, especially when they felt that being identified as a veteran would lead to uncomfortable or adversarial conversations with classmates and instructors. Importantly, these student-veterans reported that "faculty members who insisted on violating anonymity could make the veteran attempting to blend in feel uncomfortable." Corey Rumann and Florence Hamrick point out, similarly, that "some professors made inappropriate disclosure requests of student veterans in class or regarded student veterans as spokespersons for all veterans" (Rumann and Hamrick 2009, 30). At the same time, however, DiRamio,

Ackerman, and Mitchell (2008, 89) noticed that "a consistent message from the participants was that they hoped faculty members would acknowledge their veteran status and attempt to understand them as a student population." These findings, as well as corroborating advice from Joel, shaped my methodology for this pilot, from the means of collecting data to the decision to offer a cohort group within our existing and proposed composition course structures rather than a veterans-only composition course.

LEARNING COMMUNITIES AND STUDENT SUCCESS

The 2010 National Survey of Student Engagement (NSSE) drew attention to the experiences of student-veterans in higher education, pointing out that "first-year noncombat veterans were less engaged with faculty, and first-year combat veterans perceived less campus support than nonveterans" (NSSE 2010, 18). Rooted in social-constructivist and active-learning theory, learning communities are an increasingly popular strategy for addressing engagement and academic performance, particularly for first-year students, in higher-education institutions (Laufgraben 2005; Laufgraben and Shapiro 2004). The term *learning community* has also become increasingly complex and encompasses a variety of forms and models, but learning communities have traditionally been defined as "a variety of curricular approaches that intentionally link or cluster two or more courses, often around an interdisciplinary theme or problem, and enroll a common cohort of students" (Smith et al. 2004, 20).[6] Indeed, Smith et al. (2004, 25–27) emphasize that the history of learning communities has at its roots the commitment to democratic, student-centered pedagogies and expanded access to higher education first articulated by philosophers and educators John Dewey and Alexander Meiklejohn in the early twentieth century.[7] Learning communities gained traction in several experiments on the East and West Coasts in the 1960s and 1970s, and, by the beginning of the twenty-first century, had become a national movement that is now at a crossroads: "With the resurgence of interest in civic engagement and expanding access, colleges and universities are revisiting issues about their role and responsibilities to the larger society and looking toward learning communities as a promising strategy" (Smith et al. 2004, 34–62).

Administrators and researchers in both student affairs and developmental education have championed the positive potential of learning communities. As Barbara Smith (1993) argues in "Creating Learning Communities," learning communities are a "realistic response to hard times. Their success demonstrates that we can create successful academic communities, even in difficult places, because they rely more upon the development of communities of people than the massive infusion of new resources." Rachelle L. Darabi (2006, 54–55) highlights the particular importance of learning communities to basic writing programs, many of which have come under scrutiny by administrators and legislators who question the validity and effectiveness of developmental education. She reports that learning-community participants who took a basic writing course paired with an introductory speech course demonstrated "improved attendance, increased participation, improved completion of assigned work, and lower [drop/fail/withdraw] rates" (Darabi 2006, 69). It is important to consider, however, that even as researchers and administrators are celebrating the potential and observed successes of the learning-community model, there is not a consensus on the extent to which learning communities impact students' persistence and success in their degree programs, especially if the learning community is limited to the first year (see Reynolds and Hebert 1998; Weissman et al. 2011).

Like many other programs focused on collaborative learning, my cohort-group model draws on the work of Kenneth Bruffee (1993, 28), who recommends consensus groups in which "people work collaboratively on a limited but open-ended task, negotiating among themselves what they think and know in order to arrive at some kind of consensus or agreement, including, sometimes, to disagree." Bruffee (1993, 29) explains that the independence and autonomy of consensus groups is key in reinforcing "productive collaboration among peers" rather than the "teacher's own community of knowledgeable peers." Or, as Vincent Tinto and Anne Goodsell-Love put it, "By opening up the conversation about what is known to many voices, student and faculty, the [learning-community] program allowed students to discover abilities they did not know they possessed" (Tinto and Goodsell-Love 1993). Derek V. Price (2005, 6–7) notes that cohort groups "provide ample opportunity for peer leaders—usually former interest-group students—to work as tutors and lead weekly seminars. The seminars are often used as an 'orientation' course where peer leaders help students ease the transition from high school to college." Iris M. Saltiel and Charline S. Russo are careful to point out, furthermore, that cohort groups are distinct from—and preferable to—study groups or support groups (Saltiel and Russo 2001, 3). While our cohort group also functioned as an informal study group (Joel occasionally met with John and Jeff in the library during the semester), most of their interactions happened in the classroom in workshop settings, where Joel facilitated peer review of the group's drafts.

At the root of this peer collaboration is a theory of active learning, a central tenet of learning-community scholarship. Marcia Magolda-Baxter (1992, 209) describes an educational approach that blends constructive-developmental theory (constructive in the sense that people actively construct knowledge and developmental in the sense that this construction is ordered and happens over time) with social-constructivist theory and dialectic approaches, arguing that "pedagogy must be an interdependent relationship between teachers and students to engage the students' way of making meaning in the context of the course goals." This meaning-making function of our cohort group was perhaps its most significant: both John and Jeff chose military issues and experiences for their essay topics, and the three members provided each other empathetic readings and constructive responses in ways that I, as an outsider, could not offer. Indeed, I noticed that the quality of their writing—and, specifically, their awareness of audience and rhetorical context—was consistently above the class average and often the strongest in the class. It may be impossible to prove a directly causal relationship between their work in the writing group and the rhetorical success of their projects. Still, I believe that sharing their writing with peers who shared intimate knowledge of the subject matter and intended audience, as well as a strong commitment to the writing process, account for at least some of these writers' rhetorical successes.

The meaning-making function of the student-veterans' cohort group was so strong, in fact, that their writing interests shaped my pedagogy and, specifically, the design of the final assignment in the course sequence. In an interview at the end of his first semester in Expanded Composition, Jeff told me he was interested in creating an educational presentation for his civilian classmates on the experiences of a student-veteran at the university. Even though he found most of his peers to be generally supportive, Jeff also sensed distance and perhaps discomfort. "I think people don't know how to treat us sometimes because they don't understand us," he explained. He expressed his hope that by presenting to his peers in a formal setting, he could help them understand and relate to the unique experiences of student-veterans. I immediately thought of the VA representative's ongoing work to establish a formal faculty-training session on interacting with and acknowledging the interests of student-veterans. And I also thought of the last writing project of the second semester in Expanded Composition, which asked students to write a proposal essay on an education-related issue and submit that proposal to an actual audience. When I asked Jeff if he would be interested in not only writing his proposal essay on student-veterans' experiences at our institution but also working with the VA representative on a faculty-training program, he responded enthusiastically. Because Jeff had envisioned his project as a presentation to his peers, I also decided to change the second-semester curriculum of the Expanded Composition program: in addition to writing and sending their proposals, students would also be asked to give presentations on their proposals to their classmates, giving Jeff, as well as all the students in the program, a platform to share their work with and address their peers directly.

DIVERSITY AND HOMOGENEITY IN LEARNING COMMUNITIES

While most learning-community researchers agree that learning communities produce positive outcomes for students, there is some debate among learning-community scholars and advocates on the ideal composition of learning communities. While nearly all agree that diversity and inclusion are primary values of the learning community, their recommendations regarding the extent of diversity within the learning community vary. Patricia A. James, Patrick L. Bruch, and Rashné R. Jehangir advocate for the creation of multicultural learning communities in developmental first-year courses, emphasizing the importance of helping students develop a "strong sense of how one's individual identity relates to larger cultural dynamics" (James, Bruch, and Jehangir 2006, 12). Smith et al. (2004, 109), on the other hand, note the value of learning communities developed to help special student groups, including underrepresented minorities and first-generation learners, "achieve greater academic success." Studies have noted, furthermore, that students of color are more likely to join a learning community (Engstrom and Tinto 2008, 11; Zhao and Kuh 2004, 120). Engstrom and Tinto's study observes the positive effects of learning-community involvement on low-income students of diverse backgrounds, especially racial and ethnic minorities. It seems, then, that the learning-community model has significant potential for creating inclusive spaces for students who may otherwise feel like outsiders to the academic community.

But, as sociologist David Jaffee (2004) remarks, "No plan can fully realize all of its intended objectives, and every program designed to produce some social good has the potential to also produce unanticipated problems." In the case of learning-community composition, both diversity and homogeneity can present such problems. Jaffee's concerns with the first-year learning-community model include the dangers of homogeneity (at least in terms of age and academic inexperience) and the potential to reinforce negative attitudes and spread misinformation.

While Jaffee is specifically addressing learning communities for traditional-aged first-year students, homogeneity in any group can have negative outcomes, as Bruffee (1993, 32) notes:

> Groups that are socially or ethnically too homogenous (everyone from the same home town, neighborhood, family, or fraternity; close friends, teammates, clique members) tend to agree too soon, since they have an investment in maintaining the belief that their differences on basic issues are minimal. There is not enough articulated dissent or resistance to consensus to invigorate the conversation. Worse, homogenous groups tend to find the differences that do arise difficult to endure and are quick to paper them over.

These are certainly legitimate concerns, and, from an outsider's perspective, they may seem especially applicable to such an apparently homogenous group as military veterans. Our experiences and conversations with student-veterans, however, instruct us otherwise. True, there may be a shared affiliation with the military—and there may be a noticeable lack of gender diversity, at least—but the experiences, ages, and beliefs of these student-veterans vary significantly. In fact, the student-veterans and military-affiliated students I worked with suggested to me that there is not only the possibility of but also an expectation for differences and disagreements among veterans of different branches, ranks, wars/operations, and combat experiences—not to mention political and personal differences.

Even as, in a conversation with our VA representative, I recounted friendly classroom banter between Joel, a veteran navy sailor, and another student, a marine reservist, she reminded me of the possibility for real tension between "FOBbits," personnel who stay mostly on the Forward Operating Base (FOB), and soldiers who go "outside the wire," or into combat or harm's way. In an interview, Joel expressed a similar concern about talking to veterans with combat experience and wearing his ROTC uniform to class visits.

> I was in the navy, I was on a ship. Had we even been in combat, I wouldn't have seen it. We had guns that could shoot from a mile away. So it's difficult for me to sit down and talk to someone who's been in combat because I wanted to be in combat. I joined the navy on September 4, 2001; I joined thinking I wanted to be on submarines. Had I not [already] gone to boot camp, I would have been back in my recruiter's office [after 9/11] saying I wanted to be a marine because I wanted to fight. I [recently] joined the ROTC with the purpose of going infantry and eventually Special Forces. But there is some tension with combat veterans. That's why I was worried about being in the ROTC, because I'll be in uniform on Monday and Wednesday [days he visited my classes]—but I have class and I don't have

time to change. I just don't want those guys to look at me, especially the ones who come out of the infantry, and it be weird.

There was, fortunately, no apparent tension between Joel and combat veterans John and Jeff, but they quickly acknowledged their different experiences. As we seek to provide common ground and solidarity for our student-veterans, then, we should also recognize the diversity and difference within this demographic.

Indeed, in some ways, these students may be an ideal "consensus group," to use Bruffee's term, because as Bruffee (1993, 32) also notes, groups that are "too heterogenous may have no basis for arriving at consensus—or no means for doing so: they find that they cannot 'come to terms' because they 'don't speak the same language.'" Student-veterans do bring diversity and difference to a group, but they also share a common language, literally and figuratively. While, from the beginning, our cohort-group members shared clear commonalities and interests, their focus and interests turned increasingly outward, especially in the second semester of the program. Far from becoming a clique, the cohort members seemed to draw on the confidence and trust within their group as they reached out more and more to their classmates, often choosing to work with other classmates and engaging their peers in energetic discussions about campus issues.

Still—and perhaps not surprisingly—in conversations with and surveys of my colleagues, concerns about a veterans- and military-only groups surfaced frequently. But instead of focusing on the groups' internal relationships, they were concerned about external relationships. One colleague said, simply, "I would worry about separating [veterans and military-affiliated students] from the rest of the student population: many might already feel isolated or marginalized, and might not this only further that feeling?" Another colleague offered his philosophy that "rationality unites rather than emphasizes differences," suggesting that the creation of a homogenous group might ultimately reinforce their differences with/from other classmates.

None of my colleagues, however, directly addressed the potential for conflict between an apparently homogenous learning community (specifically, a veterans- or military-only group) and the instructor, although several alluded to this issue by pointing out that they "lacked experience" or would not feel comfortable working with such a group. It is difficult to separate, in a case involving military personnel, the personal and political feelings of my colleagues from their pedagogical concerns, but they are not alone in expressing doubts. Several researchers have noted the potentially negative effects of learning communities on students' relationships with their instructors (Jaffee 2004; Saltiel and Russo 2001). Saltiel and Russo (2001, 61) describe such an effect in a learning community for adults: "When the power of the group is strong, they can weaken professors, by challenging their authority and knowledge base in such ways that at one institution an instructor was left cowering in a corner. The power of the group is the group using their power." While neither instructors nor students should be cowering in corners, we must also consider the positive possibilities of empowered groups and dialectic engagement with instructors, especially if we subscribe to a theory of education that encourages both participation and questioning on the part of students (see Shor 1992; Shor and Freire 1989). Even as Shor (1992, 24–25) acknowledges the potential for conflict among students and between students and instructors in "empowering classrooms," he maintains that the possibility of conflict is still preferable to teacher-centered settings in which "student alienation is provoked and then driven underground." And especially in the case of marginalized students, the pedagogical and social benefits of an empowered group often outweigh the negative effects of conflict—which, of course, can also be productive.

Still, these concerns about the pedagogical and social limitations of learning communities—and especially groups organized around similar interests or identities—shaped the design of our program. Just as much of the scholarship on student-veterans focuses on transitions, our veteran-led cohort group is a point in transition, a means rather than an end, a dynamic rather than a static experience, and perhaps the most important facilitator of that transition for student-veterans is the student-veteran peer tutor leading the cohort group. While student-veteran peer tutors are especially effective in relating to their veteran and military-affiliated peers, the practice of employing peer tutors in writing courses and studios, especially for basic writers, has a long history of success, beginning in the 1970s (see Bruffee 1980; Hartwell 1980). The peer-tutoring model quickly gained traction outside of writing programs as well (see Martin and Hurley 2005). And in a National Center for Academic Transformation (NCAT) report on redesigning introductory courses, Carol Twigg (2005, 11) notes that undergraduate tutors were particularly effective at relating to and assisting their peers, and with tangible results: the more peer-tutor-led studio sessions students attended, the better they performed in their introductory course. Still, despite the wealth of evidence demonstrating the effectiveness of peer tutors in first-year and developmental education—not to mention the cost effectiveness, as Twigg points out—some faculty and administrators are wary, at best, of the peer-tutoring model. "I find the term *peer tutor* deeply contradictory," one colleague said of our proposed veteran-led learning community.[8]

REFLECTIONS AND RECOMMENDATIONS

Given the limitations of this case study, there is certainly room for further research: it remains to be seen, for example, what effect, if any, the veterans-cohort group will have on the student-veterans' future academic work and completion of their degrees. In the meantime, though, writing program administrators and faculty considering adopting a veterans-cohort group model should consider, in addition to student population, interest, and flexibility within basic writing course structures, the following important factors: faculty attitudes toward the veterans-cohort model, possibilities for administrative partnerships (especially with a VA representative), and the positioning of the student-veteran peer tutor.

My institution is perhaps not unlike many public, four-year institutions in its staffing of first-year writing courses with graduate-student instructors and contingent faculty (with the exception of the director of composition and myself). Full-time, tenured/tenure-track faculty almost never teach English 101, and the two or three faculty who do teach this course instruct honors college sections only. I found, in my surveys, that while graduate students and contingent faculty expressed unanimous support for the veterans-cohort group, just half of full-time faculty surveyed expressed support (see table 10.5).[9] In interviews, I also found that full-time faculty were far less supportive of the peer-led cohort model than were graduate students and contingent faculty (many of whom began their careers at this institution working in the university writing center as tutors). The less enthusiastic response of full-time faculty may be attributed to a lack of awareness of veterans' issues since our institution is just beginning to formally address these issues. As the survey data reveal, full-time faculty reported encountering fewer student-veterans and military-affiliated students in their classes. Several of them also expressed reluctance to support peer tutoring as an instructional model. On the other hand, perhaps the immediacy of their teaching (and tutoring) experiences in first-year writing causes graduate students and contingent faculty to be more supportive of alternative instructional models and initiatives for veterans and military students. While I have adopted an informal model in my classes and have anchored my model in a partnership with the VA representative, I imagine that a formalized peer tutor/cohort-group model would be more viable in departments in which all or most full-time faculty are teaching first-year composition.

Table 10.5 Faculty Responses to Veterans Issues Survey

Survey Question	Full-Time Faculty (Tenured, Tenure-Track and Non-Tenure-Track)	Graduate Student and Contingent Faculty	Combined Faculty
Average Number of Semesters Teaching FYW	18.1	5.1	8.9
Average Percent of Military Students Encountered in FYW	1.8%	2.7%	2.4%
Observed Tension between Military and Nonmilitary Students	37.5%	31.6%	33.3%
Observed Military Students Writing about Military Experiences	37.5%	42.1%	40.7%
Taught at Institution Offering Veterans Learning Community	0%	10.5%	7.4%
Expressed Support for Veterans-Cohort Group at USM	50.0%	100.0%	85.2%
Would Teach a Course with Veterans-Cohort Group	37.5%	78.9%	66.7%

Source: English department faculty survey, fall 2011.

Given the limited interest and support from my full-time colleagues in the English department, as well as my logistical limitations, including an inability to contact student-veterans before the start of the semester, I knew I needed to look beyond the department for partnership opportunities. Charles C. Schroeder (2005, 204) maintains that collaboration is "the only way to bridge the great divide between the curriculum and the cocurriculum—between academic affairs and student affairs—that has existed for decades." He adds that "building partnerships between the two groups on campus most committed to students is the best way to create a truly integrated and coherent experience and, in the process, realize the full educational potential of the first college year." Learning-community researchers have noted, moreover, the importance of administrative partnerships in sustaining learning-community programs beyond the tenure of one enthusiastic faculty member or administrator (Laufgraben and Shapiro 2004, 24–25).

Because formal campus resources for student-veterans were scarce, I initially designed the group to function without the support of other campus services. I would locate the self-identified veterans and military-affiliated students already enrolled in our basic writing companion course and offer them the opportunity to join a veteran-led cohort group and, possibly in the future, to seek employment in the program as peer tutors, thus providing community, academic support, and employment opportunities. And while the original plan still stands, we are fortunately no longer limited to our basic writing classes, or even first-year writing classes; the current VA representative, who is married to a veteran and plans to pursue doctoral research in veterans' issues in education, eagerly agreed to a collaboration. Beyond the obvious practical implications of a partnership between a student-affairs initiative and a basic writing program that serves some 30 percent of all first-year students, this collaboration is significant as a means of creating a more holistic experience for first-year student-veterans and as a means of stabilizing and maintaining the services we offer them. This symbiotic relationship benefits both the composition program efforts and the VA representative's efforts: our pilot group also doubles as a focus group for her efforts to assess veterans' interests in additional campus services and programs. Furthermore, the VA representative helped secure payment from the VA for our student-veteran peer tutor, further professionalizing the veterans-cohort program. And because, as I mentioned in my discussion of our first-year writing survey results, the VA representative and I believe many of our student-veterans may not be in our first-year writing courses, I have committed to training a student-veteran to work as a collaborative-writing tutor in the academic study area of the proposed veterans' lounge, which will be under the supervision of our VA representative.

There is much room for growth in our understanding of and efforts to reach out to student-veterans. But beyond acknowledging their presence, needs, and interests, involving student-veterans, as well as the campus VA representative, in the design and implementation of military/veteran-friendly spaces can offer us new insights and opportunities for turning academic checkpoints into points of access. The strategies discussed in this study may not be effective for every campus; indeed, as we have seen, programs and services for student-veterans must be tailored to their unique local circumstances. But the underlying principles—creating space for student-veteran voices and addressing their needs and interests by involving them in the initiative—resonate with core values of our work in composition.

Notes

1. Students' names have been replaced with pseudonyms. This project was approved by the university's Institutional Review Board for Human Subjects, and all participants in the study gave their informed consent.

2. In full implementation, most basic writing students will be placed into Expanded Composition; state policy, however, requires that students whose ACT English subscores are below 17 take, in addition, a noncredit bearing course. We have reenvisioned this course, English 099E, as a companion course to the first semester of Expanded Composition, drawing on the Accelerated Learning Project model at the Community College of Baltimore County. In the vein of the basic writing studio model, or to use Judith Rodby and Tom Fox's term, an "adjunct workshop," students in English 099E will work in a cohort group, facilitated by a faculty instructor, on their writing projects for Expanded Composition (Rodby and Fox 2000, 91). My survey results suggest that most of our student-veterans who qualify for a basic writing course will be placed in Expanded Composition but not in English 099E.

3. I use the term *instrumental case study* as Robert Stake (2005, 445) defines it—"a particular case . . . examined mainly to provide insight into an issue"—though my case certainly has elements of an intrinsic study, especially since "in all its particularity *and* ordinariness, this case itself is of interest."

4. My study did not include students or faculty on our gulf-coast campus, nor did it include online sections of English 101 or honors-college sections of English 101.

5. It should be noted, however, that in the weeks after I surveyed the first-year students in English 099, 100E, and 101, nearly fifty students moved from English 101 into English 100E or English 099. Furthermore, while students in basic writing classes constitute only 21 percent of the total first-year writing student population, in our proposed full implementation of Expanded Composition, we estimate that some 30 percent of students—all those scoring below a 20 on the English portion of the ACT—will be placed in our basic writing program.

6. Scholars frequently include in their discussions definitions of several common iterations of the learning community: (1) clustered or paired courses, (2) cohorts in large courses (also referred to as freshman interest groups or FIGs), and (3) a team-taught, interdisciplinary model (Darabi 2006; Laufgraben 2005; Laufgraben and Shapiro 2004; Malnarich and Dusenberry 2003; Price 2005). Variations on these themes are nearly infinite, and many learning communities also include a common residence for members (Laufgraben and Shapiro 2004, 5).

7. Meiklejohn first coined the term *learning community*; Patrick Hill popularized the term in the 1970s by applying it to the federated learning communities he developed at SUNY-Stony Brook (Smith et al. 2004, 49).

8. Indeed, the director of composition and I had, at first, envisioned an Expanded Composition writing studio as a large-course section in which all students—not just student-veterans—would be placed in cohort groups led by peer tutors under the supervision of an instructor. But as full implementation drew closer, the residual concerns of colleagues and administrators, as well as limited resources to recruit and train tutors, led us to redesign the studio as small, one-hour sections led by instructors rather than peer tutors.

9. Less than one-third of the main-campus English department faculty—and just under half of graduate-student instructors and contingent faculty—responded to my request to survey and/or interview them (eight of twenty-nine faculty, nineteen of forty-three instructors).

References

Boone, Stephanie D. 2010. "Thin Skin, Deep Damage: Addressing the Wounded Writer in the Basic Writing Course." *Arts and Humanities in Higher Education* 9 (2): 227–42. http://dx.doi.org/10.1177/1474022210360192.

Bruffee, Kenneth A. 1980. "Staffing and Operating Peer-Tutoring Writing Centers." In *Basic Writing: Essays for Teachers, Researchers, and Administrators*, edited by Lawrence N. Kasden and Daniel R. Hoeber, 141–49. Urbana, IL: NCTE.

Bruffee, Kenneth A. 1993. *Collaborative Learning*. Baltimore: Johns Hopkins University Press.

Cook, Bryan J., and Young Kim. 2009. *From Soldier to Student: Easing the Transition of Service Members on Campus*. Washington, DC: American Council on Education. http://www .acenet.edu/news-room/Documents/From-Soldier-to-Student-Easing-the-Transition -of-Service-Members-on-Campus.pdf.

Darabi, Rachelle L. 2006. "Basic Writers and Learning Communities." *Journal of Basic Writing* 25 (1): 53–72.

DiRamio, David, Robert Ackerman, and Regina L. Mitchell. 2008. "From Combat to Campus: Voices of Student-Veterans." *NASPA Journal* 45 (1): 73–102.

Engstrom, Cathy McHugh, and Vincent Tinto. 2008. "Learning Better Together: The Impact of Learning Communities on the Persistence of Low-Income Students." *Opportunity Matters* 1: 5–21.

Ford, Deborah, Pamela Northrup, and Lusharon Wiley. 2009. "Connections, Partnerships, Opportunities, and Programs to Enhance Success for Military Students." In *Creating a Veteran-Friendly Campus: Strategies for Transition and Success*, edited by David DiRamio and Robert Ackerman, 61–69. Special issue, *New Directions for Student Services* 126. San Francisco: Jossey-Bass. http://dx.doi.org/10.1002/ss.317.

Glau, Gregory R. 1996. "The 'Stretch Program': Arizona State University's New Model of University-Level Basic Writing Instruction." *WPA: Writing Program Administration* 20 (1–2): 79–91.

Hartwell, Patrick. 1980. "A Writing Laboratory Model." In *Basic Writing: Essays for Teachers, Researchers, and Administrators*, edited by Lawrence N. Kasden and Daniel R. Hoeber, 63–73. Urbana, IL: NCTE.

James, Patricia A., Patrick L. Bruch, and Rashné R. Jehangir. 2006. "Ideas in Practice: Building Bridges in a Multicultural Learning Community." *Journal of Developmental Education* 29 (3): 10–18.

Jaffee, David. 2004. "Learning Communities Can Be Cohesive—and Divisive." *Chronicle of Higher Education* 50 (44): B16.

Kattner, Therese. 2009. "Low-Cost Ideas for Serving Veterans." *Recruitment and Retention in Higher Education* 23 (8): 2–3.

Kelty, Ryan, Meredith Kleykamp, and David R. Segal. 2010. "Military and the Transition to Adulthood." *Future of Children* 20 (1): 181–207. http://dx.doi.org/10.1353/foc .0.0045.

Laufgraben, Jodi Levine. 2005. "Learning Communities." In *Challenging and Supporting the First-Year Student*, edited by M. Lee Upcraft, John N. Gardner, and Betsy O. Barefoot, 371–87. San Francisco: Jossey-Bass.

Laufgraben, Jodi Levine, and Nancy S. Shapiro. 2004. *Sustaining and Improving Learning Communities*. San Francisco: Jossey-Bass.

Leonhardy, Galen. 2009. "Transformations: Working with Veterans in the Composition Classroom." *Teaching English in the Two-Year College* 36 (4): 339–52.

Magolda-Baxter, Marcia. 1992. *Knowing and Reasoning in College: Gender-Related Patterns in Students' Intellectual Development*. San Francisco: Jossey-Bass.

Malnarich, Gillies, and Pam Dusenberry. 2003. *The Pedagogy of Possibilities: Developmental Education, College-Level Studies, and Learning Communities. National Learning Communities*

Project Monograph Series. Olympia, WA: Evergreen State College, Washington Center for Improving the Quality of Undergraduate Education, in cooperation with the American Association for Higher Education.

Martin, Deanna C., and Maureen Hurley. 2005. "Supplemental Instruction." In *Challenging and Supporting the First-Year Student*, edited by M. Lee Upcraft, John N. Gardner, and Betsy O. Barefoot, 308–19. San Francisco: Jossey-Bass.

McBain, Lesley, Young M. Kim, Bryan J. Cook, and Kathy M. Snead. 2012. *From Soldier to Student II: Assessing Campus Programs for Veterans and Service Members*. Washington, DC: American Council on Education. http://www.acenet.edu/news-room/Documents /From-Soldier-to-Student-II-Assessing-Campus-Programs.pdf.

National Survey for Student Engagement (NSSE). 2010. *Major Differences: Examining Student Engagement by Field of Study—Annual Results 2010*. Bloomington, IN: Indiana University Center for Postsecondary Research.

Otte, George, and Rebecca Mlynarczyk. 2010. *Basic Writing*. West Lafayette, IN: Parlor Press.

Palmer, Clark. 2011. "Improving Services for Student Veterans." *Recruitment and Retention in Higher Education* 25(2): 6–7.

Price, Derek V. 2005. "Learning Communities and Student Success in Postsecondary Education: A Background Paper." *MDRC*. www.mdrc.org/sites/default/files/full_421 .pdf.

Reynolds, Katherine C., and Hebert, F. Ted Hebert. 1998. "Learning Achievements of Students in Cohort Groups." *Journal of Continuing Higher Education* 46 (3): 34–42. http://dx.doi.org/10.1080/07377366.1998.10400354.

Rodby, Judith, and Tom Fox. 2000. "Basic Work and Material Acts: The Ironies, Discrepancies, and Disjunctures of Basic Writing and Mainstreaming." *Journal of Basic Writing* 19 (1): 84–99.

Rumann, Corey B., and Florence A. Hamrick. 2009. "Supporting Student Veterans in Transition." In *Creating a Veteran-Friendly Campus: Strategies for Transition and Success*, edited by David DiRamio and Robert Ackerman, 25–34. Special issue of *New Directions for Student Services* 126. San Francisco: Jossey-Bass. http://dx.doi.org/10.1002/ss.313.

Saltiel, Iris M., and Charline S. Russo. 2001. *Cohort Programming and Learning: Improving Educational Experiences for Adult Learners*. Malabar, FL: Krieger.

Schroeder, Charles C. 2005. "Collaborative Partnerships Between Academic and Student Affairs." In *Challenging and Supporting the First-Year Student*, edited by M. Lee Upcraft, John N. Gardner, and Betsy O. Barefoot, 204–20. San Francisco: Jossey-Bass.

Shor, Ira. 1992. *Empowering Education: Critical Teaching for Social Change*. Chicago: University of Chicago Press.

Shor, Ira, and Paulo Freire. 1989. *A Pedagogy for Liberation: Dialogues on Transforming Education*. Westport, CT: Bergin & Garvey.

Smith, Barbara Leigh. 1993. "Creating Learning Communities." *Liberal Education* 79 (4): 32–39.

Smith, Barbara Leigh, Jean MacGregor, Roberta S. Matthews, and Faith Gabelnick. 2004. *Learning Communities: Reforming Undergraduate Education*. San Francisco: Jossey-Bass.

Stake, Robert E. 2005. "Qualitative Case Studies." In *The Sage Handbook of Qualitative Research*, 3rd ed., edited by Norman K. Denzin and Yvonna S. Lincoln, 443–66. Thousand Oaks, CA: Sage.

Tinto, Vincent, and Anne Goodsell-Love. 1993. "Building Community." *Liberal Education* 79 (4): 16–22.

Twigg, Carol. 2005. "Increasing Success for Underserved Students: Redesigning Introductory Courses." *National Center for Academic Transformation*. http://www.then-cat.org/Monographs/IncSuccess.htm.

Weissman, Evan, Kristin F. Butcher, Emily Schneider, Jedediah Teres, Herbert Collado, and David Greenberg. 2011. "Learning Communities for Students in Developmental

Math: Impact Studies at Queensborough and Houston Community Colleges." *MDRC.* http://dx.doi.org/10.2139/ssrn.1782120.

Zhao, Chun-Mei, and George D. Kuh. 2004. "Adding Value: Learning Communities and Student Engagement." *Research in Higher Education* 45 (2): 115–38. http://dx.doi.org /10.1023/B:RIHE.0000015692.88534.de.

APPENDIX A: SURVEY INSTRUMENT FOR FIRST-YEAR WRITING STUDENTS*

Survey I: First-Year Students in English 099, 100E, and 101

Please respond to the following questions.

1. Which of the following best describe(s) your current status? Please mark all that apply.

   a. Civilian

   b. Active military

   c. Retired military

   d. Reserves

   e. Military veteran

   f. Military beneficiary/relative

2. Mark the sources that are covering your living and colleges expenses while you attend the University of Southern Mississippi. Please select all that apply.

   a. Scholarships

   b. Grants

   c. Loans

   d. On-campus job

   e. Off-campus job

   f. Parents

   g. Siblings

   h. Employer

   i. Military/VA/GI Bill

   j. Other (please specify):

3. Please select your age range:

   a. 18–23

   b. 24–30

   c. 31–40

   d. 41–50

   e. 51–Above

4. Military Personnel (active, reserve, veteran, and retired): If a centrally located space on campus were dedicated to student-military personnel for socializing, accessing records, working with the Financial Aid VA Representative, and studying, how likely would you be to utilize the space?

   a. Very likely

   b. Likely

   c. Somewhat likely

   d. Unlikely

   e. Very unlikely

5. Military Personnel (active, reserve, veteran, and retired): We are piloting a classroom model in which students meet in small groups facilitated by an undergraduate peer leader. If you had the opportunity to join a small group of other military-affiliated students in first-year composition that is led by an undergraduate student-veteran, would

you do so? *Note: This group would also serve as a focus group for efforts to improve campus resources for military-affiliated students.*

a. Yes   b. No   c. Maybe

Why?

*This survey was approved by the Institutional Review Board for Human Subjects at the University of Southern Mississippi. Before the surveys were administered, all participants gave their informed consent after hearing a presentation on the study and reading and signing an informed consent letter.

11

THE VALUE OF SERVICE LEARNING FOR STUDENT-VETERANS

Transitioning to Academic Cultures through Writing and Experiential Learning

Bonnie Selting

> *For the things we have to learn before we can do them, we learn by doing them . . .*
> —Aristotle, *Nicomathean Ethics*,
> Book 2, part 1

INTRODUCTION

In 2008, an assistant director of a service-learning program at a large, midwestern research-one university shared with her military husband stationed in Iraq that their state's government was making moves to cap tuition for veterans returning to postsecondary education. She was surprised that her husband did not seem to share her excitement about the moves being made to help ensure military veterans could afford college. When she asked him about his lack of enthusiasm, she found that he and several of his returning-vet buddies were uncomfortable with the idea of sitting in a classroom filled with the eighteen- to twenty-year-olds they once were. This situation mirrors research findings (Broder 2011; Katopes 2009; McDaniel 2004; Nesser 2011; in a report by the Student Veterans Task Force ("Student Veterans Task Force" 2011) that show many veterans find it frustrating to return to an uncertain environment like academia where there is no one who will instinctively "watch their backs" or assume the kind of responsibility they have come to expect from many months or years of war-zone realities. No matter the duty— from mechanics ensuring the efficient operation of aircraft carriers to engineers eluding snipers while building a bridge to front-line combatants—these veteran soldiers' value systems contrast decidedly from

DOI: 10.7330/9780874219425.c011

those of a "traditional" student. For example, after researching and compiling lists of the characteristics veterans bring with them to campus, James Mason University contends that "while not all veterans have experienced combat, all have experienced the stresses of a 'no-front' war in which serious threats to their lives are present" ("Resources for Returning War Veterans" 2012). Both *high magnitude* events and circumstances like "reality-based fear of their own serious injury or death" or "the requirement to attempt to kill the enemy" and *low magnitude* stressors like "unfamiliar living conditions [causing] irregular sleep and eating patterns. . . harsh climates . . . heavy physical demands with long work days, and . . . sexual, gender, or racial harassment" are logically bound to shape a veteran's attitude toward, and perception of, an academic environment ("Resources for Returning War Veterans" 2012). In light of these realities, then, many of our returning veterans need a kind of pedagogy not always available in a traditional classroom format.

Also at issue is the need to recognize that even though these veterans are threatened by a milieu drastically different than the one from which they have recently returned, research has shown that a large number of them are also eager to learn ways they can continue serving their communities and country. Alex Nesser, in a 2011 compilation of research done by the George Washington University Center of Civic Engagement and Public Service, underscores the needs of veterans to continue serving as they did in the military, preferably with those who have shared similar experiences. Drawing from a survey of fifty national veteran service projects, thirty university-led service projects, and twenty-five student-veterans, Nesser's (2011, 7) report identifies the five "most prevalent themes discovered in successful veteran service projects," with the last being the most provocative for my purposes here:

- The vast majority of veterans want to continue serving their nation once out of the military.
- The foundation for successful programs is a peer-to-peer community of veteran volunteers.
- Veterans enjoy service projects that are meaningful and in line with their past experiences.
- Well-structured community-service programs can help ease the transition home for veterans.
- Very few university-led projects exist that seek to engage student-veterans in community service.

Ninety percent of the veterans surveyed agreed that service was a basic responsibility of every American; 78 percent served when asked to do so by a veteran service organization, yet only 13 percent agreed their transitions home were going well. This low percentage of successful transitions tells us that it is no picnic to come out of the military and rejoin society, especially the select college or university society. Nesser's (2011, 5) report also demonstrates that "veterans involved in community service have higher adjustment rates than those that are not involved in service."

To be sure, we cannot valorize all returning veterans as if they are now eager to sacrifice their time and energy only to community service and to dedicate their future careers to helping others. Characterizing this demographic is not so simple, and creating useful, successful university courses for them means taking into account the complex natures they bring to the classroom. For instance, in 2009, the Naval Health Research Center in San Diego reported that 77,881 enlisted marines with at least one combat deployment and diagnosed as having posttraumatic stress disorder (PTSD) were six times more likely to be arrested on drug charges than marines without PTSD, and eleven times more likely to be discharged for misconduct (Wood 2012). Many are plagued with alcoholism, drug addiction (Cucciare, Darrow, and Weingardt 2011; Wood 2012), and abusive tendencies that make it almost impossible for them to cope—like "Sam," who took an almost unmanageable anger back to campus. He says,

> The most difficult aspect of readjustment is dealing with my anger. I react sharply because I still have quick reflexes. I have an aggressive streak that I am afraid of. One day I had a fight with my baby brother and I started to strangle him. (Zinger and Cohen 2010)

These students also can display paranoia manifested in a certainty of danger around every corner, in every classroom (Cucciare, Darrow, and Weingardt 2011; Katopes 2009; Lin 2012; Wood 2012). Indeed, as one veteran comments, "When I first came back, a lot of stuff made me uncomfortable. It's almost embarrassing to admit. We do like being near the exit or in the corner (of a classroom), somewhere we can see everything" (Lin 2012). For many, the 9/11 GI Bill is just too tempting to let go, so they return to school nonengaged, troubled, and often insensitive to opportunities college can offer. It can be argued that "War veterans" are, "of course, responsible for their actions, like everyone else. And some doubtless would have gotten in trouble no matter what their wartime experiences" (Wood 2012). But even though common sense and statistics tell us many veterans are not interested in saving the world or their communities, we also have ample evidence characterizing many as altruistic and ethical enough to make us rethink how we can best meet their pedagogical needs as they reach for a college degree, often an allusive, seemingly impossible goal (Brainard 2011). We need to listen to the Sam's of our campuses when they say, "I feel so far behind in life and am struggling to catch up" (Zinger and Cohen 2010).

Many of college-bound veterans' needs can be met by guiding the veterans toward solid, well-planned *service-learning* courses, the types of courses that allow this student population to work with people who need their skills and experiences (Bowenn and Kiser 2009; Carrington and Selva 2010). A service-learning "approach . . . is often considered a time to critique and reflect on knowledge learned at university and by doing so become more aware of our own and others' beliefs and practices that contribute to a more just society" (Carrington and Selva 2010, 47). So, for thousands of military veterans, service-learning pedagogy coincides with the visions of the just society, solid democracy, and participation in civic responsibilities that drew many of them to military service in the first place.

For example, Peter Katopes (2009), Vietnam veteran and Vice President of Academic Affairs at LaGuardia Community College is well acquainted with veterans' general characteristics. In his article "Veterans Returning to College Aren't Victims, They're Assets" he tacitly assumes a interconnectedness between service-learning pedagogies and student-vets when he says, "[Veterans returning to higher education] are for the most part mature and accomplished young women and men [bringing] with them a wealth of knowledge . . . experience and a depth of character which is worthy of our deep regard." He considers returning veterans to be "valuable resources" able to help "transform our institutions to better meet the challenges of a complex and rapidly changing world."

Similarly, Joe Klein, author of "The Next Greatest Generation" for *Time* magazine, discusses his experience with, and his research on, returning veterans in an open-source website called SWAMP.Time. Klein (2011), who was embedded with the soldiers in their camps downrange from immediate combat zones, watched them learn skills that were new to them, and as he watched, he became convinced that they were becoming "well-suited for public service." Klein points out that these soldiers appeared not only to be leaders but also to "represent exactly what America needs to rebuild its economy and propel its future: leadership, resilience and commitment to serve" (Klein 2011). He illustrates his point with specific examples from his follow-up of soldiers after their tours of duty. He describes posttraumatic stress disorder (PTSD) sufferers building homes for handicapped veterans; a Phi Beta Kappa graduate of Johns Hopkins going back to his hometown of Baltimore and starting a mentoring program for first-time offenders between the ages of eight and twelve; two sergeants taking their learned "ability to keep a cool head in chaotic circumstances" and using it to create a company that "provides medical logistics in the midst of disasters like the Haiti earthquake and the Joplin, Mo., tornado." They bring home, says Klein, "a history of service and sacrifice that most Baby Boomers have not had, and a sense of pride and accomplishment that our Vietnam veterans never experienced." All of these characteristics— ability to lead, entrepreneurship, altruism, awareness of need—align with the essence of service-learning pedagogy, which rests on a type of student-centered environment that acknowledges the importance of (1) respect for the experiences brought to its courses by students and (2) a belief that activating learning situations in communities rather than testing content knowledge in a classroom could foster more meaningful, sustainable knowledge.

Yet, there are times when returning veterans are not directed toward these courses because traditional pedagogies trump those that heed the life experiences students bring to the classroom. One reason might be that it is difficult to recognize the extraordinary response veterans' presence on campus elicits from their nonmilitary classmates. As Katopes (2009) found in his brief investigation, the "kids," the traditional students with whom vets share classrooms, characterize them in light of the many Vietnam-induced myths told about veterans since the days when anyone in the military was considered a "half-crazed Vietnam vet" or "ticking time bombs . . . not only in newspaper stories but in casual conversations as well" (Katopes 2009). The generation these returning vets meet in college classrooms know little, if anything, about Vietnam, but they have grown up with the myths perpetuated by society's contempt for that war and the vets who served in it. Today's veterans are still compared to the "losers" of the Vietnam era, when it was fashionable for the upper and middle classes to avoid the draft while anyone who did serve was "either not very smart or a member of a relatively powerless and ill-defined underclass" (Katopes 2009).

Drawing on the data from her survey of students from six midwestern universities, Laura McDaniel (2004, 19) confirms Katopes's assertions. She notes that "today's generation of college students remains out of touch with veterans and their values." Indeed, a senior majoring in English and history says, "I tend to find most military figures very frightening . . . . I think that my generation simply pities most veterans. Maybe there is a sense of pride attached to relatives who are veterans, but for the most part my generation is rather removed from military service" (McDaniel 2004, 18). And from a junior majoring in political science and journalism: "It has been many years since Vietnam veterans returned and were for a time reviled by many Americans. It's just hard to comprehend that my generation will soon have its own veterans" (McDaniel 2004, 19). Apparently, this responder does not realize that "will soon" is already here. Also, McDaniel's study was in 2008, thirty-three years after the fall of Saigon. It is stunning that this "generation of college students" hangs on to an image of military veterans established in an era completely unrelated to anything they have lived through.

In turn, this tension between "traditional" college students and non-traditional military veteran college students is perpetuated by the vets' own characterizations of whom they face in the classroom. I share here, with permission, some comments from casual e-mail conversations with veteran acquaintances.

> We served our country; now, we want to come back and make sure we didn't waste our time. But then I see these 18 year olds in our classrooms, and it pisses me off that they don't care. They don't do the assignments; they don't read the stuff; they miss class. They're rude to professors. If anyone acted like that on my aircraft carrier it could cost some lives.

His friend added,

> I really dislike the carelessness of a lot of students. On a ship you constant-ly have to be aware of your surroundings because a moment of inattention could get you or someone else killed. To see someone walk across a street without even looking at traffic bothers me a lot.

These issues may seem irrelevant to us, and certainly to traditional students, but they connect veterans to a *sensed* incongruity between obli-gations they assumed as part of the military and their responsibilities as students. Whether returning to school from combat or combat-support zones, these students have stepped from those *high* and *low magnitude stressors* related to the military into an equally stressful situation related to academia. It is my belief that higher education's faculty, advisors, and administrators would do well to read and learn from the several recently published studies explaining veterans' specific needs as returning stu-dents, needs that can directly relate to service and serving. Accordingly, I suspect that paying attention to studies like Nesser's (2011), Katopes's (2009), Klein's (2011), and Bringle and Hatcher's (1999; 2009) can heighten consciousness of the need for service-learning approaches to teaching these students. Often, such studies demonstrate, either implic-itly or explicitly, how well service-learning courses fit, especially those service-learning courses integrated into composition-studies pedagogy.

SERVICE-LEARNING COURSES AND COMPOSITION STUDIES

Fostering excellent written-communication skills is often a fundamental element of learning in service-learning courses. In fact, these courses are sometimes referred to as "community-based writing" courses (Davis 2008, 18) with direct connections among writing, critical reflective thinking, and civic responsibility. Service-learning courses connect with a veteran's need to be of service to a community. They also connect to increasing students' communication abilities through writing. Veterans are accustomed to first-rate communications, and at one time or another, a veteran's life may have depended on clear, concise, and correct communications, not just veterans in combat situations but also mechanics responsible for maintaining aircraft carriers; office clerks responsible for relaying accurate instructions and messages; or healthcare personnel far from the front lines but responsible for accurate triage and training. Consequently, veterans appreciate skillful communication abilities and tend to respond enthusiastically to such (Nesser 2011, 10).

Elements of composition theory, then, can be essential for veterans who frequently appreciate the value of learning to organize, explore, and complicate messy, inchoate thoughts and make meaning out of rote data dumps through learning skillful writing. So, when either service-learning educators or composition educators, or both, meet these particular students, who are returning in droves to higher education excited about learning, meeting goals, and feeling accomplished in ways dictated by the sensibilities they have developed as military personnel (Broder 2011; Katopes 2009; Nesser 2011), those educators need to be aware of the value returning-veteran students sometimes place on learning-to-write and writing-to-learn opportunities. Because most of these students have been out and about in the world, it is logical to believe they can sense growing empowerment as they become able to write successful documents like grant proposals for nonprofits, or letters on behalf of women looking for employment while living in battered-women shelters, or any type of written communication that will aid an organization to which they have been assigned—rhetorically astute memos, reports, white papers, and e-mails. This is real-world stuff, and these students have been active citizens in that world. The aim is primarily what Kim Davis (2008, 19) calls "traditional academic writing . . . . that represents the discourse of the power elite in the academy." Veterans could be identified as "outsiders," as David Bartholomae (2003) would see it, until they meet the requirement that all writers must meet. They "must imagine for themselves the privilege of being 'insiders'—that is the privilege of both being inside an established and powerful discourse and of being granted a special right to speak" (quoted in Davis 2008, 19). Specifically, we can design those opportunities in the form of writing assignments and projects that will help them move from simple to complex. They can move from narrative to academic writing as they actively take part in community and classroom discourse. And one of the first steps to accomplish this move is to learn the power of writing *reflectively*. These students can be guided into this powerful discourse through service-learning courses because it is usually second nature for those designing effective service-learning courses to include written reflection, a cornerstone of service-learning pedagogy (Furco 2001; Lukenchuk 2009; Novak 2010; Schutz and Gere 1998).

From what we know of returning veterans' attitudes and learning needs, it is not a stretch to imagine they do not welcome a curriculum filled with lectures and bubble tests, grade obsession, and apathy. Some might agree with Jeffery Wilhelm in *Teaching Literacy for Love and Wisdom* when he states, "It is high time for us to figure out a way to bring life and human substance back into education, introducing a thoroughly thought-through life-enhancing agenda to replace this systematically deadening regime" (Wilhelm 2011, 9). Wilhelm is speaking for the importance of devising ways to loosen up thought processes with just such strategies as reflective writing. Writers can usually engage in this sort of thinking with words because it is often ungraded and always their own. As a veteran said to me recently when I asked him about his thoughts on being allowed to simply *write* as an initial exercise in a writing-intensive service-learning course:

> Writing is therapeutic to me now whereas I used to loathe it. There are things in my head that for whatever reason end up going un-said. When I write it all gets to come out. I think it's because everyone wants to talk. Can you imagine if I came in your office and read this to you or anyone else? There's no way I could have gone this long without someone asking a question or giving their input. That's where these words would have been cut off and the subject possibly changed. Whatever I had intended on saying would now never come into existence. So it's kind of like conversation is the abortion of thought and story but with writing I can continue.

This comment hints at the importance writing can have for students who really wish to self-examine, feel quiet, and ponder. Perhaps these veterans lack opportunities to meet reflective writing on these terms. Perhaps they need to before they go on. The point is, a writing opportunity offered in a service-learning course can be especially valuable.

On one hand, compositionists who infuse their courses with service-learning experiences can appreciate the ways in which reflective writing almost always proves "to be a rich source of information for . . . insight into students' service-learning experiences" (McClam et al. 2008). And on the other hand, reflective writing offers the writers themselves chances to really listen and engage with what others have said (their community agency, organization, or client). Recognizing these chances helps produce meaning and the need to communicate that meaning, much like Burke's (1941, 110–11) "parlor" metaphor, which was used to argue that writing begins with listening, listening until we find a spot where we can "put in our oar." By being required to write in this manner, veterans can become cognizant of the fact that entering conversations means listening to others and finding or creating a space they want to fill with their own words (Bazerman 1980; LeFevre 1987). Such experiences play into the ethos most veterans develop during their service days when comradeship was more than a slap on the back. Depending on others and listening to what went on around them saved lives. Practicing the discipline drilled into them helps them stick to projects (which for some are now the dreaded writing assignments) and have patience with the people assigned to work with them for a semester.

We must remember that these students come to service-learning courses and writing assignments from a code of conduct unlike one any other students we teach have experienced. If they have been US Army personnel, they have memorized the US "Soldier's Creed" written as part of the 2003 Warrior Ethos program and have lived by it for at least several years. It is difficult to imagine this creed not seeping into the psychology and behavior of these students with its thirteen stern dictates, some of which are "I am a Warrior and a member of a team"; "I will never accept defeat"; "I am an expert and I am a professional"; "I stand ready to deploy, engage, and destroy, the enemies of the United States of America in close combat"; and "I will never quit" ("Soldier's Creed" n.d.). With mindsets influenced by these kinds of dictums, soldiers who find themselves in academia require opportunities to listen, interpret, analyze, and reflect in conjunction with real-world experiences and real people, problems, purposes, and audiences. They can then more successfully discover their power as learners, as academicians in their own right, and engage in a process that enables them "to generalize, to reason abstractly, to evaluate evidence and critique ideas, and so on" (Bizzell 1982, 131). In other words, they can participate in the whole writing process at a "deep level, at the idea level rather than the word level" (Bird 2010, 6). As mentioned, however, critical to this process is the ability of the writing assignments we design to complicate the term *reflection*.

To more fully develop this issue, we can compare student-veterans' learning needs with those of adult learners. For more than twenty years, educators have grappled with defining service-learning pedagogy in terms that signify real, complex learning situations separated from "volunteerism, community service, fieldwork, and/ or internships" (Sedlak et al. 2003, 99). This separation can be especially important for adult learners and/or returning veterans who wish to feel they are contributing as they make learning meaningful and transfer classroom lessons to doable projects on the ground, so to speak. Once again, neither all adult learners nor all returning veterans fall in this category. A proper definition of who cares about such learning depends on the extent of student involvement, specifically those students who wish to take the time to develop legitimate forms of inquiry into problems resounding in our civic, democratic, and institutional lives (Cushman, 1999, 47).

Similar thoughts are expressed by Bruce Hertzberg (1994) in his article "Community Service and Critical Thinking." Hertzberg worries that when he incorporates a service-learning element into his writing classes, his students who tutor illiterate citizens tend "to see their [tutees] . . . as persons with personal problems" rather than transcending "their own deeply-ingrained belief in individualism and meritocracy" when they analyze "reasons for the illiteracy they see." Hertzberg (1994, 312) would like to see students "take on a specific kind of self and ideology, embodying relationships . . . beyond the context of the activity itself" and talk about their thoughts in class." Likewise, Henk Procee (2006) defines writing as reflection when it allows students opportunities to hone their intellectual skills because as they write, they conceptualize how to fit the facts they discover with what those facts might mean. Thus, if we understand veterans as students who have lived closely with facts—the pragmatic, the concrete, and the questions so often answerable only through action—we "intellectualize the act of reflection" (Procee 2006, 239). They can better learn when "concept remains elusive, is open to multiple interpretations, and is applied in a myriad of ways in education and practice environments" (Kinsella quoted in Procee 2006, 239). A writing assignment in a service-learning course, then, would not generalize the term *reflect on* without expanding on it by explaining the thought processes reflection demands, once again an act that connects service learning to an intellectual enterprise. With encouragement and guidance, veterans can use their military experience and attitude toward getting the job done to exercise more the "mental capacity to formulate and grasp logical relationships, concepts, and theories" in order to "come to a deep and finely tuned interpretation of the situation at hand" (Procee 2006, 246).

Another element of a composition-studies approach to learning found in service-learning courses and essential to integrating veterans back into academia is student-centered classrooms. The notion that students write more skillfully when they, not teachers, have agency over their own thoughts and the expression of those thoughts has been supported for many years through composition-research-studies literature (Berlin 1988; Faigley 1992; Hertzberg 1994; Lauer 2004; Marback 2009). Of course, even though the term *student-centered learning environments* sounds great, we can see that veterans may not understand this concept of knowledge acquisition. Rather, they have just returned from a structured environment in which they became used to taking orders. Many, however, like the veteran quoted below, are able to jump right into this new, unregimented pace.

> Being in school is a lot better for me than being in the navy. I think what I like the about school over the military is the freedom. If I have a teacher who I think is incompetent, I just take the class with someone else. If I don't like my campus, I can transfer. If I don't like my major, I can change it, easy as that. I didn't have that kind of freedom in the navy and it was suffocating. Of course, along with that freedom comes a certain degree of uncertainty that isn't present in the military, which is why I think a lot of people stay in, or go back. Personally I'll take the freedom to succeed, or fail, on my own.

In this context, it helps once again to see the learning needs of veterans as closely mirroring those of adult learners, whom educators have studied for many years (Brookfield 1992; Merriam 1993; Mezirow 1996). Adult learners are especially tuned to service-learning pedagogy because it encourages them to take agency in civic projects, risk making assumptions, and write about their experience. When they learn in this way, they are enacting what veterans mean to do as learners who have fought for their country, producing "full citizenship in democracy" (Mezirow, 1996). Mezirow is talking here of adult-learning issues, but the connections to military-veteran-learning issues is clear. Both adult learners and veterans need opportunities to become "critically reflective of assumptions, . . . open to other perspectives, . . . [and] make tentative best judgements to guide actions." And this connection becomes even more logical when we understand that veterans—like adult learners—have already learned a great deal outside the "control and confines of formal education institutions" (Merriam, 1993). They have acquired job skills and insights into managing families and marital relationships. Some have children. Many have traveled the world and owned their own homes, and most are no longer emotionally or financially dependent on anyone. So, writing in service-learning courses is not only a way to promote intellectual growth for these veterans; it also fulfills their rather dichotomous needs for both agency and control when learning.

ENACTING A PEDAGOGY

Nesser's (2011) study shows us many of the efforts of postsecondary academic institutions to accommodate veterans returning to school. Yet even though the study references over fifty such institutions, few of the descriptions of university-led service projects for veterans seem to accommodate them academically. For example, Arizona State University offers career counseling services; Hawaii Pacific University contributes a Spouse Scholarship Program; the University of Michigan offers a Student Veterans Assistance Program that "helps veterans transition to the campus lifestyle"; and the University of Maryland has advocacy groups, a central office for veterans affairs, and "social events such as football, games and happy hours, career development services, [and] Volunteer service trips" (Nesser 2011, 15). These services are all valuable for veterans, but what more campuses need are (1) well-designed, organized, approved service-learning courses that use writing as a main learning source and (2) instructors capable of guiding them through semester-long activities serving nonprofits and other civic organizations in their communities.

Indeed, over the course of ten years, the director of the service-learning program introduced earlier has become increasingly swamped with guiding at least 100 discipline-specific faculty from across campus in their required service-learning courses, plus teaching service-learning courses in the program, itself—not connected to a particular department or college. The university has a comprehensive Veterans Assistance Program for help with funding, admissions, availability of campus facilities, and so forth, but nothing geared specifically toward meeting veterans' academic needs, including an academic advisor dedicated only to this student group. So, five years ago this director designed a service-learning course specifically for veterans. The director hired an assistant director, and together they have created relationships with over 200 agencies and organizations (*recipients*) from which students can choose their projects. The majority of returning vets, it seems, gravitate either to veteran homes and hospitals or to schools. The director is not a composition specialist, but writing is integral to everything taught, everything experienced. In other words, there are educators out there fully aware of this growing student demographic and of the need to incorporate writing-to-learn strategies into their curricula. Furthermore, educators who have taught veterans are aware that these students do not always know the process of learning in higher academia and that professors should take time to sit down and explain it. What do individual professors expect from their students and why? Why are reflective writing assignments assigned? Are the students just jumping through hoops or does this assignment have a reason, purpose, goals, and objectives? As the director who designed veteran-specific courses says,

> There is no specific academic advising formula for vets, but they do deserve to know why they are being asked to do whatever they're being asked to do. Even if I make them read a poem, if I can't tell them why, I shouldn't be assigning it. It takes time and trouble to explain ourselves in the classroom, and often vets are uncomfortable about individualized attention so they won't ask. Then they'll do poorly and be oh, so defeated. We have to understand the returning military veteran. Teaching them is not for the faint of heart!

There are many specific goals to keep in mind when designing these courses for veterans. Often writing-across-the-curriculum (WAC) tenets become viable in these situations because disciplines across the educational spectrum are incorporating writing into lesson plans and syllabi in place of exams and lectures. Veterans can, for instance, explore questions about public policy by taking an active part in community politics in a service-learning component of a political science program. Such opportunities can come about in any type of course, as Sherman and MacDonald report in "Service-Learning Experiences in University Science Degree Courses." They studied a service-learning program that "examined how professors and students became involved through science and mathematics course work and related activities" (Sherman and MacDonald 2009, 235). The professors in the study realized that when they taught courses with service-learning components, they were "bound to give up some control and autonomy" in order to allow students to be more responsible for their own learning. In the end, the professors "[created] more student-centered courses. [They also found they] needed to use different types of assignments in course-based service-learning situations so as to tap [students'] full learning potential" (Sherman and MacDonald 2009, 242). This study demonstrates that the nature of service-learning courses demands the type of student-centered environment valued by compositionists.

In fact, service-learning courses for military veterans will thrive when university personnel at all levels learn more about the fit between veterans and the valorization of writing in service-learning pedagogy. One idea is to have the first writing assignment be an organization and job profile paper. Students are asked to research their service-learning sites, interview the leaders with whom they are working, and write an essay that

- defines the vision, mission, and goals of the office;
- describes the constituency and population served;
- details their role within the organization and the job they will perform;
- outlines both what they hope to learn and what they hope to contribute through their internship.

In line with thoughts of pacing assignments sequentially from narrative to more complicated reflective thinking (analyses, interpretation, questioning, persuading), this assignment would help military students reintegrate into school by being unthreatening in what it asks for: simply going out and meeting a recipient in the community and actually starting on their service-learning projects. Pure description, itemizing tasks, and thinking in fairly concrete terms about what they hope to get out of this connection are writing tasks to which veterans can easily acclimate because they have been trained to get things done in a step-by-step manner. The idea is to complicate this first writing assignment by calling for more complex thinking tasks as work progresses at the job site, that is, with the community organization.

And *job site* is the key term here because we are talking about learning simultaneously with experiencing. Traditional composition classes may be less likely than composition classes that incorporate service-learning to provide student-veterans with optimal opportunities to engage because in traditional classes the rigor of being challenged by rhetorical issues is so often short-circuited by the lack of real audiences and real purposes. In a good service-learning project, learners do not have to make up audiences. They do, however, need to concern themselves with how to find recipients with real community needs. "One of the most significant ways in which service learning differs from many other community-related campus-based initiatives lies in its insistence that the needs to be met [are] defined by the community, not the campus" (Carracelas-Juncal, Bossaller, and Yaoyuneyong 2009, 36). In addition, instructors must concern themselves with how to help veterans pay attention to their writing—whether the writing is a grant for a nonprofit, a veteran history for the National Veterans' History Project, a policy to help administer a homeless shelter, or instructions for a

second-grade elementary school math game—in terms of its effect
on the community recipient of their actions. When guided to do so,
student-veterans can manage to engage reciprocity such that their service-learning projects will have a valuable, significant, positive impact
on the community.

From what we know so far about returning military veterans' distinc-
tive learning needs and the strong connection between those needs and
principles of service-learning/composition-studies theory, we can see
that this is an important area for further research, perhaps in the form
of field studies or ethnographies, using grounded-theory-based methodology. Such research will shed more light on best practices for teaching veterans as they return to an academic environment. It should also
be clear by now that when our teaching methods "[engage] ordinary
citizens with voluntary associations, social institutions, and government
in local communities" (Lukenchuk 2009, 246), we will better be able
to get at the core values and passions of our returning military veterans. Writing teachers are in a prime position to couple these methods
with service-learning pedagogy and guide this significant student group
toward academic success.

References

Bartholomae, David. 2003. "Inventing the University." In *Cross-Talk in Comp Theory*, 2nd
    ed., edited by Victor Villanueva, 623–54. Urbana, IL: NCTE.
Bazerman, Charles. 1980. "A Relationship between Reading & Writing: The
    Conversational Model." *College English* 41 (6): 656–61. http://dx.doi.
    org/10.2307/375913.
Berlin, James. 1988. "Rhetoric and Ideology in the Writing Class." *College English* 50 (5):
    477–94. http://dx.doi.org/10.2307/377477.
Bird, Barbara. 2010. "Meaning-Making Concepts: Basic Writer's Access to Verbal
    Culture." *Basic Writing e-journal.* http://bwe.ccny.cuny.edu/Meaning-Making%20
    Concepts-%20%20Basic%20Writer%E2%80%99s%20Access%20to%20Verbal%20
    Culture.pdf.
Bizzell, Patricia. 1982. "Literacy in Culture and Cognition." In *A Sourcebook for Basic
    Writing Teachers*, edited by Theresa Enos, 125–37. New York: Random.
Bowenn, Glen A. M., and Pamela Kiser. 2009. "Promoting Innovative Pedagogy and
    Engagement through Service-Learning Faculty Fellows Program." *Journal of Higher
    Education Outreach and Engagement* 13 (1): 27–43. http://openjournals.libs.uga.edu
    /index.php/jheoe/article/view/86.
Brainard, Jeffrey. 2011 "Veterans Report Less Preparation for College and Less
    Confidence in Their Prospects." *Acedeme Today.* https://chronicle.com/article
    /Veterans-Report-Less/127768/.
Bringle, Robert G., and Julie Hatcher. 2009. "Innovative Practices in Service-Learning
    and Curricular Engagement." Special issue, *New Directions for Higher Education* 2009
    (147): 37–46. http://dx.doi.org/10.1002/he.356.
Bringle, Robert G, and Julie Hatcher. 1999. "Reflection in Service-Learning: Making
    Meaning of Experience." In *Introduction to Service Learning Toolkit*, 179–85.

Broder, Judith. 2011. "Combat Veterans Returning—To College—But Can They Succeed?" *California Progress Report*. http://www.californiaprogressreport.com/site/combat-veterans-returning-college-can-they-succeed.

Brookfield, Stephen. 1992. "Developing Criteria for Formal Theory Building." *Adult Education Quarterly* 42 (2): 79–93. http://dx.doi.org/10.1177/0001848192042002002.

Burke, Kenneth. 1941. *The Philosophy of Literary Form*. Berkeley: University of California Press.

Carracelas-Juncal, Carmen, Jenny Bossaller, and Gallayanee Yaoyuneyong. 2009. "Integrating Service-Learning Pedagogy: A Faculty Reflective Process." *Insight: A Journal of Scholarly Teaching* 4: 28–44. http://www.researchgate.net/publication/26842934_Integrating_Service-.

Carrington, Suzanne, and Gitta Selva. 2010. "Critical Social Theory and Transformative Learning: Evidence in Pre-Service Teachers' Service-Learning Reflection Logs." *Higher Education Research & Development* 29 (1): 45–57. http://dx.doi.org/10.1080/07294360903421384http://eprints.qut.edu.au/31994/.

Cucciare, Michael A., Maura M. Darrow, and Kenneth R. Weingardt. 2011. "Characterizing Binge Drinking among U.S. Military." *Addictive Behaviors* 36: 362–67. http://digitalcommons.unl.edu/publichealthresources/167.

Cushman, Ellen. 1999. "The Public Intellectual, Service-Learning, and Activist Research." *College English* 61 (3): 328–36. http://dx.doi.org/10.2307/379072.

Davis, Kim M. 2008. "Twenty-First Century Academic Writing: The Blending of the Personal and the Academic in the Context of Community-Based Writing." *Language Arts Journal of Michigan* 23 (2): 18–22. http://dx.doi.org/10.9707/2168-149X.1119.

Faigley, Lester. 1992. *Fragments of Rationality: Postmodernity and the Subject of Composition*. Pittsburgh: University of Pittsburgh Press.

Furco, Andrew. 2001. "Advancing Service-Learning at Research Universities." *New Directions for Higher Education* 2001 (114): 67–78. http://dx.doi.org/10.1002/he.15.abs.

Hertzberg, Bruce. 1994. "Community Service and Critical Thinking." *College Composition and Communication* 45 (3): 301–19. http://compositionawebb.pbworks.com/f/Herzberg_Community_Service_Learning_and_Critical_Teaching_1994%5B1%5D%5B1%5D.pdf.

Katopes, Peter. 2009. "Veterans Returning to College Aren't Victims, They're Assets." *Community College Week* March 23. http://connection.ebscohost.com/c/opinions/37199802/veterans-returning-college-arent-victims-theyre-assets.

Klein, Joe. 2011. "The Next Greatest Generation." *Time Swampland*. http://swampland.time.com/2011/08/18/the-next-greatest-generation.

Lauer, Janice. 2004. Invention in *Rhetoric and Composition*. West Lafayette, IN: Parlor.

LeFevre, Karen B. 1987. "Invention as a Social Act." *Rhetoric Review* 6 (1): 107–11.

Lin, Ho. 2012. "Veterans Facing Challenges: Going Back to School." *Military.com*. http://jobsforveterans.military.com/520/veterans-facing-challenges-school/#ixzz2NkApXZMT.

Lukenchuk, Anotonina. 2009. "Living the Ethics of Responsibility through University Service and Service-Learning: 'Phronesis' and 'Praxis' Reconsidered." *Philosophical Studies in Education* 40: 246–257. http://eric.ed.gov/ERICWebPortal/search/detailmini.jsp?_nfpb=true&_=&ERICExtSearch_SearchValue_0=EJ864325&ERICExtSearch_SearchType_0=no&accno=EJ864325.

McClam, Tricia, Joel F. Diambra, Bobbie Burton, Angie Fuss, and Daniel L. Fudge. 2008. "An Analysis of a Service-Learning Project: Students' Expectations, Concerns, and Reflections." *Journal of Experiential Education* 30 (3): 236–49. http://jee.sagepub.com/content/30/3/236.full.pdf+html.

McDaniel, Laura. 2004. "Can They Connect on Campus?" *VFW, Veterans of Foreign Wars Magazine*, September, 18–21. http://www.fredonia.edu/tlc/ses/sesinfo/pdf/Can%20They%20Connect%20on%20Campus.pdf.

Merriam, Sharan. 1993. "Adult Learning: Where Have We Come From? Where Are We Headed?" In *An Update on Adult Learning Theory*, edited by Sharan Merriam, 5-14. San Francisco: Jossey-Bass. http://dx.doi.org/10.1002/ace.36719935703.

Mezirow, Jack. 1996. "Toward a Learning Theory of Adult Literacy." *Adult Basic Education* 6 (3): 115–27.

Marback, Richard. 2009. "Embracing Wicked Problems: The Turn to Design in Composition Studies." *College Composition and Communication* 61 (2). http://www.ncte .org/library/NCTEFiles/Resources/Journals/CCC/0612-dec09/CCC0612Embracing. pdf.

Nesser, Alex J. 2011. "Engaging Student Veterans in Community Service." Washington, DC: Corporation for National and Community Service, 1–18.

Novak, Jeanne. 2010. "Learning through Service: A Course Designed to Influence Positively Students' Disability-Related Attitudes." *Journal of Education for Teaching: International Research and Pedagogy* 36 (1): 121–23. http://dx.doi.org/10.1080 /02607470903462263.

Procee, Henk. 2006. "Reflection in Education: A Kantian Epistemology." *Educational Theory* 56 (3): 237–53. http://dx.doi.org/10.1111/j.1741-5446.2006.00225.x.

"Resources for Returning War Veterans." 2012. *James Madison University.* https://www .jmu.edu/counselingctr/resources/for-veterans.shtml.

Schutz, Aaron, and Anne Ruggles Gere. 1998. "Service-Learning and English Studies: Rethinking 'Public' Service." *College English* 60 (2): 129–49. http://dx.doi.org/10 .2307/378323.

Sedlak, Carol A., Margaret O. Doheny, Nancy Panthofer, and Ella Anaya. 2003. "Critical Thinking in Students' Service Learning Experiences." *College Teaching* 51 (3): 99–104. http://dx.doi.org/10.1080/87567550309596420.

Sherman, Ann, and Leo MacDonald. 2009. "Service-Learning Experiences in University Science Degree Courses." *Innovative Higher Education* 34 (4): 235–44. http://dx.doi .org/10.1007/s10755-009-9110-7.

"Soldier's Creed." n.d. *Military.com* http://m.military.com/join-armed-forces/military -creeds.html.

"Student Veterans Task Force." 2011. *TILT.* http://tilt.colostate.edu/sotl/taskforces /veterans/.

Wilhelm, Jeffery. 2011. *Teaching Literacy for Love and Wisdom: Being the Book and Being the Change.* New York: Teachers College Press; Urbana, IL: National Council of Teachers of English. Berkeley: National Writing Project.

Wood, David. 2012. "Veterans: Coming Home." *Huffington Post.* http://www.huffington post.com/2012/10/02/veterans-coming-home_n_1932366.html.

Zinger, Linda, and Andrea Cohen. 2010. "Veterans Returning From War into the Classroom: How Can Colleges Be Better Prepared to Meet Their Needs." *Contemporary Issues in Education Research* 3(1): 39–51.

12

"FRONT AND CENTER"
Marine Student-Veterans, Collaboration, and the Writing Center

Corrine E. Hinton

Over the last ten years, the growing body of research on student-veterans has provided scholars and educators with new insights about the transitional challenges student-veterans entering (or reentering) college often face. Only recently have we started to learn about the experiences and perceptions of student-veterans in undergraduate composition courses and the importance of considering these experiences and perceptions within the context of previous learning and writing interactions in the military. We know even less about the possible implications of these students' experiences and perceptions on student-veteran collaborations in college and university writing centers. As more student-veterans enter or reenter college and begin accessing the academic support services in place at their institutions, writing center administrators should begin thinking about how and why student-veterans engage with or disengage from writing center services.

In 2010, as the focus of my dissertation, I conducted a small, qualitative, interview-based research study in order to learn directly from marine student-veterans themselves about their teaching, learning, and writing experiences in college composition. I grew up in an air force family and married into the Marine Corps, so I developed a professional interest in what had already made such an impact on my personal life and identity. With a husband about to retire and complete his undergraduate degree program, I was especially interested in whether student-veterans' previous experiences as active-duty marines might have an impact on their college writing experiences. Over a six-month period, I had the opportunity to speak with twelve marine veterans (eleven men and one woman), all of whom were formerly enlisted personnel from a variety of military

DOI: 10.7330/9780874219425.c012

occupational specialties (MOSs).[1] The participants had served between four and twelve years as active-duty marines in the Corps. They represented nine four-year institutions, public and private, from five states across western, midwestern, and southeastern parts of the United States. Ten of the student-veterans were enrolled in college at the time of their interviews, while two of them had graduated within the last year.[2]

Scholarship on the effects of prior knowledge on current learning experiences prompted me to think about how the marine student-veterans' previous experiences with composition in the Corps affected their experiences with and perceptions of college-level writing. Specifically, I wanted my interviewees to characterize themselves as writers; describe their writing processes; tell me about the amount and kinds of writing they were exposed to in the Corps—either as producers or consumers; describe the features of military or Marine Corps written discourse and how they learned it (formally or informally); and consider the ways in which their acquisition of military written discourse had an impact on their learning academic discourse in undergraduate composition courses.[3] From their responses, I discovered that the composition experiences of some marine student-veterans in many ways significantly shaped their perceptions about writing faculty and academic writing tasks.

The results of my study complicate the nature of the transitional experiences student-veterans face when entering college. In many ways, studies that explore the individual journeys of student-veterans help highlight the intricate and unique features of these journeys, from veteran to veteran, school to school. And while the purpose of my study did not deliberately focus on investigating student-veteran experiences with writing centers, my attempt to capture the essence of their composition experiences exposed overlapping areas of strengths, challenges, and opportunities for composition and writing center professionals. Such knowledge not only gives us a clearer picture of how complex the experiences of student-veterans are, but more important, it continues to raise questions and possibilities about how we might serve student-veterans in writing centers in ways that intentionally acknowledge and address these complexities.

Both student-writers and peer consultants[4] benefit from collaborating in the writing center (see, for example, Dinitz and Kiedaisch 2009; Harris 1995; Hughes, Gillespie, and Kail 2010; Williams and Takaku 2011; Williams, Takaku, and Bauman 2006). Yet, the ideal collaborative environment most center directors or coordinators attempt to achieve within their centers is not without both theoretical and practical challenges. Contributing scholars throughout the 1980s and 1990s primarily raised concerns about negotiating dynamics of power and authority within sessions (Lunsford 1991; Severino 1992; Sollisch 1985; Trimbur 1987) and defended the ethicality of the writing center's collectivist collaboration approach (Behm 1989; Clark and Healy 1996; Lichtenstein 1983; Young 1992). Recently, these conversations have shifted from broader, conceptual discussions of power and ethics to the ways in which collaborations may be further complicated by the particular characteristics of institutions (Papay 2002), of consultants (Applequist 2004; Truesdell 2008), and of student-writers (Blau and Hall 2002; Papay 2002). Writing center consultants, administrators, and scholars have highlighted the intricacies of and effective strategies for collaborating with English language learners, students with specific disabilities, graduate students, online students, international students, students in two-year colleges, and adult learners. Few, however, are currently exploring collaborative opportunities with one of the fastest growing undergraduate populations in the United States.

While scholarship considering the needs of student-veterans in higher education has grown across several disciplines, it has yet to formally enter writing center studies. Effective consultants, like effective teachers, use what they know about students to increase engagement and to improve opportunities for learning. Previous military service can affect the knowledge student-veterans possess and help shape their cultural identities. However, the average civilian's understanding of the military is, in many instances, largely limited to suppositions about a servicemember's *professional experiences* (DiRamio, Ackerman, and Mitchell 2008; Jennings et al. 2006). Here, I will expand that understanding to include the educational experiences and rhetorical practices of enlisted marines and how those experiences and practices have affected their perceptions of classroom (and by extension, writing center) authority, help-seeking behaviors, rhetorical awareness, and collaboration.

Educators now have access to a growing amount of multidisciplinary literature and research on student-veterans. Recognizing that many student-veterans enter college writing courses every semester, composition scholars have taken their experiences and research public to share success stories, propose challenges, offer suggestions, and raise questions. Infrequently recorded during the course of these conversations is the significance of culture on student-veterans' transitions, negotiations of the academic institution, and perceptions. *Repatriation* refers broadly to the process of reentering one's home culture after spending significant time in a host-culture environment; generally, cultural studies and sociology scholars have investigated the repatriation experiences of domestic workers overseas, missionaries, and students studying abroad. By extension, then, student-veteran repatriation refers to the process of reentering civilian and/or academic culture after adjusting—wholly or in part—to military culture and service-specific subcultures. A brief overview of applicable findings in repatriation scholarship, as well as transition identity theory, provides a useful starting point for conceptualizing this study. Before doing so, I find it equally important to provide some background on education in the Marine Corps in order to help the reader understand the instructional culture from which the participants in my study emerged.

TEACHING AND LEARNING IN THE MARINE CORPS

Servicemembers undergo a professional military education in a complex organizational learning system. The primary goals of this system are to impart skills, institutional policies, educational philosophies, and organizational culture to students using a systematic and transferable approach (Reed et al. 2004, 47). Involvement in such a complex educational system, even for a single enlistment period, can potentially influence how military students and student-veterans perceive their own learning. Education in the Marine Corps, as in other service branches, takes on several different forms, although an emphasis on practical application is a core feature. Marine students are also encouraged to be critical, strategic, and reasoned thinkers; self-motivated; detail oriented; and assertive, confident communicators in class (Herrmann et al. 2009; US Marine Corps 2008). They are also expected to ask questions, participate actively, volunteer for leadership roles, and support struggling marines (US Marine Corps 2011). When I asked Stephen, a thirty-four-year-old who grew up in a Marine Corps family, to talk a little about his learning experiences during his eleven years of active duty, he told me, "I'm a team player. I'm always gonna help the weaker person . . . 'Cause that's the way I was trained. I was trained to help people out . . . and to make them stronger . . . I've been a leader. I've been a teacher. I know what it's like on the other side. So when I'm in a classroom, I'm up front, my eyes are on him, my ears are open, and I'm there to learn. And when the professor asks a question, my hand's going up. I'm answering it." Stephen's description of the way he was trained to be responsible for others' learning and accountable for his own performance as well as the ways in which these characteristics carried over into his participatory approach to college learning was echoed by the other student-veterans I interviewed.

Aside from the implicit authority granted by way of rank, the teacher-learner relationship in the Corps contains its own cultural hierarchy. The authority and respect marine students grant to their instructors derives from both the specialized knowledge they have of the course material and the trust vested in their ability to teach it effectively. Authorized instructors complete a formal instructor school through the Marine Corps Training & Education Command's (TECOM) Train the Trainer School (T3S). T3S courses employ highly structured delivery sequences; this approach is common to several of its sister services (Reed et al. 2004, 46; US Marine Corps 2011). One example of a frequently employed sequence is the GOLMEST method. Instructors must Gain the audience's attention, provide a course Overview, review the Learning objectives, state the Methods and Media to be used, explain the Evaluation measures and Safety procedures, and Transition to the first module with an opportunity to ask questions (US Marine Corps 2004). This structured, sequential learning environment exists to ensure that every marine receives knowledge in the same way and for the same purpose.

Aside from this formal instructor training, marine instructors learn to value simplicity in their approach because they work with a wide range of learner styles and speeds. Most often, this approach is referred to as "barney style," or simplifying material and/or tasks for the lowest-performing learners in the group to ensure every marine has gained mastery of the material. The *Systems Approach to Training* manual (US Marine Corps 2004), used or referenced in formal Marine Corps instructor courses, indicates that simplicity can be accomplished in several ways: by teaching in sequential groupings of simple to complex, avoiding jargon or acronyms that may confuse students, providing handouts with only the essential information, and designing assessment items that allow for simple recall of material. The simple approach used in military teaching did not escape criticism from the study's participants. Although fairly effective, "barney-style" can also be distracting and frustrating at times. Justin, who completed a five-year enlistment and spent time as a Marine Corps instructor, addressed both the positives and negatives: "You gotta make everything like really simplistic so that the lowest common denominator can always understand what you're talking about, and . . . a lot of times it's tedious for the people who are faster learners, but for those who aren't, you know, it's good." Ultimately, providing instruction in the simplest way possible, according to the marines I interviewed, allowed them to focus not just on the content for its own sake, but on the utilization of that content through practical application, task completion, or as a foundation for more complex material.

MILITARY CULTURE, CULTURAL IDENTITY, AND REPATRIATION

The military serves as one example of an organizational culture whose impact goes beyond regulating workplace behaviors or socializing members to the organization's values; rather, it has the ability to influence—at varying levels—an individual's identity. Servicemembers are expected to participate, first as learners and then as mentors, in the expressed integration of values, behaviors, and belief systems systemic to each service subculture. Hence, student-veterans who depart the military and enter the university represent not only individuals in transition from one phase of their lives into another, but also individuals who must undergo some level of repatriation back into civilian culture. Cultural readjustments, according to cultural psychologist and repatriation expert Nan M. Sussman (2000, 363), are "prompted by the lack of fit between one set of cultural cognitions and behavior no longer appropriate within the new cultural context" and require that the individual first become aware of differences in cultural values. Sussman, who has studied the effects of repatriation on domestic workers, students, and educators for more than thirty years, asserts that the cultural readjustment process is even more complicated for repatriates. These individuals have separated themselves from their home cultures, spent time adjusting to the values and behaviors of a host culture, and then returned home to undergo yet another period of cultural adjustment.

Sometimes referred to as *reverse culture shock*, repatriation was initially likened by sociologists and cultural psychologists to the cultural readjustment process, but the growing body of literature has prompted scholars to suggest that the adjustment experiences during repatriation may be even more difficult than cultural adjustments (Adler 1981; Black, Gregersen, and Mendenhall 1992; Clague and Krupp 1978; Howard 1974; Selmer 2007; Sussman 2000). Empirical studies have investigated the repatriation experiences of domestic workers and/or their partners returning home after overseas assignments (Allen and Alvarez 1998; Black and Gregersen 1991; Briody and Baba 1991; Hammer, Hart, and Rogan 1998; Sussman 2000), missionaries (Moore, Van Jones, and Austin 1987; Stringham 1993; Wiemer 2011), and students studying or living abroad (Martin 1987; Rohrlich and Martin 1991; Uehara 1986). When viewed as a body of literature, empirical findings on the repatriation process are inconsistent; however, they have contributed a framework through which we may start to understand the repatriate's experience. Sussman's (2000) transition identity model traces adjustments during repatriation and identifies the four affective responses sojourners may experience: additive, subtractive, affirmative, and intercultural.

In essence, these responses vary based upon (1) the strength of the connection between an individual's identity and their home culture and (2) the strength of the connection between an individual's identity and the host culture. Her model establishes one possible lens through which we may interpret the experiences of marine student-veterans as they (re)orient themselves to the civilian and academic worlds. This lens became an equally useful tool when I sought to understand if and how learning and writing experiences in the Marine Corps affect marine student-veterans during their undergraduate composition courses or with academic writing broadly.

INTERVIEW ANALYSES

In order to identify emerging themes from the interviews, my data-analysis techniques included both phenomenological reduction and cross-case analysis. After an initial surface reading of each transcript, I wrote a brief summary of my initial impressions to establish a broad context (Seidman 2006). I then reread the transcripts, highlighting particularly interesting and potentially significant passages (Christiansen and Brumfield 2010; Seidman 2006). I also noted recurring phrases, and I then identified possible categories based on these passages (Christiansen and Brumfield 2010). After I identified meaning units from the individual transcripts, I then set off to locate possible overlaps in meaning units across transcripts using an analysis technique known as *cross-case analysis.* I explored the data, searching for deliberate patterns, categories, and relationships among individual meaning units. I then retraced particular theme patterns back to their individual sources and compared those against the participant profile information (age, service length, MOS, etc.) to further contextualize the nature of the veterans' experiences because they may or may not relate to these individual differences. Finally, all themes and subthemes were reviewed against the research questions and separated into domains. From these findings emerged themes about teaching and learning, rhetorical experiences, composing practices, and collaboration most relevant to writing center professionals.

Discoveries

Repatriation, like cultural adjustment, is a process. Thus, the experiences the participants describe suggest they are operating at various and individualized stages in that process, marked by moments filled with challenges, rewards, and self-discovery. After collecting and analyzing the data, I extracted various themes that provide some insight into how this group of marine student-veterans perceive and articulate their experiences with learning and writing in college. Of these, four themes in particular may be helpful to writing center administrators and consultants because these themes speak specifically to the participants' perceptions of and attitudes toward group learning activities, collaboration, and feedback during the writing process, or they expose features of prior—and potentially useful—rhetorical knowledge and writing processes.

Community and Teamwork

Eight of the study participants cited the important role the Corps's community-based environment played in enhancing their military educational experiences. Joseph, Justin, and Stephen characterized the community of the Corps as conducive to learning, a conclusion perhaps best articulated by Joseph: "When you're in the military, you have this built-in social structure, [a] support network that's there, everywhere you go, that's based off shared experiences, shared culture . . . When you're working as a team, the best way you're gonna accomplish anything is if you care about the other people and if you care about their success as much as you care about yours, and you need to know about people." This community, designed so that individuals operate together within a bond of a "shared culture," as Joseph describes it, is not as explicit in college, according to some of the participants I interviewed. Joseph continued by recollecting his initial experiences after coming to college: "So not having those friends and that support network, you do feel like you're in an ocean a little, you know, to an extent, because no one understands what you've been doing." Several of the student-veteran participants disclosed seeking both assistance and camaraderie from their institution's veteran centers. Joseph explained, "I love it that I can go into the veteran department . . . and eat my lunch, and if someone I never met before and I can sit down and we can talk and I know exactly what he's been through and he knows exactly what I've been through. And then we can shoot the breeze and we can talk about our experiences, 'cause . . . I can't do that with my friends now and friends here." For some marine student-veterans like Andrew—just one year out of the service and into his degree program—these centers served as primary points of contact with other military students or student-veterans in an effort to recreate a sense of community seemingly absent from the institution at large.

Only one of the study's participants, Samuel, disclosed feeling more at home at his university than he did during his time in the marines. Like some of the other marines, he confessed not enjoying group work or projects because "it's hard to trust people these days." As a corporal in the Corps, Samuel worked in nuclear, biological, and chemical defense systems. While he credited the Corps with instilling confidence in him, he told me he felt isolated as a marine. "Maturity was totally out the window," Samuel said of the Corps, but when he started his education at a private Christian university in the Southeast, he immediately felt a shift. "I'm finally in an environment which is kinda meaningful, with people who understand the concept of respect and maturity . . . spiritual maturity and regular maturity." His perceptions of comfort and community in his institution make his experience an important one for student-veteran scholars to recognize because it may be indicative of the varying degrees to which marine student-veterans respond to their repatriations.

Not all student-veterans rely on the institutional community as a part of their college experience. The two married marine student-veterans, Miriam and Bradley, indicated they did not pursue college as a way to meet other people or to feel supported by their colleagues; rather, they saw their families (partners and children), neighbors, and friends closer to their homes as the source of support. Miriam, for example, told me, "I feel a lot of my social needs are filled at home versus at school." Bradley, who took the majority of his coursework online, grew accustomed to feeling "available" to his family and still able to work to provide income for them—attitudes common to other adult-learner populations.

Many universities and colleges pride themselves on the communities they help create for their students through student-affairs programming, residential life, learning communities, or other deliberate attempts to get students working, learning, and socializing together. In terms of working cooperatively, most of my study's participants agreed that while they saw the benefits in working in teams, many of them disliked doing so primarily because of what they perceived as inequitable partnerships. David, a sergeant in the infantry who completed three deployments in his five-year enlistment, considered what happens when students are not given the opportunity to form their own groups: "Usually, when they allow you to pick your group members, that's handy, 'cause you can get stuck with some slackers . . . and some people just don't work well with groups and . . . I've been fortunate enough to get to pick my group almost every time and choose who's in and who's not." Notice David wants the responsibility of choosing "who's in and who's not"; this need to control his own group formation and, by extension, the group's performance may hamper his ability to exercise tolerance for working with others unlike him. Thomas echoed David's sentiments about wanting to choose groups and admitted, "I always try to pair up with someone who was in the military because I know . . . they're not gonna mess around." What may be a sign of a student-veteran's motivation to get the project completed efficiently and successfully may also indicate isolationist or separatist attitudes toward working with students without service-related backgrounds or working with less prepared, less motivated students in general.

Miriam—the study's only female participant—had a similar but distinct experience working with her classmates. As the only participant in a science, cohort-based program, Miriam offered a unique perspective on interactions with her classmates. She described the dynamics in her most recent course group: "I love my tablemates, and we joke around because our table is the best table, because we poke fun at the people . . . who ask questions that we think are stupid . . . We *should* be taking things seriously and we shouldn't be making fun of people. But, you know, the people that . . . I'm around in the classroom are definitely really intelligent people." While Miriam's experiences working with others was more positive, she still exhibits some intolerance for those whose intellects she perceives as lower than her own. Later in the interview, she explained, "In my program, I think it's super important, because we need to be able to help each other make clarification, you know? We have a Facebook group, so if somebody has a question about the homework . . . they want to clarify. I think that's important so that we can be helping each other." Miriam recognizes the value in approaching difficult learning tasks by working with others and capitalizing on their strengths in order to bolster her own chances at success.

The marine student-veterans participating in my study seemed to fall on various points along the spectrum of belonging, or closeness to their institutions. Some, like Andrew and Joseph, are early in the adjustment and find greater comfort with members of the military (host) culture than students without military backgrounds. Others seemed to prefer complete avoidance of nonmilitary students whenever possible while still others, like Miriam and Bradley, have found alternative means of social contact. For some student-veterans, like Samuel, the institutional community can feel more inclusive and comfortable than the military. The perceptions some of the study participants described may initially suggest that educators exercise caution with partner- or group-based activities; however, these attitudes demonstrate the varying degrees of acceptance and patience some student-veterans may exercise when learning, working, or socializing with others.

Rhetorical Knowledge Is Present but Not Always Salient

Another applicable finding of my research to the writing center community focuses on the rhetorical knowledge marine student-veterans bring with them into college. Overall, I found many of the marine student-veterans I interviewed possess a good amount of knowledge useful in college composition contexts; however, they were generally unaware of these transferable skills or knowledge until asked to articulate their experiences with writing in the Marine Corps. Most of them did not think of themselves as mass producers of military writing. Only one participant, Miriam, expressed having produced a large amount of writing, an experience she credits with her transfer into the publications office during her pregnancy and her work in the company office after the birth of her first daughter. Miriam's exposure to formal Marine Corps writing was not representative of the group's collective experiences, but it is still significant. Many marine student-veterans occupy MOSs that include frequent contact with military writing (as readers and as writers); these student-veterans bring forward even more prior knowledge and rhetorical experiences applicable to academic writing tasks than those in MOSs with less contact with writing. During their enlistments, most of the study participants produced a limited amount of writing because, they often remarked, writing was a task primarily relegated to staff noncommissioned officers (staff NCOs) and officers. However, all of the study participants concluded they did write during their time in the service; these experiences included formal correspondence, standard operating procedures (SOPs), training plans, orders, forms, after-action reports, commendations or recommendations for promotion, and requests.

Even marine student-veterans with more limited exposure to military writing had been able to amass some important rhetorical knowledge, knowledge they were able to identify during the course of my interviews. Some identified the ways in which particular Corps genres helped with formulating college essays; for example, Thomas and Ivan indicated that their knowledge of how to write the formulaic Marine Corps order helped to "communicate the information in an organized manner" in college-level writing assignments (Ivan). Miriam stated that her exposure to formalized Marine Corps formatting made the transition to learning formal academic reference styles, like APA or MLA, easier. Andrew, another recently discharged combat marine, explained how his audience awareness had improved based on his experience writing to his mother during combat operations: "I would write to her . . . and there's so much that I *wanted* to say. But that [operational security] would control what I wanted to say and how I said it . . . What that did was give me different ways of saying the exact same thing. I can say one thing ten different ways, just because I know the right verbiage to put behind something." Overall, nearly half the student-veterans I interviewed attributed improvements in their own writing styles to the stylistic qualities of military writing. In particular, they credited the directness and conciseness valued in Marine Corps writing with ensuring that, as writers, their messages are clear, understandable, and precise. Bradley, an older participant in the study and a recent graduate, articulated the compatibility of military and academic writing styles: "I think they fuse together pretty nice, 'cause . . . with military writing, you get to the point . . . But at the same time, you kind of elevate the military writing to not be so direct, kind of like a conversation. So, I . . . like my papers sound . . . like a conversation that is leading somewhere and try to get the reader to be a part of that conversation." Bradley and Miriam were the only participants to directly convey how military discourse has influenced their own approaches to academic writing tasks; most of the other study participants seemed to compartmentalize the two discourses until I prompted them to consider the possible connections. While the stylistic features of military and academic discourses may have little in common, the commonalities may be one way for student-veterans to approach new academic writing tasks.

Sometimes, the marine student-veterans I interviewed seemed to be at odds with the expectations of academic writing, having become accustomed—pedagogically and compositionally—to the direct, concise, informational style of military writing. The results of what one participant, Thomas, described as a "painful" adjustment to academic writing standards are often negative perceptions of the value of academic writing as well as a lack of motivation to write in college. When I asked my participants to compare the military writing style to the academic writing style, only Bradley had something positive to say about academic writing. The others focused generally on the differences in development demands, isolating specifically what they perceived as laborious page length requirements, the mandated inclusion of "unnecessary fluff," or the apparent repetitiveness of words or ideas (Andrew, David, Samuel, Stephen, Thomas). These negative perceptions seem to suggest a couple of conclusions. First, some marine student-veterans have allowed their familiarity and/or comfort with military discourse to obstruct a tolerant attitude toward understanding the purposes of academic discourse. Second, such attitudes may also merely reflect their lack of understanding about the features or expectations of and/or approaches to academic written discourse. For example, student-veterans might wonder *why* particular features have become features of the discourse, or what purpose they serve for the writer, audience, or discipline.

Seeking Assistance Is Part of the Culture

Most of the marine student-veterans with whom I had the opportunity to speak indicated they had received little or no formalized instruction in writing for the Marine Corps. Instead, they learned how to communicate and how to express themselves in writing by reading and modeling their work after existing pieces considered acceptable, referencing official manuals or publications for guidance, and/or seeking assistance from other marines they felt were more experienced or more knowledgeable. Generally, I will refer to these as *help-seeking behaviors*, a term adopted by psychologists to describe the behaviors people exhibit when they attempt to receive assistance from others, and I will examine the ways help seeking with regards to writing tasks emerged during the interviews.

More than half the study's participants revealed they learned military writing standards through the informal mentorship of fellow marines. When I asked Andrew how he acquired his knowledge about how writing in the Marine Corps is supposed to look, he recalled, "One of my good friends was our . . . head administrative clerk. I worked right in the office next to him when I was a training chief. And . . . I'd go to him and say, 'What's the best way to say this?' And I remember us sitting down a lot and just working through ideas: this is what I want to say, this is what I want to accomplish, what's the best way to say this?" Bradley also mentioned the inevitability of soliciting feedback from knowledgeable, more senior personnel when he wrote counseling statements for the marines who reported to him. "Your boss will look at the counseling statements you write for those under you. So you say, 'Hey, I've written this. What do you have to say about it? Is this good?'" Looking to more senior or knowledgeable personnel for guidance during writing is not an uncommon practice; in fact, the collaboration between marines on writing tasks is almost encouraged and is viewed, as Stephen explained, as one way marines can better themselves: "I started surrounding myself with people who were educated that had the literacy skills, that knew how to write . . . and, and, you know, I wanted to be like them . . . you always want to improve yourself." Seeking guidance from others, as far as the study participants were concerned, was critical to writing successfully in the Marine Corps, especially for those who did not attend formal courses (like the sergeant's course) that may include a unit on genres specific to particular billets. Such practices suggest that marine student-veterans may be open to collaborating with others on writing tasks because, in many ways, such collaboration has already become part of their culture's discourse. On the other hand, based on their experiences, some conditions may be in place that echo earlier perceptions of group projects (e.g., usefulness of collaboration and trustworthiness of members).

Feedback on College Writing Tasks Is Solicited and Welcomed

The final theme that emerged from my research with ten marine student-veterans encompasses the role of feedback on college writing tasks. Specifically, I will examine two findings that lend support to this theme: when and from whom marine student-veterans ask for feedback and the desire for more (both quantity and quality) instructor feedback.

Nearly all the student-veterans interviewed indicated they often sought feedback on their college-level writing tasks; however, the nature and direction of this solicitation varied. The enthusiasm for actively showing their college essays to others for feedback varied along the spectrum, from "I love showing my work to others" (Justin) to "only if I think it's necessary" (Ivan). For some, the desire to ask others for assistance was conditional, based on either the assignment's importance to the course (in Andrew's case) or subject matter (in Ivan's and Mariam's cases). For half the veterans I interviewed, showing work to friends, family, or spouses/partners was a permanent part of their writing processes. In many cases, the people they asked for feedback were chosen thoughtfully, deliberately, and with the same sense of purpose as when they sought assistance from other marines during their time in the Corps. For example, Bradley asked his wife or friend to read his papers for clarity of his intended meaning, so "if they don't understand it or it doesn't make sense to them, then I change it, so anybody who picks up that piece of paper knows exactly what I'm going for." For others, like Andrew, the experience or knowledge of the other person plays a major role: "The person who edits the majority of my papers is my mother. She's an English major—she's got her master's in it [and] she was a college professor for a while. So, I'd email my papers to her and . . . we'll talk about it . . . she'll call me on the phone and say, 'Why are you saying this, why are you doing this?' And just from that, that's what I started looking for in my papers." When I asked Andrew why he goes to his mom or close friends, as opposed to the instructor or his writing center, for feedback, he replied, "I'm more comfortable with who I know. I think I like their opinions . . . or I guess I trust their opinions a little more." Several of the other participants also indicated that their ability to trust in the feedback they received from responders was critical to involving those responders in their feedback process.

Most of the study's participants expressed a desire for more feedback on their course assignments, particularly from their instructors. Some of this desire may be attributable to components of Marine Corps training to which some student-veterans may be socialized. For some, a marine can always be a better marine, and this philosophy seemed to apply in part to the participants' perceptions of themselves as writers. Thomas, a former ground communications repair sergeant from Chicago, admitted, "I'm sure I didn't get an *A+* on every single paper I've written, so it would be nice to get that feedback and actually learn something. Because right now, I'm still thinking that that paper I turned in was *A+*, but maybe it *wasn't.* Maybe I could have learned that this is how you put these words together, or this is how you group the sentences to make this paragraph a better example of what it should be." Joseph reiterated that the purpose of a college writing course is "to become a better writer," something he says only happens by "writing and then having someone critique it, and then going back and writing some more, and then having someone critique that." Largely, the marine student-veterans participating in my study seem to portray a welcoming attitude toward specific feedback on their writing that would lead to improvements in their understanding of college writing and/or their ability to perform better on college writing tasks.

Another possible source of some participant's demands for more feedback may stem from the directed feedback common in Marine Corps training. Recall the "barney-style" instructional method, during which information may be repeated and simplified to ensure all marines can access, understand, and implement content. While this method is effective for the Marine Corps, it may also develop particular behaviors in or expectations from students, which may then manifest themselves in college classrooms. In particular, they desire for faculty to be direct, concise, and specific in their communications, show models of acceptable work, or provide repeated feedback at all stages of an assignment. These kinds of expectations are not always met, nor do instructors always intend to meet them at the postsecondary level, where deductive reasoning, critical thinking, and creative problem solving often become pillars of student success. When viewed through the lens of repatriation, marine student-veterans may be carrying forward practices and expectations acceptable in the military (host) culture into situations where these practices and expectations are not as readily applied or accepted.

Limitations

Limitations are inherent in qualitative research studies, particularly those attempting to capture the essence of particular human experiences (Creswell 2003); therefore, limitations to this study, its design, and its findings are plausible. Because of my close connections with the military—personally and professionally—researcher bias may have occurred. While I made every attempt to keep biases in check, it is possible that the participants' responses were colored by my reactions or affected by leading questions and/or that I missed opportunities that would have allowed me to probe and reflect upon particular experiences further (including more writing center-specific inquiries). The responses I collected from my interviews came from participants who volunteered, which limits the generalizability of my findings. That is, marine student-veterans who did not choose to participate in the interviews may not have shared experiences similar to the experiences of those who did.[5] The interview structure allowed me to spend between twenty-five and ninety minutes with each participant. While this time was ample for gathering data rich enough to thoroughly analyze each marine student-veteran's experience, it was not enough to allow each participant to fully explore and analyze the meaning of a lifetime of experiences. While I made efforts to choose participants who represented a broad range of demographic, geographic, and personal backgrounds, the results, while valuable for increasing our understanding of marine student-veteran experiences, may not be generalizable to the entire population of marine student-veterans or to student-veterans from other services. However, it is important to note that generalizability is not a primary goal of phenomenological interviewing; rather, comparing common themes among participants replaces surface-level considerations of generalizability (Seidman 2006, 52). Student-veterans, even when categorized into service subpopulations, do not possess a stock set of characteristics or personal attributes; however, their interviews revealed similar characteristics, attitudes, perceptions, and experiences.

IMPLICATIONS FOR PRACTICE

After having the opportunity to learn more from the marine student-veterans' perceptions of and experiences with teaching, learning, and writing (both in college and in the Marine Corps), it is equally important to consider the findings and their implications for those working with student-veterans in the writing center: improving the writing center's visibility and perceived value to student-veterans, educating peer consultants to support and challenge student-veterans, and using student-veterans' existing rhetorical knowledge to improve the student-consultant relationship.

The first practical implication highlights the importance of a writing center's visibility and perceived value to student-veterans as a useful resource. Many of the marine student-veterans I spoke with acknowledged the importance of receiving feedback on their written work but chose to share that work with family or friends rather than access writing center services. In some instances, introductions to the writing center via classroom visits or general student-orientation presentations may be valuable. Such typical marketing efforts may help attract some student-veterans, but for others, a change of approach may be more effective. Existing veterans' resource centers provide one opportunity to bring the writing center to veterans as a way to meet student-veterans in a place in which many of them already feel more comfortable. For many institutions, veterans' centers have already established themselves as places of comfort, community, and/or productivity away from the general student population; placing a writing consultant within the veterans' center on a drop-in or walk-in basis improves visibility of writing center services for veterans. By conducting sessions in a less visible location, consultants may reduce any anxiety or embarrassment student-veterans may feel in asking for assistance. Another opportunity to demonstrate the writing center's worth to student-veterans is by coordinating efforts with individual instructors, particularly in courses with higher student-veteran populations. Sending one or more consultants into writing classrooms to work regularly with student writers, particularly student-veterans, provides consultants the opportunity to demonstrate their collaborative skills and develop trust and rapport. Student-veterans may also see the instructor's incorporation of consultants into the classroom as validation, both of the consultants' abilities and of the veterans' help-seeking behaviors.

Assisting student-veterans effectively in writing center sessions begins with educating consultants to work productively with this unique student population. Younger student-veterans occupy an interesting, albeit ambiguous, space between traditional college student and adult learner. While younger student-veterans may appear to be at or slightly above the average age of a traditional undergraduate, they bring with them a wealth of experiences (professional, educational, and rhetorical) that should encourage faculty, administrators, and consultants to rethink how we communicate with and assist student-veterans in a way that invites exploring and sharing (or concealing) those experiences (Herrmann et al. 2009, 59).

Writing center administrators should help their consultants (especially those without any previous military experience or knowledge) learn about military life and culture and how to use that understanding to shape their approach. Frances Applequist (2004) states simply, "Nationality is not the only cultural consideration in a writing center" (11). A one-size-fits-all approach cannot be used to consult student-veterans because even within their own subcultures, they bring a unique collection of experiences, expectations, and goals. Hence, a solid consultant-training program designed to educate civilian consultants to work with student-veterans is one that begins by asking consultants to explore and challenge their own assumptions about military life and culture. Open, honest, and productive dialogue is the key to developing an understanding of and sensitivity to veterans' experiences; writing center personnel or more appropriate members of the institutional community (e.g., veterans' services offices, military liaisons, etc.) would be better suited to facilitate this dialogue. The discussion might begin with investigating what consultants already know (or think they know) about the military (or a particular branch if the institution has a prevailing veteran population on campus) and the origins of that knowledge (family experiences, mass media, literature/films, political ideologies). In general, few consultants may explicitly recognize the educational and rhetorical skills student-veterans bring with them into college (Herrmann et al. 2009). Hence, an explanation about the experiences beyond the work of the military (i.e., educational and communicative) is warranted. Discussions about military experiences that may challenge the assumptions or expectations of administrators and/or consultants helps reinforce the writing center's function as a nonevaluative, judgment-free space for students.

Another significant element in educating consultants about working productively with student-veterans is an articulation of the differences between adult or nontraditional learners and student-veterans. Generally, the terms *adult learner* or *nontraditional student* evoke images of older workers who are beginning or continuing their postsecondary educations after a change (forced or voluntary) of career paths (Haynes-Burton 1990), and it is this primary vision that guides the ways in which many writing center administrators prepare their consultants. For the most part, these suggestions (such as being considerate of a learner's time, cognizant of one's demeanor, the need for structure in sessions, etc.) are also applicable to student-veterans (Ryan and Zimmerelli 2010, 72). These strategies, which often stem from theoretical models that emphasize the physical, social, and psychological transitions that adult college students commonly experience, have also been applied to discussions about assisting student-veterans (Bauman 2009; DiRamio, Ackerman, and Mitchell 2008; Haynes-Burton 1990; Rumann).

Aside from professional or combat-related experiences, what sets student-veteran learners (particularly marine student-veterans) apart from other adult or nontraditional learners? While adult learners' individual experiences vary considerably (professional, educational, rhetorical), less consistent is the sense of community more apparent in the military. While service subcultures (US Air Force, Army, Coast Guard, Navy, and Marine Corps) differ, the importance of collective success forms the backbone of many military training and education programs. Such experiences can result, for some student-veterans, in an interpretation of teamwork that differs from that of adult learners whose experiences, even in their own professions, may have still favored individual achievements over community successes. For those student-veterans who still desire veteran-to-veteran contact, a less explicit sense of community on a college campus may be disheartening. However, for a variety of personal reasons, many servicemembers do not wish to associate with any other veterans or anything military related after they leave the service. Faculty, administrators, and staff should recognize identification and association as a space student-veterans may occupy or leave at will throughout the course of their readjustment.

Student-veterans unaccustomed to learning experiences in tutoring or writing centers may be uncomfortable with a learning environment that is less formal, less structured, and more individual-learner centered than a classroom. While most writing center directors would agree that a writing center is not and should not be a microclassroom where students are taught by peers who are more like "little teachers," the writing center is a space where learning happens (Beck et al. 1978, 446). *How* that learning happens, however, is unique to each collaborative experience and defined by the participants. While some consultants may look (especially if they are traditional aged) less authoritative than a faculty member, some student-veterans may assume the consultant must know something they do not know and that part of the consultant's responsibility is to help them gain access to that information. "Programs to impart college-learning skills to veterans should begin by explaining the difference between learning from training and learning in college" (Herrmann et al. 2009, 101). Part of assisting student-veterans with expanding or reshaping their understanding of teaching and learning is through forthright and honest discussions about roles, boundaries, and expectations. Knowing that many marine student-veterans seek writing assistance from fellow marines during their service-writing experiences, and then using that knowledge as a starting point for a discussion about roles, may assist consultants in helping student-veterans become comfortable with the authoritatively ambiguous relationship that develops between student writers and their consultants. Once they can work together to define roles, boundaries, and expectations, the student-veteran and the consultant are more likely to flourish within the writing center environment.

Advocating for a more directive approach when consulting some student-veterans may, on the surface, seem to subvert how many writing center administrators train their team members. However, positioning directive and nondirective approaches as oppositional forces may actually reinforce the hierarchy of the consultant (i.e., the consultant may have information and be unable to tell students what they need to know). Previous writing center scholars have advocated for more directive approaches in working with nonnative English speakers or nontraditional/adult learners (Blau and Hall 2002). Ultimately, an approach that appreciates varying degrees of directivity (and the different techniques that may be classified as more or less directive) would allow consultants the flexibility to initiate approaches that work for students without appropriating their work (Carroll 2004; Clark 2001). With this flexibility, consultants and student-veterans can work together toward establishing a comfortable middle ground (Haynes-Burton 1990, 4).

One final implication of this study's findings is in regards to the ways in which both consultants and student-veterans may utilize their growing rhetorical knowledge more deliberately during sessions. If consultants are trained to understand the kinds of rhetorical practices in which marine student-veterans (or other student-veteran populations) may have been likely to engage during their service, then they can use that knowledge to assist student-veterans as they become familiar with the features of formal academic writing. Many of the marine student-veterans interviewed for this study eventually recognized the ways in which their writing experiences in the Marine Corps could be beneficial to academic writing; however, for some, these connections were not explicit. Writing center consultants can assist student-veterans in accelerating their awareness of rhetorical similarities and differences in audience, style, structure, expression, and delivery.

CONCLUDING REMARKS

When we talked about teamwork, Joseph provided a thoughtful metaphor I think works well with my discussion of marine student-veterans, collaboration, and the writing center. He explained, "When you're working as a team, the best way you're gonna accomplish anything is if you care about the other people and if you care about their success as much as you care about yours, and you need to know about people. So, the only way a car is going to move is if all four wheels are turning at the same speed, and that's how a unit operates as well: everybody needs to be on the same page; everybody needs to have the same goals." If I build upon Joseph's metaphor, collaboration is the engine of every writing center session. Even if the engine is running smoothly, the slightest compromise in the balance of one tire has the potential to affect the whole ride. Are there bumpy rides in the writing center? Absolutely. As long as writing centers continue to serve as spaces where differences "meet, clash, and grapple with each other," bumpy rides are sure to follow (Pratt 1991, 34). Writing center administrators can ease the journey by preparing consultants who are just as interested in learning from their students as they are in helping their students learn. From the stories throughout this collection, I can say there is still much for us to learn from student-veterans and from each other.

APPENDIX A
Interview Protocol

Background Questions

1. Tell me a little bit about yourself—perhaps where you grew up, if you were raised in a military family, your family structure, and perhaps some of your early educational experiences.
2. Tell me a little bit about your military experiences: what prompted you to join the Marine Corps? How long did you serve? What, if any, experiences stand out to you as particularly significant? What was your MOS and what did you do for the Marine Corps?

Questions about Learning Experiences & Preferences

1. How would you describe yourself as a learner?

2. How would you describe your learning style or process?

3 At what point in your life did you become aware of your learning preferences?

4 How did that awareness come about?

Questions about Writing Experiences & Processes

1. How would you describe yourself as a writer?

2. What does your writing process look like, from the time you're given an assignment to the time you submit it to an instructor?

3. Do you ever show your work to anyone else for feedback (family, friends, a writing center, etc.)?

4. What kind of criteria—yours, your instructor's, or the course's—are important for you to be successful in a college writing course?

5. What kind of exposure did you have to writing in the Marine Corps, either as a consumer or as a producer?

6. How would you describe writing in the Marine Corps?

7. If you had experiences writing in the Marine Corps, how did you learn the style (e.g., a formal school, from other marines, from following models, etc.)?

Questions about Relationships between the Military and College

1. How would you describe your learning experiences in the Marine Corps? In college?

2. Have there been any obstacles or challenges for you in moving from learning in the Marine Corps to learning in college?

3. Have you had the opportunity to work in groups with other college students? How would you describe those experiences?

4. Is there a particular style of writing the Marine Corps, and if so, how might that compare to the writing style preferred in college?

5. What skills, attitudes, or behaviors that you learned in the Marine Corps have you been able to apply in college? Have any of these been obstacles rather than helpers for you?

Final Questions

1. What role do you think your education will play in the next steps of your life?

2. What role do you think writing or written communication skills will play in the achievement of your professional goals?

Notes

1. While men outnumbered women nine to one, a gender overrepresentation is proportionate to the current makeup of the Marine Corps. Currently, female enlisted personnel represent only 7 percent of enlisted personnel (United States Marine Corps 2011).

2. Ultimately, two participants were excluded from my final study as I determined during their interviews that they no longer met the criteria for inclusion.

3. See Appendix A for the complete interview protocol.

4. Generally, *tutor* and *consultant* are interchangeable; for consistency, I have opted for the latter.

5. Robert Rosenthal and R. L. Rosnow (1975, 198–99) outline several guidelines for combating volunteer bias and increasing the validity of research, several of which were employed in this study, including designing the call for volunteers in a non-threatening way, stating the explicit purpose and importance of the research, and identifying the ways in which the target population is valuable to the research.

References

Adler, Nancy J. 1981. "Re-Entry: Managing Cross-Cultural Transitions." *Group & Organization Studies* 6 (3): 341–56. http://dx.doi.org/10.1177/105960118100600310.

Allen, Douglas, and Sharon Alvarez. 1998. "Empowering Expatriates and Organizations to Improve Repatriation Effectiveness." *Human Resource Planning* 21 (4): 29–39.

Applequist, Frances. 2004. "The Challenges and Contributions of Nontraditional Tutors." *Writing Lab Newsletter* 28 (10): 10–3.

Bauman, Mark C. 2009. "Called to Serve: The Military Mobilization of Undergraduates." PhD diss., Pennsylvania State University.

Behm, Richard. 1989. "Ethical Issues in Peer Tutoring: A Defense of Collaborative Learning." *Writing Center Journal* 10 (1): 3–13.

Black, J. Stewart, Hal B. Gregersen, and Mark E. Mendenhall. 1992. "Toward a Theoretical Framework of Repatriation Adjustment." *Journal of International Business Studies* 23 (4): 737–60. http://dx.doi.org/10.1057/palgrave.jibs.8490286.

Black, J. Steward, and Hal B. Gregersen. 1991. "When Yankee Comes Home: Factors Related to Expatriate and Spouse Repatriation Adjustment." *Journal of International Business Studies* 22 (4): 671–94. http://dx.doi.org/10.1057/palgrave.jibs.8490319.

Blau, Susan, and John Hall. 2002. "Guilt-Free Tutoring: Rethinking How We Tutor Non-Native English Speaking Students." *Writing Center Journal* 23 (1): 23–44.

Briody, Elizabeth K., and Marietta L. Baba. 1991. "Explaining Differences in Repatriation Experiences: The Discovery of Coupled and Decoupled Systems." *American Anthropologist* 93 (2): 322–44. http://dx.doi.org/10.1525/aa.1991.93.2.02a00030.

Beck, Paula, Thom Hawkins, Marcia Silver, Kenneth A. Bruffee, Judy Fishman, and Judith T. Matsunobu. 1978. "Training and Using Peer Tutors." *College English* 40 (4): 432–49. http://dx.doi.org/10.2307/376266.

Carroll, Beth. 2004. "A Pragmatist Approach to Writing Center Staff Education." *Praxis: A Writing Center Journal* 1 (2). http://praxis.uwc.utexas.edu/praxisarchive/?q=node/94.

Christiansen, Teresa M., and Kristy A. Brumfield. 2010. "Phenomenological Designs: The Philosophy of Phenomenological Research." In *Counseling Research: Quantitative,*

Qualitative, and Mixed Methods, edited by Carl J. Sheperis, J. Scott Young, and M. Harry Daniels, 135–50. Upper Saddle River, NJ: Pearson Education.

Clague, Llewellyn, and Neil Krupp. 1978. "International Personnel: The Repatriation Problem." *Personnel Administrator* 23:29–33.

Clark, Irene. 2001. "Perspectives on the Directive/Non-Directive Continuum in the Writing Center." *Writing Center Journal* 22 (1): 33–58.

Clark, Irene L., and Dave Healy. 1996. "Are Writing Centers Ethical?" *WPA* 20 (1/2): 32–48.

Creswell, John W. 2003. *Research Design: Qualitative, Quantitative, and Mixed Method Approaches.* 2nd ed. Thousand Oaks, CA: Sage Publications.

Dinitz, Sue, and Jean Kiedaisch. 2009. "Tutoring Writing as Career Development." *Writing Lab Newsletter* 34 (3): 1–5.

DiRamio, David, Robert Ackerman, and Regina L. Mitchell. 2008. "From Combat to Campus: Voices of Student-Veterans." *NASPA Journal (Online)* 45 (1): 73–102. http://www.degruyter.com/view/jsarp.2008.45.1.xml.

Hammer, Mitchell R., William Hart, and Randall Rogan. 1998. "Can You Go Home Again? An Analysis of the Repatriation of Corporate Managers and Spouses." *Management International Review* 38 (1): 67–86.

Harris, Muriel. 1995. "Talking in the Middle: Why Writers Need Writing Tutors." *College English* 57 (1): 27–42. http://dx.doi.org/10.2307/378348.

Haynes-Burton, Cynthia. 1990. "'Thirty-Something' Students: Concerning Transitions in the Writing Center." *Writing Lab Newsletter* 18 (8): 3–4.

Herrmann, Douglas, Charles Hopkins, Roland B. Wilson, and Bert Allen. 2009. *Educating Veterans in the 21st Century.* Charleston, SC: Book Surge.

Howard, Cecil G. 1974. "The Returning Overseas Executive: Cultural Shock in Reverse." *Human Resource Management* 13 (2): 22–6. http://dx.doi.org/10.1002/hrm.3930130204.

Hughes, Bradley, Paula Gillespie, and Harvey Kail. 2010. "What They Take with Them: Findings from the Peer Writing Tutor Alumni Research Project." *Writing Center Journal* 30 (2): 13–46.

Jennings, Patricia A., Carolyn M. Aldwin, Avron Spiro, III, and Daniel K. Mroczek. 2006. "Combat Exposure, Perceived Benefits of Military Services, and Wisdom in Later Life: Findings from the Normative Aging Study." *Research on Aging* 28 (1): 115–34. http://dx.doi.org/10.1177/0164027505281549.

Lichtenstein, Gary. 1983. "Ethics of Peer Tutoring in Writing." *Writing Center Journal* 4 (1): 29–35.

Lunsford, Andrea. 1991. "Collaboration, Control, and the Idea of a Writing Center." *Writing Center Journal* 12 (1): 3–11.

Martin, Judith N. 1987. "The Relationship between Student Sojourner Perceptions of Intercultural Competencies and Previous Sojourn Experience." *International Journal of Intercultural Relations* 11 (4): 337–55. http://dx.doi.org/10.1016/0147-1767(86)90031-3.

Moore, L., B. Van Jones, and C. N. Austin. 1987. "Predictors of Reverse Culture Shock among North American Church of Christ Missionaries." *Journal of Psychology and Theology* 15 (Winter): 336–41.

Papay, Twila Yates. 2002. "Collaborating with a Difference: How a South African Writing Center Brings Comfort to the Contact Zone." *Writing Center Journal* 23 (1): 5–22.

Pratt, Mary Louise. 1991. "Arts of the Contact Zone." *Profession* 33–40.

Reed, George, Craig Bullis, Ruth Collins, and Christopher Paparone. 2004. "Mapping the Route of Leadership Education: Caution Ahead." *Parameters* (Autumn): 46–60.

Rohrlich, Beulah F., and Judith N. Martin. 1991. "Host Country and Reentry Adjustment of Student Sojourners." *International Journal of Intercultural Relations* 15 (2): 163–82. http://dx.doi.org/10.1016/0147-1767(91)90027-E.

Rosenthal, Robert, and R. L. Rosnow. 1975. *The Volunteer Subject.* New York: Wiley.

Ryan, Leigh, and Lisa Zimmerelli. 2010. *The Bedford Guide for Writing Tutors*. 5th ed. Boston: Bedford/St. Martin's.

Seidman, Irving. 2006. *Interviewing as Qualitative Research: A Guide for Researchers in Education and the Social Sciences*. 3rd ed. New York: Teachers College Press.

Selmer, Jan. 2007. "Reverse Culture Shock." In *International Encyclopedia of Organizational Studies*. Edited by Stewart R. Clegg and James R. Bailey, 1386–88. Thousand Oaks, CA: Sage.

Severino, Carol. 1992. "Rhetorically Analyzing Collaborations." *Writing Center Journal* 13 (1): 53–64.

Sollisch, James. 1985. "From Fellow Writer to Reading Coach: The Peer Tutor's Role in Collaboration." *Writing Center Journal* 5 (2): 10–5.

Stringham, Edward M. 1993. "The Reacculturation of American Missionary Families: A Dynamic Theory." *Journal of Psychology and Theology* 21 (Spring): 66–73.

Sussman, Nan M. 2000. "The Dynamic Nature of Cultural Identity throughout Cultural Transitions: Why Home Is Not So Sweet." *Personality and Social Psychology Review* 4 (4): 355–73. http://dx.doi.org/10.1207/S15327957PSPR0404_5.

Trimbur, John. 1987. "Peer Tutoring: A Contradiction in Terms?" *Writing Center Journal* 7 (2): 21–29.

Truesdell, Tom. 2008. "Problems with Bruffee: Post-Process Theory and Writing Center Opposition." *Praxis: A Writing Center Journal* 5 (2): 16. http://praxis.uwc.utexas.edu /praxisarchive/?q=node/197.

Uehara, Asako. 1986. "The Nature of American Student Reentry Adjustment and Perceptions of the Sojourn Experience." *International Journal of Intercultural Relations* 10 (4): 415–38. http://dx.doi.org/10.1016/0147-1767(86)90043-X.

United States Marine Corps. Marine Corps Community Services (MCCS). 2011. *The Marine Corps "A Young and Vigorous Force"*: Demographics Update June 2011.

US Marine Corps. 2004. *Systems Approach to Training (SAT) Manual*.

US Marine Corps. 2008. *Marine Corps Education Programs Student Guide*. Enlisted Professional Military Education, Sergeants Course. MCCS-LDR-I004.

US Marine Corps. 2011. *Train the Trainer School*. Training & Education Command. http://www.t3s.marines.mil/.

Wiemer, B. J. Wandersee. 2011. "The Third Culture Kid in the First Culture Classroom: School Experiences of Missionary Children during Home Ministry Assignment." PhD diss., Saint Louis University.

Williams, James D., and Seiji Takaku. 2011. "Help Seeking, Self-Efficacy, and Writing Performance among College Students." *Journal of Writing Research* 3 (1): 1–18.

Williams, James D., Seiji Takaku, and K. Bauman. 2006. "Effects of Self-Regulatory Behavior on ESL Student Writing." *Tohoku Psychologica Folia* 65:24–36.

Young, Art. 1992. "College Culture and the Challenge of Collaboration." *Writing Center Journal* 13 (1): 3–16.

ABOUT THE AUTHORS

SUE DOE, associate professor of English at Colorado State University and an army spouse, served on the original student-veteran task force at CSU, teaches student-veteran cohort classes in composition, and works with her colleague Lisa Langstraat on faculty-development workshops at CSU relating to student-veteran issues. She was coeditor of a special issue of *College English* (March 2011) on the topic of academic labor.

LISA LANGSTRAAT is an associate professor of English and the Director of Composition at Colorado State University. She teaches veterans-cohort composition courses and co-facilitates faculty-development workshops about working with student-veterans at CSU. With Sue Doe she is coordinating the first community writing workshop for veterans and military families in the Ft. Collins, Colorado, area. Her work has appeared in an array of journals, including *Michigan Journal of Service Learning* and *JAC*.

ASHLY BENDER is a doctoral candidate in the University of Louisville's Rhetoric and Composition program. Her research interests include military rhetoric, student-veterans, and composition in digital environments.

LINDA S. DE LA YSLA is an assistant professor in the Department of English at the Community College of Baltimore County in Baltimore, Maryland. Dr. De La Ysla serves on the leadership team for the nationally acclaimed CCBC Accelerated Learning Program in Basic Writing as well as on the college-wide Veterans Success Committee. She has been teaching college writing at both two- and four-year institutions for more than twenty years.

DOUG DOWNS is an associate professor of Rhetoric & Composition in the Department of English at Montana State University (Bozeman). His research interests center on research-writing pedagogy in both first-year composition and across the undergraduate curriculum. The author of *i-Cite: Visualizing Sources* and coauthor (with Elizabeth Wardle) of *Writing About Writing: A College Reader*, he is currently studying student reading habits in our age of screen literacies and rhetorical conceptions of writing.

ERIN HADLOCK, MAJ, United States Army, is a rotating instructor of composition and literature at the United States Military Academy, West Point. She has served in the US Army for twelve years as an aviator and military intelligence officer, and upon her completion of three years at USMA, she will return to an operational unit to continue working with fellow soldiers.

ALEXIS HART is an associate professor of English and the Director of Writing at Allegheny College in Meadville, Pennsylvania. A US Navy veteran, Hart has published several articles related to the US military and veterans' issues. She was the corecipient, with Roger Thompson, of a Conference on College Composition and Communication (CCCC) Research Grant to study veterans returning to college writing classrooms, serves as cochair of the CCCC Task Force on Veterans, and is codirector of research for the volunteer organization Military Experience and the Arts.

The daughter of two retired air force personnel and the wife of a retired US Marine, **CORRINE E. HINTON** received her PhD from SLU and is an assistant professor of English at Texas A&M Texarkana with nearly a decade of experience working with university writing and learning centers. She has presented her research at several national conferences.

Hinton's dissertation, *The Experiences of Marine Student Veterans in Undergraduate Composition Courses: A Phenomenological Study*, explores ten marine student-veterans' perceptions of and experiences with college and academic writing.

IVY KLEINBART teaches academic writing and creative nonfiction at Syracuse University and has been a coleader of the Syracuse Veterans' Writing Group since the group's inception in March 2010. She holds an MA and an MFA from Syracuse University. Her poems have appeared in *Stone Canoe, Bateau,* and *NoTellMotel.org*.

ANN SHIVERS-MCNAIR is a doctoral student in language and rhetoric at the University of Washington. Her research interests include basic writing and composition studies, and she is currently working on an analysis of peer review data collected during her work as the basic writing coordinator at the University of Southern Mississippi.

ANGIE MALLORY is a six-year military veteran who served two tours as an aircraft technician and safety specialist in the US Navy. She has a BA in English-Writing from Montana State University. She is pursuing her PhD in Rhetoric and Professional Communication at Iowa State University, where she also teaches writing.

SEAN MORROW is an infantryman in the United States Army. A graduate of West Point, Boston College, and the Army Command and General Staff College, his assignments have included leadership positions in combat as well as an assistant professorship in West Point's Department of English and Philosophy. He currently resides in New York with his wife, Meghan, and their children.

EILEEN E. SCHELL is associate professor of Writing and Rhetoric at Syracuse University. She served as the chair and director of the Writing Program at Syracuse from 2007 to 2012. Schell is the author of *Gypsy Academics and Mother-teachers: Gender, Contingent Labor, and Writing Instruction* (Heinemann 1998), the coauthor of *Rural Literacies* (SIUP 2007) as well as the coeditor of three essay collections. She is also the cofounder and coleader of the Syracuse Veterans' Writing Group, a community writing group for military veterans in Syracuse, New York.

BONNIE SELTING completed her undergraduate work at the University of Colorado and received her PhD from Purdue University, specializing in rhetoric and composition. She is a coordinator for the University of Missouri's interdisciplinary Campus Writing Program (CWP) and specializes in researching writing-across-the-curriculum (WAC) issues. Amongst the many courses she has taught are first-year and advanced composition, technical writing, composition theory, and an array of related courses.

KAREN SPRINGSTEEN is Senior Lecturer in the English Department at Wayne State University. She works with veterans and conducts writing workshops as a part of the national Warrior Writers project. She has also published on art and activism in the collection *Composing(Media) = Composing(Embodiment)* and reviewed veterans' creative work for the nonprofit *Military Experience and the Arts*.

ROGER THOMPSON is currently an associate professor in Stony Brook University's Program in Writing and Rhetoric. He is also senior fellow at the Institute for Veterans and Military Families at Syracuse University and is coauthor with Shannon Meehan of *Beyond Duty: Life on the Frontline of Iraq*, a bestselling Iraq War memoir that has been adopted at more than a dozen schools and was covered by major media outlets, including the *New York Times*, CNN, the CBC, and NPR.

TARA WOOD is an assistant professor of English at Rockford University in Illinois. Her publications include "Overcoming Rhetoric: Forced Disclosure and the Colonizing Ethic of Evaluating Personal Essays" in *Open Words: Access and English Studies* and the WPA-CompPile

Bibliography on *Disability Studies*, collaboratively written with Margaret Price and Chelsea Johnson. Her current projects include "Subversion of the Violent Gaze: Sins Invalid and the Aesthetics of Disabled Bodies" for the forthcoming edited collection *Violence, Beauty, Representation*; "Suggested Practices for Syllabus Accessibility Statements" for the *Kairos PraxisWiki*; and a dissertation project on accommodations, universal design, and composition pedagogy in higher education.

INDEX